Shakespeare's English

Shakespeare's English

A practical linguistic guide

Keith Johnson

Harlow, England • London • New York • Boston • San Francisco • Toronto • Sydney • Auckland • Singapore • Hong Kong
Tokyo • Seoul • Taipei • New Delhi • Cape Town • São Paulo • Mexico City • Madrid • Amsterdam • Munich • Paris • Milan

Pearson Education Limited
Edinburgh Gate
Harlow CM20 2JE
Tel: +44 (0)1279 623623
Website: www.pearson.com/uk

First published 2013 (print and electronic)

© Pearson Education Limited 2013 (print and electronic)

The right of Keith Johnson to be identified as author of this work has been asserted
by him in accordance with the Copyright, Designs and Patents Act 1988.

Pearson Education is not responsible for the content of third-party internet sites.

ISBN: 978-1-4082-7735-5 (print)
      978-0-273-78610-8 (PDF)
      978-0-273-78613-9 (eText)

British Library Cataloguing-in-Publication Data
A catalogue record for the print edition is available from the British Library

Library of Congress Cataloging-in-Publication Data
Johnson, Keith, 1944-
  Shakespeare's English : a practical linguistic guide / Keith Johnson.
    pages cm
  Includes bibliographical references and index.
  ISBN 978-1-4082-7735-5 (limp)
  1. Shakespeare, William, 1564-1616--Language.   2. Shakespeare, William, 1564-1616--
Literary style.   3. English language--Early modern, 1500-1700--Style.   I. Title.
PR3072.J64 2013
822.33--dc23

2012040981

10 9 8 7 6 5 4 3 2 1
17 16 15 14 13

Cover image: Getty Images

Print edition typeset in 9/13.5pt Stone Serif by 35
Printed in Malaysia (CTP-VVP)

NOTE THAT ANY PAGE CROSS REFERENCES REFER TO THE PRINT EDITION

To the memory of my grandfather, Frederick Charles Owlett
(1883–1965)

Contents

Author's acknowledgements

At the beginning, when this book was just a twinkle in the eye, I was much encouraged by the support of Geoffrey Leech, Mick Short, Jonathan Culpeper, and David Crystal. When the idea became a proposal, the comments of anonymous reviewers helped give my thoughts direction. When a first complete draft was ready, anonymous reviewers again provided invaluable feedback, and their comments significantly shaped the final version. Sincere thanks to all of these people, and also to Kate Ahl, Sarah Turpie and Helen Savill at Pearson Education for their help. Also to Alison Bowers for her excellent copy editing.

As well as providing encouragement, David Crystal's influence is everywhere to be seen. His own book, *Think on my Words*, leads the field in its particular genre, and one can but follow, paying appropriate attention to his various other Shakespeare contributions (some produced with Ben Crystal).

Thank you Helen for your usual support, and for being the constructive critic that you are.

The book is dedicated to the memory of my grandfather, Frederick Charles Owlett, whose lifeblood was the Elizabethan writers, particularly Shakespeare and Marlowe. In the nineteen-thirties he set up the *Globe-Mermaid Association* with the intention of having the Globe Theatre rebuilt in London. The war put paid to his efforts. Sam Wanamaker was, later, more successful. Johnson (2010) describes FCO's work.

Publisher's acknowledgements

We are grateful to the following for permission to reproduce copyright material:

Figures

Figure 2.1 from *Treasure-House of the Language: The living OED*, Yale University Press (Brewer, C. 2007); Figure 4.1 and 4.2 from *Historical Sociolinguistics: Language change in Tudor and Stuart England*, Pearson Education (Nevalainen, T. & Raumolin-Brunberg, H. 2003) p. 178 and p. 123; Figure 4.3 from *Early Modern English*, Revised edn, Edinburgh University Press (Barber, C. 1997) Fig. 5.1, www.euppublishing.com; Figures 8.1, 8.4, 8.5 and 10.1 by permission of the Folger Shakespeare Library; Figures 8.2 and 8.3 images taken from sources in the collection of Lancaster University Library and photographed by Folio Photography at Lancaster University.

Text

Extract on page 2 from Christopher Sykes Productions, Carl Feynman and Michelle Feynman, BBC TV, *Horizon*, The Pleasure of Finding Things Out (1982); Poetry (6 lines) on pages 212–3 from *Beowulf: A verse translation*, edited with an introduction, glossary and notes by Michael Alexander (Penguin Classics, 1995). Copyright © Michael Alexander, 1995. Reproduced by permission of Penguin Books Ltd.; Song Lyric on page 213 from 'It's My Thing' written by Erick Sermon, Tyrone Thomas, August Moon, Parish Smith. Performed by EPMD. Published by Talpa Music BV, administered by Bucks Music Group.

In some instances we have been unable to trace the owners of copyright material, and we would appreciate any information that would enable us to do so.

Chronology of Shakespeare's works

When exactly Shakespeare wrote each of his works is not known for certain, and is the subject of scholarly debate. While recognising such uncertainties, Wells, Taylor and Jowett (2005) come up with a 'conjectured order of composition', and the list here is based on this. The abbreviations used in this book for plays and poems are also given here.

1589–91	The Two Gentlemen of Verona (TGV)
1590–1	The Taming of the Shrew (TS)
1590–1	Henry VI, Part 2 (2H6)
1591	Henry VI, Part 3 (3H6)
1592	Henry VI, Part 1 (possibly with Thomas Nashe) (1H6)
1592	Titus Andronicus (Tit)
1592–3	Richard III (R3)
1592–3	Venus and Adonis (VA)
1593–4	The Rape of Lucrece (Luc)
1594	Edward III (with other authors) (E3)
1594	The Comedy of Errors (CE)
1594–5	Love's Labour's Lost (LLL)
1595	Richard II (R2)
1595	Romeo and Juliet (RJ)
1595	A Midsummer Night's Dream (MND)
1596	King John (KJ)
1596–7	The Merchant of Venice (MV)
1596–7	Henry IV, Part 1 (1H4)
1597–8	The Merry Wives of Windsor (MWW)
1597–8	Henry IV, Part 2 (2H4)
1598–9	Much Ado About Nothing (MA)
1598–9	Henry V (H5)
1599	Julius Caesar (JC)
1599	The Passionate Pilgrim (PP)
1599–1600	As You Like It (AYLI)

Phonetic symbols used

Sounds found in RP

p	pet
b	boy
t	tell
d	dad
k	key, car
g	go
tʃ	child, nature
dʒ	jail, age
f	father
v	vote
θ	think, Athens
ð	this, rather
s	sit
z	zip, rise
ʃ	sheep, ratio
ʒ	pleasure
h	hope
m	music
n	now
l	love
r	right
j	yet
w	war, square
ɪ	hit, rabbit
e	bet, many
æ	cat, attack
ɒ	hot, what
ʌ	shut, love

ʊ   good, should

iː   sea, me

eɪ   lay, face

aɪ   cry, lie

ɔɪ   boy, choice

uː   do, spoon

əʊ   throw, no

aʊ   how, foul

ɪə   dear, here

eə   fair, wear

ɑː   car, heart

ɔː   saw, shore

ʊə   sure, poor

ɜː   bird, earn

ə   about, teacher

Non RP

ɤ   Used in EModE where RP has [ʌ]. See the box in 9.4.1 for an indication of tongue position. For an audio example, listen to how Crystal pronounces *blood* and *lovers* in the *Romeo and Juliet* passage transcribed in 9.2.

ɛː   As in the French word *même*. See the box in 9.4.1 for an indication of tongue position. There is an audio example at http://en.wikipedia.org/wiki/Open-mid_front_unrounded_vowel

eː   As in German word *sehen*. See the box in 9.4.1 for tongue position. Audio recording at http://en.wikipedia.org/wiki/Close-mid_front_ unrounded_vowel

oː   As in the German word *Sohn*, and the French *chose*. Audio recording at http://en.wikipedia.org/wiki/Close-mid_back_rounded_vowel

əɪ   As a West Country British speaker would say the word *line*. The sound is discussed in 9.4.2.

ɹ   Discussed in 9.3.1. A pronunciation of pre-consonantal or word-final [r] in rhotic versions of English. As in American or West Country British *were*.

hw   Also written [ʍ]. As in Scottish and American *when*. Audio recording at http://en.wikipedia.org/wiki/Voiceless_labio-velar_ approximant

CHAPTER 1

Why, What, and How

1.1 Shakespeare's language? Why study it?

This book is about Shakespeare's language. When a book declares this as its topic, it can be one of two things. Perhaps it will be written by a literary critic with an interest in language. Maybe it will talk about the poet's imagery, about his use of metaphor, and his literary style. Frank Kermode's famous and excellent book entitled (yes!) *Shakespeare's Language* – is of this first type. On the other hand it may be a book written by a linguist with an interest in literature. Less on imagery and literary style here perhaps, and more on 'down-to-earth' linguistic matters – nouns and verbs, definite articles and adjectives. David Crystal's equally excellent *Think on my Words* is like this. And so is this one.

Books of the second sort sometimes meet with hostile scowls. A common objection is that studying the nuts and bolts of Shakespeare's masterpieces will detract from their glory. As soon as you start to analyse it, the magic will turn to dust. A closely allied objection (not so hostile perhaps, but equally damning) – is to ask: 'Why bother? What good does it do to study nouns, verbs, articles, adjectives? Will it change your view of Macbeth's crimes to study the tenses that he uses? Or is the sincerity of Romeo's love revealed by his adjectives?' The next few paragraphs will offer some thoughts on these questions. Before you read them, think about the questions yourself. Is the 'magic to dust' argument credible? What counter-arguments are there? More generally: what is the point in studying Shakespeare's language? Does it really tell us something valuable about his work? Or, principally, something about the English language and its development? Why study all this?

Here is what one scientist has to say about the 'magic to dust' question. He is Richard Feynman, a Nobel prize winner who (among many other things) expanded our understanding of quantum electrodynamics. Here is part of an interview he gave for the BBC's *Horizon* programme in 1982:[1]

> *I have a friend who is an artist and has sometimes taken a view which I don't agree with very well. You hold up a flower and say 'look how beautiful it is', and I agree, I say; and he'll say 'I as an artist can see how beautiful it is. But you as a scientist take all this apart and it becomes a dull thing'. And I think that he's kind of nutty. First of all, the beauty that he sees is available to other people and to me too. I believe, although I may not be quite as refined aesthetically as he is, that I can appreciate the beauty of the flower. At the same time, I see much more about the flower than he sees. I could imagine the cells in there, the complicated actions which also have a beauty. I mean it's not just beauty at this dimension of one centimetre, it's beauty at a smaller dimension – the inner structure; also the processes. The fact that the colours in the flower evolved in order to attract insects to pollinate it, is interesting. It means that insects can see the colour. It adds a question: does this aesthetic sense also exist in the lower forms? Why is it aesthetic? All kinds of interesting questions [which the scientist's] knowledge only adds to the excitement, the mystery and the awe of a flower. It only adds. I don't understand how it subtracts.*

But even if you are in sympathy with Feynman's argument, the question remains: what is the *value* of reading about Shakespeare's language (in the nouns, verbs, articles, adjectives sense)? There is a general argument that goes like this: Shakespeare's 'medium' was language; therefore if we want to understand him well, the more we know about the language of his time, and how he used it, the better. But what about the particulars: how *exactly* will linguistic knowledge help? Here are two concrete examples of how such knowledge might enrich our understanding and appreciation of Shakespeare. The first is to do with sounds and comes from a book dedicated to the study of Shakespearean pronunciation, Kökeritz (1953).[2] It relates to a speech by Jaques, a melancholic character in *As You Like It*. Wandering in the Forest of Arden, Jaques meets the court jester Touchstone. Something Touchstone says makes Jaques laugh for a whole hour – no mean feat given Jaques' melancholic nature. Why? What is the joke? Probably reading the passage will not reveal much. Here is Jaques' description of the meeting (AYLI 2.7.20; the *he* in the first line is Touchstone):

> *And then he drew a dial from his poke,*
> *And looking on it, with lack-lustre eye,*
> *Says, very wisely, 'It is ten o'clock.'*
> *'Thus we may see,' quoth he, 'how the world wags:*

> *'Tis but an hour ago since it was nine,*
> *And after one hour more 'twill be eleven,*
> *And so from hour to hour we ripe, and ripe,*
> *And then from hour to hour we rot, and rot,*
> *And thereby hangs a tale.'*

The joke? Kökeritz observes that the word *hour* would have been pronounced like our present-day *oar*, which would also be the way the word *whore* would have been pronounced. If you read the passage again, replacing *hour* with *whore*, it takes on a quite different, and humorous, air (and perhaps the word *tale* also assumes a new dimension, but let that be).

The second example is based on the word *thou* (and the associated forms *thee, thy, thine*). It means 'you' ('your', 'yours'). But the word *you* is also used in Shakespeare. So what is the difference? When does a Renaissance person use *thou*, and when *you*? Perhaps you have learned a language like French, German or Italian where there are two forms of address – like French *vous* and *tu* – and where (in very simplistic terms) the second is only used in the singular, and suggests an intimate relationship. The *you/thou* of Shakespeare's time is comparable. Selecting which form to use can be extremely complex and express subtle shades of meaning. Look for example at this speech from *The Taming of the Shrew* (2.1.268). Katherina (the shrew) comments that Petruchio (the one who will 'tame' her) needs to keep himself warm. Go through his reply noting every use of a *you* and a *thou* form (the latter including the related words *thy* and *thee*). What is the sequence in their use? What can possibly account for the changes from *thou* to *you* and vice versa?

> *Marry, so I mean, sweet Katherine, in thy bed.*
> *And therefore, setting all this chat aside,*
> *Thus in plain terms: your father hath consented*
> *That you shall be my wife; your dowry 'greed on,*
> *And, will you, nill you, I will marry you.*
> *Now, Kate, I am a husband for your turn,*
> *For by this light, whereby I see thy beauty,*
> *Thy beauty that doth make me like thee well,*
> *Thou must be married to no man but me,*
> Enter Baptista, Gremio, Tranio [disguised as Lucentio]
> *For I am he am born to tame you, Kate,*
> *And bring you from a wild Kate to a Kate*
> *Conformable as other household Kates.*
> *Here comes your father. Never make denial,*
> *I must and will have Katherine to my wife.*

The sequence is *thou → you → thou → you*. The shades of meaning expressed by *you* and *thou* will be considered in detail in Chapter 5 (Section 5.5). For the moment it suffices to raise the issue, and suggest that an important linguistic distinction is at play here, and that shades of meaning will indeed be missed unless we know something about the uses of *you* and *thou* in Shakespeare's time.

Perhaps these two examples will convince you that knowing about Shakespeare's language will reveal interesting things about his work. But, you might argue, 'is it worth reading a book devoted to Shakespeare's English just to be able to understand the odd pun, or to know more about how characters addressed each other?' It is a good point. If you are tempted to answer 'no', think first in cumulative terms. The odd pun missed is inconsequential, as is failing to notice the occasional switch from *you* to *thou* or vice versa. But knowing something about Shakespearean pronunciation, and knowing that the two forms of address – *thou* and *you* – were used at the time, will inevitably sharpen your focus as you read or watch Shakespeare. There is of course a lot you will understand without any special knowledge about the language of his time. But with that knowledge you will understand a useful amount more. Everything is likely to make a little more sense.

Many readers will approach this book with more interest in Shakespeare than in language. Of course, studying Shakespeare's language will tell us something about the development of the English language, and indeed it would be possible for a book on the topic to do no more than use Shakespeare's works as linguistic examples. This is not the aim here; Shakespeare is the main topic, not just a provider of examples. But at the same time we certainly will not shy away from introducing linguistic concepts when (as quite often) they help to clarify aspects of Shakespeare's English. So there is a good amount of linguistics in this book, and no apology is made for that. Certainly no harm at all will be done if a reader starts this book interested in Shakespeare, and leaves it enthused not just by the writer but with a new curiosity about linguistic analysis, and about the development of the English language.

1.2 What is Shakespeare's language like? An initial look

In the early 1960s a group of young British 'wits' wrote a stage review called *Beyond the Fringe*. It was very funny, hugely popular, and made the actors – Peter Cook, Dudley Moore, Alan Bennett and Jonathan Miller – famous. One of their sketches was a parody of Shakespeare.

Parodies work by picking up essential characteristics of their victim, and making fun of these. So one initial approach to identifying the essential characteristics of the way Shakespeare writes is to take a look at the *Beyond the Fringe* parody. Part of their Shakespeare sketch is below.[3] After an initial read-through, spend some time listing the characteristics that make it like Shakespeare. Some of them will have little or nothing to do with language – identify these too, though you will not want to spend much time on them. When you concentrate on language matters, you will find that many of the characteristics are in fact ways in which the English of Shakespeare's time differs from English today.

As this part of the sketch begins, a group of lords are making plans:

Miller: *Get thee to Gloucester, Essex. Do thee to Wessex, Exeter.*
            Fair Albany to Somerset must eke his route.
            And Scroop, do you to Westmoreland, where shall bold York
            Enrouted now for Lancaster, with forces of our Uncle Rutland,
            Enjoin his standard with sweet Norfolk's host.
            Fair Sussex, get thee to Warwicksbourne,
            And there, with frowning purpose, tell our plan
            To Bedford's tilted ear, that he shall press
            With most insensate speed
            And join his warlike effort to bold Dorset's side.
            I most royally shall now to bed,
            To sleep off all the nonsense I've just said.

They exit. Re-enter all four as rustics.

Miller: *Is it all botched up, then, Master Puke?*
Bennett: *Aye, and marry is, good Master Snot.*
Moore: *'Tis said our Master, the Duke, hath contrived some naughtiness*
            against his son, the King.
Cook: *Aye, and it doth confound our merrymaking.*
Miller: *What say you, Master Puke? I am for Lancaster, and that's to say for*
            good shoe leather.
Cook: *Come speak, good Master Puke, or hath the leather blocked up thy tongue?*
Moore: *Why then go trippingly upon thy laces, good Grit.*
Cook: *Art leather laces thy undoing?*
Moore: *They shall undo many a fair boot this day.*
All: *Come, let's to our rural revel and with our song enchant our King.*

Like all good Shakespeare it ends with a battle:

Enter Cook and Miller, with swords.

Miller: *Why then was this encounter nobly entertained*
            And so by steel shall this our contest be buckled up.
            Come, sir. Let's to it.
Cook: *Let's to it.*
            Good steel, thou shalt thyself in himself embowel.
Miller: *Come, sir.* (They fight)
            Ah ha, a hit!
Cook: *No, sir, no hit, a miss! Come, sir, art foppish i' the mouth.*

They fight again. Cook 'hits' Miller.

Miller: *Oh, God, fair cousin, thou hast done me wrong.* (He dies)
            Now is steel twixt gut and bladder interposed.
Cook: *Oh, saucy Worcester, dost thou lie so still?*

Enter Bennett.

Bennett: *Now hath mortality her tithe collected*
            And sovereign Albany to the worms his corpse committed.
            Yet weep we not; this fustian life is short,
            Let's on to Pontefract to sanctify our court.

Here are some of the characteristics you may have listed (roughly in the order in which they appear):

- Use of *thee* (*thy* and *thou*) – forms rarely used today;

- *Do* used to substitute for another verb (*do thee to Wessex*, where *do* means *get* or *go*);

- Curious word order, sometimes resulting in the main verb coming late in the sentence (*Fair Albany to Somerset must eke his route*);

- Complicated sentences with many clauses (for example, the third sentence of Miller's opening speech – *Fair Essex . . . I've just said*);

- Lots of adjectives, some strange to our ears, often sounding as if they come from a 'Romance' language like Latin or French. *Insensate* is an example;

- Omission of a movement verb like *go* (*let's to our rural revel*);

- A speech ending with rhyming lines (*bed/said* at the end of the first speech);

- Words no longer used (though you may have some inkling of what they mean). *Marry* might be an example;

- Words used today but found here in a rather unfamiliar context. The word *naughtiness* is for example used to suggest something more seriously evil than usage today suggests;

- Asking a question by inverting the subject and verb, without *do* (*what say you?* Instead of *what do you say?*);

- Extended word play, sometimes rather difficult to follow (the exchange about shoe leather, laces, etc. is an example);

- *This* and *our* used together before a noun (*this our contest*);

- Addressing objects as if they were people (*Good steel . . .*);

- Exclamations (sometimes odd-sounding ones), used in situations where we would not use them (*Ah ha*);

- Unusual contracted forms (*i'the*);

- A negative formed without *do* (*weep we not* instead of *we do not weep*);

- Verse which has a regular rhythm but usually no rhymes; mixed with prose.

Try to make a rough classification of the items on this list according to the linguistic areas they deal with. Some items, for example, are to do with word meanings, while others are grammar points. Then take a look at the contents page of this book. Different chapters cover different linguistic areas. Identify which chapters you might expect the various characteristics to appear in.

1.3 How hard is Shakespeare's English?

Here is a thought about time scales. In this book mention will occasionally be made of the version of English spoken in Chaucer's time, now called Middle English (ME). Chaucer was born in around 1343. The language spoken in Shakespeare's time (born 1564) is known as Early Modern English (EModE). Today the language I am writing in is the British version of Present Day English (PDE). These dates show that in terms of years, Shakespeare and Chaucer were much closer to each other (just 221 years between their birth dates) than Shakespeare is to the present day (449 years between his birth and 2013). You might therefore expect Shakespeare's English to be closer to Chaucer's than it is to PDE. Measuring how 'close' languages are to each other is of course difficult to do precisely. But take a look at the two passages below, one from Chaucer and the other from Shakespeare. Focus first on the Chaucer. Form an impression of how many unknown words there are, and how many grammatical expressions are strange to you. Then do the same for the Shakespeare passage. Given this small amount of impressionistic evidence, what are your thoughts about the closeness of the three versions of English to each other?

The opening sentence of the Prologue to Chaucer's *Canterbury Tales*:

Whan that aprill with his shoures soote
The droghte of march hath perced to the roote,
And bathed every veyne in swich licour
Of which vertu engendred is the flour;
Whan zephirus eek with his sweete breeth
Inspired hath in every holt and heeth
The tendre croppes, and the yonge sonne
Hath in the ram his halve cours yronne,
And smale foweles maken melodye,
That slepen al the nyght with open ye
(so priketh hem nature in hir corages);
Thanne longen folk to goon on pilgrimages,
And palmeres for to seken straunge strondes,
To ferne halwes, kowthe in sondry londes;
And specially from every shires ende
Of engelond to caunterbury they wende,
The hooly blisful martir for to seke,
That hem hath holpen whan that they were seeke.

And a piece of Shakespeare, from *Coriolanus* 5.3.41:

Like a dull actor now
I have forgot my part and I am out,
Even to a full disgrace. (Rising and going to her) *Best of my flesh,*
Forgive my tyranny; but do not say
For that, 'Forgive our Romans.' O, a kiss
Long as my exile, sweet as my revenge!
Now, by the jealous queen of heaven, that kiss
I carried from thee, dear, and my true lip
Hath virgined it e'er since. You gods! I pray,
And the most noble mother of the world
Leave unsaluted. Sink, my knee, i'th' earth;
He kneels
Of thy deep duty more impression show
Than that of common sons.

The chances are that you will feel Shakespeare's English is significantly closer to present-day English than ME is. So as our exploration of Shakespeare's language begins, here are two thoughts to bear in mind. One is that there are indeed differences between PDE and EModE. The listed characteristics of the *Beyond the Fringe* sketch make this clear; there are indeed things that need to be pointed out to the modern reader about Shakespeare's language. But the other thought is that EModE is really quite like PDE, much more than ME is. So those who say 'Shakespeare's language is very different from modern English. It is just like Chaucer's English' are not really being accurate.

But despite the degree of similarity between EModE and PDE, the fact remains that many readers find Shakespeare difficult. Plenty of people say they would love to know more Shakespeare, but have been put off by the difficulty of the language. For these people, here is a further thought. Look again at the passage from *Coriolanus*. The words and the grammar may be largely familiar to you. But what on earth is the character talking about? The words may be decipherable, but the sense is hard to scan. Though this is true, there are two sorts of information that can dramatically help comprehension. One is information about the context. You have been presented with the *Coriolanus* passage 'cold', and text is often very difficult to interpret 'cold'. Here is some information about the context in which the speech occurs.

Coriolanus, a celebrated Roman soldier, has been banished from Rome, leaving behind his wife Virgilia, his mother Volumnia and his young son Martius. He misses them very much, but despite this is determined to revenge his banishment by attacking Rome, the city in which his family still lives. He and his army are now camped near to Rome. The Romans fear his military prowess, and attempts are made to persuade him against attacking the city. In this scene, his mother, wife and son arrive at the camp to try persuasion once more. Coriolanus has not seen his family for a long while. He is moved by their appearance, but determined not to let personal feelings affect his military decision to attack. His wife speaks to him. He feels tongue tied as he starts to respond.

Read the speech again. The chances are that it will make much more sense now that some context has been provided.

The other sort of information which greatly helps comprehension is supplied by the actors. Here are some notes based on the BBC's DVD performance of *Coriolanus* (the BBC set of Shakespeare's complete dramatic works is an excellent way to get to know the plays). The notes provide a good deal of information about what is going on:

- The first words of the speech, up to *a full disgrace*, are said as soliloquy, not addressed to the other characters;

- On the words *Best of my flesh* Coriolanus begins to address his wife;

- After the words *Forgive our Romans* Coriolanus and Virgilia kiss passionately, and at length;

- After the words *e'er since*, Coriolanus turns towards his mother, and addresses her;

- On the words *Sink, my knee*, Coriolanus kneels in front of his mother.

Read the speech one last time, bearing the two sorts of information in mind. They probably make a very great difference to your understanding of what Coriolanus is saying. The moral is clear. Shakespeare can be very hard to follow. But many who say so, and are put off by this, do not bear in mind how much easier it is to understand plays when you know what is going on and when you can see what is happening. This is a message of hope and optimism; it should make Shakespeare easier to live with.

Shakespeare without words

You may be interested to try an informal experiment to find out how much Shakespeare it is possible to understand by watching actors perform it, but without hearing the actual words. To do this, you will need a copy of a Shakespeare play on DVD (the BBC series mentioned earlier will be useful here). It must be a play you do not know at all well. Watch a few scenes with the sound turned down. There will of course be plenty that cannot be understood. But you may be surprised at just how much can be worked out, both in terms of what is happening and of how the characters relate to each other.

1.4 Something about this book and how to use it

This book is subtitled *A practical linguistic guide*. Activities are integral to it, but this does not mean that every one must be done. You are expected to pick and choose. Frequently, throughout the book, you are invited to stop and do an activity (or simply to think about an issue) before reading the next paragraph which discusses the issue (and hence provides the 'answers' to the activity). This procedure gives you the option to avoid an activity if you so wish. But if you decide to do it, you will of course need to do so *before* you read the following paragraph. In order to alert you to such activities which need to be done there and then, the letters (**NP**) (for 'Next Paragraph') are used.

As well as 'normal' activities, there are also 'extended' ones. These are more open-ended, and are usually either suggestions for discussion topics, or involve focusing on a play of particular relevance to you – one perhaps that you are studying.

There may on occasions be not just activities, but actual sections of the text that you wish to leave out, because you already know about what is being discussed. For example, Chapter 6, Section 2 looks at compound and complex sentences, and the difference between the two. If you already know about these concepts, simply miss the section out. Incidentally, when new pieces of linguistic terminology are first introduced, they are underlined.

Each chapter (except for this one) has an *Answer Section* which gives solutions to questions raised in the chapter and its activities. An (**AS**) in the text signals that solutions appear in this *Answer Section*. Where (as often happens) solutions are given in the text itself, they are not repeated in the *Answer Section*.

Two of the chapters – 6 and 7 – have 'Text Pages' which consist of a number of example texts. This is because these chapters deal with areas which need longer stretches of text to make their points.

All main chapters suggest further reading to follow up topics discussed in the text. One book: Crystal's excellent *Think on my Words* (2008, Cambridge: Cambridge University Press) is not mentioned chapter by chapter, simply because it is relevant to *all* chapters. It provides a highly readable introduction to all areas of Shakespeare's language, and is the one main further reading recommendation.

Some more points:

- The book is, of course, full of quotations from Shakespeare. Often brief notes on the context of the quotation are given because (as was mentioned earlier in this chapter) context aids comprehension very considerably.

- There is a Glossary at the end of the book. It is not a full Shakespearean glossary, and it only contains words appearing in the book's quotations. Words explained in the text are not included in the Glossary.

- Internet sites are mentioned throughout the book. Two are mentioned particularly frequently because they have facilities for searching Shakespeare's works (looking for uses of a particular word, for example). These are Crystal and Crystal's site at www.shakespeareswords.com/. This is referred to as 'Shakespeare's Words'. The other is www.opensourceshakespeare.org/, referred to as 'Open Source Shakespeare'. Another useful site is internetshakespeare.uvic.ca/Library/facsimile/, which includes a facsimile copy of the First Folio. All websites referred to are as accessed in June 2011.

- Act, scene and line references from Shakespeare have been taken from the 'Shakespeare's Words' site. References are given from that source, even when, on a very few occasions, another edition is being cited. The notational system employed uses Arabic numerals only, so Act 1, Scene 2, line 145 is written as 1.2.145.

- Usually full play titles are given in the text, but at some points, for example where a number of quotations are given together (particularly in activities), abbreviations are used. A list of these is given before the main text of the book, which also provides a chronological order in which Shakespeare's works were written.

A final note on boxes: there are quite a few of them, and they usually contain interesting additional pieces of information, brief reports on research, historical notes. Here, to introduce the concept, is a box dealing with two print formats which will be mentioned throughout the book:

Quartos and folios

Quartos and folios are printing formats. Take a piece of A4 typing paper. The following instructions will show you the different formats (though the resulting pages will be much smaller than Elizabethan ones). Fold the paper in half, then in half again, so that you have a rectangle very close to being a square. If you then unfold the page, the fold marks will show that you have divided it into quarters (hence the word 'quarto'). Each of these quarters would make a page, so with both sides printed on, you will have eight pages in all. Fold the page again as before, and use scissors to cut through the shorter edges. You will then have an eight-page spread. A collection of these eight page spreads ('gatherings' or 'quires', as they were called) would make up a quarto book. The size would be roughly 16 × 12 cms.

   In Elizabethan times the quarto format was used for everyday printing purposes. The folio format was more elegant, and was reserved for more prestigious publications. To form a folio, simply fold a piece of paper in half. You then have four pages. The word folio is from the Latin word meaning 'leaf', and a folio book's size would be around 30 × 22 cm.

   Fear of piracy prevented Elizabethan authors and theatre companies from producing too many written copies of plays, which might be stolen by rival companies who would use them to put on their own versions of the play. In fact, attempts were often made to have just one copy of a play in general circulation – the prompt-book, containing full production notes, including stage directions.

But like DVD pirates today, Elizabethan pirates went to great lengths to lay hands on copies of popular productions. Sometimes prompt-books themselves were stolen, and texts were often produced based on notes taken during performances, plus memory work.

The result was that, according to the British Library, by 1642, 21 of Shakespeare's plays had appeared in no fewer than 70 quarto editions. Among the plays particularly well-circulated were *Romeo and Juliet*, *Hamlet*, *The Merry Wives of Windsor*, and *King Lear*. Some of the editions were based on notes and memory, and were full of errors (the so-called 'bad' quartos). Here for example is how Hamlet's famous *To be, or not to be* appears in one quarto: *To be or not to be. Aye, there's the point/To die to sleep, is that all? Aye all.*[4] There were, however, 'good' as well as 'bad' quartos, sometimes produced by the bona fide theatre companies themselves who wanted accurate versions of plays to be available for posterity.

As time went on, people began to want to read as well as see plays, and in 1623 two of Shakespeare's fellow actors (and admirers) collected most of his plays together and produced them as a nine-hundred-page book entitled *Mr William Shakespeare's Comedies, Histories & Tragedies*. Their names were John Heminge and Henry Condell, and the printer publisher was William Jaggard. The book was printed in folio form, and has come to be known as the First Folio. Later versions appeared in 1632, 1663 and 1685 – the Second, Third and Fourth Folios.

An informative website about the First Folio is http://www.william-shakespeare.info/william-shakespeare-first-folio.htm. There are also several copies of the Folio itself online, including at http://internetshakespeare.uvic.ca/Library/facsimile/). This is the site of the 'Internet Shakespeare Editions', and contains quarto and various folio versions of many plays. A facsimile of the First Folio is readily available in book form – Hinman (1996). This is the version that has been used whenever the First Folio is mentioned in this book.

1.5 Shakespeare's English? Which Shakespeare? Whose English?

The *Quartos and folios* box above introduces the issue of 'transmission' – how Shakespeare's original manuscripts have been transmitted down to us today, becoming the versions that we now use. As the box suggests, there were often many more than one version of a play in circulation. So when it came to producing an 'authoritative' published edition, part of an editor's job was to sift through the available versions and choose which one to use. This was what the First Folio editors Heminge and Condell did, and they took the task very seriously.

As well as selecting 'which Shakespeare' (which version to use, that is), editors were also capable of altering text in order to fit in with their own (or their readers') prejudices. One of Maguire's (2003: 590) examples relates to some of Shakespeare's sonnets which seem to have been written to a man. A 1640 printing of some of these 'arbitrarily changed some masculine posses- sive pronouns to feminine, making selected sonnets more palpably hetero- sexual'. Over the centuries, editors have altered Shakespeare in even more drastic ways – a particularly well-known case is the seventeenth-century edi- tor Nahum Tate, who gave *King Lear* a happy ending, to avoid the bleakness of the conclusion that Shakespeare himself supplied.[5]

As Maguire (2003: 589) puts it: 'an editor is a mediator'. But they were far from being the only mediators. The manuscript which Shakespeare produced would have formed the basis for the prompt-book from which actors worked. If the manuscript was unclear in any way, the 'scriveners' (clerks) would have tidied it up, or even on occasions rewritten it. So even at this early stage in the production process, there is the possibility of two slightly differing versions of a play in existence: Shakespeare's own original and a 'tidied-up' version. Then there were the 'compositors' (typesetters). Their job was to transfer text from a manuscript to the plate which was used for printing. They saw it as part of their job to add their own corrections, regularising spelling or punctuation. Sometimes their work reveals that they were following principles, but often it was simply a question of personal whim.

The existence of these various intermediary steps means that we need to question how much of what we read today is actually Shakespeare, and how much the work of others involved over time in the production and editing process. 'Whose English?' indeed. The transmission issue is particularly relevant to Chapter 8, which focuses on spelling and punctuation. Is a par- ticular spelling Shakespeare's or that of a scrivener or compositor? Often we cannot know. But as the example of changing pronouns in the sonnets suggests, intervention can go far beyond the mechanics of writing. 'Which Shakespeare?' and 'whose English?' are questions which need to be borne in mind throughout this book.

Notes

1 The extract can be found on YouTube at http://www.youtube.com/watch?v=
   zSZNsIFID28. The passage also became the opening paragraph of *The Pleasure of
   Finding Things Out* (Feynman, 2001), whose first chapter describes Feynman's
   youth and the growth of his interest in science. For more Feynman on YouTube,
   there is the *Symphony of Science: We are connected* which he performed with Carl
   Sagan and others. It is at www.youtube.com/watch?v=XGK84Poeynk&feature=
   player_embedded.

2 The example is also used in Crystal (2008).

3 Various versions of the sketch can be seen on YouTube, for example at
   http://www.youtube.com/watch?v=QCoZhMip-eM&feature=related).

4 This information is taken from Mabillard (2000).

5 The way that Shakespeare's works have been adapted over the centuries is
   particularly well described in Wells (2002) and Taylor (1989). Murphy (2010)
   provides a useful short account of the transmission process.

CHAPTER 2

Inventing Words: The 'great feast of languages'

Key phrases:
unruly growth; adaptation and innovation

2.1 Admiring Shakespeare's vocabulary

Shakespeare's fan club is very large indeed. In fact you may have come across the word *bardolatry* – a mixture of *bard* and *idolatry* – used to describe the way people idolise the man. You might be interested to use the internet and other sources to identify some of the famous Shakespeare fans (and for that matter, others among the famous who were Shakespeare detractors). The novelist Virginia Woolf was a fan. Here is what she says about him in her diary:[1]

> I read Shakespeare directly I have finished writing. When my mind is agape and red-hot. Then it is astonishing. I never yet knew how amazing his stretch and speed and word coining power is, until I felt it utterly outpace and outrace my own, seeming to start equal and then I see him draw ahead and do things I could not in my wildest tumult and utmost press of mind imagine.

Analysing the specifics of Shakespeare's 'word coining power' is a central concern of this chapter. But it is appropriate that before analysis should come admiration – of his huge, rich vocabulary, and his use of unexpected, memorable words. Almost every page of his works has its examples. Some of the ones below illustrate the richness – particularly when it comes to insults! Others contain particularly striking images created by unexpected word choices. The passages are here to be read and admired, and for this it is not important to understand every word. But as a first step towards analysis, try to explain to yourself how the effects of the words come about. In the first passage, for example, think what it might mean to 'descant on one's own deformity'. Shakespeare's images often link up to others, and indeed in the next chapter (3.3) we will discuss what has been called his 'never-broken chain of imagery'. So one might also consider how the notions of *descant* and *piping* connect. Where the focus is on one particular word, it is underlined:

(a) **Richard Gloucester** is a hunch-back, and feels excluded from some of the pleasures of peace-time (R3 1.1.24):
   Why I, in this weak piping time of peace,
   Have no delight to pass away the time,
   Unless to spy my shadow in the sun
   And <u>descant</u> on mine own deformity.

(b) **Lady Macbeth** is contemplating a murderous crime (Mac 1.5.48):
               Come, thick night,
   And pall thee in the dunnest smoke of hell,
   That my keen knife see not the wound it makes,
   Nor heaven peep through the <u>blanket</u> of the dark
   To cry, 'Hold, hold!'

(c) Antony has made his followers weep, and **Enobarbus** joins them (AC 4.2.34):
               Look, they weep,
   And I, an ass, am <u>onion-eyed</u>. For shame,
   Transform us not to women.

(d) After a fight at sea, this **soldier** is pleased to see night fall (2H6 4.1.1):
   The <u>gaudy</u>, <u>blabbing</u>, and <u>remorseful</u> day
   Is crept into the bosom of the sea;

(e) **Cleopatra** remembers the indiscretions of her youth (AC 1.5.73)
               My <u>salad days</u>,
   When I was green in judgement,

In the next two examples it is the passage as a whole, rather than individual words, which deserve attention:

(f) Here is how **Berowne** in *Love's Labour's Lost* describes Cupid (3.1.176):
   This wimpled, whining, purblind, wayward boy,
   This senior-junior, giant-dwarf, Dan Cupid,
   Regent of love-rhymes

(g) **Falstaff** can be very rude to the future king of England, Prince Hal. For example (1H4 2.4.240):
    'Sblood, you starveling, you eel-skin, you dried neat's tongue, you bull's-pizzle, you stock-fish! O for breath to utter what is like thee! You tailor's-yard, you sheath, you bow-case, you vile standing tuck!

For more extended examples of lexical (the word means 'verbal') richness, take a look at one or more of the following:

- Mercutio's 'Queen Mab' speech in *Romeo and Juliet* (1.4.53)
- Oberon describing to Puck where to find Titania at night (MND 2.1.249)
- Enobarbus describing Cleopatra in her barge (AC 2.2.196)

If you want elaborate, rich insults, Thersites in *Troilus and Cressida* is the man to watch. Try *Troilus and Cressida* 5.1.17.

Before we focus in on the mechanics of Shakespeare's word coinage, it will be useful to look in some detail at the linguistic context in which he was writing.

2.2 The Renaissance and words

2.2.1 English vocabulary, and the struggle for linguistic supremacy

Probably most people's knowledge of King Henry V, who reigned in England from 1413 to 1422, comes from Shakespeare's play of that title, and includes little more than that he was a strong patriot, made Churchill-like speeches (*Once more unto the breach, dear friends, once more*), and won the Battle of Agincourt. The real king Henry was indeed a patriot, and a friend of the English language, being responsible for its adoption as the official language of government. He even, we are told, used English in his own correspondence. It is curious for us today to think that an English king could have used any other language for that. We are perhaps accustomed to thinking that English people use English (and only English), just as Germans use German and the French use French. But in fact the 'one language for one country' model did not apply to England in mediaeval times. Instead there was a situation of what sociolinguists call diglossia (a Greek-based word meaning 'bilingual'), where more than one language, or different varieties of the same language, are in use for different purposes. In situations where diglossia occurs (including in very many parts of the world today), there is characteristically a 'Higher' (or H) language, used for formal or literary purposes, and a

'Lower' (L) language, used for everyday communication.[2] In the mediaeval period, English served very much as an L language. There were two H ones. The first was French. It was brought by the Norman invaders in 1066, and had thereafter established itself as the language of administration and of the upper classes. If we find Henry V's use of English surprising, it is interesting to know that his father, Henry IV, born in 1367, was the first king of England after the conquest to speak English as mother tongue. In Shakespeare's time, French was losing its sway, though it is worth recalling that Shakespeare himself clearly had a command of the language, and could expect his audience to have the same: there is an entire scene in *Henry V* (3.4) in French, where princess Katharine of France is trying to learn some English from her attendant, Alice.

Latin was even more H than French. England had of course been a Roman colony, but long after the Romans departed, the influence of their language remained. Christianity spread to England at the end of the sixth century, accompanied by its own language – Latin, very much the language of early Christianity. Church services were held in Latin throughout the Middle Ages, and it was spoken in the monasteries. Religious texts were written in Latin, 'the language reserved for God's highest mysteries'.[3] Indeed, because the Bible appeared in Latin, it was the 'word of God'. Translation of any part of holy Scripture into English was prohibited in 1407 by the Archbishop of Canterbury, Thomas Arundel.

Latin was also the language of learning, used by scholars whatever their mother tongue, if for no other reason than because its use would guarantee international readership. The influential Renaissance humanist, Sir Thomas More, was for a time counsellor to Henry VIII (and like many who had to do with Henry VIII, he ended up without a head). He chose to write his famous book *Utopia*, which appeared in 1516, not in English but in Latin. Incidentally, he, an Englishman born in London, was also a strong advocate *against* the translation of the Bible into English. The oddness of using Latin for scholastic works is brought home by the fact that in 1568 (Shakespeare was alive by then), another Sir Thomas (Smith this time, 1513–1577, who held many positions including that of Vice Chancellor of Cambridge University) produced a book about the pronunciation and writing of English. The book's title proclaims the language Smith chose to write in. It is *De recta et emendata linguae Anglicae scriptione, dialogus*. That English was indeed the L, and not the H, language of the time, is suggested by the fact that in 1605 there were nearly 6000 books in the University of Oxford's Bodlean Library, but only 36 of these were in English.[4] In fact the practice of writing scholastic works in Latin to ensure international readership persisted into the late seventeenth century, when Newton chose to write his 1687 *Philosophiae Naturalis Principia Mathematica* in Latin. The book was not translated into English for 32 years.

Education was a third area where Latin played its H role. Everyone wanted their children to learn Latin. As Roger Ascham put it in his influential 1563 book, *The Schoolmaster*, 'all men covet to have their children speak Latin: and so do I very earnestly too.' Ascham acted as Latin tutor to Princess Elizabeth, who later as Queen put his teaching to good use by giving the occasional address in Latin, at the Universities of Oxford and Cambridge, for example. Latin was indeed the language of higher education, with universities throughout Europe using it for texts, lectures, disputations, and examinations. But it was also an important part of the curriculum in English grammar schools, including Shakespeare's own, the King's New School in Stratford, where a 'central educational principle was total immersion in Latin'.[5] Indeed, a fragment of a Latin lesson makes its way into *The Merry Wives of Windsor*, where Evans questions the schoolboy William. Shakespeare adds a characteristic bawdy note at the end (4.1.52):

Evans:	*What is your genitive case plural, William?*
William:	*Genitive case?*
Evans:	*Ay.*
William:	*Genetivo: 'horum, harum, horum'.*
Mistress Quickly:	*Vengeance of Jenny's case! Fie on her! Never name her, child, if she be a whore.*

In fact by the time Shakespeare was writing this, in the late sixteenth century, the wheels of change had long since been in motion, and English had already 'mostly supplanted Latin as the primary medium for written discourse'.[6] Why this change of fortune for English? It was partly a question of education. Reading and writing were increasingly being taught, for example at the so-called 'petty schools' – low level primary schools run by educated housewives – and the language used was English. Adult male literacy in London was as high as fifty per cent in Shakespeare's time, and the development of printing (a topic Chapter 8 considers in more detail in relation to spelling) was making reading material more available to more people. Increasingly also, English was gaining vocal supporters. One such was the schoolmaster Richard Mulcaster. In 1582 he wrote an influential book about English and English teaching, called *The Elementarie* (we will also consider his work in Chapter 8). 'I do not think that any language', he said, 'is better able to utter all arguments, either with more pith, or greater plainness, than our English tongue is ...' By the mid seventeenth century, support of English had gained in strength to the point of arrogance. In 1644 (just 28 years after Shakespeare's death), Milton seems to be suggesting in his *Areopagitica* that the English have a special relationship with God who, Milton says, will reveal himself to his servants, and 'first to his English-men' – in English of course.

But for all the positive qualities of English that writers like Mulcaster celebrated, there was a general awareness that the language needed to develop and grow. If this was to happen, it was essential that prescriptive attitudes should be avoided. Masses of rules and regulations about what the language should be like, laid down by scholars, would only stifle language growth. Of course, without these things, one is likely to have a degree of chaos, and indeed McDonald (2001) talks of the 'unruliness of the English language' at the time. But unruliness is not always a bad thing. There was a feeling in the air that 'anything goes', and for vocabulary (the concern of this chapter) this created an atmosphere of 'creative chaos' which encouraged people to invent new words, to modify existing ones for new uses, and to borrow words from other languages.

It is also important to realise that development and growth, adventure, exploration and innovation, were all part of the spirit of the times, evident in many spheres and activities. There was of course geographical exploration, with sailors like Drake and Raleigh travelling the world, finding new territories, bringing their spoils back to England and the Queen. The nineteenth-century English poet, Francis Thompson, captures this spirit of the age by saying it was a time 'when a man got up in the morning and said "I have an idea. If you have nothing better to do, let us go continent-hunting". And he that had not found an island or so was accounted a fellow of no spirit'.[7] But it was also a time of great exploration in architecture, music, poetry, science, philosophy. Horizons of many types were being extended, and what was happening to the English language was just one example of this.[8]

Foreign travel and exploration was indeed one major source of vocabulary expansion in the Renaissance. Raleigh came back to Elizabeth's court laden with potatoes and tobacco, from the Spanish *patata* and *tabaco*. The English travelling in France returned with such words as *bigot, bizarre, entrance*. When they returned from Italy, they imported *algebra* (originally an Arabic word), *balcony, violin*, while Spanish and Portuguese gave them *alligator, banana, mosquito*.[9] English, it seems, has quite a reputation for widespread borrowing, even to this day. The Canadian science fiction enthusiast James D. Nicoll has a vivid, indeed lurid, way of putting it: 'English is about as pure as a . . . whore. We don't just borrow words; on occasion, English has pursued other languages down alleyways to beat them unconscious and rifle their pockets for new vocabulary.' The Renaissance was very much such an occasion, and as the examples above show, lexical borrowings (or loan words as they are called) were taken from a variety of languages. But there was one language from which English took a particularly large number of words at this time: Latin. Here is a box which says a little more about borrowing in general, and borrowing from Latin in particular:

Latinate borrowings, and how to recognise them

English has always borrowed from other languages, even when it has equivalent words already existing. This preparedness to welcome new words has resulted in a rich and complex vocabulary. At different times, different languages have dominated English borrowing habits. In ME, after the Norman invasion of 1066, French was the source. Because Anglo-Saxon (a Germanic language) tended to be spoken by 'ordinary' people, and French by the upper classes, there are plenty of examples of Germanic/French lexical doublets where the Germanic word tended to be more 'down to earth', and the French version more 'fancy'. Examples of Germanic/French doublets are *cow/beef; calf/veal; sweat/perspire*. Anglo-Saxon speakers sweated, French speakers perspired.

Though some Latinate (Latin-based) words came into English during the ME period, it was the Renaissance that opened the floodgates. The word 'renaissance' means 'rebirth', and what was being 'reborn' at this time – starting in Florence in the fourteenth century and spreading across Europe – was an interest in classical culture. During the time of this huge 'renaissance' of interest in classical times, it was natural for Latin (and Greek) words to make their appearance in English. It was partly a question of translation: as learned books were translated from Latin, the translators often had to invent new words to express the ideas they came across. Naturally such words were often Latin-based.

With French and Germanic words already in English, the influx of Latin words created lexical triplets of Germanic/French/Latin words. Here are some, all still in use today. If the Germanic words tend to be 'down to earth' and the French 'fancy', what can be said about the Latin ones?

Germanic	French	Latin
rise	mount	ascend
ask	question	interrogate
kingly	royal	regal
holy	sacred	consecrated
fire	flame	conflagration

Since Shakespeare's language is full of Latinate words, it is relevant to ask how these can be recognised, in both EModE and PDE. It is not easy. If you know

Latin well, this will help, though even then you may have problems: many words went from Latin into French; so if they then came into English, it is difficult to say whether it was from Latin or French. Take the word *port* (= 'harbour'), for example. It is clearly from Latin *portus*, and so is the French *port*. Does the English word come from French or Latin? Often in such cases only careful scholarship will provide answers. In the case of *port*, the *Oxford Dictionary of Word Histories* (Chantrell, 2002), gives Latin as the root, but acknowledges that it comes into English 'reinforced' by Old French usage.

Sometimes affixes will help with identification. Prefixes like *ex-* (e.g. in *exit*) suggest Latin, as do suffixes like *-ate* (e.g. *interrogate*), *-us* (*campus*), *-ex* (*index*) and *-a* (*diploma*).

Earlier you were asked about the 'style' of the Latin words in the lexical triplets. This table from Culpeper (2005) captures the differences between Germanic and Latin sources:

Germanic	Latin
spoken	written
frequent	rare
informal	formal
private	public
simple (monosyllabic)	complex (polysyllabic)
affective (= conveying feeling/emotion)	neutral
concrete	abstract

So, to summarise: in the Renaissance, English was increasing in use and status, but there was a realisation that it needed to grow and develop, in terms of lexis ('vocabulary'; the noun associated with the adjective *lexical*) as much as anything else. Foreign borrowing was one major means of expansion. But was this the best way to enlarge the vocabulary? An alternative would be to expand native sources, reviving English words which had fallen out of use, inventing new words based on English rather than foreign models. Foreign or native sources? It is a question of how best to manage change, and became the basis of one of the big linguistic debates of the age, to which we now turn.

2.2.2 The Inkhorn Controversy

An *inkhorn* is a vessel used for holding ink (what some today call an *inkwell*). *Inkhorn terms* are pedantic, bookish expressions, and the *Inkhorn Controversy* relates to the argument which raged during the English Renaissance about the importation and use of strange and often foreign words into the language.

There were, of course, two main points of view. The 'purists' believed in staying with English roots, and using English basics to develop the vocabulary. Then there were the 'neologisers' (from the word *neologism* meaning a newly coined word, and the practice of introducing innovative words in a language). In the next paragraph some of the arguments on both sides are briefly summarised. Before reading it, take a look at Activity 1 (*To borrow, or not to borrow*). It contains some quotations from writers on both sides of the Inkhorn Controversy, and allows you to see for yourself the kinds of arguments put forward (**NP**).

To summarise what the quotations say: On the purists' side were writers like the literary critic George Gascoyne and the statesman Sir Thomas Chaloner. They argued that borrowing from foreign languages ends up in a strange mixture of tongues. It is fashionable, they observe, for people who have been abroad to pepper their talk with foreign words, partly to show off how well-travelled they are. English has the advantage of using short (monosyllabic), no-nonsense words, and should be kept clean and pure. The neologisers included authors who were concerned with specialist areas where English lacked vocabulary to express certain ideas. Among their number were George Pettie who translated an Italian book about Renaissance manners, and the unknown author of a *Discourse on War*. Foreign languages, the common argument runs, are sometimes rich in vocabulary and where this is the case, there is no harm in taking words from them to enrich English and make it possible to express 'new' concepts and ideas. All languages borrow in this way, and though foreign words may take a time to learn, they will eventually become a part of the language, and their foreign origin will be forgotten.

The Inkhorn Controversy came about because of the extent of foreign borrowing at the time. It was a central part of the linguistic spirit of the age. To gain a sense of the lexical furore of the time, there is no better place to look than at one of Shakespeare's early plays, *Love's Labour's Lost*.

2.2.3 'Honorificabilitudinity': *Love's Labour's Lost* and linguistic excess

One might almost say that *Love's Labour's Lost* is 'about linguistic excess'. As one literary scholar puts it: the play lives through 'words sought for their own sake, words dancing to unexpected rhythms, and twisting themselves into fantastic shapes, words robbed from the rhetoricians and strung out, half mockingly, into patterns borrowed from the grammarians'.[10] One of the most linguistically interesting parts of the play is Act 5, Scene 1, and the paragraphs below take you through some moments from this scene.

The main characters in it are a pedantic schoolmaster (Holofernes), a 'fantastical Spaniard' (Don Adriano de Armado) with his page (Moth), a curate (Sir Nathaniel), and a clown (Costard) – perfect ingredients to create a powerful mixture of bizarre language use.

These extracts are intended to give you a flavour of the linguistic excess of the times, and it is not essential to understand every word (though the glossary at the end of the book will help you if you want to do this). Let the fountain of exotic language wash over you. At the same time it is worth keeping a special eye open for the following characteristics:

- florid expressions which you suspect might have a Latin or Italian source. The box earlier (*Latinate borrowings, and how to recognise them*) may help identify these;

- any words which you suspect may have been coined especially for the occasion;

- the habit of repeating the same idea more than once, using different words, as if the speaker were deliberately trying to explore the various linguistic resources available for expressing an idea. There is an example in the next paragraph with Nathaniel's three ways of saying 'named';

- though we will not be concerned with rhetoric until Chapter 6, you may also note how structures are repeated for rhetorical effect (as in the first extract below where the structure is *his* + noun + adjective – e.g in *his discourse peremptory*).

So, to the scene. At the beginning, Sir Nathaniel mentions that he has had a conversation with the man 'entitled, nominated, or called' Don Adriano de Armado. Holofernes replies – in Latin: *Novi hominem tanquam te* ('I know him as well as I know you'). He then proceeds to describe Armado thus:

his humour is lofty, his discourse peremptory, his tongue filed, his eye ambitious, his gait majestical, and his general behavior vain, ridiculous, and thrasonical. He is too picked, too spruce, too affected, too odd, as it were, too peregrinate, as I may call it. (5.1.10)

In the next part of his description, it is not only the words Holofernes uses that are of interest. He also has something to say to linguists about the pronunciation of certain words. His lines well illustrate how 'matters linguistic' were topics of discussion at the time. He is, as before, talking about Armado:

He draweth out the thread of his verbosity finer than the staple of his argument. I abhor such fanatical phantasimes, such insociable and pointdevice companions, such rackers of orthography, as to speak 'dout' sine 'b'

> *when he should say 'doubt,' 'det' when he should pronounce 'debt' – d, e, b, t,*
> *not d, e, t. He clepeth a calf 'cauf', half 'hauf'; neighbour vocatur 'nebor',*
> *neigh abbreviated 'ne'. This is abhominable, which he would call*
> *'abominable.' It insinuateth me of insanie.* (LLL 5.1.16)

Words like *debt*, *calf* and *abhominable* all contain silent letters ('b', 'l' and 'h' respectively). Pedants like Holofernes believed that these letters should be pronounced, and you can almost hear him sneering at the poor ignoramuses who do not pronounce the 'b' in *debt*! We return to this speech and look at it in more detail in 9.6.1.

Now Armado himself appears, accompanied by Moth and Costard. Nathaniel, Armado and Holofernes in conversation together put on a colourful linguistic firework display. As Moth witheringly comments: *They have been at a great feast of languages, and stolen the scraps.* Costard agrees; as you read, continue to look for examples of the characteristics mentioned earlier:

> *O, they have lived long on the alms-basket of words. I marvel thy master*
> *hath not eaten thee for a word; for thou art not so long by the head as*
> *honorificabilitudinitatibus: thou art easier swallowed than a flap-dragon.*
> (5.1.38)

Honorificabilitudinitatibus?!? A fascinating word, but not a Shakespearean invention. It means 'the state of being able to achieve honours', and according to Samuel Johnson is 'often mentioned as the longest word known'. It has even been rendered into English, as *honorificabilitudinity* (a wonderful word for Scrabble players, but unfortunately the board is not big enough). Try looking for the Latin version on an internet search engine. It has quite an interesting history.

Armado is proud of the fact that he is a companion of the King. Here he brings word from the King that a celebration for the princess is planned for that afternoon (5.1.82). Notice particularly the bizarre way in which he expresses the notion of 'afternoon':

Arm: *Sir, it is the king's most sweet pleasure and affection to congratulate*
      the princess at her pavilion in the posteriors of this day, which the
      rude multitude call the afternoon.
Hol: *The posterior of the day, most generous sir, is liable, congruent and*
      measurable for the afternoon: the word is well culled, chose, sweet and
      apt, I do assure you, sir, I do assure.

It would be an interesting linguistic challenge to attempt a 'translation' of these Armado/Holofernes speeches into PDE, with the help of the glossary at the end of the book.

The scene does indeed provide a flavour of the linguistic times. Do not fail to note how much conscious interest is shown to words and forms of expression. Holofernes' rant about the pronunciation of silent letters is a case in point, as is also his expressed admiration for the phrase 'the posterior of the day'. For him, like many in his day, how you expressed yourself was a matter of some importance. Chapter 6, which deals with rhetoric, shows just how important an issue this was.

2.3 Shakespeare's word coining

2.3.1 New words: but how many? Multifarious ifs and buts

There is no doubt that the Elizabethan period was one of great invention, linguistically as well as in other spheres. One reliable source has around 6000 new words introduced during the time that Shakespeare was writing.[11] But how many of those new words was Shakespeare responsible for? Since he is regarded as England's greatest writer, people want to believe that he must have been a prolific linguistic inventor as well. He was. But just how prolific? This is not an easy question to answer, as you will gather from the multifarious ifs and buts that fill the following paragraphs . . .

In 1906 the scholar Harold Bailey claimed that Shakespeare coined almost 10,000 words.[12] Bailey arrived at this figure – generally regarded today as highly excessive – by using the *Oxford English Dictionary* (the *OED*). This impressive dictionary will be mentioned many times in this book, and it plays a central role in attempts to calculate the extent of Shakespeare's coinages. So some background will be useful. It all began in 1857 when the Philological Society of London called for a new English Dictionary. Between then and 1928, the *OED* appeared in instalments. Because a dictionary compiler's work is never done, the production of Supplements began soon after. Dictionary plus Supplements formed the basis of the Second Edition, which appeared in the 1980s, and in 1992 the first CD-ROM version was published. The *OED* is currently being revised with new material appearing online. It is a staggeringly large work, not only listing words (600,000 of them), definitions and origins, but also providing examples of each word in use – there are two and a half million such 'quotations'. The *OED*'s website, (http://www.OED.com/) includes a short history of the dictionary, while Brewer (2007) provides a fascinating detailed account of its development. The website also gives information about how to access the dictionary. There are three ways of doing this today. One is online, either by an individual subscription, or by going through a public or university library which has paid for institutional access. Another is to purchase a CD-ROM copy. The CD version currently available is 4.0, of the Second Edition, and it includes new material prepared up to 1997. Revisions have taken place since then, so the CD-ROM version is not entirely up-to-date, but it costs considerably less than an individual subscription for online access. For those with sufficient bookshelf space, a third possibility is to buy the twenty-volume printed version of the dictionary.[13]

The *OED* was not finished at the time that Bailey was doing his neologism count. His method was to scrutinise the available parts of the dictionary, counting how many words had a Shakespeare quotation as the first example of use. He then made the assumption that that a 'first quotation' in the *OED* strongly suggested that Shakespeare invented the word. Those doing similar neologism counts in more recent times have at least had the advantage of a more 'complete' dictionary to work with (to the extent that any dictionary is ever complete). But the assumption that 'first quotation means first use' is a fraught one, as the box below explains.

First quotations and first use

The *OED* lexicographers (as dictionary compilers are called) collected their quotations by sifting through a large collection of texts. But their sample was uneven, and some types of text received much more attention than others. In the preface to the dictionary's first volume, the editors openly admit that quotations were to be taken from 'all the great English writers of all ages'. Calculations of the number of quotations by source clearly show this literary bias. Walter Scott, Milton, Chaucer, Dryden and Dickens are all in the top ten of *OED* quotations sources. But at the very top is Shakespeare, providing no fewer than 33,000 quotations.[14] Because his vocabulary was so rich and extensive, one would expect him to be a major quotation source. But it is also likely that while the lexicographers were looking closely at him (and other well-known literary figures), they were ignoring others who may well have used particular words before him. There are also quotation biases according to period, and not all historical periods were scrutinised with the same thoroughness. For example, in the early days of the *OED* medieval texts were not so available as they are today. Hence there are not so many *OED* quotations from that period. Perhaps if there were, many first quotations from Shakespeare would not be 'Shakespearean firsts' any more.

The graph in Figure 2.1 illustrates these points. It shows *OED* quotation numbers per decade. Notice the peaks and troughs, revealing unevenness in

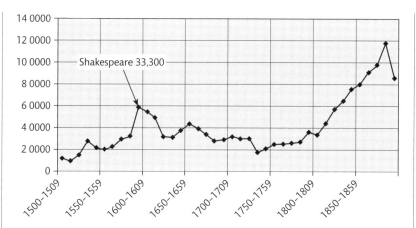

FIGURE 2.1 The OED's quotations: numbers rise as Shakespeare is included. From Brewer (2007)

sampling according to period. Notice also the peak around 1600. This 'is in large measure due to the *OED* lexicographers' devoted documentation of Shakespeare's vocabulary over this period'.[15] It is easy to see how such 'devoted documentation' could lead to exaggerated claims regarding his neologisms.

Scholarship in the last few decades has made many more texts available for scrutiny, and this has helped to rectify some of the exaggerations. But there is one other point to bear in mind: even if every text ever written had been examined by the *OED* lexicographers, how would one ever know that the first use of a word was spoken as opposed to being written down? There may well be many cases of words which others 'invented' but Shakespeare was first to put into print. So Shakespeare may falsely take the credit.

The points made in the box show that (in this book and elsewhere) claims about Shakespearean coinages must be expressed with a great deal of caution. But there is even more to it than that. If you are calculating neologisms, it is natural to focus only on words still in existence today. But Shakespeare con- tains a good number of what have been called <u>stillborn</u> neologisms – words like *acture* ('action'), *adoptious* ('connected with adoption'), and *repasture* ('food', 'repast') which were invented then but did not make it into PDE.[16] A true calculation of neologisms would have to bear these in mind. Then there is the issue of what counts as a new word. Crystal (2008) considers this in detail (as part of what he calls the 'The Quantity Myth' associated with Shakespeare's creativity). An example he gives is the word *nation*. Think of all the associated words like *national, nationally, nationhood, nationalise, nationalisation*. Do these count as separate words, or just different realisations of the same underlying form? Six words or one? How you answer this question will clearly dramatically affect the number of neologisms you arrive at. Questions of meaning can cause similar problems. Take the word *irritate* for example. It can mean 'to annoy', but also 'to cause inflammation/discomfort to' (e.g. the skin). One word or two? One reason why Bailey's coinage count was so high was that he regarded each different meaning of a word as a separate item. He counted the word *go*, for example, no less than 22 times, because he calculated it had 22 different meanings.[17]

When all these multifarious ifs and buts have been borne in mind, Crystal's estimate is that there are around 1,700 words which may be considered as plausible Shakespeare neologisms. Though this figure is much lower than Bailey's extreme claim, it is still a very large figure indeed – for one author. But there is another aspect of Shakespeare's neologisms that needs considering to appreciate the extent of his lexical achievement. This involves a kind of analysis known as type/token ratio, which measures the frequency of occurrence of each word within a body of work. So it does not tell you how many different words a writer uses, but how often words re-occur. Bolton (1992) uses this kind of analysis for Shakespeare and concludes that 'the real versatility of Shakespeare's vocabulary lies in the variety of his diction'. In comparison with other authors, he uses a very large proportion of his words a few times only.

As well as words, there are very many idioms too. Here are some of the idioms which are first found in Shakespeare (and may thus be neologisms; after all the discussion in earlier paragraphs, the 'may' really does need underlining):

Blinking idiot, breathe one's last, cheer up, crack of doom, do famously, fob off, foregone conclusion, foul play, full of sound and fury, good riddance, green-eyed monster, hoist with his own petard, household names, it's Greek to me, one's pound of flesh, tower of strength, what the dickens.[18]

A partial list of some reputed Shakespearean word coinages can be found on the website www.enotes.com/shakespeare-quotes/appendix-household-words-1. You could use this list to do your own mini type-token analysis which will indicate how infrequently invented words were re-used. Select a few words from the list. Then look them up on another website already mentioned – Crystal and Crystal's 'Shakespeare's Words' – http://www.shakespeareswords.com/. If you put a word you have selected into the search box on the home page, the site will give you a list of all occurrences in Shakespeare.[19] The chances are that you will find a good number of coinages that are used once or twice only. I tried this with all the words beginning with 'a' on the enotes site – a list of fourteen items. According to a search in Crystal and Crystal, only three of these fourteen were used by Shakespeare more than twice, and an astonishing seven just once only. The man was inventing words for a particular context, and often not using them again.

2.3.2 Neologisms: how Shakespeare did it

In the next few sections we will look at how neologisms were created in the Renaissance. As our discussion of the Inkhorn Controversy showed, there is more than one source for new vocabulary. One can (as James Nicoll put it) rifle words from the 'pockets' of other languages. Or one can make new words from ones that used to exist in English (in Anglo-Saxon times for example). A third possibility – and a major source of neologisms – is to make new words from already-existing English ones, adapting lexical items already in use, for example by adding a prefix or a suffix to them. 'Adaptation' is indeed a key word in the creation of all neologisms, whatever their original source, and this very much includes foreign words. So if a new word has a foreign origin, it is likely that an English ending will be added to it, to make it 'fit in' with English. The process of adding (or sometimes subtracting) elements to make new words is called <u>derivation</u>.

2.3.3 Derivation

<u>Prefixes</u> go on the front of words, <u>suffixes</u> on the end, and together they are called <u>affixes</u>. Sometimes it is difficult to specify exactly what an affix 'means', but often it is quite easy. A common use of the suffix -er for example (in PDE as well as EModE) is to indicate a person who undertakes or causes an action. It is used to change a verb into a noun. So PDE *teacher* refers to someone who *teaches* ('undertakes teaching'), and Shakespeare's neologism *injurer* changes the verb *injure* to a noun meaning 'a person who has caused an injury'. You do not of course have to be Shakespeare to be creative with affixation. We all do it all the time. For example, recently a new word, *defriend*, has been invented to describe the process of removing someone from your list of friends on a social network site like Facebook. And if you could not remember the word *watering can*, you might find yourself inventing the term *flower waterer*, which would doubtless convey your message adequately.

Here are some more affixes whose meanings are quite easy to work out. Try to specify what each 'means', and give a thought also to what parts of speech they change into what other parts of speech:

dis-   counter- (contra-)   un-
-y   -ship

The short passages below use these affixes in words that you have probably never seen outside Shakespeare. The underlined words are taken from Garner's (1982) list of Shakespeare's neologisms involving some Latin-based element. Use these passages to confirm your views on the meanings of the affixes above. Try also to provide definitions for the neologisms:

(a) The **Senators** are discussing Coriolanus' great deeds, in his presence. He is embarrassed and gets up to leave. The senators ask him to stay. One of them says (Cor 2.2.69):

> Sir, I hope
> My words <u>disbenched</u> you not.

(b) **Coriolanus** wants the enemy to return with peace conditions certified as accepted (Cor 5.3.206):

> you shall bear
> A better business back than words, which we
> On like conditions, would have <u>counter-sealed</u>.

(c) Here is **Lady Macbeth** wishing she were not a woman (Mac 1.5.38):

> Come, you spirits
> That tend on mortal thoughts! <u>Unsex</u> me here,
> And fill me . . . . full
> Of direst cruelty;

(d) The Welshman **Glendower** tries to convince everyone of his superhuman powers (1H4 3.1.53):

> I can call spirits from the <u>vasty</u> deep

(e) In *Henry VI, Part 1* (5.5.55), the **Earl of Suffolk** is arguing that there should be more to marriage than a legal and financial agreement:

> Marriage is a matter of more worth
> Than to be dealt in by <u>attorneyship</u>

Activity 2 (*Some interesting inventions*) gives you an opportunity to look at some more examples of Shakespeare's neologisms using affixes.

Though most derivations involve adding an affix, one could also be taken away. Subtraction of an affix is known as <u>back formation</u>. A common one was to take the suffix -ion from a noun to create a verb ending in -ate. For example, the verb *castigate* comes from the noun *castigation* and has its first citation in the *OED* from Shakespeare's *Timon of Athens* (4.3.240), where Apemantus says to Timon *If thou didst put this sour cold habit on / To castigate thy pride, 'twere well*. Similarly Shakespeare was an early user of *arbitrate* and *adulterate*. The nouns *castigation*, *arbitration* and *adulteration* all occurred much earlier – the first two are in Chaucer.

Sometimes the back formations are not obvious at all, and you need to be told this is what they are before you can work out what they mean. In *Cymbeline*, for example, Posthumus describes his wife Innogen as acting with a *pudency*. The word is a back formation from *impudency* (associated with *impudent*), and it means 'modesty'. Similarly, in *Romeo and Juliet*, when the Nurse talks about the '*versal* world' (2.4.201) she is using a back formation of 'universal'.[20]

Sometimes affixes were used to introduce new words when an old one already existed, and in some cases the new word was used for metrical reasons. In Chapter 7 we will consider metre in more detail. But you do not need a technical knowledge of the subject to appreciate the value of some neologisms. The word *blast*, for example, is old, the first *OED* citation being in the year 1000. Why then did Shakespeare bother to invent the noun *blastment*, which occurs in this line of *Hamlet*: *Contagious blastments are most imminent* (1.3.42)? To appreciate how the answer might be to do with metre, read the line replacing *blastments* with *blasts*. The change plays havoc with the rhythm of the line. The same reason may explain why *vasty* was used in example (d) earlier, even though the adjective *vast* was in use in Shakespeare's time. Again, try reading the line with *vast* instead of *vasty* and see the effect on the metre.[21]

The neologism *blastment* comes from another noun (*blast*), and *vasty* comes from another adjective, *vast*. But often affixes are used to change one part of speech to another – nouns into verbs and so on. Look through the neologisms introduced in the Activity 2, and find an example of a noun changed into a verb by the addition of an affix (the example will make an appearance in the next section). When the grammatical category of a word is changed without any substantial alteration to its form, this is called a functional shift (also called conversion), which we will now focus on.

2.3.4 Functional shift

A common form of functional shift is making verbs out of nouns (sometimes called 'verbing'). We all do it: the process of using the search engine *Google* has become so common that we soon made a verb of it, and talk about *to google* and *I googled it*. The American cartoonist Bill Watterson has a cartoon about verbing. In it the young boy, Calvin, announces that he likes to 'verb words. I take nouns and adjectives and use them as verbs. Remember when "access" was a thing? Now it's something you **do**. It got verbed.' He concludes by introducing his own new verb: 'verbing weirds language,' he announces.

Calvin's companion is a stuffed tiger named Hobbes. His reaction to Calvin's comments captures the irritation that some people feel towards functional shift. 'Maybe we can eventually make language a complete impediment to understanding,' he observes sardonically. Here is how angry one blogger became at an example of verbing from recent times – use of a verb *to podium* to mean winning a medal at a games meeting: 'these linguistic absurdities continue, aided and abetted by the network people. The latest is truly bizarre, from the Olympic coverage: "She was unable to podium." Arrrrgh. Grrrrr. Comment unnecessary'.[22]

Though functional shift does attract such responses, it is a very powerful tool for expanding the lexical resources of a language. As in the *podium* example above, nouns and verbs are usually involved, but in fact any part of speech can be subject to the process. One of Culpeper's examples (his 2005 book is a highly accessible account of the history of English) uses the adverbs/prepositions *up* and *down* which become nouns when we talk of *the ups and downs of life*. Since functional shift is still very common, you might like to think of a few examples you have come across in recent times.

Shakespeare indulges in functional shift a great deal. Here are ten examples. In each case, first identify the word which has been 'shifted', then try to paraphrase its meaning in the passage:

(a) **Iago** is saying to Othello that sexual licence is common yet despicable (Oth 4.1.70):
   O! 'Tis the spite of hell, the fiend's arch mock,/ To lip a wanton in a secure couch/ And to suppose her chaste

(b) Vincentio, the Duke, has gone away, leaving Lord Angelo as Duke in his place. Angelo, **Lucio** says, is really acting the part. (MM 3.2.90):
   Lord Angelo dukes it well in his absence

(c) At the beginning of *The Two Noble Kinsmen* (1.1.43), three **queens** talk about the cruelty of Creon, who will not let their dead husbands be properly buried:
   He will not suffer us to burn their bones,/ To urn their ashes,

(d) **Ulysses** is railing against Achilles who is full of self-importance and anger. (TC 2.3.173):
   Kingdomed Achilles in commotion rages

(e) Bolingbroke addresses the Duke of York: *My gracious uncle*. But the **Duke** is angry with him, as this reply shows (R2 2.3.86):
Tut, tut! Grace me no grace, nor uncle me no uncle

(f) **Hamlet** is warning the visiting actors against over-acting. Herod was a tyrannical ruler who appeared in the Bible (3.2.14):
It out-herods Herod; pray you, avoid it

(g) The Theban **Palamon** asks why he should make his appearance suit the image ('glass') of someone he wants to please. Should he be out of favour because his beard is not liked? (TNK 1.2.54):
My poor chin too, for 'tis not scissored just/ To such a favourite's glass?

(h) In *Cymbeline* (1.7.64), **Iachimo** is describing the pangs of love felt by a Frenchman he knows:
There is a Frenchman . . . that, it seems, much loves/ A Gallian girl at home. He furnaces/ The thick sighs from him

(i) Antony has sent his friend Enobarbus some treasure. A **soldier** warns him to give safe-conduct to the messenger who brought it, protecting him from the army ('host') (AC 4.6.26):
I tell you true: best you safed the bringer/ Out of the host

(j) In *Antony and Cleopatra* (4.14.72), Antony asks his friend Eros to kill him. Eros refuses, and **Antony** asks him whether he would like to see his master (Antony) taken prisoner back to Rome:
Eros,/ Wouldst thou be windowed in great Rome and see . . .   Thy master thus . . . submissive, docile, subjugated

Activity 3 (*Shakespeare 'weirding' language*) provides some additional tasks using the examples above. If you want more examples of functional shifts, Crystal and Crystal (2002: 191) contains a long list.

There is a branch of linguistics known as neurolinguistics which looks at brain functioning in relation to language activity. Occasionally, though not very often, neurolinguists venture into the world of literature. Here is an example where functional shift in Shakespeare is the main concern.

Shakespeare's functional shifts and electroencephalograms

Philip Davis, at the University of Liverpool (in collaboration with colleagues) undertook some research which interestingly combines literary study with neuroscience. The results are described in a paper, Davis (2006). The research is focused on the area of functional shift that we have been considering. Davis finds that 'the effect [of such functional shifts] is often electric . . . like a lightning-flash in the mind'. With neuroscientific colleagues he sets out to explore whether this 'electricity' can be actually detected in the brain when a functional shift is encountered. For his experiment he uses sets of four sentences. Think particularly about the italicised words:

(a) I was not supposed to go there alone: you said you would *accompany* me.

(b) I was not supposed to go there alone: you said you would *charcoal* me.

(c) I was not supposed to go there alone: you said you would *incubate* me.

(d) I was not supposed to go there alone: you said you would *companion* me.

Sentence (a) in each set is a normal English sentence. (b) is odd both syntactically and semantically (that is, in terms of both grammar and meaning): in the example above there is a noun where there should be a verb, and its meaning does not relate to the sentence. Sentence (c) each time is semantically unacceptable, but syntactically all right (*incubate* does not make sense here, but it is at least a verb, and is being used as one here). Sentence (d) is the most like Shakespearean functional shift; *companion* is semantically clear (we know immediately what it means), but syntactically odd because the word is a noun being used as a verb.

Subjects were asked to read each of the four sentences. Using various experimental techniques including electroencephalogram tests which involve placing electrodes on various parts of their brains to measure brain-events, the subjects' reactions to the different sentence types were assessed. It was found that type (d) sentences had 'distinct and unique' effects on the brain. One of these effects was to 'alert' the brain to further possible anomalies. Davis concludes that 'Shakespeare is stretching us; he is opening up the possibility of further peaks, new potential pathways or developments'.

The experimenters admit that this work is a 'small beginning'. Perhaps in the future interdisciplinary work like this will throw more light on how Shakespeare's verbal effects are registered in the brain.

Derivation, you could say, is the process of adding bits to (or taking bits away from) words. The third major way of creating new words, also much used in the Renaissance, involves a process of joining rather than adding or subtracting. It is called compounding.

2.3.5 Compounding

A compound is a word made up of two or more elements joined together. It has always been a popular means of word creation in English. Culpeper

(2005) shows that it was extremely common in Anglo-Saxon times. His example uses the AS word *folc* meaning 'people' or 'tribe'. He gives six instances of *folc* joining together with other words to form compounds. These include *folcmære* (literally 'people famous', meaning 'celebrated'), *folctalu* ('people tale', meaning 'genealogy'), and *folcweleg* ('people rich' meaning 'populous'). It was also a rich source of language development in Shakespeare's day, and it continues to be popular today. Culpeper gives statistics about the relative occurrence of various ways of generating vocabulary over the past fifty years. Compounding comes out to be by far the most popular.

Creating new compounds is something we particularly associate with poetry – we expect our poets to show off an array of creative new combinations, and it was particularly expected in the Renaissance, where poets and dramatists displayed a clear liking for the striking compound – particularly adjectives. Sometimes (as we will see in a moment) Shakespeare introduces compounds for some 'technical' reason, such as to avoid an awkward stress pattern. But often, particularly in his later works, the compounds he invents are imaginative and thought-provoking. Below are some examples. First just read through them enjoying the compounds and their effects. Then attempt to 'unpack' them by paraphrasing the underlined words, or even the entire passages (not always so easy):

(a)   *Let us rather*
    Hold fast the mortal sword; and like good men
    Bestride our <u>down-fallen</u> birthdom (Mac 4.3.2)
    [*birthdom* = native land]

(b) *. . . Lord Angelo, a man whose blood*
    Is very <u>snow-broth</u>, one who never feels
    The wanton stings and motions of the sense, (MM 1.4.57)

(c) *And that which should accompany old age,*
    As honour, love, obedience, troops of friends,
    I must not look to have, but in their stead
    Curses, not loud but deep, <u>mouth-honour</u>, breath
    Which the poor heart would fain deny and dare not (Mac 5.3.24)

(d) *A <u>care-crazed</u> mother to a many sons*
    A <u>beauty-waning</u> and distressed widow (R3 3.7.183)

(e) *Strives in his little world of man to <u>out-storm</u>*
    The <u>to-and-fro conflicting</u> wind and rain.
    This night, wherein the <u>cub-drawn</u> bear would couch,
    The lion and the <u>belly-pinched</u> wolf
    Keep their fur dry, . . . (KL 3.1.10)

In these examples, the words are joined by a hyphen. But because of all the uncertainties surrounding spelling conventions (as will be discussed in Chapter 8), there were various ways of representing compounds. So an *adjective + adjective* construction like *honest-true* (in *The Merchant of Venice* 3.4.46, Portia says she has always found Balthasar *honest-true*), could be written with a hyphen, but might equally well be *honest true*, or even *honest, true*. These different ways have persisted over time, and indeed into the present day. Nicholas Rowe, the eighteenth-century Shakespeare editor, for example, has a comma (*honest, true*) in the example above. In the First Folio of *Julius Caesar*, Cassius speaks of an enterprise which is *of honourable dangerous consequence* (1.3.124). Some modern editors (like Bate and Rasmussen, 2007) have the same, while others (like Craig, 1905, and Crystal and Crystal's 'Shakespeare's Words') have a hyphen (*honourable-dangerous*).

How can compounds be classified? One reason why compounding is popular as a means of increasing vocabulary is that it allows great scope in terms of what grammatical elements can be joined together. Thus one means of classification is in terms of the elements involved. The compound in passage (a) above is *down-fallen*. This comes from the verb 'to fall down', and consists of a particle (*down*) followed by the past participle of the verb (*fallen*). A very common way of forming compound adjectives is by *noun + present participle*, as in Lear's *oak-cleaving thunderbolts* (KL 3.2.5). Another common one is *noun + past participle (or adjective ending in -ed)* – as in *rash-embraced despair* (MV 3.2.109), or as when Juliet's father rather rudely describes his daughter's body as *tempest-tossed* (RJ 3.5.137). The five passages above in fact illustrate most of the main ways of compounding Shakespeare uses: noun + present participle; adverbial + present participle; particle + past participle; noun + past participle; noun + noun; particle + infinitive. Look through the compounds illustrated in all the passages and associate each with one of the above combinations (**AS**).

Another way of classifying compounds is in terms of how they function. Of the uses which Salmon (1970) considers, a major one is to describe some physical or mental attribute of a person. Here the form is often an adjective made up of a noun or adjective plus an *-ed* form. In *The Tempest* (4.1.99), Cupid is described as Mars' *waspish-headed son* (what do you think this adjective might mean?) Often the 'attribute' will be a term of abuse, as when Puck, in *A Midsummer Night's Dream*, describes Lysander as a *lack-love* and a *kill-courtesy* (2.2.83). Describing the natural world is another major function (of the sort exemplified by Homer's famous description of the dawn as 'rosy-fingered'). In *Romeo and Juliet* (2.2.31) Romeo uses the evocative compound *lazy-pacing* (or *puffing* as it is in many editions) to describe the clouds.

Looking at the semantic relations involved in compounds is yet another way of classifying them. For example, you might say that *waspish-headed* means 'having a head which is like a wasp's', or in abstract terms 'having a y which is x'. Sometimes the semantic relations expressed in compounds are very unexpected. Here is one where the relations seem to be 'x and yet y': in *Troilus and Cressida* (4.4.89), Troilus is (rightly as it turns out) worried that Cressida will be seduced by the charms of the Grecians, in whose graces *there lurks a still and dumb-discoursive devil*. *Discoursive* means 'communicative', almost the opposite of *dumb*. One wonders how this phrase could be translated into PDE. Juxtaposing opposites (as in this compound) is certainly not unknown elsewhere in Shakespeare, and indeed passage (f) in 2.1 (from *Love's Labour's Lost*) has elements of this. There is a longer example in *Romeo and Juliet*, when Juliet finds out that her beloved Romeo has killed her cousin Tybalt. She expresses her love-hate towards Romeo in a long passage made up of contrasting opposites, including (3.2.75): *Beautiful tyrant, fiend angelical,/ Dove-feathered raven, wolfish-ravening lamb.*

Occasionally you find nonce compounds. *Nonce* means 'for a particular occasion', and the word has interesting roots. It is derived from the old ME expression *for þan anes* meaning 'for the once' (the þ is a kind of 'th'). The final letter of *þan* became attached to the following word, giving *for the nonce*. There is an example of a nonce compound in *Love's Labour's Lost* (5.2.169). Moth, trying to catch the attention of the ladies, talks of their *sun-beamed eyes*. The ladies pay no attention to him, and Boyet suggests – playing on the *sun/son* pun – that since they are ladies, Moth would do better to call their eyes *daughter-beamed*. A typical nonce word.[23] Activity 4 (*More interest-rousing compounds*) provides a further opportunity to classify compounds.

As with derivation, Shakespeare sometimes uses compounds for reasons to do with the technicalities of metre. For example, *King John* (3.3.43) has the line: *Had bak'd thy blood, and made it heavy-thick*. A possible alternative to the compound *heavy-thick* would be to have *heavy and thick*, or even *thick and heavy*. As you did earlier with derivations like *blastments*, try substituting the compound with each of these alternatives. Read the revised lines aloud, concentrating on the rhythm, and you will notice that the alternatives lead to rhythmic irregularity. The technicalities of this will be discussed in Chapter 7.

2.3.6 Portmanteau words

Another way of joining existing words together to form new ones is by portmanteau words (sometimes called blends), which are simply words 'telescoped together'. One of the most famous examples in English is the word *slithy*, invented by Lewis Carroll in *Through the Looking Glass* to describe the creature he calls a *tove*. The word is a telescoped version of *slimy* and *lithe*. In fact it was Lewis Carroll who first used *portmanteau* in this linguistic sense; the word refers to a kind of travelling bag 'into which things are packed together'. Portmanteau words (consisting of two words 'packed together') are even today a productive means of creating new vocabulary. Think what words are telescoped together to form these three fairly recent blends: *motel*, *brunch* and *smog*. Look back to the first paragraph of this chapter and you will find another example of a portmanteau word. Another example is the word *spork* (sometimes also called a *foon*). If you cannot guess what one of these eating implements looks like, search the internet for a picture.

Creating portmanteau words was one of the techniques of word creation used by Shakespeare and the Renaissance. The examples below are all from Shakespeare, though not necessarily his own neologisms. Work out what words are being blended to form the underlined words. Once you have done this, the meaning of the words should be clear enough (**AS**):

(a) In *Hamlet* (4.5.102), **Laertes** is approaching very fast. The ocean, it is reported, *eats not the flats with more <u>impiteous</u> haste* than Laertes

(b) In *Antony and Cleopatra* (5.2.303), **Cleopatra** addresses the snake which is about to kill her. The word she uses is a Renaissance, but not a Shakespearean, neologism: *With thy sharp teeth this knot <u>intrinsicate</u> / Of life at once untie*

(c) Times are troubled! In *Julius Caesar* (1.3.20) **Casca** reports: *I met a lion, / Who <u>glazed</u> upon me, and went surly by*

2.4 Shakespeare and the spirit of the age

In section 2.3.1, we saw that there was massive vocabulary expansion in English during the period 1500 to 1659 in general, and during Shakespeare's lifetime in particular. We have considered the various sources for new words, and various ways of creating them. Shakespeare participated in this massive growth, and a main theme of this chapter is indeed that he was acting very much within the spirit of his age as regards his vocabulary usage. This means that if you take a look at other contemporary writers, like Marlowe and Jonson, you will find the characteristics that we have been discussing here. A quick skim through a few pages of one of Marlowe's or Jonson's plays will not be enough to reveal these processes in detail, but it may give you a sense of their presence. In the next chapter we will again find Shakespeare acting in the spirit of his age, in relation to another linguistic practice, which he also entered into with great gusto – 'playing with words'.

Activity section

1 To borrow, or not to borrow

These quotations from purists and neologisers have been taken from Baugh and Cable (2002) and McDonald (2001). Put them into the purist or neologiser camps; sometimes you will have to be guided by the 'tone' of what is said, rather than by any actual argument put forward. Then look more closely at what arguments are in fact made. Why, according to the purists, should we use native words and avoid foreign imports? And what about the neologisers' side of things? Taken together, the quotations will enable you to discern the main points used by both sides in the Inkhorn Controversy. The quotations are all from Renaissance writers, except for one from a much more recent writer. This has been included to show that the controversy has persisted into later times.

(a) *the most ancient English words are of one syllable, so that the more monosyllables that you use the truer Englishman you shall seem, and the less you shall smell of the inkhorn* George Gascoigne (1535–1577, an Elizabethan poet, dramatist and early literary critic who wrote an essay entitled *Certayne notes of instruction concerning the making of verse or rhyme in English*).

(b) *I know no reason why I should not use them* [foreign words]*: for it is in deed the ready way to inrich our tongue, and make it copious, and it is the way which all tongues have taken to inrich them selves.* George Pettie (c. 1548–89, best known as a writer of romances), in the 1581 preface to his translation of a book about Renaissance manners: Stefano Guazzo's *The Civile Conversation.*

(c) *I knowe no other names than are given by strangers, because there are fewe or none at all in our language* The [unknown] author of a *Discourse of Warre* justifying his use of foreign military terms.

(d) *I have thought good to borowe . . . littell of the Rethoriciiens of these saies, who plainely thynke theirm selfes demigods, if like horsleches thei can shew two tongues, I meane to mingle their writings sought out of strange langages as if it were alonely thing for theim to poudre theyr bokes with ynkehorne termes . . .* Sir Thomas Chaloner (1521–1565, a statesman and writer of Latin verses).

(e) *for as the Romanes and other Latin writers, notwithstandinge the copiouse and abundant eloquence of their tongue, haue not shamed to borrow of the*

Grecians these and many other terms of arte: so surely do I thinke it no reproche, either to the English tongue, or any English writer, where fit words faile to borrow of them both. Thomas Digges (1546–1595, a mathematician and astronomer: the first to describe in English the ideas of Copernicus about the planets revolving round the sun).

(f) *He that commeth lately out of Fraunce will talke French English and never blush at the matter. An other chops in with English Italianated and applieth the Italian phrase to our English speaking . . . I know them that thinke Rhetorique to stande wholie upon darke wordes, and he that can catche an ynke horne terme by the taile, him they coumpt to be a fine Englisheman, and a good Rhetorician.* Thomas Wilson (1524–1581, a diplomat and scholar who wrote a book called *The Arte of Rhetorique*).

(g) *I intend to augment our Englyshe tongue, whereby men shude as well expresse more abundantly the thynge that they conceived in theyr hartis . . . having wordes apte for the pourpose: also interprete out of greke, latyn, oor any othere tonge into Englysshe as sufficiently as out of any other of the said tongues into an other.* Sir Thomas Elyot (c. 1490–1546; he helped the cause of English by publishing a book about medicine – *The Castell of Helth* – which replaced Greek medical words with English ones).

(h) We have already come across Richard Mulcaster (1531–1611, a headmaster and educationalist, best known today for his 1582 book *Elementarie*). When we come across something new, he says, we must get to know it *and make the thing familiar if it seme to be strange. For all strange things seme great novelties, and hard of entertainment at their first arrival, till theie be acquainted: but after acquaintance theie be verie familiar, and easiee to entreat . . . Familiaritie and acquaintance will cause facilitie, both in matter and in words.*

(i) *I am of this opinion that our own tung should be written cleane and pure, unmixt and unmangeled with borrowing of other tunges, wherein if we take not heed of tijm, euer borrowing and neuer paying, she shall fain to keep her house as bankrupt.* Sir John Cheke (1514–1557, a scholar and statesman) in letter appended to a translation of Castiglione's *The Courtier* (1528).

(j) *Also ye finde these wordes, penetrate, penetrable, indignitie, which I cannot see how we may spare them, whatsoever fault we finde with Ink-horne termes: for our speech wanteth wordes to such sense so well to be used.* George Puttenham (1529–1590: scholar, and author of *The Arte of English Poesie*).

(k) [There are] *more things than there are words to express them by* Ralph Lever (c. 1530–85, a clergyman who in his *Art of Reason*, 1573, made strenuous efforts to express traditional philosophical ideas in English).

(l) *Bad writers, and especially scientific, political, and sociological writers, are nearly always haunted by the notion that Latin or Greek words are grander than Saxon ones, and unnecessary words like expedite, ameliorate, predict, extraneous, deracinated, clandestine, subaqueous, and hundreds of others constantly gain ground from their Anglo-Saxon numbers.* George Orwell (1903–1950; writer, best known for novels like *Animal Farm* and *Nineteen Eighty-Four*. The quote comes from *Politics and the English Language*).

2 Some interesting inventions

Table 2.1 has some of the more interesting Shakespearean neologisms involving some Latinate element. They have been taken from the long list

TABLE 2.1 Some Shakespearean neologisms with Latinate element (from Garner 1982)

Word	Reference	Example	Meaning
bemonster	KL 4.2.63	*Thou changed and self-covered thing, for shame, / Be-monster not thy feature.*	make monstrous
enwheel	Oth 2.1.85	*And the grace of heaven, / Before, behind thee, and on every hand, / Enwheel thee round.*	encircle
fishify	RJ 2.4.38	*O flesh, flesh, how art thou fishified?*	turn into fish
lieutenantry[24]	Oth 2.1.168	*If such tricks as these strip you out of your lieutenantry,*	position as lieutenant
oathable	Tim 4.3.136	*You are not oathable, / Although I know you'll swear,*	suitable to take an oath
outstorm	KL 3.1.10	*Strives in his little world of man to outstorm / The to-and-fro conflicting wind and rain.*	rage more violently than a storm
razorable	Tem 2.1.253	*till new-born chins / Be rough and razorable*	Ready for shaving
rumourer	Cor 4.6.48	*Go see this rumourer whipped.*	someone who spreads rumours
under-honest	TC 2.3.122	*If you do say we think him over-proud / And under-honest,*	wanting in honesty
unscissor'd	Per 3.3.29	*Unscissor'd shall this hair of mine remain*	Uncut
unfool	MWW 4.2.108	*Master Page, have you any way then to unfool me again?*	remove the suggestion of folly from

supplied by Garner (1982). Look first at the leftmost column, perhaps covering the other columns, and make a guess at the meanings of the words. Then use the third column to check (and perhaps modify) your view. The rightmost column provides you with an 'answer'.

3 Shakespeare 'weirding' language (AS)

Here are some other ways of using the ten examples in the text from Section 2.3.4:

(i) Nearly all the passages show nouns becoming verbs (noun → verb), but there is one (and possibly a second) which involves other shifts. Find this.

(ii) Salmon (1970) identifies some functions which Shakespeare uses functional shift for. Here are three: (i) to express anger; (ii) to express disgust by referring to a body part; (iii) meaning 'to act as'. Find an example of each.

(iii) Find an example of a person's name (a proper noun) being turned into a verb.

4 More interest-rousing compounds (AS)

(i) Here are some more instances of interesting compounds. Look for examples:

■ used as a term of abuse;
■ describing the natural world;
■ where the semantic relations seem to be 'x and yet y' (like the *dumb-discoursive* example in the text).

(a) Here is how **Roderigo** describes the Moor Othello (Oth 1.1.67):
What a full fortune does the <u>thick-lips</u> owe

(b) **Helena** is commenting on the huge confusion of lovers caused by Puck's magic potion (MND 3.2.129):
When truth kills truth, O <u>devilish-holy</u> fray!

(c) **Malcolm** is speaking about his time in England (where the scene takes place; Mac 4.3.148):
Which often since my <u>here-remain</u> in England

(d) **Iachimo** is observing the beautiful Innogen asleep (Cym 2.2.19):
the flame o'th' taper
Bows toward her, and would <u>under-peep</u> her lids

(e) *like the herald Mercury,*
    New lighted on a <u>heaven-kissing</u> hill
    (Ham 3.4.60)

(f) *My people did expect my <u>hence-departure</u>*
    Two days ago.
    (WT 1.2.450)

(g) *Before the always <u>wind-obeying</u> deep*
    (CE 1.1.64)

(h) The 'mourner' being described here is a dog (Ven 920):
    Another <u>flap-mouthed</u> mourner, black and grim,

(ii) As an additional activity, look at the examples from a syntactic point of
     view. In the first you have an adjective and noun combined to make a
     noun: adjective + noun → noun. Go through the examples saying in
     each case what grammar forms are combined, and what the resulting
     form is. The grammatical terms you will need to use are: adjective;
     noun, adverb, *-ing* participle; *-ed* participle.

Extended activities

1 2.1 draws attention to some particularly noteworthy word or phrase
   used in Shakespeare, and the point is made that 'almost every page of
   his works has its examples'. Make your own selection of (say five) words
   or phrases you particularly admire from a work of your choice. Try and
   articulate the reasons why you find them particularly memorable. It may
   also be interesting to compare your selection with that of a friend also
   interested in the same work.

2 2.3.4 contains an example of how angry people can become even today
   about linguistic change. Think of examples of how someone you know
   (it might even be you) gets angry about some aspect of the way your
   native language is changing.

3 Sections 2.3.2 onwards deal with the main processes of word
   formation in Shakespeare: derivation, functional shift, compounding
   (including portmanteau words). Select a scene from a work that
   particularly interests you. Go through it identifying words which
   seem to illustrate these processes. If you have the available resources
   (e.g. a copy of the *OED*), check whether the words may be Shakespearean
   neologisms.

Answer section

Compounding combinations (section 2.3.5)

Down-fallen: particle + past participle; *snow-broth*: noun + noun; *mouth-honour*: noun + noun; *care-crazed*: noun + past participle; *beauty-waning*: noun + present participle; *out-storm*: particle + infinitive; *to-and-fro conflicting*: adverbial + present participle; *cub-drawn*: noun + past participle; *belly-pinched*: noun + past participle.

Portmanteau words (section 2.3.6)

Impiteous is *impetuous* and *piteous*; *intrinsicate is intricate* and *intrinsic*; *glaze* is *glare* and *gaze*.

Activity 3 Shakespeare 'weirding' language

(i)   *Safed* is an adjective become a verb; *kingdomed* might be regarded as a noun become an adjective (the part participle being used adjectivally);

(ii)   Example (e) suggests anger; (a) refers to a body part, and (b) has the sense of 'act as'.

(iii) Herod (in f) is a proper noun.

Activity 4 More interest-rousing compounds

(i)   terms of abuse: (a) and (h); describing natural world: (e) and (g); 'x and yet y': (b).

(ii)   (b) is adjective + adjective → adjective; (c) is adverb + verb → noun; (d) is adverb + verb → verb; (e) is noun + *-ing* participle → adjective; (f) is adverb + noun → noun; (g) is noun + *-ing* participle → adjective; (h) is noun + *-ed* participle adjective.

Notes

1 *A Writer's Diary* (London: Hogarth Press, 1953), entry dated April 13th, 1930.

2 Most introductory textbooks on sociolinguistics, such as Spolsky (1998), contain discussion on the notion of diglossia. Ferguson's seminal paper on the topic (1959) is reproduced in various edited collections, Giglioli (1972) for example. For discussion of diglossia from a historical perspective, see Nevalainen and van Ostade (2006).

3 Dillon (1998).

4 The information is taken from Miola (2000: 11).

5 Greenblatt (2004: 25).

6 McDonald (2001: 11).

7 From 'The Poet's Poet', an essay on Spenser, available in Thompson (2003), p. 140.

8 Books which describe Renaissance 'exploration' in a variety of fields include Kraye (1996), Burke (1998), Rabb (2000), and Palliser (1992).

9 These examples are taken from Baugh and Cable (2002).

10 Evans (1964).

11 The figure is taken from Wermser (1976), as cited in Nevalainen (1999).

12 Information from Garner (1982).

13 The version used in this book is the CD-ROM Version 4.0 of the Second Edition. This includes when the *OED* is used for word definitions.

14 The information is taken from Brewer (2007: 233).

15 The graph and quotation are taken from http://OED.hertford.ox.ac.uk/main/, which describes a large research project in this area. The graph also appears in Brewer (2007: 128).

16 The examples are taken from Nevalainen (1999), which contains a longer list (p. 340).

17 This is pointed out by Theobald (1906).

18 The list is taken from Hughes (2000).

19 But be careful. The 'Shakespeare's Words' site often lists different forms of the 'same' word separately. So *house* and *houses*, for example, are listed as separate items.

20 Crystal and Crystal regard *versal* as a malapropism of the Nurse in *Romeo and Juliet*. Malapropisms are discussed in 3.1.3.

21 The examples come from Salmon (1970), who considers some of the motives for Shakespearean word formation.

22 The cartoon is from Bill Watterson's Sunday Strip. The website containing the blog is called 'Language Log' and is run by phonetician Mark Liberman (http://languagelog.ldc.upenn.edu/nll/). The blogger's comments on *to podium* can be found at http://itre.cis.upenn.edu/~myl/languagelog/archives/003968. html). There is a publication – Liberman and Pullum 2006 – which contains some of the more interesting blog comments from Liberman's site.

23 The example is taken from Salmon (1970).

24 According to the latest online revision of the *OED*, *lieutenantry* is used early by Shakespeare but was not invented by him.

Further reading

A lengthy and authoritative treatment of lexis is given in Nevalainen, T. (1999) 'Early Modern English Lexis and Semantics'. In Lass, R. (ed.) (1999) *The Cambridge History of the English Language, Volume 3*, Cambridge: Cambridge University Press, 332–458. Similarly in Kastovsky, D. (2006) 'Vocabulary', in Hogg, R. and Denison, D. (eds) (2006) *A History of the English Language*, Cambridge: Cambridge University Press, 199–270.

For background information on the Renaissance, various books are mentioned in note 8, including Kraye, J. (ed.) (1996) *The Cambridge Companion to Renaissance Humanism*, New York: Cambridge University Press. For a highly readable set of brief portraits of important Renaissance figures, see Davis, R. C. and Lindsmith, B. (2011) *Renaissance People*, London: Thames & Hudson.

A look through Vickers, B. (ed.) (1999) *English Renaissance Literary Criticism*, Oxford: Oxford University Press, will reveal the importance given to self-expression and rhetoric in the English Renaissance.

CHAPTER 3

Using Words: The fatal Cleopatras

Key phrases:
artifice; self-consciousness; wordplay

3.1 Playing with words

3.1.1 Artifice; self-consciousness about language

The Two Gentlemen of Verona was, according to some, Shakespeare's first play. In Act 2, Scene 4, Silvia witnesses an exchange of word-play between her two suitors – Valentine (one of the title's 'two gentlemen'), whom she comes to love, and the dull, conventional Thurio, whom her father wants her to marry – the first of many Shakespearean situations where child and parent come into conflict over choice of a partner. Since Silvia is present, Valentine and Thurio are out to impress her with their wit, while at the same time belittling each other with clever insults. It is a little piece of theatre, with Silvia as audience, and she shows her appreciation at the end with a compliment: *A fine volley of words, gentlemen, and quickly shot off* (2.4.32). In the BBC DVD production of the play the audience is enlarged to include a group of onlookers, who clap when particularly witty remarks are make – rather as today one would applaud a particularly funny joke of a stand-up comedian, or even (as one meaning of the word 'volley' suggests) an exceptional volley in a tennis match.

This element of 'performance' was characteristic of the Renaissance attitude towards language use. An important keyword of the time was *artifice*. Today we tend to look down on artifice, associating it with artificiality and hence lack of true feeling. But in the Renaissance, it was 'not a term of oppro-brium . . . but of praise . . . Readers and playgoers were expected to notice and to admire the skill with which artistic materials were arranged and presented'[1] – just as Silvia noticed, admired – and commented on – the performance of Valentine and Thurio.

We will look in detail at Renaissance ideas about good writing in Chapter 6, which focuses on rhetoric. In 6.3, we will note that the Renaissance saw the emergence of a large number of rhetorical handbooks, largely based on classical models, which provided guidance on how to write well. In these, the notion of artifice is central. There was an old classical proverb, of uncertain origin, which said *orator fit, poeta nascitur* ('the orator is made, the poet born'), suggesting that poetry was a natural thing, produced without artifice. But one of the rhetorical handbooks from classical times, mentioned in 6.3, the anonymous *Rhetorica ad Herennium*, put forward another point of view. It stated that the poet is formed by 'art, imitation, exercise'.[2] By 'art' is meant 'artifice' or 'theory'. The handbook was one of the most popular in Renaissance England, and a number of writers took up the idea. George Puttenham, whose 1588 *Arte of English Poesie* was another influential book, put it like this: 'Speech is not natural to man . . . as to the form and action of his speech, it cometh to him by art and teaching, and by use or exercise'.[3] Likewise Sir Philip Sidney in his *Defence of Poetry* urges poets to use 'art, imitation and exercise'. Ben Jonson says as much in relation to Shakespeare. He wrote a poem which appeared at the beginning of the First Folio, entitled *To the memory of my beloved, the author Mr William Shakespeare: and what he hath left us*. In it, he says: *For a good poet's made, as well as born/And so wert thou*. Later in the same poem he praises Shakespeare for his *well turned, and truly-filed lines*.

Often the artifice which the poet uses may be well concealed, and indeed Chapter 25 of Puttenham's book is entitled: *That the good poet or maker ought to dissemble his art; and in what cases the artificial is more commended that the natural, and contrariwise*.[4] But even when disguised, it is still there. Your enjoyment and understanding of Renaissance writing will be increased if you can come to terms with their attitude towards artifice. A look through the collection of Renaissance literary criticism in Vickers (1999) will help to develop that understanding.

A related key concept, whose importance you will have picked up in what has been said so far about language attitudes (and which is well shown in both the *Two Gentlemen of Verona* example, and the last chapter's extracts from *Love's Labour's Lost*) was 'self consciousness about language'. In the Renaissance, language was something you thought about, talked about, explored and experimented with. And it was something to be played with, knocked around rather like a kitten knocks around a ball of wool. Word-play was important to the Renaissance and to Shakespeare. Two aspects of this which we shall concentrate on in the following sections are puns and malapropisms.

3.1.2 Puns

What is a pun? Before looking at the definition below, try to come up with your own. Think of an example of a pun to illustrate your definition (**NP**).

Here is what the *OED* says: 'The use of a word in such a way as to suggest two or more meanings or different associations, or the use of two or more words of the same or nearly the same sound with different meanings, so as to produce a humorous effect; a play on words'. As the box below shows, puns have slipped in and out of fashion over time.

Puns in and out of fashion

Puns were a common feature in Shakespeare's day, used by many poets and prose writers. John Donne (1572–1631, sometimes called the 'Monarch of Wit') is a good example. He even punned on his own name, about his marriage to Anne which had a disastrous effect on his career: 'John Donne, Anne Donne, Un-done', he wrote.

But only fifty years after Shakespeare's death puns were out of fashion, and attempts were made to 'banish' them. In 1670, John Eachard, an English divine and satirist, wrote a book entitled *The Ground and Occasions of the Contempt of the Clergy.* He wanted to drive puns from the pulpit, wondering 'whether or no punning . . . and such other delicacies of wit . . . might not be very conveniently omitted'. In his 1656 poem, *Ode to Wit,* the poet Cowley asks the question 'what kind of thing is Wit?' Here is a negative part of his answer: *Tis not when two like words make up one noise; / Jests for Dutch men, and English boys.* ('Dutch man' sometimes just meant 'foreigner'; and 'double Dutch', incidentally, meant 'very foreign', when applied to a language – i.e. gibberish).

As we are about to see, the eighteenth-century critic, Dr Johnson, saw the pun as Shakespeare's weakness. According to his biographer, Boswell, he had a 'great contempt for that species of wit', and a 'general aversion to a pun'. They hindered, he thought, 'what is taken to be the function of language: the clean transmission of a pre-existing, self-sufficient, unequivocal meaning'.[5] Every idea had a word to fit it, and double meanings were something to be fought against, rather than admired.

Despite such views, we find in the eighteenth century some memorable examples of puns. Here is an example from Pope's poem, *The Dunciad* (4: 201–2). In these lines, the poet is ridiculing Richard Bentley – scholar, critic, and Master of Trinity College, Cambridge from 1700. Bentley had a reputation for being turbulent, but also, as the pun on the word *port* suggests, led a somewhat sleepy existence, possibly involving the use of alcohol on occasions:

> *Where Bentley late tempestuous wont to sport*
> *In troubled waters, but now sleeps in port.*

Empson (1977) characterises the nineteenth-century view of verbal ambiguities by looking at the editors of Shakespeare's works. When a word in the text has multiple meanings, they assiduously list and discuss these in their notes, weighing up what chances each has of being the meaning Shakespeare intended. They do not take on board the notion that multiple meanings may have been deliberate.

The twentieth century embraced wordplay vigorously. One writer who particularly comes to mind in this respect is James Joyce, whose novels *Ulysses* and *Finnegan's Wake* are celebrated for their word inventions, many of which are portmanteau words (discussed in 2.3.6). Here is the view of puns of the twentieth-century writer Anthony Burgess: 'plurality of reference is in the very nature of language, and its management and exploitation is one of the joys of writing'. A view diametrically opposed to the eighteenth-century one stated earlier.

Shakespeare loved puns, so much so that the aforementioned Dr Johnson describes them (or *quibbles* as he called them), as if they were some kind of drug to which Shakespeare was addicted. Here is what Dr Johnson famously said in his *Preface to Shakespeare*:

> '*A quibble is to Shakespeare what luminous vapours are to the traveller; he follows it at all adventures; it is sure to lead him out of his way and sure to engulf him in the mire. It has some malignant power over his mind. . . . A quibble was for him the fatal Cleopatra for whom he lost the world, and he was content to lose it.*'

There are certainly very many 'fatal Cleopatras' in the plays. Mahood (1957) – a book entitled *Shakespeare's Wordplay* – counts over 100 in *Much Ado About Nothing* and in *All's Well That Ends Well*, 150 in each of the *Henry IV* plays, and over 200 in that play which is all about linguistic excess – *Love's Labour's Lost*. The average for all the plays is 78. Before reading the next paragraph, consider which characters in the plays that you know well pun the most (**NP**).

The biggest punner of them all is Hamlet. Falstaff probably comes next. Villains do it a lot – Iago in *Othello*, and Richard III for example. So do lovers, particularly the women. Juliet and Cleopatra pun, and Beatrice outpuns Benedick (in *Much Ado About Nothing*). Not surprisingly, fools and clowns – like Feste in *Twelfth Night*, and Touchstone in *As You Like It* – also do a lot of punning. That is partly how they earn their living. Puns are indeed everywhere. Take a look perhaps at a few speeches made by one of the characters just mentioned, and see how far you have to read before coming across a pun. For more examples, look at Activity 1 (*Some fatal Cleopatras*) which provides the opportunity to identify some double meanings.

One sign of how deep in the Elizabethan psyche puns are lodged is Shakespeare's use of them in sad, tragic situations, where serious-minded critics like Dr Johnson regard them as inappropriate. So as Antonio in *The Merchant of Venice* is preparing to let Shylock take his pound of flesh (from the heart area), he says: *I'll pay it presently with all my heart* (4.1.278). And as Mercutio in *Romeo and Juliet* lies bleeding to death, he comments: *Ask for me tomorrow and you shall find me a grave man* (3.1.97). But perhaps the best example of all comes in *Richard II* when the man whose name is made for punning – John of Gaunt – is dying. He delivers a long speech (almost his final words) playing on his name and the gauntness associated with illness and death. *Gaunt am I for the grave, gaunt as a grave*, he concludes (2.1.82). So noticeable is this morbid word-play that King Richard, witnessing the scene, is moved to comment: *Can sick men play so nicely with their names?*

As mentioned earlier, high on the list of punners are men and women flirting with each other. Mahood (1957: 29) has a phrase which captures this banter of lovers, flirters (or just good friends for that matter). She speaks of the 'wordplay of good company'. The banter is often quite extended and involves puns and images that are developed at great length. It is a clear characteristic of Shakespeare, and you may be able to think of examples of it yourself. Beatrice and Benedick in *Much Ado About Nothing* do it all the time. The example below is from *Love's Labour's Lost* (2.1.114).[6] To appreciate the passage, you do not need to know anything about the situation except that the man (Berowne) is flirting, the woman (Rosaline) is resisting, and that both are wearing masks. Their banter involves a comparison between wit and riding/hunting, and puns are right at the centre of it. Identify the lines in which this comparison is developed, and what puns are involved. But identification and comparison aside, do not fail to enjoy the play of wit which runs through the passage as a whole:

Berowne: *Did I not dance with you in Brabant once?*
Rosaline: *Did I not dance with you in Brabant once?*

Berowne:	*I know you did.*
Rosaline:	*How needless was it then to ask the question!*
Berowne:	*You must not be so quick.*
Rosaline:	*'Tis long of you that spur me with such questions.*
Berowne:	*Your wit's too hot, it speeds too fast, 'twill tire.*
Rosaline:	*Not till it leave the rider in the mire.*
Berowne:	*What time of day?*
Rosaline:	*The hour that fools should ask.*
Berowne:	*Now fair befall your mask!*
Rosaline:	*Fair fall the face it covers!*
Berowne:	*And send you many lovers!*
Rosaline:	*Amen, so you be none.*
Berowne:	*Nay, then will I be gone.*

Just as with the *Two Gentlemen of Verona* scene described at the beginning of this chapter, you can here imagine a group of onlookers applauding this display of wit.

If you want a more extended example, take a look at *The Two Gentlemen of Verona* 3.1.273 on. Launce and Speed, both described as 'clownish servants', are talking about the milkmaid Launce claims to love. The wordplay comes thick and fast.

Mahood (1957: 51) lists some of the most common words Shakespeare uses to pun with. Here are some of them: *dear, heart, son, bear, light, blood, bond, arms, stomach*. In the case of the first four of these, the pun is based on words pronounced the same way, but with different spellings, like *dear* and *deer*. Give the alternative spellings for the other three (of the first four). For the rest of the list, identify the possible alternative meanings that make them usable as puns (**AS**).

3.1.3 Malapropisms: 'misplacing language'

Another of Shakespeare's wordplay favourites is the malapropism. The *OED* defines this as the 'ludicrous misuse of words'. The name comes from the character of Mrs Malaprop in Richard Sheridan's play *The Rivals*, first performed in 1775. Here are a couple of examples from Mrs Malaprop herself. You can probably guess what words were intended for the underlined malapropisms:

She's as headstrong as an allegory on the banks of the Nile
He is the very pineapple of politeness

The words Mrs Malaprop was looking for here are *alligator* and *pinnacle*. Another name for malapropisms is dogberryisms, after Constable Dogberry in *Much Ado About Nothing* – perhaps a fairer name, given that Dogberry was using them over 170 years before Mrs Malaprop came on the scene. You might also call the practice 'misplacing language', a term used in *Measure for Measure* in relation to one of Shakespeare's other major users of malapropisms, Elbow (also, one notes, a constable – perhaps this says something about Shakespeare's views of the police). *Do you hear how he misplaces?* Escalus says (2.1.85).

Talking of major users, Schlauch (1965), in a paper devoted to the topic, has (in rough chronological order of the plays): Moth, Armado, Holofernes, and Dull (all in *Love's Labour's Lost*), The Nurse in *Romeo and Juliet*, Gobbo (*The Merchant of Venice*), Slender, Shallow, Nym in *The Merry Wives of Windsor*, Mistress Quickly (*Henry IV, Parts 1 and 2* and *Henry V*), Pistol (*Henry IV, Part 2*), Fluellen (*Henry V*); Dogberry in *Much Ado About Nothing*, the first gravedigger (*Hamlet*), Elbow (*Measure for Measure*), the third servant in *Coriolanus*. As this list suggests, their use is mostly in the earlier plays.

Here are some Shakespearean malapropisms, with the 'misplaced words' underlined.[7] You are invited to work out what the intended words were – not always that easy (**AS**):

(a) **Constable Dogberry** (in MA 3.5.42) reports that he has made some arrests:
    One word, sir: our watch, sir, have indeed comprehended two aspicious persons, and we would have them this morning examined before your worship.

(b) Malapropisms clearly run in families. Here, Shylock's servant **Launcelot** wants to work for **Bassanio**. Launcelot and his father **Gobbo** approach Bassanio (MV 2.2.126):
    Launcelot: *In very brief, the suit is impertinent to myself, as your worship shall know by this honest old man, and though I say it, though old man, yet poor man, my father.*
    Bassanio: *One speak for both. What would you?*
    Launcelot: *Serve you, sir.*
    Gobbo: *That is the very defect of the matter, sir.*

(c) Here the other constable – **Elbow** in *Measure for Measure* (2.1.46) – is reporting an arrest, again with a malapropism. Notice also the play on the name Elbow (to do with leaning):
    Elbow: *If it please your honour, I am the poor Duke's constable, and my name is Elbow. I do lean upon justice, sir, and do bring in here before your good honour two notorious benefactors.*

(d) Juliet's **Nurse** is looking for Romeo, and finds him (RJ 2.4.124). Romeo's friend, **Benvolio**, makes fun of the Nurse's malapropism by using one of his own:

Nurse: *If you be he, sir, I desire some <u>confidence</u> with you.*
Benvolio: *She will <u>endite</u> him to some supper.*

(e) In *The Merry Wives of Windsor* (1.1.161), **Bardolph** expresses the view that Slender had had too much to drink:

Bardolph: *Why, sir, for my part, I say the gentleman had drunk himself out of his five <u>sentences</u>.*

(f) **Bottom** is acting Pyramus in a play (in MND 5.1.283). His love, Thisbe, has been killed by a lion. He laments:

O wherefore, nature, didst thou lions frame,
Since lion vile hath here <u>deflowered</u> my dear?

If you enjoy deciphering malapropisms, there are some more in Activity 2 (*Classifying malapropisms*). If you are going to look at this, now is the time to do so, since the following paragraph includes the 'answers' to part of that Activity (**NP**).

Schlauch (1965) classified malapropisms according to which part of the word has been 'misplaced'. She identifies three main types. The most common is making a mistake with the prefix. There are a number of examples in Activity 2, for example when Dull says *collusion* and *pollution* instead of *allusion*. The second type is when a suffix is mistaken, as when Mistress Quickly says *infinitive* for *infinite*. Another example in the Activity is the Welshman Evans' *virginity* for *virgin* – a common type of mistake for him and others in Shakespeare whose first language is not English (an issue discussed in 3.5 below). It often, as in this case, comes down to using the wrong noun, or (on other occasions) the wrong part of speech. The third type is when the roots of words are confused, as when Elbow uses *cardinally* for *carnally*, or Mistress Quickly *indite* for *invite*.

3.2 'Kitchen diction'

Part of the definition of the word 'diction' in the *OED* is 'choice or selection of words and phrases; wording; phrasing; verbal style'. Here is a passage from a poem which was highly influential in Elizabethan times, and which was written in a type of diction common then. The poem was Spencer's *Faerie Queene*, published in 1590, and the diction was a highly 'artificial', poetical one. Identify a few words in the stanza that exemplify this <u>poetic diction</u>.

Phoebus is the sun, and what is being described here in such florid terms is what we today more mundanely call 'dawn':

> *At last the golden oriental gate*
> *Of greatest heaven gan to open fair,*
> *And Phoebus, fresh as bridegroom to his mate,*
> *Came dancing forth, shaking his dewy hair*
> *And hurls his glistening beams through dewy air*

Look now at this passage from Shakespeare's early play, *Henry VI, Part 3*. As in the Spenser passage, it is dawn that is being described (though you may be puzzled by the notion of morning saying 'farewell' to the sun at dawn; the idea is that Aurora, the goddess of dawn, is saying goodbye to the sun as it begins its journey round the skies). Parts of Shakespeare's description are also clearly poetic in their diction, and again you are invited to identify words and phrases which show this:

> *See how the morning opes her golden gates,*
> *And takes her farewell of the glorious sun!*
> *How well resembles it the prime of youth,*
> *Trimmed like a younker prancing to his love!*

But there are at least two words in this passage which strike a chord quite different from the Spenserian world of Phoebus and his 'glistening beams'. You may be able to identify them, even though one is no longer in use. It is the word *younker*, meaning a 'fashionable young man'. The other word is *prancing*. These examples are used by Bland (1951) to show that Shakespeare had 'a fondness for the "ordinary" word, and an ability to put it to effective use that is outside the usual canons of Elizabethan prosody.' Indeed, Bland goes on to say, Shakespeare's 'poetic speech derives strength from common speech to a degree that far surpasses anything that, say, Wordsworth tried to do'.[8] To capture this notion of common speech, we will use the term 'kitchen diction' (some writers prefer the term 'household words').

Shakespeare's use of 'kitchen diction' made him unpopular with critics who felt that poetry should use its own special 'elevated' means of expression (poetic diction). Samuel Johnson, the eighteenth-century disliker of puns, was one of these. He took particular exception to one famous speech of Lady Macbeth's (which we have already seen in 2.1) where she is gearing herself for evil deeds. Here are the concluding lines. You may be able to guess which words gave offence to Johnson (though again this is made more difficult by the fact that not all the words are used much today):

> *Come, thick night,*
> *And pall thee in the dunnest smoke of hell,*
> *That my keen knife see not the wound it makes,*
> *Nor heaven peep through the blanket of the dark*
> *To cry, 'Hold, hold!'*
> (Mac 1.5.48)

In the journal called *The Rambler* which Johnson published from 1750 to 1752, he took exception to three words/phrases.[9] First there was *dun* (meaning 'dingy brown') which, he said, was 'an epithet now seldom heard but in the stable'. Then Johnson complained that the 'sentiment is weakened by the name of an instrument used by butchers and cooks in the meanest employments' – the word *knife*. As for the phrase which many today see as a highly creative and exciting one – *peeping through a blanket* – Johnson can only ask: 'who, without some relaxation of his gravity, can hear of the avengers of guilt *peeping through a blanket*?' Just about a century later, Coleridge, in his 1849 book *Shakespearian Criticism*, agreed with Johnson. In fact, he went so far as to suggest that Shakespeare could not have intended the 'kitchen diction' word *blanket* at all. He suggests it should be *blank height* instead.[10]

In Activity 3 (*Spotting 'kitchen diction'*) you can see more examples of 'ordinary words' upsetting the flow of poetic diction in a way that was characteristic of Shakespeare. The example below shows another unexpected 'kitchen touch' carried in an image. In the passage, Macbeth is having doubts about whether to kill Duncan. If he does, the spirit of pity will never let him forget. Notice the poetic diction of the first three lines. In contrast, the image in the fourth line is the everyday one of 'getting something in your eye'.

> *And pity, like a naked new-born babe,*
> *Striding the blast, or heaven's Cherubins, hors'd*
> *Upon the sightless couriers of the air,*
> *Shall blow the horrid deed in every eye*
> *That tears shall drown the wind.*
> Mac 1.7.21

One nineteenth-century critic, Andrew Becket, was moved to comment: 'the images . . . have more of the ludicrous than the effecting in them, and should not here find place'.[11]

3.3 'Never broken chain of imagery'

Activity 1 (*Some fatal Cleopatras*) contained an 'extended pun' passage from *The Merry Wives of Windsor*, joking about Falstaff's large stomach (*I am in the waist two yards about*). Shakespeare liked to develop images in this extended way. Coleridge talks about it in his *Biographia Literaria* where he says Shakespeare has 'a never broken chain of imagery, always vivid, and because unbroken, often minute [detailed]'.[12] It is almost as if he is thinking in terms of images. They 'take over'.

The Sonnets are full of examples; very often an entire poem is constructed around one central image. It is possible to turn to almost any sonnet to find an example of this, and you might wish to do just that. Or here are two to look at: Sonnet 135 (*Whoever hath her wish, thou hast thy Will*) involves an extended play on the name *Will*, while 127, one of the 'Dark Lady' sonnets (*In the old age black was not counted fair*), plays with the notion of blackness (and fairness) from beginning to end. The example below is not from a sonnet, but from *Antony and Cleopatra*. Antony has returned from the wars defeated, and he thinks that Queen Cleopatra has abandoned him. In a desperate condition he talks to his knave (boy) Eros about a sense of having lost his identity (a 'body' no longer holding its 'visible shape'). The word *knave* does not just mean 'boy'. It also refers to the playing card called a 'jack'. Using this word leads Shakespeare into extended playing card imagery. There is *triumph* which can mean 'trump', and *pack* with the possible meaning of 'shuffle'. Read through the passage tracking how the card images develop (do not let *Queen* and *heart* escape your attention):

My good knave Eros, now thy captain is
Even such a body. Here I am Antony,
Yet cannot hold this visible shape, my knave.
I made these wars for Egypt; and the Queen –
Whose heart I thought I had, for she had mine,
Which, whilst it was mine, had annexed unto't
A million more, now lost – she, Eros, has
Packed cards with Caesar, and false-played my glory
Unto an enemy's triumph.
(AC 4.14.12)

For some, the extended episodes of wordplay in Shakespeare can be a little tedious – and obscure for us when they involve words carrying meanings that they no longer hold today. The 'shoe scene' in 1.2's extract from *Beyond the Fringe* parodies this characteristic of Shakespeare. Here is another similar parody, based on the Gravediggers Scene in *Hamlet,* which will be discussed in 5.5.2. It is by the early twentieth-century English essayist, Max Beerbohm:[13]

Second Policeman: *Canst tell me of this prize-fight? Is't within the law?*
First Policeman: *Aye! To't. For what does a man prize highest? A fight.*
                      But no man fights what he prizes, else he is no man,
                      being not manly, nor yet unmannerly. Argal, if he
                      fight the prize, then is not the prize his, save in
                      misprision, and 'tis no prize-fight within the meaning
                      of the act.
Second Policeman: *Marry, I like thy wit . . .*

3.4 Words then and now: historical false friends

How difficult are Shakespeare's words for us today? How much do they
impede our understanding? Crystal (2008) argues that the database on which
the Crystal and Crystal (2002) glossary is constructed has 47,365 examples of
words which either existed then and are no longer used today, or which still
exist but with a change in meaning. But with a total of 884,647 words in
Shakespeare, he argues, this represents only just over 5%. You also have to
bear in mind that many of the meaning changes are really very small. Crystal's
examples are words like *morn* for 'morning' and *plumpy* for 'plump'. Nevertheless,
there <u>are</u> hard words in Shakespeare. Some are difficult because they express
complex ideas, and others because they bear no obvious resemblance to PDE
words (words like *scroyle* which meant 'ruffian'). But in this section we will
concentrate on another set of words: ones that are difficult precisely because
of the (misleading) resemblance that they <u>do</u> have to PDE words.

   Here are two examples. In 1608 John Chamberlain, a celebrated letter
writer, wrote to a friend saying 'I am sorry to hear Sir Rowland Lytton is so
crazy'. To us today, 'crazy' means 'mad', but the older meaning was 'damaged' (retained in the expression 'crazy paving' which we still use), and it
could refer to physical as well as mental health. The same use of the word is
found in *Henry VI, Part I* (3.2.89), where Talbot talks about 'crazy age'.[14] In his
book on the language of English Renaissance literature, Ronberg (1992) gives
a second example of a student who had trouble with some lines of Queen
Elizabeth in *Richard III*. She is grieving:

Give me no help in lamentation.
I am not barren to bring forth complaints.
All springs reduce their currents to mine eyes,
That I, being governed by the wat'ry moon,
May send forth plenteous tears to drown the world.
(R3 2.2.66)

The student's problem is with the word *reduce*. It does not seem to make sense in the context. The Queen is talking about 'plenteous tears', yet at the same time apparently mentioning a reduction in tears. The explanation is that the word *reduce* at that time did not mean 'lessen', but 'bring back'.

These words *crazy* and *reduce* are what are called <u>false friends</u> – words which you think you know but you do not, because they have an unexpected meaning. Such 'weasel words' are a real problem when you are learning a foreign language. The French noun *front*, for example, is a false friend. It looks as if it should mean the same as 'front' in English, but in fact the meaning is 'forehead' or 'brow'. So the English learner of French who uses the word when talking about the 'front of a building', will mystify native French speakers because he is in fact speaking about the 'forehead of the building'.

Studying 'historical false friends' leads one into the fascinating world of word sources (<u>etymology</u>), into which we will take a short digressionary step. The Elizabethan meaning of *reduce* makes perfect sense when you realize it comes from the Latin *reducere*, where *ducere* means 'lead', and *re-* means back. This meaning is still found in a medical context where 'reducing a dislocated shoulder' means putting it back to its proper position. Chantrell's *Oxford Dictionary of Word Histories* (2002) describes the change to modern meaning like this: *reduce* came to mean 'bring to a different state', then 'bring to a simpler or lower state', and finally 'diminish in size or amount'. Activity 4 (*Friends, oh so false*) identifies historical false friends in Shakespeare. Now is the time to do part (i).

Linguists like Ullmann (1964) have classified the way words change their meaning over time. One of the most common movements is <u>restriction</u>. This is where a meaning becomes 'narrower', or more specific. For example, according to the *OED*, in Old and Middle English the word *worm* referred to 'any animal that creeps or crawls; a reptile; an insect'. Shakespeare often uses it to refer to a snake or dragon. In *Antony and Cleopatra*, for example, Cleopatra calls the asp snake which poisons her a *worm*. Now of course we use the word only to refer to a specific type of creeping creature, one which would have done Cleopatra no harm at all. The contrary movement, <u>extension</u>, is less common. It is where a meaning widens, becomes more general. The word *bird*, for example, originally meant a 'young bird' or 'chick', and this is how Lavinia uses it in *Titus Andronicus* (2.3.153): *Some say that ravens foster forlorn children / The whilst their own birds famish in their nests.* Now of course the word refers to the same creature, but of any age. More common is where a word changes for the worse, becomes <u>pejorative</u>. An example is *cunning*, which in Shakespeare's time could mean 'knowledgeable', 'skilful'. In this meaning it is related to the PDE verb *can*, and you can still find remnants of this meaning in phrases like *D'you ken John Peel* (='know'), and the phrase *beyond our ken* (= 'understanding'). Today *cunning* has pejorative overtones, but these were not present when Suffolk in *Henry VI, Part 2* (4.1.34), talking of a fortune teller, says *A cunning man did calculate my birth*. Words can also change meanings in the opposite direction, becoming <u>ameliorative</u>. In Shakespeare, *nice* could have various pejorative meanings. One is 'lascivious' (Moth in *Love's Labour's Lost* talks of *nice wenches*). Another is 'trivial', as when Cassius (JC 4.3.8) says: *In such a time as this it is not meet / That every nice offence should bear his comment*. It is true that something close to this second meaning can still be found today (we can talk of a *nice distinction* for example); but now the word's main meaning carries positive senses: *kind, friendly, pleasant*.

Part (ii) of Activity 4 asks you to classify false friends using the above categories.[15]

3.5 Register, and other levels of variation

Section 3.2 focused on one particular <u>variety</u> of English – poetic language. Linguists use the term <u>register</u> to describe a variety of the language associated with some particular use, or with a group of people sharing some specific area of interest. As well as having a poetic register, English also has a military register, a legal register, a nautical register, and a computer register – among many others. It is particularly in relation to lexis that these areas differ – they all have their own specialised vocabularies which are likely to be baffling to the outsider. But there will be other linguistic features involved as well, such as syntax.

A register which frequently gets discussed in relation to Shakespeare is the legal one. One play where legal English is particularly prominent is *The Merchant of Venice*, because it includes a lengthy court scene, where Shylock's claim to take a 'pound of flesh' from his debtor Antonio is put to legal test. But there are other plays where legal language abounds. *Coriolanus*, for example, is full of discussion about the affairs of state, and the legal technicalities associated with electing representatives to power in Roman times. One particular scene steeped in law is 3.3. Coriolanus has been accused of various misdemeanours, and he wants to have these treated in a legal manner – as if he were on trial. Tanselle and Dunbar (1962) is a study devoted to the legal language of *Coriolanus*. They find no fewer than 194 legal words and phrases used in the play. They also show that the areas of law covered are diverse, including criminal law, civil law, procedural law (dealing among other things with the procedures followed in court cases), and even commercial law. Legal imagery fills the play, they argue, even when specifically legal matters are not being discussed. For example, at one point in the play Coriolanus decides to launch an attack on Rome. Two of the Roman characters – Menenius and Sicinius – fear for their lives, because they know just how good a soldier Coriolanus is. Menenius expresses this fear by using legal terms: *Our throats are sentenced*, he says (5.4.7), *and stay upon execution.*

But there is a great deal more legal register in Shakespeare than is found in just *The Merchant of Venice* and *Coriolanus*.[16] In 2000 Sokal and Sokal produced a book entitled *Shakespeare's Legal Language: A Dictionary*. It is 400pages long. Their conclusion: 'it is our view, derived from cumulative evidence, that . . . Shakespeare shows a quite precise and mainly serious interest in the capacity of legal language to convey matters of social, moral, and intellectual substance.' (2000: 3). Indeed, there is so much 'law' in Shakespeare that it raises a very Big Question indeed. Here is a box which discusses it:

Stratfordians versus Oxfordonians

The Big Question that Shakespeare's use of legal language raises is eloquently posed by Mark Twain, in an article entitled 'Is Shakespeare dead?' Here is what he says: 'The man who wrote [the plays] was limitlessly familiar with the laws, and the law-courts, and law-proceedings, and lawyer-talk, and lawyer-ways—and if Shakespeare was possessed of the infinitely-divided star-dust that constituted this vast wealth, *how* did he get it, and *where*, and *when*?'

Shakespeare, as we all know, received a sound education in Stratford, but is that enough to give him the kind of legal knowledge that is displayed? One group of people who answer 'no' are the so-called 'Oxfordonians'. They argue that Shakespeare's plays were not written by the man from Stratford, but perhaps by Edward de Vere, the 17th Earl of Oxford, who lived from 1550 to 1604. It seems that he may have received legal training at Gray's Inn, and only such training, it is argued, can be behind the massive legal knowledge found in the plays.

The 'Stratfordians' (who believe that Shakespeare was Shakespeare) counter with two very different arguments. One is to suggest that the plays' legal knowledge is in fact a little vague and occasionally shaky. But this is not, as we have seen, Sokal and Sokal's conclusion. The other argument was put forward by the eighteenth-century Irish scholar Edmond Malone (himself a lawyer). He argued that Shakespeare worked as a lawyer's clerk during one of those periods in his life when nothing is known about his movements.

Legal knowledge is of course only one part of the 'authorship issue'. Oxford is not the only candidate, and a major problem with his claim is that he died so early, long before some of the plays were supposedly written. The authorship debate will, of course, run and run . . .

Register is just one of a number of dimensions of variation that interest linguists, and although considering these will take us a little beyond the immediate focus on lexis in this chapter, the digression will be worthwhile. The largest dimension is of course language. Though, as we have seen, some of the characters in *Love's Labour's Lost* seem to be as happy in Latin or Italian as they are in English, Shakespeare's plays are indeed in English. But there is one very comic scene in Shakespeare which is almost entirely in French. It is when the English soldiers, including King Henry V, are in France and the local ladies are probably brushing up on their English in case possible suitors should present themselves. One such lady is Katherine, the French king's daughter no less. In *Henry V* (3.4), Katherine asks her lady-in-waiting, Alice, to help her learn some English, starting with the parts of the body. Katharine's efforts produce comedy (she says *bilbow* for 'elbow', and *sin* for 'chin', for example), and it is a language-learning strategy which is guaranteed to end up in innuendo and a suggestion of vulgarity – which is just what happens. There are also occasional instances of invented foreign languages being spoken. In *All's Well that Ends Well*, for example, the roguish Parolles is captured by some mischievous individuals who blindfold him and pretend to be foreign soldiers (Muscovites, Parolles imagines) who plan to kill him. The situation provides Shakespeare with the opportunity to indulge in exuberant linguistic creativity. Here are some of the lines illustrating the nonsense words that the individuals invent to convince Paroles of their foreign origins (from AW 4.1 and 3):

Bosko chimurchno   *Boblibindo chicurmurco*
Portotartarossa   *Boskos thromuldo boskos*
Throca movousus, cargo, cargo, cargo   *Oscorbidulchos volivorco*
Manka revania dulche

The French scene in *Henry V* is perhaps the best example of a comic theme which Shakespeare plays on more than once: foreign or non-standard English speakers trying to speak English. Sometimes (as with French speakers) the level of variation is language, but often it occurs at another level of variation: dialect.[17] The Welsh are a common target, particularly in *Henry IV, Part 1*, *Henry V* and *The Merry Wives of Windsor*, but the Scottish and the Irish do not escape. Shakespeare's accents, it has to be admitted, were not always very accurate, as some of the examples in Activity 5 (*English as she is (sometimes) spoken*) may suggest. There is often an element of ridicule in Shakespeare's representations – he is making fun of people who speak in an odd way. One instance where there is no ridicule involved occurs in *King Lear*, where Edgar uses a West Country accent to disguise his identity. In 4.6 he is asked to let go of blind Gloucester's arm. His response (4.6.235): *Ch'll not let go, zir, without vurther 'cagion.* ("Cagion' means 'occasion', or, in this context, 'cause'.) The line illustrates one very salient feature of British West Country dialects, using 'z' for 's' and 'v' for 'f' at the beginning of words – in linguistic terms replacing initial unvoiced consonants with their voiced equivalents.

A further dimension of variation deals with personal character, and is known as <u>idiolect</u>. It is one person's individual way of speaking – a 'personal style' which separates that person off from the next. Shakespeare has a memorable array of characters with their own idiolects – verbal characteristics which contribute significantly to making them fully-rounded, as opposed to cardboard, characters. One that is sometimes discussed in this respect, because he is particularly distinctive, is Pistol – Falstaff's rumbustious companion who appears in *Henry IV Part 2*, *Henry V*, and *The Merry Wives of Windsor*. Here is part of a scene from *Henry V* which illustrates some important characteristics of Pistol's idiolect. Try to identify what these characteristics are before you read the paragraphs following the passage. To set the scene: two followers of Falstaff – Nym and Pistol – are quarrelling, because Pistol has married the person Nym had designs on, Mistress Quickly. When Pistol enters, Nym draws his sword to fight, and Bardolph, another of Falstaff's crew, tries to separate them with a threat. Drawing his own sword, Bardolph says (2.1.60): *he that strikes the first stroke, I'll run him up to the hilts, as I am a soldier.* Nym and Pistol sheathe their swords, and Pistol is ready to shake hands (or 'fists'). He says:

Give me thy fist, thy forefoot to me give; Thy spirits are most tall.

But Nym is not so sure he wants to be pacified. He says: *I will cut thy throat one time or other, in fair terms, that is the humour of it.* This is Pistol's reply:

'Couple a gorge!'
That is the word. I thee defy again!
O hound of Crete, think'st thou my spouse to get?
No, to the spital go,
And from the powdering tub of infamy
Fetch forth the lazar kite of Cressid's kind,
Doll Tearsheet she by name, and her espouse.
I have, and I will hold, the quondam Quickly
For the only she; and – pauca, there's enough.
Go to!
(**NP**)

Like much of Pistol's speech, exactly what he is saying is difficult to follow. But here are some characteristics:

- Like some of the outlandish characters in *Love's Labour's Lost*, there is a love of foreign expressions, not always used correctly. *Couple a gorge* is Pistol's version of the French *couper la gorge* – 'cut the throat', so he is just repeating (in a foreign language) what Nym has said to him. Then, at the end of his speech, he uses the Italian word *pauca*, literally meaning 'few', and associated with the expression *pauca verba* meaning 'few words' – an expression, incidentally, which the pedant Holofernes in *Love's Labour's Lost* uses (4.2.162). Pistol's sense is 'in short', or 'that's all there is to it'.

- There are also archaic words. *Mickle* for example, meaning 'great'.

- Pistol is fond of using curious word order. Sometimes this makes his prose sound like poetry, as if he were altering the normal word order to achieve a rhyme, as in *think'st thou my spouse to get?* Other examples of curious word order in the passage are *thy forefoot to me give* and *No, to the spital go*.

- Another effect which gives his prose a touch of poetry is alliteration. This is where the front of words, rather than their endings, rhyme (and indeed we describe it in 6.4.1 as 'front-rhyme'). It was a technique popular in Old English poetry. Examples in the passage are *Give me thy fist, thy forefoot to me give* (two words beginning with both 'g' and 'f' here), and *I have, and I will hold, the quondam Quickly* (with two 'h' words and two 'q's). As well as making Pistol's speech curious, the effect was also to make him sound archaic.

- Pistol also had a love of classical and literary allusions. In the passage, Cressida is mentioned. She is the unfaithful lover of Troilus in the story set in the Trojan wars (though in fact it seems to have been a twelfth century French invention rather than classical Greek). The story was popular in medieval and Renaissance times, and indeed Shakespeare wrote a play about the pair (*Troilus and Cressida*). Because of Cressida's unfaithfulness, she is often maligned, and Pistol here calls her a *lazar kite*, meaning a 'leprous scavenger'; apparently the phrase *kite of Cressid's kind* occurs frequently in literature of the time.[18] The phrase suggests Pistol's predilection for citing 'half remembered or misremembered scraps of old plays'.[19]

- Curious, bombastic phrases are Pistol's particular speciality, and the passage has several examples. Consider particularly *thy fore-foot to me give*. A *fore-foot* is 'one of the front feet of a quadruped' – the definition is from the *OED*, which cites this quotation as the only case where the word is used to refer to a human hand. So the phrase means something like 'give me your paw'.

In this section we have considered three dimensions of linguistic variation: register, dialect and idiolect. There are of course many others, and you are invited to consider what these are. Some will be touched on in later chapters, particularly in Chapter 5 which deals with pragmatics. There we will note (5.5) that the difference between *thou* and *you* is related to the dimensions of social status as well as degree of personal intimacy, while in 5.3.1 variations in forms of address according to social class will be briefly discussed.

A realisation of the many different levels of linguistic variation is important because it leads towards a proper understanding of the richness and diversity of all languages, including EModE. Crystal (2004a) captures this well in the title of his book, *The Stories of English*. Perhaps we should similarly be using a plural form when talking about Early Modern English, with all its varieties. Not Early Modern English, perhaps, but Early Modern Englishes.

3.6 Fine volleys of words

The last section of Chapter 2 (2.4) emphasised that word creation was part of the 'spirit of the age': everyone was doing it. The same can be said about wordplay. 'Artifice' and 'self-consciousness about language' – key phrases for the present chapter – were characteristics not just of Shakespeare but of most English Renaissance writers, and 'playing with language' was not merely accepted: it was expected almost. Renaissance writers loved to produce 'fine volleys of words'.[20]

Activity section

1 Some fatal Cleopatras   (AS)

(i) Here are some of Shakespeare's 'fatal Cleopatras'. Most depend on two different words having the same pronunciation. In (a), for example, the wordplay involves the two words *tide* and *tied* which are pronounced in the same way. You also sometimes find two different words which are written in the same way (*recover* is an example). In the passages below, establish what the play of words is; the words to focus on are underlined:

(a) **Launce** (and his dog Crab) are awaited on board ship, ready to set sail (TGV 2.3.33):

Pantheno: *Away, ass! You'll lose the <u>tide</u> if you tarry any longer.*

Launce: *It is no matter if the tied were lost; for it is the unkindest tied that ever any man tied.*

Pantheno: *What's the unkindest tide?*
Launce: *Why, he that's tied here, Crab, my dog.*

(b) **Romeo**, sinking under 'love's heavy burden', does not feel like
dancing, but **Mercutio** tries to persuade him (RJ 1.4.13):
Mercutio: *Nay, gentle Romeo, we must have you dance.*
Romeo: *Not I, believe me. You have dancing shoes*
With nimble <u>soles</u>. I have a soul of lead
So stakes me to the ground I cannot move

(c) In *Julius Caesar*, **Flavius** is trying to find out the job of the man he is
questioning (1.1.20):
Flavius: *Thou art a cobbler, art thou?*
Cobbler: *Truly, sir, all that I live by is <u>with the awl</u>: I meddle with no*
tradesman's matters, nor women's matters; but withal I am,
indeed, sir, a surgeon to old shoes: when they are in great
danger, I <u>recover</u> them.

(d) In the opening words of *Richard III*, the future king observes that the
fortunes of the House of York are changing for the better (R3 1.1.1):
Now is the winter of our discontent
Made glorious summer by this <u>son</u> of York,

(e) Duncan (the *he* in the passage) is dead. **Lady Macbeth** wants his
grooms (attendants) to take the blame, so she will smear them with
blood (Mac 2.2.55):
If he do bleed,
I'll <u>gild</u> the faces of the grooms withal,
For it must seem their guilt.

(f) You have to know something about fruit to understand this one.
Count Claudio, Benedick's companion, is looking sad. **Beatrice**
comments (MA 2.1.269):
The Count is neither sad, nor sick, nor merry, nor well; but civil count,
<u>civil</u> as an orange, and something of that jealous complexion.

(g) Think here about possible meanings of the whole phrase *little
seeming substance*. **Lear** is offering Cordelia's hand in marriage
to Burgundy. Lear is upset with Cordelia because she refused to
express her love for him in a superficial way, just for appearances
(KL 1.1.198):
If ought within that little <u>seeming</u> substance
. . . . may fitly like your Grace,
She's there, and she is yours.

(ii) Here is a slightly longer passage containing a short series of connected puns. It comes from *The Merry Wives of Windsor* (1.3.35) where **Falstaff** is telling his mates Nym and **Pistol** about his plans to try and seduce Mistress Ford. Identify the puns and plot how one leads to another (Note: the glossary will reveal that *thrift* has two meanings):

Falstaff: *My honest lads, I will tell you what I am about.*
Pistol: *Two yards, and more.*
Falstaff: *No quips now, Pistol. Indeed, I am in the waist two yards about. But I am now about no waste – I am about thrift. Briefly, I do mean to make love to Ford's wife. I spy entertainment in her.*

2 Classifying malapropisms   (AS)

Schlauch's (1965) classification of Shakespeare's malapropisms has three main categories made according to which part of the word is mistaken. The purpose of this Activity is to look at some more examples of malapropisms, and use these to identify Schlauch's categories.

The passages below contain examples of each of Schlauch's categories. Decide first what word was intended for each malapropism; like the examples you saw in the text, this is not always that easy, and you may need to consult the *Answer Section* on occasions. Write the malapropism and the intended word down side by side so that you can identify which part of the word has been mistaken. When you have done this for all twelve examples, look for common elements in the parts of the words which are mistaken, in order to work out what Schlauch's three categories are. These categories are stated in the text, and the *Answer Section* gives the category of each example.

(a) **Holofernes** (LLL 4.2.40) gives **Dull** an *allusion* (= riddle), but the latter has trouble with the word:

Holofernes: *The moon was a month old when Adam was no more,*
             And raught not to five weeks when he came to five-score.
             Th' allusion holds in the exchange.
Dull: *'Tis true, indeed; the <u>collusion</u> holds in the exchange.*
Holofernes: *God comfort thy capacity! I say, th' allusion holds in the exchange.*
Dull: *And I say the <u>pollution</u> holds in the exchange*

(b) **Evans** and Slender (MWW 1.1.42) are talking about the marital availability of Master Page's daughter. (Evans is a Welshman, and Shakespeare sometimes makes fun of his use of English; see 3.5):

Evans: *Anne Page, which is daughter to Master George Page, which is pretty <u>virginity</u>.*

(c) **Slender** (MWW 1.1.228), still on the topic of marriage:
I will marry her, sir, at your request. But if there be no great love in the beginning, yet heaven may <u>decrease</u> it upon better acquaintance when we are married and have more occasion to know one another. I hope upon familiarity will grow more content

(d) **Mistress Quickly** (2H4 2.1.21) describes the unseemly haunts and bad company Falstaff is associated with. She wants him arrested, and knows where he can be found:
he is <u>indited</u> to dinner to the Lubber's Head in Lumbert Street to Master Smooth's the silkman.

(e) **Constable Dogberry** (MA 3.3.18) is telling one of his subordinates what to do as he patrols the streets:
This is your charge: you shall <u>comprehend</u> all <u>vagrom</u> men; you are to bid any man stand, in the Prince's name.

(f) **Dull** (LLL 1.1.181) announces that he, as the Duke's representative, would like to speak to the Duke personally. (The passage contains a second malapropism. *Farborough* means *thirdborough*, a parish constable):
I myself <u>reprehend</u> his own person, for I am his grace's farborough. But I would see his own person in flesh and blood

(g) **Mistress Quickly** (MWW 2.2.91) brings Falstaff a message from Mistress Ford. She then tells him about another message, this time from Mistress Page:
Why, you say well. But I have another <u>messenger</u> to your worship. Mistress Page hath her hearty commendations to you too;

(h) Shylock has been invited to supper, but is reluctant to go. **Launcelot** makes it clear that he is expected (MV 2.5.19):
I beseech you, sir, go. My young master doth expect your <u>reproach</u>.

(i) In *Measure for Measure* the Viennese authorities are on the lookout for brothels. **Constable Elbow** knows of one (2.1.75):
Escalus: *How dost thou know that, constable?*
Elbow: *Marry, sir, by my wife, who, if she had been a woman <u>cardinally</u> given, might have been accused in fornication, adultery, and all uncleanliness there.*

(j) **Mistress Quickly** (2H4 2.1.22) has ordered Falstaff's arrest, one reason being that he never pays his bar bill:
I am undone by his going, I warrant you, he's an <u>infinitive</u> thing upon my score. Good Master Fang, hold him sure; good Master Snare, let him not 'scape.

(k) **Quince** (MND 4.2.11) extols the acting virtues of his colleague Bottom:
Yea and the best person, too; and he is a very _paramour_ for a sweet voice.

(l) **Mistress Quickly** (2H4 2.4.22) comments on the state of mind and health of Doll Tearsheet:
I'faith, sweetheart, methinks now you are in an excellent good _temperality_.
Your _pulsidge_ beats as _extraordinarily_ as heart would desire, and your colour,
I warrant you, is as red as any rose, in good truth, la!

3 Spotting 'kitchen diction' (AS)

Bland (1951) is all about Shakespeare's use of 'the ordinary word'. The following examples are all taken from his paper. Which word (or words) in each passage do you think Bland selects as 'the ordinary word', standing out in otherwise more poetic diction? It is possible that you may find more 'ordinary words' than Bland does in any passage, and you may well disagree with some of his choices, as given in the *Answer Section*.

(a) *God take King Edward to his mercy,*
And leave the world for me to bustle in
(R3 1.1.151)

(b) *Because I cannot flatter and speak fair,*
Smile in men's faces, smooth, deceive and cog,
Duck with French nods and apish courtesy,
I must be held a rancorous enemy
(R3 1.3.47)

(c) *Thus have I shunned the fire for fear of burning,*
And drenched me in the sea.
(TGV 1.3.78)

(d) *I cannot come to Cressid but by Pandar,*
And he's too tetchy to be woo'd to woo,
As she is stubborn, chaste, against all suit.
(TC 1.1.97)

(e) *Let Rome in Tiber melt, and the wide arch*
Of the ranged empire fall! Here is my space.
Kingdoms are clay. Our dungy earth alike
Feeds beast as man.
(AC 1.1.33)

(f) *These blue-veined violets whereon we lean*
Never can blab, nor know not what we mean.
(VA 125)

(g) *You cram these words into mine ears against*
The stomach of my sense. Would I had never
Married my daughter there!
(Tem 2.1.108)

(h) *Thou sure and firm-set earth,*
Hear not my steps, which way they walk, for fear
Thy very stones prate of my whereabouts
(Mac 2.1.56)

4 Friends, oh so false   (AS)

(i)   Here are ten examples of historical false friends. Many are taken from
Crystal (2008), who has a useful Appendix listing a number of false
friends in Shakespeare. Think first about the modern meaning of the
underlined word. Then try to work out what it means in the passage.
This will not always be easy. Sometimes trying to think of similar, related
words in PDE may help. If all fails, there is always the *Answer Section*.

(a) In *The Merchant of Venice* (5.1.89), **Portia** is returning home and sees
the light of home. She philosophises:
That light we see is burning in my hall;
How far that little candle throws his beams!
So shines a good deed in a <u>naughty</u> world.

(b) **Hamlet** hears that his father's ghost has been seen (1.2.255):
My father's spirit! In arms! All is not well.
I <u>doubt</u> some foul play. Would the night were come!

(c) In *Much Ado About Nothing* (1.3.54), **Borachio** eavesdrops on the
Prince and Claudio in conversation. Their talk is not 'sad' in the
modern sense of the word:
as I was smoking a musty room, comes . . . the Prince and Claudio, hand
in hand, in <u>sad</u> conference. I whipt me behind the arras, and there heard it
agreed upon that the Prince should woo Hero for himself,

(d) **Macbeth** thinks that his enemies are dead, but he finds out that some
are still alive. He feels 'cabined' (caged up) and 'cribbed' (shut up):
But now I am cabined, cribbed, confined, bound in
To <u>saucy</u> doubts and fears
(Mac 3.4.23)

(e) In *As You Like It* (4.1.18), **Jaques** is trying to explain his melancholy
to Rosalind:
often rumination wraps me in a most <u>humorous</u> sadness.

Humour and humorous are, by the way, favourite words of **Nym**, a follower of Falstaff who appears in *Henry V* and *The Merry Wives of Windsor*. *My humour shall not cool*, he says in *The Merry Wives of Windsor* (1.3.92).

(f) There are two passages to clarify this example. **Portia** (in MV 4.1.335) assures the court that Shylock will receive justice:
He hath refused it in the open court.
He shall have merely justice and his bond.
And in *Antony and Cleopatra* (3.7.47), **Enobarbus** advises Antony that chance and nothing else is what will assist him:
Give up yourself merely to chance and hazard
From firm security.

(g) **Iago** tells Othello that he will deal with Cassio (4.1.210):
And for Cassio, let me be his undertaker. You shall
hear more by midnight.

(h) **Ophelia** is distraught at the sight of Hamlet's apparent madness:
And I . . .
Now see that noble and most sovereign reason
That unmatched form and feature of blown youth
Blasted with ecstasy. O, woe is me
(Ham 3.1.156):

(i) **Buckingham** is flattering the future king (R3: 3.7.209):
As well we know your tenderness of heart
And gentle, kind, effeminate remorse

(j) **Hamlet** (3.4.19) suggests to Gertrude that she should take a good look at herself:
Come, come, and sit you down. You shall not budge.
You go not till I set you up a glass
Where you may see the inmost part of you.

(ii) The last four examples above illustrate Ullmann's processes of restriction, extension, pejorative, ameliorative, but not in this order. Decide which example illustrates which process ('answers' in the *Answer Section*). Remember that you are looking at change from <u>then</u> till <u>now</u> (and not vice versa). So *nice* is regarded as ameliorative because <u>then</u> it had pejorative meanings, and <u>now</u> has a positive meaning.

(iii) As an additional activity, choose a couple of the examples above and look up in an etymological dictionary how the words have changed sense over the centuries. There are some such dictionaries online, including at http://www.etymonline.com/.

5 English, as she is (sometimes) spoken   (AS)

Here are some passages spoken by Shakespearean characters using non-standard English. The speakers are: Irish, French, Scottish and Welsh (but not in that order). Try to identify which is which: some are very easy and others almost impossible! Specify what characteristics the speeches have that make them non-standard, and assess (as best you can) how accurate they are as examples of their variety. Then specify any linguistic characteristics that you associate with these varieties, but which are not found in the speeches. Are you led to any conclusions about the accuracy of Shakespeare's representations of non-standard English?

(a) *Vat is you sing? I do not like des toys. Pray you, go and vetch me in my closet*
     un boitier vert, a box, a green-a box: do intend vat I speak? a green-a box.
     You jack'nape, give-a this letter to Sir Hugh; by gar, it is a shallenge: I will cut
     his troat in dee park; and I will teach a scurvy jack-a-nape priest to meddle or
     make. You may be gone; it is not good you tarry here.

(b) *To the mines? Tell you the Duke, it is not so good to come to the mines,*
     for, look you, the mines is not according to the disciplines of the war. The
     concavities of it is not sufficient; for, look you, th' athversary, you may discuss
     unto the Duke, look you, is digt himself four yard under the countermines.
     By Cheshu, I think 'a will plow up all, if there is not better directions.

(c) *By the mess, ere theise eyes of mine take themselves to slomber, ay'll de gud*
     service, or ay'll lig i'th' grund for it, ay, or go to death! And ay'll pay't as
     valorously as I may, that sall I suerly do, that is the breff and the long.
     Marry, I wad full fain hear some question 'tween you tway.

(d) *By Chrish, la, 'tish ill done! The work ish give over, the trompet sound the*
     retreat. By my hand I swear, and my father's soul, the work ish ill done: it ish
     give over. I would have blowed up the town, so Chrish save me, la, in an hour.
     O, tish ill done, 'tish ill done – by my hand, 'tish ill done!

Extended activities

1   At two points in this chapter (3.1.1 and 3.5), the 'authorship question'
    is raised – that is, the question of who wrote Shakespeare. A huge
    amount of scholastic effort has been put into this issue, and a number
    of candidates for authorship have attracted passionate following.
    Spend some time (using the internet perhaps) finding out who the main

candidates are. Then consider whether it really matters. What difference does it make who wrote Shakespeare? Once you have thought about this, you might like to consult an article by a law professor, Peter Jaszi, entitled 'Who cares who wrote "Shakespeare"?' (available on the internet at http://www.wcl.american.edu/journal/lawrev/37/jaszi3.pdf?rd=1).

2   One of the dimensions of variation considered in 3.5 is idiolect. Focus on a play that particularly interests you and identify one character who has a particularly distinctive way of speaking. Identify the linguistic characteristics which make their speech so distinctive. What do these characteristics tell us about their personality or social position?

3   3.3 is about 'chains of imagery' in Shakespeare. Considering again a play of your choice, seek out some examples of such chains, where an image, or a play on words, is extended over a few lines or more.

Answer section

Common punning words (section 3.1.2)

The other spellings are *hart*, *sun* and *bare*. *Light* can mean the opposite of dark, or of heavy; *blood* can refer to the red bodily fluid, or to family descent (as well as, also, a person's temperament); *bond* can mean a tie, connection or even agreement (e.g. between people), but also a shackle or restraint; *arms* can be limbs, but also weapons; *stomach* can refer to the digestive organ, but also to a person's inclination to do something (especially an action requiring bravery).

Malapropisms (section 3.1.3)

(a) *comprehend* for *apprehend*; *auspicious* for *suspicious*; (b) *impertinent* for *pertinent*; *defect* for *effect*; (c) *benefactors* for *malefactors*; (d) *confidence* for *conference*; *endite* for *invite*; (e) *sentences* for *senses*; (f) *deflowered* for *devoured*.

Activity 1 Some fatal Cleopatras

(a) *tide* and *tied*; (b) *sole* and *soul*; (c) *with the awl* and *withal*; *recover* and *recover*; (d) *son* and *sun*; (e) *gild* and *guilt*; (f) *civil* and *Seville*; (g) In one sense, *little* and *seeming* go together to mean '*apparently small*'; here *substance* refers to Cordelia's size. In the other sense, *seeming* goes with *substance*, almost as a compound. Here *seeming* means 'paying attention to superficialities', and *substance* means 'essential nature'.

Activity 2 Classifying malapropisms

(a) *collusion* and *pollution* for *allusion*; (b) *virginity* for *virgin*; (c) *decrease* for *increase*; (d) *indited* for *invited*; (e) *comprehend* for *apprehend*; *vagrom* for *vagrant*; (f) *reprehend* for *represent*; (g) *messenger* for *message*; (h) *reproach* for *approach*; (i) *cardinally* for *carnally*; (j) *infinitive* for *infinite*; (k) *paramour* for *paragon*; (l) *temporality* for *temper*; *pulsidge* for *pulse*; *extraordinarily* for *ordinarily*.

Schlauch's classifications are Prefix (P), Suffix (S), and Root (R): (a) P; (b) S; (c) P; (d) R; (e) P, R; (f) R; (g) S; (h) P; (i) R; (j) S; (k) R; (l) R, S, P.

Activity 3 Spotting 'kitchen diction'

Bland's selection (which may not be the same as yours) is: (a) *bustle*; (b) *cog* and *duck*; (c) *drenched*; (d) *tetchy*; (e) *dungy*; (f) *blab*; (g) *cram* (there is an argument for *stomach* also perhaps); (h) *prate*.

Activity 4 Friends, oh so false

(a) *naughty* = wicked (a much stronger pejorative meaning than today); (b) *doubt* = suspect (a sense that you find in the Modern French *se douter de*); (c) *sad* = serious; (d) *saucy* = insolent, presumptuous; (e) *humorous* = moody (associated with the *humours*, bodily fluids which control human moods; you can probably see associations here with the word *humid*); (f) *merely* = absolutely, entirely; (g) *undertaker* = one who 'undertakes' to do a specific task; (h) *ecstasy* = frenzy, madness (the *OED* relates it to the Greek meaning insanity); (i) *effeminate* = tender, gentle (it could also carry the pejorative sense which it has today, meaning unmanly); (j) *glass* = mirror.

Examples (g)–(j) in terms of Ullmann's processes: *undertaker* = restriction; *ecstasy* = ameliorative; *effeminate* = pejorative; *glass* = extension.

Activity 5 English, as she is (sometimes) spoken

(a) This is the French doctor Caius (MV 1.4.43 and 105).

(b) The Welsh Captain Fluellen (H5 3.2.56).

(c) Captain Jamy, who is Scottish (H5 3.2.110).

(d) The Irish Captain Macmorris (H5 3.2.85).

There are some French words in (a) (like *un boitier vert*) which make the first language of the speaker clear. There are some French sounding constructions like *it is not good you tarry here*, and what would be a false friend for a French speaker of English: *entendre* means 'hear', and since *intend* sounds a little like *entendre*, Dr Caius uses it (wrongly) here. Dr Caius uses a 'v' sound for 'wh' and 'f', and a 'd' for 'th' in words like *the*. These are not really characteristics of French speakers (today at least). More convincing are 't' for 'th' in *troat*, and 'sh' for 'ch' in *shallenge*. Dr Caius also puts a vowel on the ends of some words (*green-a*, *give-a*). This is much more distinctive in Italian speakers of English, but the French may sometimes do it.

Fluellen, in (b), displays the linguistic characteristic that many associate with the Welsh – using the phrase *look you*. He also uses singular verbs after plural subjects (*the mines is not*). *Adversary* becomes *athversary*, based perhaps on the fact that Welsh people sometimes aspirate consonants (making *bad* sound like *pad* – or *blow* sound like *plow* as in this speech). *Jesu* is written *Chesu*, perhaps for the same reason.

In (c), a number of the vowel sounds are written to reflect how a Renaissance Scottish person might have pronounced them, like *slomber*, *gud*, *grund*, *wad*. You also find the Scottish version of *two* and *lie*: *tway* and *lig*.

Macmorris' Irish accent in (d) is dominated by one feature: the use of 'sh'. So *Christ* becomes *Chrish*, *tis* becomes *tish*, and *is* becomes *ish*.

Notes

1 The quotation is from McDonald (2001: 24).

2 *Rhetorica ad Herennium* 1.2.3. An English translation is available online at http://penelope.uchicago.edu/Thayer/E/Roman/Texts/Rhetorica_ad_Herennium/

3 *Arte of English Poesie*, Book 3, Chapter 4: 'Of Language'. Available online at http://www.gutenberg.org/ebooks/16420; also in Vickers (1999).

4 p. 290 in the Vickers (1999) version.

5 Attridge (1988: 140).

6 This passage is not in every edition of the play. The line reference is based on Bate and Rasmussen's (2007) edition.

7 The examples are taken from http://en.wikipedia.org/wiki/Malapropism

8 Bland (1951: 238).

9 *The Rambler*, No. 168, 26 October 1751.

10 The information for this discussion about the *Macbeth* passage is taken from Hopkins (1997).

11 Becket (1815).

12 Coleridge, S.T. (1817) *Biographia Literaria*, Chapter 15.

13 From Beerbohm (1969: 582). The example is taken from Wells (2002: 159).

14 The example from Chamberlain's letter is taken from Nevalainen (1999).

15 Culpeper (2005) uses a different taxonomy, that of Traugott (1982).

16 There is a website dedicated to Shakespeare's use of legal English: http://www.shakespearefellowship.org/virtualclassroom/Law.htm

17 In fact the dialect examples focus almost entirely on accent, and contain few examples of dialect words.

18 According to the editor of the Arden Shakespeare's *Henry V* (first edition), J. H. Walter.

19 The phrase is Hussey's (1982: 130).

20 See the first paragraph of this chapter for the origin of this phrase.

Further reading

The notions of artifice, self-consciousness, and Renaissance attitudes towards language are dealt with in a number of books, like McDonald, R. (2001) *Shakespeare and the Arts of Language*, Oxford: Oxford University Press; Hussey, S. S. (1982) *The Literary Language of Shakespeare*, London: Longman; and Ronberg, G. (1992) *A Way with Words: The Language of English Renaissance Literature*, London: Arnold. As for some other chapters, the Vickers collection of texts (Vickers, B. (ed.) (1999) *English Renaissance Literary Criticism*, Oxford: Oxford University Press) has much of relevance here.

On puns in general, Redfern, W. (2000) *Puns*, 2nd edn, London: Penguin Books, makes interesting reading. There is also an edited collection of papers: Culler, J. (ed.) (1988) *On Puns: The foundation of letters*, Oxford: Blackwell. Empson, W. (1977) *Seven Types of Ambiguity*, London: Chatto and Windus, is a classic in the field. Mahood, M. M. (1957) *Shakespeare's Wordplay*, London: Methuen is also a classic, though now somewhat dated. Schlauch, M. (1965) 'The social background of Shakespeare's malapropisms', in Salmon, V., and Burness, E. (eds) *Reader in the Language of Shakespearean Drama*, Amsterdam: Benjamins, 71–99 is a paper dealing just with malapropisms. Other papers in the Salmon and Burness collection are also relevant.

As regards variation (and register), any introductory textbook in sociolinguistics will provide basic background – Spolsky, B. (1998) *Sociolinguistics*, Oxford: Oxford University Press, for example. For more detailed coverage, specific to the period, there is Görlach, M. (1999) 'Regional and social variation', in Lass, R. (ed.) *The Cambridge History of the English Language, Volume III: 1476 to 1776*, Cambridge: Cambridge University Press, 459–538.

CHAPTER 4

Grammar: Inside the bonnet

Key phrases:
half-way house; settling down; variation

4.1 Grammar and cars

The internet site www.Wordreference.com includes a blog where people can express views on language matters. One blogger, pulling no punches, writes: 'many people think grammar is boring'. It is both amusing and ironical that this comment should stimulate extensive grammatical discussion. For example, one respondent asks: 'could you tell me if "boring" is a gerund or verb in this sentence?' Grammatical issues like this rattle round the discussion, but the central point about boredom keeps coming back. Here it is again: 'I think grammar is the most boring thing that I have ever met, if it's not please tell me why'. But here is the sensible reply this comment receives: 'Some people happily drive cars all their lives without the slightest interest in how they work or any desire to take them apart and have a look at just what all the components do, separately and together. Some people are just the opposite. It's like that with language and grammar'.

This chapter will have more than its fair share of linguistics. This is because in order to understand how Shakespeare's grammar works, and how it differs from our own, we will have to lift up the bonnet and look inside the car engine. The 'mechanic' who will help us understand what we find there is the linguist. If you are already familiar with the content of a particular section, then the expectation is that you will miss it out. This may apply to the following section, which deals with ways of conveying grammatical information by means of inflexions, function words, and word order.

4.2 Expressing grammatical information

We will start, quite a long way from Shakespeare, with some Russian. Imagine you wanted to know what the Russian word for *school* was, and you asked a native speaker. The reply might sound, roughly, like 'shkola', and would be written *школа* in the Cyrillic alphabet Russian uses. Perhaps you might ask your informant for some example sentences, to see how the word operates. Maybe at this point the informant would begin to realise that the actual form the word 'shkola' would take depends on its function in the sentence. If the word was the subject of the sentence, then indeed *shkola* would be the right form. But if it was the object, then it would be *shkoly*, and if you wanted to say 'to the school' the word would be *shkole*. If you continued to ask your informant grammatical questions, you would indeed find many different manifestations of the word *shkola* occurring according to the <u>grammatical function</u> the word was fulfilling in its context.

You might conclude that Russian is a highly complicated language, and you would be right. We do not do such things in English, you might add, and this time you would be wrong. It is true that nouns in English do not have distinct forms for subject and object function, but some pronouns do. *He*, for example, becomes *him* when it is the object of a sentence (compare *He saw the man* and *The man saw him*). And nouns do change to mark some other grammatical functions. So we can put an *-'s* on the end of one to indicate possession, as in the phrase *Helen's book*. Another occasion on which we use a suffix is to make a noun plural. What is that suffix (**AS**)? Adjectives also change; *-er* added to an adjective like *dark* (forming *darker*) indicates a concept of 'more than', called the <u>comparative form</u>. Or consider the suffix *-ed* when added to a verb. One use of this is to express past time, so the difference between *They walk to work* and *They walked to work* is in the time when it happened, and here this is marked solely by the presence or absence of *-ed*.

We have come across affixes (prefixes and suffixes) in abundance, in Chapter 2, when we were looking at word formation. The affixes we are considering now are particular, because they are fulfilling grammatical functions. They are known as <u>inflexions</u>. Languages differ widely in the degree to which they use inflexions to express grammatical notions. Some, like Russian, are <u>highly inflected</u>, and are what we call <u>synthetic</u> languages.

What about English? We have already seen that English by no means avoids inflexions, though it is not nearly so synthetic as Russian. But it was not always thus. The language of the period before the late eleventh century is known as Old English (OE) or Anglo-Saxon. It was a language very unlike PDE, and today's reader would be able to do no more than recognise a few words in a passage of the language. The most famous OE poem is *Beowulf*, and if you want to know what OE looks like, use an internet search engine to find an online copy of the *Beowulf* text; there are several available.

OE was much more inflected than PDE. To see just how synthetic it was, look at this table which shows the forms of three OE nouns, representing three different patterns, or <u>declensions</u> as they are called. Incidentally, the dash over the 'a' in *stān* is called a <u>macron</u>, and it indicates that the vowel is long (as in PDE *father*) rather than short (as in PDE *hat*):

Singular

	hunter	stone	ox
N	hunta	stān	oxa
A	huntan	stān	oxan
G	huntan	stānes	oxan
D	huntan	stāne	oxan

Plural

	hunter	stone	ox
N	huntan	stānas	oxan
A	huntan	stānas	oxan
G	huntena	stāna	oxena
D	huntum	stānum	oxum

The initials in the first column stand for linguistic terms used to describe what are called <u>cases</u>:

(a) N is the Nominative case. This expresses the subject of a sentence. For example, in the sentence *The hunter* ate the ox the underlined words are the subject;

(b) A = the Accusative case, expressing the object of a sentence. *The hunter ate <u>the ox</u>*

(c) G = Genitive, which expresses possession. *The ox ate <u>the hunter's</u> food.*

(d) D = Dative. This cases expresses *to whom* or *to what*. *The hunter gave the food <u>to the ox</u>*

The table above can be used to 'translate' the underlined words into OE. For example, in (a) *The hunter* is the subject of the sentence, and hence nominative. The table shows you that the nominative singular of 'hunter' is *hunta*. Work through the other examples in the same way, 'translating' the underlined words. Activity 1 (*Hunt the inflexions*) asks you to work out how the PDE noun *hunter* is 'declined'. If you are going to do this Activity, it should be now, before you continue reading (**NP**).

If you compare how the noun *hunta* was declined in OE with how we decline *hunter* today (which Activity 1 asks you to look at), it will confirm what we have already seen: that PDE is not without inflexions. The genitive forms (both singular and plural) adds an 's' – written *'s* and *s'* for singular and plural respectively, and all plural forms have an *-s*. Incidentally, you can see where the PDE genitive and plurals inflexions come from by looking at the *stān* declension, where the genitive singular is *stānes*, and the nominative and accusative plural *stānas*. But there are markedly fewer inflexions in PDE than there were in OE.

The question therefore arises: what other means are available for conveying grammatical information, when inflexions are not used? There are two further means. One is by using phrases which contain what are called <u>function words</u>, like *to, by, from*. The expression of 'dativeness' in PDE is a case in point. For example, the OE dative plural, which is conveyed by the ending *-um* (*stānum*), would be 'to the stones' in PDE. An alternative way of expressing possession (genitive) is also available to us in PDE, using the function word *of*. So you can say *of the hunter* as well as using the inflexion *-'s* (*the hunter's*).

But how do we, in PDE, express the information about whether a noun is the subject or object of a sentence – nominative or accusative? As we have seen, for some pronouns like *he/him* there is a different form for nominative and accusative. For nouns, the answer is by word order. Look at these PDE examples:

(a) The hunter killed the ox

(b) The ox killed the hunter

In (a) *the hunter* is in the nominative, and is the one that does the killing. In (b) *the hunter* is the object, and ends up dead. The difference is not signalled by an inflexion (it is the same word *hunter* each time), but by <u>word order</u> – the subject comes before the verb, and the object after. This is a third way of 'conveying grammatical information', and is much used in PDE.

In highly inflected languages like Russian or OE, word order is often not important. To continue the present example, the OE word for 'kills' is *abreoteth*. Notice that in the four sentences below the words and their inflexions are exactly the same, but the word order is different:

(c) Hunta abreoteth oxan

(d) Hunta oxan abreoteth

(e) Oxan abreoteth hunta

(f) Abreoteth hunta oxan

These sentences mean exactly the same. Each time it is the ox and not the hunter who gets killed. It is the inflexions and not the word order that give the information, distinguishing killer from victim.

Some languages use function words and word order more than inflexions to express grammatical information, and such languages are called <u>analytic</u> ones. As we have seen, English was once quite synthetic, but is today more analytic. As Hope (2002) puts it: 'Over time, English has shifted to being more and more analytic, hence subject and object roles are marked by word order, not inflexion'.

4.3 Shakespeare as 'half-way house'

And so to Shakespeare. Chronologically he lies exactly half way between the end of the OE period and the present day. If indeed there is a progression from synthetic to analytic, we would expect more suffixes in his language than today, but fewer than in OE. This is exactly what we find. Renaissance English is indeed a half-way house. It is always dangerous to talk about one form of the language being 'simpler' or 'more complex' than another, but at least as regards inflexions we may say that Shakespeare's language is simpler than OE, and more complex than PDE. We shall also find the characteristic of 'simpler than in the past but more complex than today' in various other grammatical areas, not just inflexions. In addition, we will be able to see a clear movement of the language in the direction of what it is today. 'Settling down into PDE' is a way of putting this.

All these characteristics suggest that the Renaissance was a time of linguistic fluctuation. As a result we will find in the area of grammar (as we have already found in earlier chapters), much variation. On more than one occasion we will be asking ourselves whether any reasons can be found for the choice of one form rather than another. Also, in the course of discussion we will be considering the role of variation in language change.

These then are the 'themes' of the chapter. In a nutshell we will be describing a version of English that:

- is more synthetic than today;
- is more complex in some areas than today;
- is 'settling down into PDE forms': aspects of today's language coming into general use;
- has much variation (which we will sometimes need to explain).

4.4 Shakespeare: an initial look inside the bonnet

As a starting-point, here is part of a scene from *Antony and Cleopatra*. To give some context: Octavia is Caesar's sister, and she has been married (for political, diplomatic reasons) to Antony, whose true love is Cleopatra. In this scene, Octavia returns quietly to Rome. Her brother, Caesar, asks where Antony is. 'In Athens', she replies. But Caesar tells his 'most wronged sister' that she is mistaken. In fact Antony and his lover Cleopatra (described here as 'a whore') are mustering troops ready for a war against Rome. Octavia is shocked (*Ay me, most wretched*).

Read through the passage (unfortunately not an easy one; the glossary will help). Pay particular attention to grammatical features. Consider how much of the grammar is different from PDE, and how much the same; this will suggest the degree of difficulty which Shakespeare's grammar is likely to cause modern readers. Then note features that are different from PDE. Some, though not all, of these grammatical features will be discussed in the following sections.

Caesar: *No, my most wronged sister; Cleopatra*
            Hath nodded him to her. He hath given his empire
            Up to a whore; who now are levying
            The kings o'th' earth for war. He hath assembled
            Bocchus, the King of Libya; Archelaus,
            Of Cappadocia; Philadelphos, King
            Of Paphlagonia; the Thracian king, Adallas;
            King Mauchus of Arabia; King of Pont;
            Herod of Jewry; Mithridates, King
            Of Comagene; Polemon and Amyntas,
            The Kings of Mede and Lycaonia;
            With a more larger list of sceptres.
Octavia: *Ay me, most wretched,*
            That have my heart parted betwixt two friends
            That does afflict each other!
Caesar: *Welcome hither.*
            Your letters did withhold our breaking forth,
            Till we perceived both how you were wrong led
            And we in negligent danger.
            (AC 3.6.65)

Perhaps your first reaction is how similar EModE and PDE grammar are. Though there are differences, we are clearly dealing with a language which in terms of grammatical structure is not that different from now. Here is a partial list of the differences, focusing only on those to be discussed in the following sections:

- *Hath.* We do not use the *-th* verb ending today, but instead have an *-s* inflexion. This latter also occurs in the passage: Octavia says *does* and not *doth.*

- *More larger.* In PDE we would say *larger* or even possibly *more large,* but not *more larger.*

- *That have, that does.* We would probably use *who* and *which* here.

- *did withhold, does afflict.* In normal circumstances, PDE would not use the verb *do* here. We would say *withheld* for *did withhold,* and *afflicts* for *does afflict.*

To give shape to the following discussion, we will divide the grammatical features to be considered into 'noun-related', and 'verb-related'. Or, to use more accepted linguistic terminology, we will talk about noun phrases and verb phrases. A noun is of course usually just one word. In the sentence *Fido bit the man,* the word *Fido* is the subject noun. But the subject might be a much longer item. In the sentence *The ugly fierce dog, which lived in the house opposite, bit the man,* the first ten words are acting like a subject noun. The term 'noun phrase' (as opposed to 'noun') is useful because it covers both single words and strings of words acting like nouns: both *Fido* and *the ugly fierce dog, which lived in the house opposite.* The same point could be made about the terms 'verb' and 'verb phrase'.

4.5 The noun phrase

4.5.1 The genitive

Here are two short speeches from Act 2, Scene 2 of *Antony and Cleopatra.* They illustrate the two main forms of the genitive in Shakespeare. Look through these passages and find the two forms. An 'original spelling' edition of Shakespeare (Wells and Taylor, 1986) has been used here; perhaps something to do with spelling in the passages will suggest why this edition was chosen.

(a) Enobarbus: *I shall intreat him*
                    To answer like himselfe: if Caesar moue him,
                    Let Anthony looke ouer Caesars head,
                    And speake as lowd as Mars. By Iupiter,
                    Were I the wearer of Anthonio's Beard,
                    I would not shaue't to day.
                    (2.2.3)

(b) Maecenas: *If Beauty, Wisedome, Modesty, can settle*
The heart of Antony, Octavia is
A blessed Lottery to him.
(2.2.246)

The two main ways of expressing the genitive are by using the inflexion -*'s* (a synthetic way of doing it), and with the function word *of* (an analytic way). As we noted earlier, both these ways are still used in PDE, where there is often a difference in the context of use. We tend to use -*'s* for people, and *of* for inanimate objects (*Helen's book* versus *the door of the house*). You find the same in Shakespeare – in *A Midsummer Night's Dream* Theseus speaks of 'the nimble spirit of mirth' (1.1.3), and Lafew in *All's Well That Ends Well* of 'the very hand of heaven' (2.3.30). But there is an example in passage (b) that shows this is not always the case. Perhaps you also noticed that the apostrophe was sometimes left out in the synthetic version of the genitive, though modern editors usually put it in. The original spelling edition is used above to show that it is sometimes there, sometimes not. Of course, whether or not an apostrophe is there is not necessarily the choice of Shakespeare, but of the scriveners who wrote down his lines. The role of these scriveners was discussed in 1.5.

There are other genitive forms in Shakespeare. Two rare but interesting ones are worth a mention. These two passages exemplify the first (the relevant forms are underlined):

(a) *Now where's the Bastard's braves and <u>Charles his gleeks</u>?*
(1H6 3.2.123)

(b) *Once in a seafight 'gainst the <u>Count his galleys</u>*
I did some service
(TN 3.3.28)

At first sight it is tempting to think that the *his* in these cases is associated with gender, since Charles and the Count are both masculine. But a non-Shakespeare example from 1607 suggests this is not true. The example is *Mrs Sands his maid* (meaning 'Mrs Sand's maid'), and here the referent is clearly feminine. The form is probably something to do with pronunciation. In Middle English the -*'s* genitive was often pronounced /ɪs/ or /ɪz/ and written *is* or *ys*. So *Count's* for example could be written *Countys*. Consequently *Countys galleys* would look and sound rather like *Count his galleys*, so people may have assumed that the two forms were the same, and used one for the other.[1]

The other rare but interesting genitive is discussed in this box:

Doing the splits

Here are two examples of a genitive form that was rather rare in Shakespeare. It was much more common earlier, thus indicating the 'half-way house' nature of Renaissance English. To show earlier usage, two more examples are added from Thomas Malory's romance *Morte d'Arthur* which appeared in 1485.

In each case, work out what we would say in PDE. Then try to explain what is happening here:

(a) *The Prince's heart of Calidon*   2H6 1.1.233

(b) *And stolest away the ladies' hearts of France*   2H6 1.3.50

(c) *The king's daughter of England*   Malory

(d) *King Howell's daughter of Brittany*   Malory

This construction is called the <u>split genitive</u>. Each example contains two genitives. So (a) for example, means *The heart of the Prince of Calidon*. In PDE we would put the -'s genitive on the last word of the phrase: *the Prince of Calidon's, the ladies of France's*. But in ME it was common to put the -'s ending on the main word of the phrase: *The Prince's, the ladies'*, etc. If you then follow this with *heart, hearts*, etc., there is no place for the *of* phrase to go than at the end.

But this structure was indeed rare in Shakespeare, and very often he follows what has become the PDE norm. So we can find plenty of examples like *The Duke of Norfolk's signories* (2H4 4.1.113); *My Lord of York's armour* (2H6 1.3.93). So it is an example of 'settling down into PDE forms'. Consider how these last two examples would be written using the split genitive construction.

4.5.2 Some noun plurals

The three OE nouns we looked at earlier were the words for hunter, stone and ox. In PDE two of these are regular, taking the normal -*s* inflexion in the plural. The third has an irregular, or what is sometimes called a <u>strong</u>, plural: *oxen*. Notice that the actual word *oxen* occurs as part of one of the OE declension forms; that is where the PDE plural comes from. Strong plurals were common in OE, but over time there has been a natural movement towards regularity and standardisation, and many have now disappeared. Consequently today they are uncommon. But they are not rare. Another PDE example is *foot* → *feet*. You may like to think of few more PDE examples.

Once again, Shakespearean English is a half-way house, simpler than OE but slightly more complex than PDE, with a movement towards 'settling down into PDE forms'. There are fewer strong plurals than in OE, but more than today. Here are two examples of irregular noun plurals in Shakespeare which today are regular. It is easy to work out what they mean:

(a) *Spare none but such as go in clouted shooen*
    (2H6 4.3.174)

(b) *Even so the maid with swelling drops gan wet*
    Her circled eien enforced, by simpathie
    (Luc 1228)

Another irregular plural found in EModE, though not in Shakespeare, is *housen*.
But even forms like *shooen* are on the way out. Hope (2002) finds just two examples of *shooen* in Shakespeare, versus 21 of *shoes*. Similarly, there are 12 examples of *eien* or *eyne* or *eine* as opposed to 706 of *eyes*. Why the variation? Sometimes Shakespeare's reason for choosing the strong plural form is obvious, as here:

(c) *If the scorne of your bright eine*
    Have power to raise such love in mine
    (AYLI 4.3.50)

Think rhyme! On other occasions Shakespeare uses strong forms to suggest archaic speech. The character of Gower in *Pericles* is a very good example. He was a real fourteenth-century poet whose work was a source for the *Pericles* story, and Shakespeare uses him as the Chorus figure in the play. If you look at all his lines on a site like 'Open Source Shakespeare' (http://www.opensourceshakespeare.org/), you will find his speech full of archaisms, including use of the *eyne* plural.

4.5.3 Adjectives: comparative and superlative forms

At the beginning of this chapter we saw that the comparative form of an adjective in PDE can be formed by adding an inflexion, *-er*. The following paragraph says more about adjectives and inflexions, but if you want to work the PDE rules out yourself, look now at Activity 2 (*Adjective comparison in PDE*) (**NP**).

Not all PDE adjectives form the comparative with *-er*. If the adjective is a particularly long one – three syllables or more – then our preference for an analytic means kicks in, and we use the function word *more* instead of adding an inflexion. So we are happy with *dark* → *darker*, but we do not like *fabulous* → **fabulouser* (a star indicates an unacceptable or impossible form). We prefer *more fabulous*. If the adjective has two syllables – and hence 'comes between' long and short, then we can accept either form. So with the two-syllabled adjective *easy*, many PDE speakers will accept both *easier* and *more easy*. There is another adjectival form which follows similar rules. It is called the <u>superlative</u> and is just what this name suggests. The inflexion this time is -*est*, and we find *darkest*, *most fabulous*, and either *easiest* or *more easy*. What Activity 2 does not show is a further complication: that adjectives taking certain endings, like -*id*, -*ain* and -*ect*, prefer the *more* rather than the -*er* form, regardless of length. So today we find *more horrid, more certain, more perfect* rather than the -*er* equivalents. A final point about the PDE rules is that we do not like 'double' comparatives or superlatives, where both methods are used together. Forms like *more easier* or *most darkest* tend to be frowned upon, and suggest that the user cannot 'speak proper'.

Given what has been said in this chapter, you will not be surprised to learn that the synthetic way of expressing comparative and superlative was the OE one, where the inflexions were -*ra* and -*ost* respectively. The analytic method – using the function words *more* and *most* – can be related to the French influence on the language. As for Shakespeare, much of the time his expressions reflect what have become the PDE rules. Here are some examples using the -*er*/-*est* versus *more*/*most* in the ways suggested above:

My legs are longer, though, to run away! (MND 3.2.343)
Why, saw you anything more wonderful? (JC 1.3.14)
Not so; but it hath been the longest night (TGV 4.2.135)
O wonderful, wonderful, and most wonderful (AYL 3.2.185)

But Shakespeare, inhabiting the half-way house between OE and PDE, sometimes uses inflexions where we would not have them, and *more*/*most* where we would use an inflexion. So when the Steward in *All's Well That Ends Well* (1.3.102) is asked whether he knows Helena, he replies: *I was . . . more near her than I think she wished me*. In *Coriolanus* (4.6.90) we find *violentest contrariety*. Indeed all the three examples given above of adjectives which in PDE prefer *more*/*most* rather than -*er*/-*est* are found with the latter: *horrider* in *Cymbeline* (4.2.331), *certainer* in *Much Ado About Nothing* (5.4.62), and *perfecter* in *Coriolanus* (2.1.76).

You also find 'double comparatives/superlatives':

With a more larger list of scepters (AC 3.6.76.1)
and for the more better assurance, tell them that I, Pyramus, am not Pyramus (MND 3.1.19)
This was the most unkindest cut of all (JC 3.2.184)

But here is how the third example continues:

For when the noble Caesar saw him stab,
Ingratitude, more strong than traitors' arms,
Quite vanquished him:
(JC 3.2.185)

Most unkindest but *more strong*. The examples show that variation was permissible. Overall, though, Shakespeare's use suggests a clear 'settling down into PDE forms'.

4.5.4 Relatives

Another area where we find English in transition is in the formation of relative clauses, usually (though not always, as we shall see) recognisable by the presence of a word like *who, which* or *whom*. These clauses modify (or give additional information about) a noun. In the sentence *The man who loves Lucy lives in Spain*, the relative clause *who loves Lucy* modifies the noun *man*. The relative word *who* refers to *the man*, and it is possible to conceptualise the sentence as two, made into one by the relative – *The man lives in Spain* and *The man loves Lucy*. Notice that in the second sentence – the one that becomes the relative clause – *the man* is the subject. When we looked at the nominative and accusative cases earlier in this chapter, we noted that there is no inflexional difference between the two in PDE nouns, though there is in some pronouns like *he* and *him*. Like *he*, the relative word *who* has a different accusative form – *whom*, and this is used when the relative word stands for the object in the sentence which becomes the relative clause.[2] Think for example of the two sentences underlying *The man whom Lucy loves lives in Spain*. They are *The man lives in Spain* and *Lucy loves the man*. Here *the man* is the object of the second sentence, the one which becomes the relative clause. This is why *whom* can be used instead of *who*. There is, incidentally, another relative pronoun associated with a case other than the nominative or accusative. It is *whose*. When is that used (**AS**)?

Below are twelve short examples of relative clauses, put into four groups. All but one are taken from Shakespeare, the one exception being the opening of the Christian Lord's Prayer, in its 1662 version – example (c). They have been chosen because they depart from PDE rules for forming the relative. In most cases it will be immediately clear that a PDE rule has been broken, but not so simple to articulate what that rule is. In each example, decide what would be said in PDE. Then attempt to state the rule that has been broken, and how (**NP**).

Group 1

(a) Here **Morocco** is describing two caskets, one of gold and one of silver:

The first of gold who this inscription bears,
'Who chooseth me, shall gain what men desire'.
The second silver, which this promise carries . . . ,
(MV 2.7.4)

(b) *John Mortimer, which now is dead*
(2H6 3.1.372)

(c) *Our father which art in heaven*
(1662 Book of Common Prayer)

(d) *Rotten opinion, who hath writ me down*
After my seeming
(2H4 5.2.128)

Group 2

(e) *Let Fame, that all hunt after in their lives*
(opening line of LLL)

(f) *The great globe itself/Yea, all which it inherit*
(Tem 4.1.153)

Group 3

(g) *And should you fall, he is the next will mount*
(2H6 3.1.22)

(h) *I have a brother is condemned to die*
(MM 2.2.33)

(i) *I have a mind presages me such thrift*
That I should questionless be fortunate
(MV 1.1.175)

Group 4

(j) *This island's mine by Sycorax my mother which thou takest from me*
(Tem 1.2.333)

(k)   *Old Lord, I cannot blame thee,*
Who am myself attached with weariness
(Tem 3.3.5)

(l) *As if it were Cain's jawbone that did the first murder*
(Ham 5.1.85)

Group 1 examples relate to the fact that in PDE we distinguish between a person and an inanimate object by using either *who/whom* or *which*. Compare *The man whom Lucy loves* and *The toy which Lucy loves*. In the last line of (a) above (*The second silver, which this promise carries . . .*), Shakespeare is following the rule which now governs PDE: the casket is inanimate, so the relative pronoun is *which*. But the first sentence – *The first of gold who this inscription bears* – shows that this was not always the case. Examples (b) to (d) show the same thing, that the person/object distinction was not always followed. It would in fact be possible to find many examples where the distinction <u>is</u> made, and what the examples here show is that the rules were not yet hard and fast. There is variability. Example (c), which is not from Shakespeare, has been put in because it is a use of *which* in relation to a person (*Father*) that many readers will be familiar with.

In the PDE sentences discussed earlier (about Lucy and Spain), *that* could be used instead of *who/whom/which*. It is possible to say *The man that loves Lucy lives in Spain*. But sometimes *that* cannot be used. This is when the relative is clearly giving you 'less important' additional information, and this is often signalled by commas being put round the clause. In the sentence *Lucy's boyfriend, whom I met last year, lives in Spain*, the information that you met the boyfriend last year is less important, additional information. The main information is very much that the boyfriend lives in Spain. EModE tended to follow this rule, and there are many examples where Shakespeare does so. Group 2 shows that there are occasional counter-examples. In (e) we would expect *which* today, and in (f) *that*.

There is a special circumstance when you can leave out the relative word in PDE, and it relates to the nominative/accusative distinction considered earlier (in 4.2). In the first paragraph of this section we saw that the sentence *The man whom Lucy loves lives in Spain* could be viewed as a combination of two underlying sentences. The one that becomes the main sentence is *The man lives in Spain*. The other one, which becomes the relative clause, is *Lucy loves the man*. The relative word *whom* is used here because *the man* is the object and not the subject of this second underlying sentence. In PDE the relative word can be omitted when it stands for the <u>object</u> of the sentence underlying the relative clause. Thus it is possible to say *The man Lucy loves lives in Spain* (omitting *whom*). But you cannot omit the relative word if it stands for the subject. So *The man who loves Lucy lives in Spain* cannot be shortened to **The man loves Lucy lives in Spain*. Group 3 examples show that this could happen in Shakespeare. This was common in OE and ME and indeed in the sixteenth century. Like many language items, it went out of use in the eighteenth century at the hands of scholars who had highly prescriptive attitudes. They found it 'ungraceful' – a typically eighteenth-century objection.[3]

Group 4 is to do with word order. In PDE it is usual for the relative word to come immediately after the noun it modifies. *Lucy's boyfriend, whom I met last year, lives in Spain* is acceptable, but **Lucy's boyfriend lives in Spain, whom I met last year* is not, even though it is clear enough that *whom* refers to the boyfriend (and could not refer to Spain). In this respect, Renaissance relatives provide an example of the point made earlier (in 4.2) about ways of conveying grammatical information. Word order, it was said, was unimportant in a language where inflexions carried grammatical information. The examples given were from OE, but the same was true of Latin, a language which had (as we saw in 2.2.1) a very great influence in the Renaissance. A relative clause in that language does not have to be put next to the noun it refers to; it could be put some distance away, since an inflexion will make it clear what the referent is.

4.6 The verb phrase

4.6.1 -th, -s, variation and language change

Look at these three short passages, concentrating particularly on the verbs and their endings. Note any that you do not find in PDE:

(a) The **Bishop of Winchester** is talking to his sworn enemy, the Duke of Gloucester –

Gloucester, whate'er we like, thou art Protector
And lookest to command the Prince and realm.
Thy wife is proud; she holdeth thee in awe
More than God or religious churchmen may.
(1H6 1.1.37)

(b) Here, in *A Midsummer Night's Dream*, **Helena** and **Hermia** are talking about the different effects they have on their menfolk –

Hermia: *I give him curses, yet he gives me love.*
Helena: *O that my prayers could such affection move!*
Hermia: *The more I hate, the more he follows me.*
Helena: *The more I love, the more he hateth me.*
(MND 1.1.196)

(c) **Antony** is asked what a crocodile is like. Here is his reply –

It is shaped, sir, like itself, and it is as broad as it hath breadth. It is just so high as it is, and moves with its own organs. It lives by that which nourisheth it, and the elements once out of it, it transmigrates.
(AC 2.7.41)

One ending that is not in regular use today is the *-est* form. It is associated with the *thou* pronoun – as in *thou lookest. Thou* is a way of saying 'you', and we will look at it in detail in the next chapter (5.5). Suffice it to say here that in Shakespeare's time *thou* was being replaced by *you*, and as *thou* died, *-est* went with it.

Much more interesting to the linguist are the forms associated with what is called the third person singular – the form of the verb associated with the pronouns *he, she, it*, and with singular nouns. There are two different forms used in EModE, and you can find examples of both in these passages. One is the *-s* ending that we have today. Examples in the passages are *gives, follows, moves, lives, transmigrates*. The other is a form which we do not have today: *-th*, as in the passages' *holdeth, hateth*, and *nourisheth*. You may associate this form with the Bible (*He that loveth not, knoweth not God* – 1 John). It is in fact the Old English form, when the 'th' was written using the letter known as 'thorn' and written /þ/; for example, the OE for *he loves* is *he lufaþ*.

The change from Old English *-th* to PDE *-s* provides the opportunity to consider some aspects of language change in general. Languages change all the time, of course, and are doing so today as much as in the past. Consider the use of *less* and *fewer* today.[4] The 'traditional' rule is that *less* is used with singular nouns, *fewer* with plurals. So we speak of *less money* but *fewer pounds*. But for over a century speakers have been using *less* for both singular and plural – *less pounds* as well as *less money*. Doubtless the fact that *more* – the form with an opposite meaning – can be used for singular and plurals has hastened this change. More conservative speakers can become very upset by what they regard as the 'ungrammatical' usage of *less* with plural nouns. But their complaints are in vain. *Less* is clearly winning the day. Once it has gained momentum, language change can rarely be stopped.

Variation – a keyword of this chapter – plays an important role in language change. The existence of two competing forms (like *less* and *fewer*, or *-th* and *-s*) provides the conditions whereby change can occur. But what processes are involved? Look at Figure 4.1 showing the regional distribution of *-s* in EModE. Concentrate on the London, North and East Anglia lines, and consider what they show (**NP**).

The figure reflects the fact that the *-s* form comes from Scandinavian languages, and was brought by the invaders from those countries who settled in the north of Britain. It started in the north and spread slowly over the country. Here is an example: in the fourteenth century, the Archbishop of York wrote a catechism (a piece of religious writing with instructional aim) which appeared in both a Northern and a Midland dialect versions. One phrase in the catechism reads (in modern English) 'as Saint John says in his gospel'. In the Northern version this is *als seint Iohn saies in his godspel*, while the Midland version has *as seynt Ion sayeth in hys gospel*.[5]

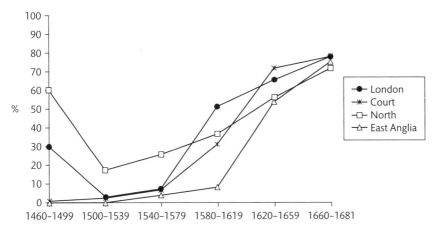

FIGURE 4.1 Replacement of -*th* by -*s* in verbs other than *have* and *do*. Regional distribution of -*s*. From *Historical Sociolinguistics: Language change in Tudor and Stuart England*, Pearson Education (Nevalainen, T. and Raumolin-Brunberg, H. 2003) 178

Supralocalisation is the name given to the process whereby a language form moves from one geographical location to another. -*s* was in a slow march southward. Notice also how much more quickly the form catches on in London – always on the lookout for new linguistic 'fashions', as opposed to rural East Anglia, with a more conservative attitude towards change.

Here is Figure 4.2 also from Nevalainen and Raumolin-Brunberg (2003). What does this one show (**NP**)?

The figure indicates that though at first men seem to use -*s* more than women, the situation very rapidly changes, and for most of the period

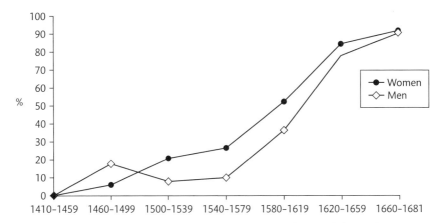

FIGURE 4.2 Replacement of -*th* by -*s* in verbs other than *have* and *do*. Gender distribution of -*s*. From *Historical Sociolinguistics: Language change in Tudor and Stuart England*, Pearson Education (Nevalainen, T. and Raumolin-Brunberg, H. 2003) 123

covered by the figure, it is women who are ahead in taking up the new form. Language change is often pushed forward by a group of individuals who adopt a linguistic form and make it dominant, and women are one group of people whose influence has been particularly studied from this point of view. As long ago as 1946, August Brun, a specialist in the Provençal dialect, found that while men in the region spoke Provençal, the younger women tended to use French. Brun regarded this fact as contributing significantly to the disappearance of the dialect.[6] Women, it seems, may be quicker to adopt new forms coming from elsewhere, while for some reason men have a tendency to stay with local forms.

The figures given above come from a recent large-scale study of language change in EModE. Here is a box about it.

An EModE corpus

From where do linguists get their information about how a language works and is used? Views can differ dramatically. In the 1960s and after, when the views of the linguist Noam Chomsky were predominant, 'native speaker intuition' – what the native speaker unconsciously knows about their language – was a prime source of information. A celebrated example involved the sentences *John is easy to please* and *John is eager to please*. On the 'surface' these sentences have identical structure. But every native speaker can tell you that while *It is easy to please John* is a possible sentence in English, *It is eager to please John* is not. Perhaps this indicates underlying differences between the seemingly identical structures. Chomsky and his followers used information of this sort to explore the structure of English.

If native speaker intuitions can reveal so much about language structure, there is little point in collecting together large quantities of instances of language use. But in more recent times, 'large quantities of instances' are exactly what linguists have collected. These take the form of corpora (the singular is corpus) – electronically-scanned collections of texts adding up to millions of words. When it comes to the study of a language's history (where native speakers are no longer available, even if we wanted to tap their intuitions), it is no exaggeration to say corpora have revolutionised the field.

The *Corpus of Early English Correspondence* (CEEC) is a 2.7 million-word electronic collection of no less than 6,000 letters written by 800 individuals between 1417 and 1681. It was compiled by Terttu Nevalainen and Helena Raumolin-Brunberg, working with a team at the University of Helsinki in 1993. They have used the data to investigate 14 areas, including the replacement of *ye* by *you*, the use of *do* in affirmative statements (both discussed later, in 5.5. and 4.6.2 respectively), and the *-s* versus *-th* suffix. In relation to these areas they consider the roles played by different variables including geographical region, social order, and gender – in eight out of the 14 areas they find that women adopt new variants earlier than men. Their research is reported in Nevalainen and Raumolin-Brunberg (2003), on which much of the discussion in this section is based.

Another corpus involving the EModE period is the *Corpus of English Dialogues, 1560–1760*. This collection of about 1.2 million words consists of 'authentic dialogues' – records of trial proceedings, for example, and 'constructed dialogues', as they appear in drama, as well as didactic works such as language teaching texts. The corpus is used by Culpeper and Kytö (2010) as the basis for their analysis of spoken interaction of the time.

As you can see from the earlier passages, both *-s* and *-th* were around in Shakespeare's day. The statistics show that *-s* was indeed winning the battle. Shakespeare's early plays (up to 1599) have 239 *-th* endings and just 68 *-s*. Thereafter you find only 29 *-th* endings and 185 *-es*.[7] 'Half-way house', 'settling down', 'variation'.

At the beginning of this chapter, we noted that when variation occurs there would be occasions for asking what factors control the choice of one or another variant. The *-s/-th* choice is a case in point. Why did Shakespeare sometimes use one and not the other? On occasions the answer may be to do with the verb being used. You may have noticed that in both the figures above, taken from Nevalainen and Raumolin-Brunberg (2003), the verbs *have* and *do* are excluded. This reflects a linguistic truth, that very commonly-used verbs are often the least susceptible to change: the strongest habits are the hardest to alter, and the sheer frequency of some verbs helps to reinforce their existing forms. This is why one of the most commonly-used verbs in English – *be* – is also one of the least regular, with three different forms in the simple present singular: *I am, you are, he is*. The verbs *have* and *do* are also very common, and perhaps this explains why, like other writers of the time, Shakespeare seems to be quite happy with the 'traditional' *-th* ending in *hath* and *doth*, using them 902 and 1985 times respectively in the plays (which is not to say that he entirely avoids the *-s* equivalents *does* and *has*). In comparison, he only uses *saith* six times in the plays, while *says* occurs 241 times.[8]

Sometimes the variation can be to do with metre. To understand this, you need to think about how many syllables there are in words ending with *-th* and *-s*. These verb pairs will enable you to work this out. Count the syllables:

likes	*liketh*	*holds*	*holdeth*
brings	*bringeth*	*loves*	*loveth*

In these examples, the *-th* ending adds an extra syllable to the word. If we think of the *-s* ending as the 'norm' (which it was for Shakespeare), then the use of the *-th* alternative will be useful to Shakespeare when the metre requires it. Look at passages (a) and (b) at the beginning of this section; replace the *-th* forms in them with an *-s* (so *holdeth* becomes *holds* and so on). See what effect it would have on the metre. It will make the lines a beat short: instead of *The more I love, the more he hateth me* (deDUMdeDUMdeDUMdeDUMdeDUM), you would have *The more I love, the more he hates me* (deDUMdeDUMdeDUMdeDUMde).

So sometimes the reason for using *-th* is metrical. But there are two circumstances where this cannot be the case. One is in prose, which is the case in the passage (c) at the beginning of this section. Metre cannot be the answer here. As for the second case, look at these verb pairs and see how they are different from the ones you saw above. Say as much as you can about why they are different:

promises	*promiseth*	*approaches*	*approacheth*
loses	*loseth*	*relishes*	*relisheth*

In these cases the *-es* and *-th* endings give words with the same number of syllables. This is because (in both PDE and EModE) if a verb ends with an *s*-like sound (and this includes [tʃ]), the *-s* you add is pronounced [ɪz], as an extra syllable. So *promises* has three syllables, like *promiseth*. Thus it cannot be for a metrical reason that in *Henry VI, Part 3*, we find:

Ah, what a shame were this! Look on the boy;
And let his manly face, which promiseth
Successful fortune, steel thy melting heart
(2.2.39)

Taylor (1976), who is the person to read on this topic in general (and who uses this example), argues that in this particular case it may be to avoid too many 's' sounds in the lines. On other occasions, Taylor says, the ending suggests grandiloquence, rhetorical flourish, possibly even great lyricism.

As a further example, here are a few famous lines from Portia in *The Merchant of Venice*. She is trying to persuade Shylock, who is about to kill Antonio, to show mercy:

The quality of mercy is not strained,
It droppeth as the gentle rain from heaven

Upon the place beneath. It is twice blest,
It blesseth him that gives and him that takes.
'Tis mightiest in the mightiest, it becomes
The throned monarch better than his crown
(MV 4.1.182)

Both the forms are here. Can it be to do with metre? Change the *-s* forms to *-th* and you will discover that the metre is indeed destroyed. If you then change the *-th* forms to *-s*, you find that the choice of *droppeth* as opposed to *drops* can indeed be accounted for by metre. But why is it *blesseth* and not *blesses* (both with the same number of syllables)? Perhaps the passage has particular 'grandiloquence'?

There are occasions where neither metre nor grandiloquence seems to be involved, and we need perhaps to remember that when a language is in flux, as English was during the Renaissance, variation is just what you would expect. As a final example: we have already seen that Antony in *Antony and Cleopatra* uses *nourisheth*. Why then, two acts later, do we also find him using the alternative form?

yet ha' we

A brain that nourishes our nerves, and can
Get goal for goal of youth.
(AC 4.8.21)

4.6.2 *do*

Do is an important word in PDE grammar. In some of its grammatical uses, it functions in a way that is comparatively rare in the world's languages. If you want to explore some of these grammatical uses, look at Activity 3 (*Just do it – NP*).

One of the main grammatical uses of *do* is in the formation of questions (or more accurately, <u>interrogative</u> sentences). Here are the examples given in the Activity. The sentences on the left are non-interrogative, or <u>affirmative</u>, and their question equivalents are on the right.

Peter likes chocolates	*Does Peter like chocolate?*
Peter and Anne like chocolates	*Do Peter and Anne like chocolates?*
Peter liked chocolates	*Did Peter like chocolates?*

For these sorts of sentences (we are dealing with just two tenses here), you form the interrogative by using an appropriate part of the verb *do* – *do* or *does* if the time is present, *did* if it is past. This is put before the subject (*Peter, Peter and Anne*). After the subject comes the verb in its infinitive form – it is invariable: *like* and not *likes* or *liked*). Activity 3 also deals with negative sentences, another important use of *do* in PDE. Once again you use the appropriate form of *do*, followed by the negative *not*: *do not, does not, did not*. These are very often shortened to *don't, doesn't, didn't*. The *do* form is then followed by the invariable infinitive. Notice that for both interrogative and negative the element which tells you when the action took place (whether present or past) is shown by the form of the verb *do*, not by the 'main verb' – you have *do/does* or *did*, while the main verb is just *like*. One might say that it is *do* which 'carries the tense'.

A further use of *do* in PDE is illustrated in the Activity. It is in positive affirmative sentences, such as *Peter does like chocolates*. You would use this form (as opposed to the more normal *Peter likes chocolates*) for emphasis, or sometimes to contradict a previous statement. For example, you might say it if someone had just asserted that John did not like chocolates.

So much for PDE. What about in the Renaissance? To start with the positive affirmative cases: in Shakespeare you do find many positive/affirmatives that are formed without the use of *do*.[9] But there are also, as in PDE, examples where *do* is used. Here are two pairs of positive affirmative sentences, which have the same main verb. In each pair, *do* is used in one case but not the other: In (a) Parolles is describing anyone who prefers to stay at home with a lover rather than going to war. In (b), Oberon has told Puck to seek out an Athenian. Puck thinks he has found the right man.

(a) *He wears his honour in a box unseen* (AW 2.3.277)

(b) *Weeds of Athens he doth wear* (MND 2.2.77)

Nestor, in (c), shows appreciation for Ulysses' advice, while in (d) it begins to dawn on Falstaff that a trick has been played on him.

(c) *Now, Ulysses, I begin to relish thy advice* (TC 1.3.387)

(d) *I do begin to perceive that I am made an ass* (MWW 5.5.119)

So there is variation. Sometimes it is clear that a form of emphasis is involved. In the following example Julius Caesar's wife, Calphurnia, is trying to persuade her husband not to go to the Senate that day. She lists the evil omens that fill her with apprehension. Perhaps her use of *did* can be accounted for in terms of emphasis:

Horses did neigh, and dying men did groan,
And ghosts did shriek and squeal about the streets (JC 2.2.23)

But often the emphasis explanation does not ring true. In the following example, King Henry is also talking about evil omens, this time occurring at the birth of Richard (whose later wickedness when he becomes Richard III is legendary). Yet there is no *do* here:

The owl shrieked at thy birth, an evil sign (3H6 5.6.44)

In *Julius Caesar* the horses did neigh, while in *Henry VI, Part 3* the owls shrieked. Or what about in *Pericles* when Helicanus says *Sir, 'tis the governor of Mytilene/ Who, hearing of your melancholy state,/ Did come to see you*? There is no apparent need for emphasis here. Perhaps in this case it is something to do with metre. This is clearly a consideration in the following two passages from *Hamlet*. Consider what would happen to the metre if *did* were dropped in both. In the first Horatio is talking about Hamlet's father's ghost, and in the second about what happened when Julius Caesar died in Rome:

It lifted up it[s] head and did address
Itself to motion like as it would speak.
(Ham 1.2.217)

The graves stood tenantless and the sheeted dead
Did squeak and gibber in the Roman streets –
(Ham 1.1.116)

Variation is also found in interrogative and negative forms. Activity 4 (*Shakespearean interrogatives and negatives*) provides examples of these and asks you to compare the rules with those of PDE (**NP**).

The examples in Activity 4 show that interrogatives and negatives could be formed as in PDE, using *do*. Hence Hamlet asks: *Why did you laugh . . . ?* (example (e)), and Henry VIII says *It does not please me* (g). But there are also alternative ways. Instead of *Do our subjects revolt?* King Richard II asks (example (d)): *Revolt our subjects?* And while Hamlet's question above uses *do*, consider how the sentence finishes: *Why did you laugh, when I said, 'Man delights not me'?* – a negative formed by simply putting *not* after the verb. Not using *do* was in fact the chief way of forming interrogatives and negatives in Old English, and the equivalent is, incidentally, very common in many languages, including perhaps ones that you know. Indeed, using a word like *do* to form questions and negatives is linguistically (considering all the world's languages) a very unusual way of performing these operations. Where does it come from? Here is a box which considers this question.

Why do we use *do*?

There are a number of theories about where the use of *do* in interrogatives and negatives comes from. In one, the positive affirmative version is thought to originate with the use of the verb *do* in what is called a causative sense – where something is caused to be done. In PDE we use the verb *make* in this sense: *It made her jump* can mean 'it caused her to jump'. The verb *do* was quite common in this causative sense in ME, and you even find it occasionally in the sixteenth-century poet Spenser, as in these lines from his poem *The Faerie Queene: So matter did she make of nought/ To stirre vp strife, and do them disagree* ('cause them to disagree').[10]

Over time, the positive affirmative use of *do* became widespread, without any causative sense remaining. Once this had happened, it is easy to see how the negative and interrogative uses of *do* followed. As noted in the text, at one time the common way of forming negatives in English was by putting *not* after the verb, and interrogatives were formed by inverting subject and verb. So the negative and interrogative of *I do like* would naturally be *I do not like* and *Do I like?* These forms stayed in the language, even after the positive affirmative *I do like* was commonly replaced by the form most in use today – *I like*.

Figure 4.3 shows a graph which plots the use of *do* from 1500 to 1700, taken from a study which focuses on the issue. Look first at the three lines showing questions and negatives (three because negative and affirmative questions are treated separately). The lines are not straight; there are some ups and downs in them, which are perhaps accidents of the samples used. But the direction they go in is very clear. Then look at the line showing affirmative declarative use of *do*. What does it show? Taking the graph as a whole, try to arrive at some statements about the use of *do* during the period (**NP**).

The graph indicates that the use of *do* for questions and negatives was gaining in strength. But for positive affirmatives the opposite is true. This use of *do* diminishes over the period, toward the position we see today, where positive affirmative *do* is the exception rather than the rule. In other words, the norms that we have today are in the process of being established; there is a 'settling down into PDE forms'. But the existence of variation shows that the process is not yet complete – we are in a 'half-way house' – and though sometimes specific reasons can be found for the use or lack of use of *do*, it often seems that variation exists because the language was in flux and more than one form was available for use.

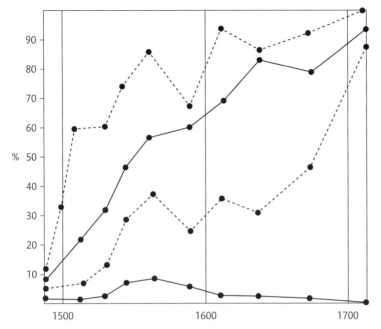

FIGURE 4.3 Auxiliary *do*. Percentage of *do* forms in different types of sentence, 1500–1700. Adapted by Barber (1997) from Ellegård (1953)

4.6.3 Modal auxiliaries

In the previous section we looked at the formation of interrogatives and negatives using *do*. We also considered alternative ways, sometimes found in Shakespeare, of forming these two sentence types – using inversion of subject and verb, and simply putting the word *not* after the verb. In fact there is a group of verbs in PDE which regularly uses these latter ways, and which do not (barring a few rare exceptions) use *do* at all. These are called <u>modal auxiliary verbs</u>, and include *must*, *can* and *may*. If (as is usual) they are followed by a main verb, then that is in the infinitive: *You must go, she can swim.* The interrogative and negative forms of this first example sentence are not **Do you must go?* and **You don't must go*, but *Must you go?*, and *You must not go*.

Many of these modal auxiliary verbs in EModE are as they are now, but there are some slight differences in meanings, just sufficient to lead to occasional comprehension problems. Activity 5 (*Some Shakespearean modal auxiliaries*) gives examples of these and invites you to speculate about meanings (**NP**).

Can is an example of a Renaissance modal auxiliary with a slightly different semantic coverage from today. In PDE its main uses are to express possibility, ability, or permission. In the sentence *He can swim* the last two are likely – it can mean 'he is able to swim' or 'he is permitted to swim'. Example (a) in the

Activity shows *can* at work as a main verb meaning 'to have skill', or 'to know how to', or simply 'to know'. We have already come across this sense of 'knowing' in 3.4 (in relation to the adjective *cunning*), and the phrase *D'you ken John Peel* was mentioned. For those of you who know German, the verb *kennen*, meaning 'to know', will come to mind. Another example of *can* interpretable in the same way occurs in *Richard III* when a messenger says: *The sum of all I can, I have disclosed* (2.4.163).

Another modal that has an interesting semantic history is *may*. Its associated form *might* gives a clue to its original meaning. In PDE it can indicate permission or possibility: *He may come* could have either one of these meanings. But originally, before Shakespeare, it was associated in meaning with the noun *might*, meaning 'power', 'strength'. *He may/might come* would have signified the power to come. Shakespeare uses *may* to indicate permission or possibility as we do today, though the phrase *as I may remember* (example (b) in the Activity) sounds odd to modern ears, and carries a sense of power ('to the extent that my powers of memory suggest' perhaps).

In PDE, some speakers make no distinction between *shall* and *will*, and will as readily say *I shall come* as *I will come*. People will, however, distinguish the associated forms *should* and *would*. *He should brush his teeth every day* suggests a moral obligation, while *He would brush his teeth every day* can suggest a habit. This difference is not found in Shakespeare, where the two forms tend to be indistinguishable. This is apparent in example (c), where *would* makes more sense to the modern reader. There is an implied condition here: *take* means 'if you take', and in EModE *should* was acceptable in this conditional sense.

Will is another modal which has a slightly different semantic coverage from PDE. Today it often simply signifies futurity: *I will go there tomorrow* can simply be indicating something that will happen in the future. Its original sense is 'wish' or 'want', and this sense is carried in the subtitle of Shakespeare's play *Twelfth Night – What You Will*. It is also carried in the Activity's example (d). Occasionally you find *will* used as a main verb, as when Mistress Quickly in *Henry IV, Part 2* (2.4.93) tries to ban the swaggering Pistol from her house by saying *I'll no swaggerers*. Does Shakespeare use *will* to indicate straight futurity (as today)? Search for the word *will* on the 'Shakespeare's Words' website. You will find 5098 instances cited. The total includes of course examples of *will* used as a noun, and these are not relevant here. It will also exclude the shortened *'ll* form (as in *I'll*), which you would want to include (though in fact there are not so many of those in Shakespeare). So the search will not throw up everything that you want, but a glance through some of the instances it does provide will make it hard to resist the conclusion that simple futurity is indeed a use.

Earlier the forms *might* and *would* were described as 'related to' *may* and *will*. There are some ways in which they can be considered as past tense forms of these verbs. But it is dangerous to call them these because in many respects they change meaning in a way that goes beyond tense. For example, the difference between *He may come* and *He might come* is not to do with tense but with degree of possibility, *might* being much more tentative than *may*. That the difference is not to do with tense is shown by the fact that both the examples have their own past forms – *He may have come* and *He might have come*. But there is one example in the Activity which shows a proper past tense form. It occurs in a word that is not used today, but which you will probably have no problem in understanding: *durst*. This is the past tense of 'dare', and example (e) shows it being used in this sense. In PDE, of course, we have the past tense form of *dared*. This form was coming into the language in the Renaissance period, and a look on the 'Shakespeare's Words' website will reveal nine uses of it in Shakespeare, in comparison with 56 uses of *durst*.

4.6.4 Double negatives

Here are four passages containing negation. Try to provide loose translations into PDE:

(a) In *Love's Labour's Lost* (5.1.144), Holofernes – a person known for his elaborate way of speaking – is talking to **Dull**, whose name says it all. Holofernes upbraids Dull for being silent – he has not said a single word. Dull's reply:
Nor understood none neither, sir.

(b) In *Henry VI, Part 2*, **Suffolk** is banished (3.2.365). He is desolate about leaving the company of Queen Margaret. There is only one thing that will please him, he says:
Live thou to joy thy life;
Myself no joy in naught but that thou livest.

(c) In *As You Like It* (2.4.8), Rosalind, **Celia** and Touchstone are trudging through the forest. Celia has had enough. She says:
I pray you, bear with me, I cannot go no further.

(d) A rather more difficult passage to paraphrase: in *Twelfth Night* (3.1.155), **Cesario** (Viola in disguise) is telling Olivia that he can never love her. He says:
I have one heart, one bosom, and one truth.
And that no woman has, nor never none
Shall mistress be of it, save I alone.

Comparing these originals with your modern translations will reveal a difference in the way negation is expressed. What is it (**NP**)?

The difference is that modern English usually allows only one negative word in a sentence. In Shakespeare's time <u>double negatives</u> (or even more than two – in (a) above there are three) were permitted. Hence Celia's *I cannot go no further*; today we would say *I cannot go any further*.

Double negatives today are often socially stigmatised. If a child says *I don't like nothing*, including the two negatives *don't* ('do not') and *nothing*, it may get told off and corrected. But they are permitted in many languages; in Italian for example, *I don't like anything* would be *Non mi piace niente* (literally 'I don't like nothing'). In ME too, negatives were often formed by using *ne* and *nat* either side of the verb – in The Prologue to Chaucer's *Canterbury Tales*, the Parson is described as being so conscientious that he never failed (*lefte*) to visit his parishioners, whatever the weather: *But he ne lefte nat, for reyn ne thonder* (line 492) – rather like French where negatives are formed by *ne* and *pas* either side of the verb.

As is often the case when someone argues against the use of a stigmatised form in language, they appeal to logic. In the case of double negatives, the logic is often mathematical – 'two negatives make a positive', teachers sometimes say to pupils learning English as a first language. Feste in *Twelfth Night* uses the same logic: *So that, conclusions to be as kisses, if your four negatives make your two affirmatives, why then, the worse for my friends and the better for my foes.* (5.1.20). To what extent language is (or can be) controlled by the laws of logic is an issue you may wish to consider.

In fact in EModE double negatives were used for emphasis. 'The more negatives in the clause, the more emphatic the negative meaning' is how Crystal (2008: 183) puts it. This is clearly the case in example (b) above, where Celia really has had enough. 'More negatives for emphasis' is reminiscent perhaps of the phrase 'not never, not nohow' which was sometimes used some years ago as a way of expressing an emphatic 'no' answer.

Yes, yea, no and *nay*

Talking of negatives, you might think that *no* and *nay* are just different ways of saying the same thing. The same may, you think, hold for *yes* and *yea*. But originally these forms had slightly different uses.

Nay was used when the preceding statement or question was positive. When it was negative, *no* was used. You can find examples of this in Shakespeare. Here, in *The Merchant of Venice*, Bassanio is telling Gratiano to behave properly (have a good 'bearing'). Gratiano agrees to behave, though he wants to make an exception of that night, when he intends to have fun, and thoroughly misbehave. Bassanio's statement is positive, so Gratiano replies with *nay*. Gratiano's reply contains the negative *You shall not gauge me*, so Bassanio replies with *no*.

Bassanio: *Well, we shall see your bearing.*
Gratiano: *Nay, but I bar tonight. You shall not gauge me*
              By what we do tonight.
Bassanio: *No, that were pity.*
(MV 2.2.186)

But the language was in flux, and *nay* was simply becoming the more emphatic way of saying no. Here is what Onions (1986: 179) says about *nay*: 'its most frequent use is to correct, amplify or emphasise something that precedes, or to express a mild protest'. His three examples:

(a) Dromio of Syracuse: *A wolf, nay worse, a fellow all in buff.*
       (CE 4.2.36)

(b) Boatswain: *Do you not hear him? You mar our labour.*
                   Keep your cabins! You do assist the storm.
       Gonzalo: *Nay, good, be patient.* (Tem 1.1.13)

(c) Isabella: *Die, perish. Might but my bending down*
                 Reprieve thee from thy fate, it should proceed.
                 I'll pray a thousand prayers for thy death,
                 No word to save thee.
       Claudio: *Nay, hear me, Isabel.* (MM 3.1.150)

A similar distinction existed between *yes* and *yea*, the former being used when the preceding statement contained a negative word, the latter when it did not. But over time *yea* was turning into a way simply 'to correct or amplify' (Onions again). Indeed, its most common meaning was something like 'and more than that'. Here is Ariel in *The Tempest* describing the storm he created:

Ariel: *the fire and cracks*
              Of sulphurous roaring the most mighty Neptune
              Seem to besiege, and make his bold waves tremble,
              Yea, his dread trident shake.
              (Tem 1.2.203)

These distinctions are not of course found today, and indeed the forms *yea* and *nay* have died out. But you may have come across a similar type of distinction in French between *oui* and *si*. The way the Harrap dictionary puts it is that *si* is 'used in answer to a negative question'. Very much what was said about *yes* earlier.

4.6.5 Tenses, simple, progressive and perfect

The main (but not the only) function of <u>tenses</u> in a language is to indicate time relations. The tense system of PDE includes three main tense types, which are formed in different ways. Examples of the <u>simple</u> tenses are *I look, she wears, we walked* and *they laughed*. Questions and negatives are formed using part of the verb *do*: *Do I look? We didn't walk* and so on. The <u>progressive</u> (or <u>continuous</u>) tenses are formed using a part of the verb *be* followed by the main verb ending in *-ing*. Examples of the present and past progressive are *I am looking, she is wearing, we were walking, they were laughing*. Think how questions and negatives are formed. The present and past <u>perfect</u> tenses use *have* followed by the past participle of the main verb (usually ending in *-ed*). Examples are *I have worked, she has worn, we had walked, they had laughed*. Notice the irregular past participle *worn* (if it were regular it would be *'weared'). Again you are left to consider how questions and negatives are formed.

The time concepts which these different tenses indicate are complex, and this makes the differences in their use equally complex. Activity 6 (*Tense differences in PDE and EModE*) looks at just some of the ways in which the simple, progressive and perfect tenses operate in both PDE and EModE. If you are going to do this Activity, do so before you read on (**NP**).

One use of the simple present (and past) in PDE is to express habitual action. Sentence (b) in Activity 6 (*I visit my aunt every year*) illustrates this. Contrast this with *I'm visiting my aunt* (sentence a), which is talking about an action taking place at the present time, explaining what is happening at a given moment. A common use of the progressive tenses is to describe an action which is taking place when another action occurs. *I was eating my dinner when he came in* (sentence e) shows this. Very often, as in the Activity's examples, adverbial phrases make the 'habitual' versus 'present' notions clear: 'every year' and 'nowadays' contrast with 'at the moment'.

The Shakespeare examples in Activity 6 indicate that these distinctions were not so clear-cut in his time. '*What letter are you reading there?*' (sentence b) uses the progressive just as we would today. But the context of Polonius' question *What do you read, my Lord?* makes it clear that he is not asking Hamlet about his reading habits in general, but about what he is reading at that particular moment. The modern reader finds this strange, as are the Friar's words in (i) – *I come, I come*. We would say 'I'm coming.'

The word Rissanen (1999: 216) uses to describe the use of the progressive tenses in this period is 'unsettled'. There was variability. There was also movement towards the PDE situation, but it was not until the second half of the seventeenth century that the progressive tenses really 'took off'. One study finds three times as many examples in texts written between 1640 and 1710 as between 1570 and 1640.[11] There are, incidentally, various views about the origins of the tense. According to some, *I am singing* started life as *I am on singing*. Over time the *on* became *a*, so you had *I am a singing*, which eventually became *I am singing*. Modern readers will be familiar with this 'a-' form (often joined to the following word with a hyphen), in somewhat archaic phrases like 'a-courting' and 'a-wooing'. The latter occurs in Shakespeare, where you also find examples like *Anne Page is . . . a feasting* (MWW 2.3.80) which is but a stone's throw from *Anne Page is feasting.* Also, incidentally, in ME and EModE the progressive could be used for a passive. Rissanen's example is *The house is building* meaning 'the house is being built'. There are a few examples in Shakespeare . . . *whilst this play is playing* says Horatio in *Hamlet* (3.2.98), meaning 'is being played', and a few where the 'a-' form is used in this way: *Let us seem humbler after it is done/Than when it was a-doing* says Brutus in *Coriolanus* (4.3.4). 'A-doing' means 'being done'.

One use of the perfect tenses in the British version of PDE (American usage is slightly different) is to express a time-span lasting up to the present, as opposed to an action which took place at one moment in the past. This difference can be seen in Activity 6's sentences (j) and (k). *I have visited France several times* means 'at unspecified times up until the present', while *I visited France last year* refers to an action taking place at a particular moment in the past. As with the simple/progressive distinction, adverbial phrases will often be associated with the tense choice. The presence of 'when he was only 15', referring to a specific point in time, would make use of the present perfect impossible to many PDE speakers (*He has read Macbeth when he was only 15* would be unacceptable to many).

Once again we find Shakespeare's usage not really following this 'rule'. The first Lord's question in (n) is just what we would say today, because it does not refer to a specific point in time (it is 'up till now'). But the Second Lord's reply *I have delivered it an hour since*, though not impossible, is a little odd; we would probably prefer 'I delivered it an hour since'. We would also today expect perfect tenses in (p) and (q). Once again, what we have is variability. As Fischer and Wurff (2006: 139) put it, the simple past and the present perfect 'were variants for a while within the tense system'. The tense system was well on its way towards its present form, but had not yet settled into it.

The aspects of tense usages that we have discussed here are indeed only a small part of the whole picture. For more complete information on how the PDE tense system works you need to consult a grammar book like Leech and Svartvik (2002). For descriptions of EModE usage, there are Rissanen (1999), Fischer and Wurff (2006), and Nevalainen (2006).

4.6.6 Verbs taking *be* in the perfect tenses

Here are some pairs of Shakespearean sentences, both using the same main verb. What is the grammatical difference between them? *Go* in the first sentence means 'walk':

(a) *I have gone all night*
  (Cym 4.2.294)
  Go in; and tell my lady I am gone,
  (RJ 3.5.232)

(b) *Forward, I pray, since we have come so far,*
  (TS 4.5.12)
  Me to proclaim the truth, and I am come,
  I dread, too late.
  (AC 4.14.126)

(c) *His Highness is fallen into this same whoreson apoplexy*
  (2H4 1.2.106)
  I'll to my brother, though he hath fallen by prompture of the blood
  (Mes 2.4.177)

These sentences are examples of the present perfect tense, discussed in the previous section where we noted that it is formed using the auxiliary verb *have*, followed by the main verb's past participle. In many European languages, but not modern English, the auxiliary *be* is sometimes used instead of *have*. This is particularly the case when the main verb describes motion, or is what is called a <u>mutative</u> verb – indicating a change of state or a change of place (verbs like *come*, *go*, *become* and *grow*, etc.). This is what happens in modern German and Dutch, and perhaps in other languages that you know; you say *I am gone* rather than *I have gone*.

It was the same in OE and ME. Describing the escape of King Croesus from death by burning, Chaucer's Monk says *Whanne he escaped was* (*Canterbury Tales*. Mk. VII.2735). As the earlier examples show, you also find *be* used as well as *have* in Shakespeare. This is particularly common with the verbs *go*, *come*, *arrive*, *turn*, *ride*, *steal away*, *set forth*, *meet*, *retire* – mostly verbs of motion, or mutative verbs (though *meet* is not at all clearly in that category).[12] Here are some more examples:

Worcester is stolen away by night (1H4 2.4.351)

Now, noble peers, the cause why we are met
Is to determine of the coronation (R3 3.4.2)

And now to London all the crew are gone (3H6 2.1.173)

As the paired examples at the beginning of this section show, you do find *have* used even with mutative verbs. So there is variability, and once again we need to ask what controls the choice of one or the other form. Some linguists have suggested that the use of *have* in cases where *be* would also be possible places emphasis on the action itself, while the use of *be* emphasises the new state reached. This explanation works well in the case of the (b) pair above. *We have come so far* emphasises the journey (the meaning being 'we have travelled so far'), while *I am come* means 'I am here'. But though this distinction might explain some examples, what is happening in Shakespeare overall is part of a movement which had been going on for centuries – towards the use of *have* rather than *be* in the present perfect tense. As Denison puts it (1993:344; he writes BE and HAVE in capitals to indicate that he is talking about the verb in all its various forms): 'the history of the BE perfect has been one of continuous retreat in the face of the advancing HAVE perfect'. The final victory of *have* came in the eighteenth and nineteenth centuries, but even in Shakespeare you can see the language settling down to a future with *have* rather than *be*.

4.7 Towards today

With one or two possible exceptions, grammatical differences between EModE and PDE do not pose many serious comprehension difficulties to today's reader of Shakespeare. The main interest in Shakespeare's grammar is that it shows the language moving away from AS and towards the present day. Two of the chapter's key phrases: 'half-way house' and 'settling down' suggest this. 'Variation' – the third key phrase – is a result of the fact that the language had not yet reached a state of stability.

In the box *Yes, yea, no* and *nay* we looked at differences in use between these pairs of words. The differences are not to do with the structure of the forms, but in how they are used. 'Use' is the area to which we turn in the next chapter. We will see there that structure and use are indeed different areas which demand separate linguistic treatment.

Activity section

1 Hunt the inflexions

Staying with hunters, but thinking now about PDE, work out how the declension for the noun *hunter* runs. Some gaps have been filled in to guide you.

Singular

N	hunter
A	
G	
D	

Plural

N	
A	
G	hunters'
D	to the hunters

2 Adjective comparison in PDE

The purpose of this Activity is to formulate the 'rules' which control the use of some adjective forms in PDE.

(i)   As was mentioned in 4.2, comparative adjectives can be formed by using the inflexion -er. But this is not the only method. Use these examples to identify the other method of forming comparatives, and to work out when one method is used and when the other (hint: counting syllables is involved):

Mont Blanc is high, but Everest is higher.
The second half of the match was more exciting than the first.
He finds languages hard, but sciences are harder.
As they approached the shore, the lights became brighter.
Swimming is much more difficult in the sea than in a pool.
Mary was friendly, but Jane was more approachable.

(ii) The above examples show that number of syllables is the important characteristic. Here are some more examples which will enable you to formulate your 'rule' a little further:

Now she'd stopped smoking she felt much healthier.
She liked England but was always more happy in Italy.
He looked much happier once the journey was over.
In recent years he had adopted a more healthy lifestyle.

(iii) The examples below enable you to find out if the same set of rules applies to another adjective form known as the superlative:

The cheapest way to go was by train.
It was the narrowest escape she had ever had.
Of the three, she was undoubtedly the most polite.
She had the most extraordinary talent of them all.

(iv) The final stage is to formulate your rules in a complete way. Before you do so, consider the following sentences. Are they acceptable English? If not, include a statement in your rules which excludes them.
Mont Blanc is high, but Everest is more higher.
He looked much more happier once the journey was over.
Of the three, she was undoubtedly the most politest.[13]

3 Just do it

Here is a PDE sentence with its question form equivalent (we call the question form <u>interrogative</u> and the non-question form <u>affirmative</u>):

Peter likes chocolates → *Does Peter like chocolate?*

(i)   Describe as precisely as you can the 'operations' performed on the affirmative form to turn it into an interrogative.

(ii) Now form interrogatives from the affirmatives below. Again, talk yourself through the operations involved.
Peter and Anne like chocolates.
Peter liked chocolates.

(iii) Now try to formulate a 'rule' for forming interrogatives in English from affirmatives like these.

Think next about modern day <u>positives</u> and <u>negatives</u>; (in the example below, you might say *doesn't* instead of *does not*):

Peter likes chocolates → *Peter does not like chocolate?*

(iv) Describe the operations involved here; then form negatives from the sentences in (ii) above, and again describe the operations involved. Try to formulate a 'rule' for making negatives in English from positives like these.
Sometimes *do* is used in positive affirmative sentences, like this:
Peter does like chocolates. When would you use this form, as opposed to *Peter likes chocolates*? Try to think of an exact context, and attempt to formulate a 'rule' for the use of *do* in positive affirmatives of this sort.

4 Shakespearean interrogatives and negatives

Below are some interrogatives and negatives from Shakespeare plays. Does he follow the same PDE rules considered in the text? To work this out systematically, begin by marking each sentence as interrogative or negative. If you find rules different from the present day ones, state what they are, and formulate how the negatives/interrogatives would be said in PDE:

(a) *I did not think to draw my sword 'gainst Pompey* (AC 2.2.159)

(b) *Or else you like not of my company* (TS 2.1.65)

(c) *Signor Gremio, came you from the church?* (TS 3.2.148)

(d) *Revolt our subjects?* (meaning 'Are our subjects in revolt?') (R2 3.2.100)

(e) *Why did you laugh, when I said, Man delights not me* (Ham 2.2.313)

(f) *Tut, I came not to hear this* (1H4 4.3.89)

(g) *No, sir, it does not please me* (H8 5.3.134)

(h) *Now, fair one, does your business follow us?* (AW 2.1.99)

5 Some Shakespearean modal auxiliaries

Here are five examples of modal auxiliaries (though sometimes being used as main verbs) in Shakespeare. All of them bar one are still used in PDE, but you will probably find the uses here a little unfamiliar. Consider what the modal auxiliaries might mean in these sentences, and what they mean in PDE.

(a) **King Claudius** pays a compliment to the French (Ham 4.7.85):
Here was a gentleman of Normandy,
I have seen myself, and served against, the French,
And they <u>can</u> well on horseback

(b) **King Henry** is trying to remember who was present when former King Richard said something prophetic:
         But which of you was by –
(to Warwick) *You, cousin Nevil, as I <u>may</u> remember –*
When Richard, with his eye brimful of tears,
Then checked and rated by Northumberland,
Did speak these words, now proved a prophecy?
(2H4 3.1.62)

(c) **Ulysses** (TC 1.3.110) expresses what happens when political order disappears:

Take but degree away, untune that string,
And hark what discord follows!
. . . . the bounded waters
<u>*Should*</u> *lift their bosoms higher than the shores,*

(d) Despite advice from the Duke of York, **King Richard** expresses his intention of confiscating everything that Bolingbroke owns (R2 2.1.209):

Think what you <u>will</u>, we seize into our hands
His plate, his goods, his money, and his lands.

(e) In *Henry IV, Part 1*, the **Earl of Worcester** talks about the hostility he feels that Prince Hal had towards him (5.1.59):

You used us so

. . . .
That even our love <u>durst</u> not come near your sight

6 Tense differences in PDE and EModE

The differences in use between the simple, progressive and perfect tenses are complex, and only some are discussed here. Use the PDE examples in (i) to work out a difference between the simple and progressive tenses today, and in (ii) for the simple and perfect tenses. Then in each case look at the examples from Shakespeare. Does he follow the distinctions you have just articulated? These issues are discussed in the text.

Simple versus progressive tenses

PDE examples

(a) John: *You're in London? What are you doing here?*
    Mary: *I'm visiting my aunt.*

(b)   *I visit my aunt every year.*

(c)   *I am reading* Macbeth *at the moment*

(d)   *I read Shakespeare a lot nowadays*

(e)   *I was eating my dinner when he came in.*

Shakespeare examples

(f) **Polonius** sees Hamlet reading a book:
What do you read, my Lord? (Ham 2.2.191)

(g) **Antonio** sees **Proteus** reading a letter:
How now? What letter are you reading there? (TGV 1.3.51)

(h) **Warwick** tells King Henry that his son the prince is approaching:
He is coming hither. (2H4 4.5.88)

(i) **The Friar** hears an urgent knocking at the door:
What simpleness is this! – I come, I come! (RJ 3.3.78)

Simple versus perfect tenses
PDE examples

(j) *I have visited France several times.*

(k) *I visited France last year.*

(l) *He has never read Macbeth.*

(m) *He read Macbeth when he was only 15.*

Shakespeare examples

(n) First Lord: *You have not given him his mother's letter?*
Second Lord: *I have delivered it an hour since.* (AW 4.3.1)

(o) *That's the worst tidings that I hear of yet* (1H4 4.1.127)

(p) *I saw him not these many years* (Cym 4.2.66)

(q) *I was not angry since I came to France/Until this instance* (H5 4.7.58)

Extended activities

1   In 4.5.3 we discuss double negatives, a form that is regarded as socially
unacceptable today. Think of some other grammatical forms which are
similarly considered socially unacceptable.
    People often have strong views about what is right and wrong
in language, and many of us have 'pet' dislikes when it comes to
grammatical or lexical usage. Some, for example, get upset about the
use of *less* instead of *fewer*, as discussed in 4.6.1 (*Ten items or less* at the
supermarket checkout, rather than *Ten items or fewer*). Others become
upset when *phenomena* is made a singular (in place of *phenomenon*).
Think of some similar pet dislikes that either you or those you know
have. Articulate what 'mistake' is being made in each case.

2 4.6.2 focuses on the use of *do* in: (a) positive affirmatives: (b) negatives; (c) interrogatives. Select a scene from a play that particularly interests you. Consider each of the categories (a) to (c) in turn. Count the number of instances when *do* is and is not used. So with (c) for example you would have a figure indicating how many interrogatives are formed using *do*, and how many use inversion (*know you?* instead of *do you know?*). Do your figures suggest that in the period *do* is becoming common in (b) and (c), and less common in (a), as suggested in the graph in 4.6.2?

   When *do* is used in positive affirmative cases, can you think of any reason (emphasis? metre?)? What about avoidance of *do* in negatives and interrogatives? Could metre be the explanation?

3 4.6.3 covers some modal auxiliaries, but not all, and there are many modal uses which are not touched on there. Stay with the same scene you used in the Activity above. Identify all the modal auxiliaries which seem to have a meaning different from how we would use them today. Use an internet source (like 'Shakespeare's Words', or 'Open Source Shakespeare') to clarify how they are being used.

   Both the sites mentioned above will enable you to find other instances of the same modal auxiliary throughout Shakespeare. Use this facility to find other meanings for the modal auxiliaries you have identified above.

Answer section

Noun plurality suffix (section 4.2)

The suffix commonly used in PDE to indicate noun plurality is -*s*.

Use of *whose* (section 4.5.4)

Whose is the genitive relative pronoun. *Lucy, whose boyfriend lives in Spain, likes chocolates* is based on the two sentences *Lucy likes chocolates* and *Lucy's boyfriend lives in Spain*.

Notes

1 The 'Mrs Sands' example is taken from Barber (1997: 146), and the suggested explanation comes from Baugh and Cable (2002: 241).

2 It is common to find *who* instead of *whom* in informal contexts.

3 This information is taken from Rissanen (1999), who is citing Lowth (1775/1979).

4 The example is used by Denison and Hogg (2006).

5 The example is from Freeborn (2006: 212). The 'thorn' has here been rendered by 'th'.

6 Brun's work is cited in Grégoire (2006).

7 This is according to Taylor (1976).

8 Noted by Barber (1997).

9 'in Shakespeare you do find . . .' How can this use of *do* be described?

10 The example comes from Barber (1997: 196).

11 The study, cited in Rissanen (1999: 216), is Elsness (1994).

12 The verb list is from Kakietek (1976), as are some of the examples given at the beginning of this section.

13 The examples have been selected to show only a partial representation of the rules. You are invited to consult a grammar of English for the full picture.

Further reading

Rissanen, M. (1999) 'Syntax', in Lass, R. (ed.) 1999 *The Cambridge History of the English Language: Volume III*, Cambridge: Cambridge University Press 187–331 provides a detailed overview of EModE syntax. Nevalainen's account (2006), *An Introduction to Early Modern English*, Edinburgh: Edinburgh University Press) has a lot on syntax, and includes exercises as well as further reading suggestions. As the titles of the following two suggest, they provide focused coverage of syntax: Hope, J. (2002) *Shakespeare's Grammar*, London: Methuen Arden Shakespeare, and Blake, N. F. (2002) *A Grammar of Shakespeare's Language*, Basingstoke: Palgrave. Barber, C. (1997) *Early Modern English, Revised Edition*, Edinburgh: Edinburgh University Press has a chapter on syntax.

On the topic of variation and language change, discussed particularly in 4.6.1, it is well worth consulting Nevalainen, T. and Raumolin-Brunberg, H. (2003) *Historical Sociolinguistics: Language change in Tudor and Stuart England*, Harlow: Pearson Education.

CHAPTER 5

Pragmatics: Shakespeare as a foreign language

Key phrases:
different from today; requiring attention

5.1 What pragmatics is

An Englishman who has been in China for a short while, but who speaks some of the language, is met by an acquaintance in the street. The acquaintance greets him by saying *Have you eaten? Yes, I have* he replies. But he is puzzled. Why is he asked such a strange question? Is the acquaintance perhaps asking him out for a meal? The answer is no; the question is not an *invitation* but a *greeting*; the acquaintance is showing concern by asking the Englishman whether he has satisfied his hunger. The question is roughly equivalent to the English *How are you?* used when two people meet. Notice that this latter question is not a *request for information*. If you treated it as such and gave the person who asked a report on your health, you would be regarded as odd. You would not be following an important <u>rule of use</u>, which says that in the meeting context *How are you?* (and *Have you eaten?* in parts of China) are fulfilling the <u>speech act</u> of *greeting*.

   There are many ways in which utterances can be analysed. A phonetician hearing *Have you eaten?* might want to point out that the final vowel sound in *eaten* is the lightly pronounced [ə] sound (which you also find at the beginning of the word *ago*, and which is never in a stressed syllable). They might also have something to say about the rising intonation pattern of the question. A grammarian/syntactician hearing the same sentence would focus elsewhere. They might describe the utterance as an example of the present perfect tense of a verb which has an irregular past participle (as we saw in

4.6.5, this form usually ends with an *-ed* inflexion, but with this verb we say *eaten*, not **eated*). We could also analyse the sentence in terms of meanings, or <u>significations</u>. On this semantic level, we would identify the meaning of *eat* as something like 'put in the mouth and consume', also noting that the subject of the sentence, *you*, is referring to a person we are addressing. The choice of the present perfect tense would indicate that the utterance asks about an action which may have occurred at any moment in the past up to the present.

Notice that none of these analyses gives us any information about the fact that the sentence could be used as a greeting. For that we need an analysis which focuses explicitly on 'rules of use', and deals with the performance of speech acts in a specific language. This level of analysis is called <u>pragmatics</u>, and it is a linguistic area which became of particular interest to linguists in the 1970s, precisely because it was realised that it existed as a separate level of analysis, which had as yet not been studied in a systematic way.

It is of course true that certain syntactic structures are associated with particular speech acts. The syntactic structure of the imperative and the speech act of *ordering* are a case in point. Imperatives like *Come here, Go away*, and *Don't talk in class* are examples of imperative forms used as orders. But it is important to realise that often imperatives are not orders at all. *Come and have dinner with us on Friday, if you're free* is one: it is clearly an invitation, not an order. Another occurs in the Christian Lord's Prayer's *Give us this day our daily bread*, which is an exhortation and certainly not an order. Similarly, there are many ways of giving an order which do not use the imperative. If an irate father says to his child *You will go to the dentist tomorrow*, that might well be intended as an order, though the grammatical form is not an imperative. Sometimes orders can be very indirect indeed. If a person in authority says *Would you please close the window*, or even just *It's cold in here* this may well be interpreted by the listener as an order to close the window. To explore different ways of ordering in PDE, and the factors which control selection of them, look at part (i) of Activity 1 (*Asking someone to get up, politely*).

Yule (1996: 133) defines pragmatics as 'the study of speaker meaning as distinct from word or sentence meaning'. There are many introductory books which will give you a background to the area, particularly Thomas (1995) and Yule (1996). Among the main concerns of the field are:

- speech acts. How we do things like *give orders*, *greet* each other, and so on;
- conversational implicature. How we know what someone 'means' when they say things indirectly. For example, what is it about a particular context that leads a speaker to believe that *It's cold in here* might be a command to close the window, rather than, say, a comment about today's weather?

■ politeness. How speakers manage not just to get their message across, but also do so in a way which does not offend. Politeness strategies are a major concern of pragmatics.

Looking at pragmatics in past times is the subject matter of <u>historical pragmatics</u>, a developing area with its own journal, *The Journal of Historical Pragmatics*. Jucker (1995) is a major publication of this area. Those interested in Shakespeare have also turned their attention to pragmatic matters, and there are a number of studies which concentrate on specific 'rules of use' in Renaissance English. Just like the Chinese way of *greeting*, it is not surprising that speech acts in Shakespeare's time should sometimes be very 'different from today' (one of the chapter's key phrases), and therefore 'requiring attention' (the other key phrase).

Perhaps one reason why linguists have only recently become interested in pragmatics is that at first sight there may appear to be little practical need to focus on it. Consider foreign language learners for example. In the past, two assumptions have been made to suggest that 'rules of use' (as well as the other areas pragmatics deals with) do not need teaching to foreign learners. One is that the rules are universal – how you greet in English is, the argument runs, the same as how you greet in other languages and cultures. The other assumption is that by teaching grammar you are providing the learners with everything necessary to know the rules of use in a language. But even this short introduction has shown both these assumptions to be false. The way of greeting in China is different from the way of greeting in Britain, so the rules are not universal; and the speech act of *ordering* cannot be associated solely with one grammatical structure – so knowing structures does not mean automatically knowing rules of use. And just as rules of use change from language to language, so they change over time. How you greet and order in Shakespeare will be different from how you greet and order today. The past, as L.P. Hartley famously put it, 'is a foreign country: they do things differently there'. Not everything, of course, and there is plenty of 'Shakespeare's pragmatics' that makes sense to us today. But there is enough that is different – enough of the 'foreign language' in Shakespeare – for the topic to require a chapter of its own.

The chapter begins with a look at how to exclaim in EModE, intended as a brief introduction to thinking in pragmatic terms and working out pragmatic meaning. It then covers the three areas associated above with pragmatics. We look at the speech acts of *greeting*, and *giving directives*. Politeness is an important issue in relation to both of these. There is a section dealing with the differences between *you* and *thou*, and the final section deals with implicature.

5.2 Working out pragmatic meaning: exclamations

Studying pragmatics requires a particular 'mind-set', where focus is put not on language structure but on language use. This short section centres around Activity 2 (*Exclamations and the pragmatic mind-set*), and aims to help establish the 'pragmatic mind-set'. It concentrates on the area of exclamations. Part of the definition of 'exclamations' in the *OED* is 'the action of exclaiming or crying out; the loud articulate expression of pain, anger, surprise, etc.'. As this definition suggests, there are indeed many emotions – both positive and negative – that can be conveyed through exclamations. Usually it is immediately clear what the emotion is (though it is often very difficult to describe such emotions in a clear and objective way), but sometimes only the context will clarify. *What a book!* for example can be used to express either a positive or a negative opinion of the book.[1]

Many of Shakespeare's exclamations are either still used today or are still understood. Like his characters, we still say *come, come* to express annoyance or disagreement, and we understand clearly what the word *alas* means, even though we may not use it ourselves. But other Shakespearean exclamations have passed out of use and are not so easily understood by the modern reader. Activity 2 is a lengthy exercise which explores the uses of some of these.

If you wish to undertake a small-scale exploration of your own into the meanings of some Shakespearean exclamations, the word *la* might be one to look at. There are a number of sites on the internet where you can find all instances of a word in Shakespeare. One already mentioned is 'Shakespeare's Words'. When you type the word *la* in the search box you will come up with 67 instances. Many of these are not exclamations at all, but the French word *the* (for feminine nouns – for example the character Joan of Arc, who appears in Shakespeare's *Henry VI, Part I*, is Joan la Pucelle). When these and other irrelevant examples are discounted, you will have approximately 20 instances left. Click on some of these to see the contexts in which they appear, and make an attempt to specify the meaning (**AS**). Other words you can search for are *forsooth* and *marry* (the latter has as many as 375 instances, though the vast majority are not exclamations at all, but the verb 'to marry').

5.3 How to be polite in Shakespeare

As we have seen, a major area of pragmatics is looking at speech acts – what forms are used to 'do things with words' (the phrase is the one used by the twentieth-century British philosopher of language, John Austin). In this section we will focus on forms of address (what you call people). These are an important element of a speech act we have already mentioned – *greeting*. They also involve another area important in the study of pragmatics: politeness – the ways used to ensure one acts in a linguistically appropriate and polite way. It is easy to give offence if you address someone in an inappropriate way. This is as true today as it was in the Renaissance. For example, the modern learner of English as a foreign language needs to know that (in British English at least) it is not normal to follow *Mr, Mrs* or *Miss* with a first name. Unlike in some languages and cultures, *Mr John* or *Mrs Mary* are unacceptable (though interestingly *Sir John* and *Lady Mary* are fine). Even today, decisions as to whether to use a first or family name when addressing someone can be difficult to make. In many cultures, it is becoming more and more the custom to use a first name when talking to a stranger you are meeting for the first time. Some people find this refreshingly informal, though others (particularly of the older generation) find it impolite. Address forms are indeed important to politeness.

In a paper entitled 'Shakespeare's salutations: a study in stylistic etiquette' Replogle (1973) discusses <u>honorifics</u>: expressions which convey respect used when addressing someone. To our modern ears, Renaissance honorifics were excessive and exaggerated. As an example, Replogle cites one John Bossewell's dedication to his 1572 book *Works of Armorie*. It runs:

> *To the right honourable and his singular good lord, Sir William Cecil, Baron of Burghleigh, knight of the most noble order of the garter, Lord High Treasurer of England, master of the courts of wards and liveries, Chancellor of the University of Cambridge, and one of the Queen's Majesty's Privy Council.*

(The courts of wards and liveries was set up by Henry VIII to look after legal cases related to the rights of minors.)

In the next few paragraphs, the usage of some Shakespearean address forms is discussed. Activity 3 (*Who would say it, to whom? When?*) invites you to think about these forms. If you wish to do the Activity, do so before you read the following paragraphs (**NP**).

Three of the features that play an important role in address forms are status or position, family relationships and endearment. In PDE these are exemplified by *doctor* (a position), *auntie* (a family relationship) and *darling* (a term of endearment). You may like to think of more examples in each of these categories. In Shakespeare's time, the same features naturally applied, and we will look at each in turn. The following paragraphs will show just how complex a business it was to address someone appropriately.

5.3.1 Status/position[2]

As the example above from John Bossewell's dedication shows, there was a rich store of terms to indicate different high statuses, some of them of remarkably specific use. The term *dread* for example, was only used to royalty; you can check this out by looking at an internet site which has a search facility. The actual form of the adjective could also be important for status. For example, the superlative form (like *most gracious, most honourable*) was usually reserved for superiors, and the norm was to use no more than three adjectives. Another convention was to repeat titles many times when talking or writing to an important person. Replogle's example is of William Cecil, Queen Elizabeth's chief advisor who uses a title for her no less than twelve times in a 230-word letter. Another term of great respect, used only to a person of note, was *your worship*, though it could of course be used in a mocking way. Today the term is usually reserved for use to such people as justices of the peace or mayors.

Professional people could be addressed as *master*. It can prefix an occupation – *Master constable* is used several times in *Much Ado About Nothing*, and a search on an internet site will reveal a few other examples related to other professions. The title is also used by inferiors to refer to the son of a superior. In *The Merchant of Venice* the old Gobbo is looking for his son. *Talk you of young Master Launcelot?*, he is asked (2.2.43). The use of *Master* here suggests to him that his son is being credited with a social station he does not have. Hence his reply: *No master, sir, but a poor man's son*. A common use of the word *mistress* today is to describe a woman involved in an extra-marital sexual relationship. Its main sense in Shakespeare implied status. It was a woman who 'ruled' – in a school, in the house, etc. This meaning is also found today, even when the domination is over an animal (one can speak of a dog's 'mistress'). It was also used as a term of respect when addressing a woman (rather like the modern *Madam*) – *Mistress, look on me*, says Berowne to Rosaline in *Love's Labour's Lost* (5.2.826). When used in front of a name it could be equivalent to the modern *Mrs* (which indeed originated as an abbreviation of *Mistress*). But you could use it to an unmarried lady too (equivalent to *Miss*). It was also found in front of a first name: in *Henry IV, Part 2*, Doll Tearsheet is addressed by Falstaff and others as *Mistress Doll*.

Sirrah in Shakespeare is a form of address which looks down rather than up; it is used to inferiors (including females). Often it expresses contempt, though it can also be familiar and playful. If it is used by an inferior to a superior, this would express over-familiarity, even contempt. This happens when Poins, a colleague of Falstaff, uses it to the future Henry V, telling him that they have some rough cloth (*buckram*) to disguise their clothes – *And, sirrah, I have cases of buckram for the nonce* (1H4 1.2.177). Very cheeky. It can also be used with a name: *Sirra Costard, I will enfranchise thee*, says Armado in *Love's Labour's Lost* (3.1.118). Though it can be used for a woman, the *OED* speculates that the origin might be *Sir* (plus the additional syllable *ah*, of indefinite origin).

5.3.2 Family relationships

As regards family relationships, use of the words *cousin* and its abbreviation *coz* are so common in Shakespeare that one might be tempted to wonder that so many of his characters seem to be related. It is indeed often used to describe a blood relative, though not one in the immediate family circle – relatives like cousins, nieces, nephews, aunts, and uncles, that are formally called 'collateral' relatives. But it is also used to close friends as a term of intimacy. It can even be used by monarchs to each other. Another word associated with family relations is *nuncle*. It means 'uncle'; indeed *mine uncle* sounds a lot like *my nuncle*, and this is probably the derivation. Incidentally, this process of phonetic confusion is not a common form of word derivation, but we did in fact see another example in 2.3.5 in relation to the word *nonce*; it is also found in the word *newt*, which was originally *an ewt*. But *nuncle* can also indicate a master, and this is the way a licensed fool (employed by Renaissance households for entertainment) usually addressed his superior. In Shakespeare it is used only by the Fool in *King Lear*.

When an important person is also a relative, the demands of status and those of family relations conflict, and then you find different uses according to situation. Intimate forms might be used when the addressee was unaware of being addressed. Cordelia for example calls Lear *My dear father* when he is sleeping. When he wakes, it is *How fares your majesty*?

Using an actual name was a way of addressing equals or inferiors – not superiors – though it could also signal a moment of high passion. In *Henry VI, Part 2*, for example, Queen Margaret addresses her husband King Henry formally (on one occasion with *Great King of England, and my gracious lord* – 1.1.24). But when the life of her lover the Duke of Suffolk is threatened, she addresses the king thus: *O Henry, let me plead for gentle Suffolk* (3.2.289).

5.3.3 Endearment

Terms of endearment form a fascinating category of address forms, and one of the more interesting is the word *bully* which in the Renaissance meant 'fine fellow' or 'good friend'. You will find 18 instances of this use on the Open Source Shakespeare website (including the two in Activity 3). According to the *OED* it was originally applied to both sexes, then to men only. In the eighteenth century, the good sense of 'gallant' turned into the bad sense of 'hired ruffian', following the process of pejorative semantic change discussed in 3.4; hence today's meaning of someone who intimidates people. But today the word maintains its 'good' sense in the phrase *bully for you*. The word *wench* has suffered a similarly pejorative semantic change, and today has an entirely bad connotation (if it is used at all). It is also used in this pejorative sense in Shakespeare, to mean a 'wanton woman'. But this was by no means always the connotation, and it could be used as a term of affectionate or familiar address to a young lady. A father might for example use it to his daughter, or to a wife or a sweetheart. On occasions it could also suggest a peasant background, or refer to a servant. Another term of endearment which is found in Shakespeare is *chuck*. It means 'chicken' or 'chick', and indeed Dr Johnson's celebrated *Dictionary of the English Language* (published in 1755) has 'chick' as the derivation. In fact, you do find *chick* itself used in the same sense, as in *The Tempest* (5.1.317) when Prospero refers to Ariel as his *chick*.

This section has shown the richness of address forms which existed in Renaissance Britain. Since they deal with the sensitive area of human relationships, it was important for the Renaissance person to master the system of etiquette. Otherwise the results could be dire. It is important too for our attempts to understand how characters are relating to each other, and Replogle (1973) lists some of the mistakes we can fall into by not understanding the conventions. 'We have seen insults where there are none', she says, 'and have ignored them where they exist' (p. 101).

5.4 A speech act: directives

A speech act area mentioned early in this chapter was 'giving an order'. Orders are often referred to as <u>directives</u>, defined as 'speech acts by means of which the speaker requests the hearer(s) to do (or not to do) certain things'.[3] Part (i) of Activity 1 focused on PDE, and now would be the time to look at part (ii), where the examples are from EModE (do not look at part (iii) yet – **NP**).

Earlier we saw that in PDE the imperative is a structure often associated with the directive speech act. The same held in Shakespeare's time. *Go forth, Agrippa, and begin the fight* says Caesar to Agrippa in *Antony and Cleopatra* (4.6.1). To make the imperative more polite, you can add a pronoun to it:

Then go thou forth, the Duke of Florence says to Bertram in *All's Well That Ends Well* (3.3.6.2). But interestingly, sometimes the pronoun is in the accusative rather than the nominative. Hamlet's famous example is the accusative addressed to Ophelia: *Get thee to a nunnery* (rather than *Get thou*), he suggests to her (3.1.121). Another alternative is to omit any verb. *Peace sirrah* the Duke of Cornwall rudely says to the Earl of Kent (KL 2.2.66). This 'verbless' imperative is, according to Brown and Gilman (1989), 'not polite and not neutral but rudely brusque' (which is also the case in PDE). A further possibility is to use *do*. Section 4.6.2 was devoted to the use of that important verb, but one PDE use was not mentioned: placing *do* in front of an imperative to make it an emphatic offer, as in examples like *Do come to dinner on Saturday*, or *Do sit down*. In Shakespeare *do* can be used with an imperative, but not necessarily for an offer. Thus when Prince Hal wants Poins to leave his company, he says *prithee do thou stand in some by-room* (1H4, 2.4.28).

But, as we also saw earlier, there are very many ways of issuing directives using other grammatical forms, and *Would you please close the window* was one PDE example given. Another was *It's cold in here*. This is what is called an indirect speech act; it sounds like a statement about temperature, but can in fact stand as a directive. Frequently speech acts do not reveal themselves in obvious ways.

Activity 1 asked you to look at the differences between PDE and EModE directives. These differences are important: as Brown and Gilman put it (1989: 182): 'even a very incomplete analysis of the forms of indirect request in Shakespeare adds a little something to our understanding of the plays'. You may notice the PDE examples include a *would you* (and *could you* is also used in the same way), but neither of these occurs in the EModE examples. The PDE instances also include two uses of *please*. According to Busse (2008) *please* was not used alone in this way until later. In Shakespeare you find longer forms like *if it please you* or *and please you*. There are no requests or directives using the phrase, so common in PDE, *Would you please . . .* You will perhaps be surprised that ways of issuing directives that are so common in PDE should be absent in Shakespeare.

Using expressions like *if it please you, may it please you* is a way of being polite by appealing to hearer willingness. Another major way of issuing directives (in Brown and Gilman's scheme) is by expressing speaker wish, focusing on what you want done by using such phrases as *I beseech you, I pray* and *prithee* (which comes from *I pray thee*). Brown and Gilman (1989) are interested to find out the differences in politeness between these three phrases, and their study offers a good example of how research into speech act use can be done. For their work they use the *Harvard Concordance to Shakespeare* (Spevack 1967). A concordance is a list of words taken from a collection of texts – in this case the complete works of Shakespeare. The large version of Spevack's concordance is no less than nine volumes and contains separate concordances for each play. The *Harvard Concordance* is a one-volume version dealing with the plays as a whole. There are 884,647 words covered (different inflectional variants of a word counting as separate items). Each instance of each word is given, together with a context (in Spevack's case 48 letters spread before and after the key word), so that it is possible to see what words <u>co-occur</u> ('go together') with the item you are interested in. Spevack's concordance is in book form, but as we have seen, there are several others online. Two which have been referred to a number of times are 'Shakespeare's Words' and 'Open Source Shakespeare'. Both provide the facility to search for all instances of a word in Shakespeare, and have sight of its context. When Brown and Gilman searched for the word *beseech* they found that 40% of the entries co-occur with titles like *Your majesty* or *Your grace*. In 96% of cases the pronoun of address was *you* not *thou* (something discussed in the next section – *you* is the form of address used with strangers). This leads to the conclusion that *beseech* is a polite, even deferential, word. With *I pray you*, only 10% of co-occurrences involve a title, and *thou* is found as well as *you*. The conclusion is that *I pray you* is less deferential. A similar analysis shows *prithee* to be even less deferential, co-occurring a lot with forms like *my son*, or *good friend*.

What factors make a directive more or less polite? Look now at part (iii) of Activity 1, which asks you to consider this question (**NP**).

Here is part of the list Givón (1993) gives as his answer:

- increased length (so *Please would you get up* is more polite than *Get up*)
- use of question forms (*Do you think you could get up?* is more polite than *Please would you get up*)
- explicit mention of the person you are talking to (*With every thing that pretty is, my sweet, arise*)
- use of a form like *could, would*
- use of a negative form (*Will you not arise now, sir?*)

At the beginning of this chapter, it was said that the area of pragmatics came to interest linguists in the 1970s. Analysis of this 'new' level of language use is indeed exciting, and the box below captures some of the excitement associated with finding ways of analysing politeness (and, incidentally, impoliteness) strategies in the work of Shakespeare.

How to be polite in a Shakespearean tragedy

Brown and Gilman (1989) is an influential paper which looks at politeness strategies in *Othello*, *Hamlet*, *Macbeth* and *King Lear*. Their study is based on an equally influential 'theory' of politeness developed in Brown and Levinson (1987). A central part of this theory is that there are three factors which control degree of politeness – how polite a person will be in a given situation:

(a) The power relationship (P) holding between speaker and hearer. If the speaker is socially superior to the hearer, he is likely not to bother much with politeness, and might even go for the brusque imperative. But if the hearer is socially powerful and the speaker not, then a more polite approach will be required. This factor can be described as <u>vertical social distance</u>; to do with whether the speaker is higher up or lower down on a vertical axis.

(b) The distance relationship (D) between speaker and hearer. If they know each other well and are friends, then you might expect a more informal, less polite, interaction. But if the two are strangers, politeness may be required. This factor can be described as <u>horizontal social distance</u>; to do with whether speaker and hearer are close or distant on a horizontal axis.

(c) Ranked extremity (R). This is the 'size' of what is being considered. If you are just asking someone to lend you a pen for an hour, a large amount of politeness is not required. But if you are a young adult asking your parents to lend you several thousand pounds towards your first house purchase, then all your politeness skills will be brought into play.

Brown and Gilman's purpose is to find out whether these factors – (P), (D) and (R) – are the important determiners of politeness in the plays they are considering. Their research method is interesting. They develop a method of 'giving utterances scores' for how polite they are. So the brusque imperative would score low, and a request using *Could you possibly* . . . would score high. Then they identify pairs of Shakespearean utterances which differ in terms of just one of the three factors. For example, in some pairs both the distance between the interactants (D) and the (R) that is involved are roughly the same. The only difference is the (P). In other pairs the difference will be between (D) but not (P) and (R), and so on. This enables them to see how degree of politeness (as measured by their 'scores') is related to (P), (D) and (R). Do the utterances of socially inferior speakers score more on the politeness scale than the utterances of a socially superior speaker? What about when the conversation is *stranger → stranger* as opposed to *friend → friend*? Or when the (R) is very high?

Their results? For the factors (P) and (R) these are generally as Brown and Levinson's theory predicts. Both factors are seen to be important. As regards (D), the theory predicts that more distant interactants will be more polite with each other. But in fact Brown and Gilman find that 'the more the speaker likes the hearer, the greater the concern with the hearer's face and so the more polite the speech; the less the liking, the less the concern and also the politeness' (p. 193). Sometimes people – in our world as well as Shakespeare's – are more polite to friends than to strangers.

One of the paper's other interesting observations concerns 'excessive politeness'. Sometimes, they note, a character uses more politeness than a situation seems to require. In such cases, there is sometimes an off-record element – something more important is being suggested than is being stated. For example, Brown and Gilman note that 'one of the politest speeches' in *Macbeth* (according to their politeness scores) is when Macbeth suggests to Banquo that they need to talk about something relatively unimportant (the witches' prophesies). A small amount of (R) would be involved, you might think. But in fact Macbeth is really asking Banquo, indirectly, whether he will be a part of the conspiracy which will involve murder. Given this off-record intention, the degree of politeness is not excessive at all.

5.5 *Thou* and *you* (and *ye*)

It is impossible to discuss pragmatics in Shakespeare without devoting a great deal of time to the various ways of saying 'you'. The main issue is the difference between *you* and *thou*, but before considering pragmatic complexities, here is some of the grammar involved.

5.5.1 *You, ye, thou, thee*: case and number

For many today, the word *ye* suggests a kind of romantic antiquity which you are invited to experience when you buy food from *Ye olde cake shoppe*. The *ye* here is in fact a version of *the*, where the 'y' is a modernised version of the OE letter thorn [þ] which stood for 'th' (mentioned earlier in 4.6.1). But the *ye* we are concerned with here is another one – the variant of *you* found for example in the Christmas carol title: *God Rest Ye Merry Gentlemen*. In 1500 the difference between *ye* and *you* was one of case. *Ye* was the nominative (subject) pronoun, *you* was for other cases – like the difference between *I* (nominative) and *me* (other cases). The same distinction held between *thou* (nominative) and *thee* (other cases). Here are a few lines from Tyndale's translation of the New Testament (Matthew 5). The words *you* and *ye* have been omitted. Given that Tyndale, writing in around 1522, maintained the case distinction, it is possible to put the words in (**AS**):

Blessed are ____ when men revile ____ and persecute ____, and shall falsely say all manner of evil sayings against ____ for my sake . . . ____ are the salt of the earth . . . ____ are the light of the world.

But by Shakespeare's time, things were different. If you would like to work out how these words operated then, look now at Activity 4 (*You and ye* – **NP**).

Activity 4 shows that by the time Shakespeare was writing 'there was very little feeling any more for the different functions of the two words'.[4] They were used interchangeably. We need say no more about *ye*. Much more interesting – and problematic – are *thou* and *you*. The former is hardly used at all today, except in a few fixed phrases like *fare thee well* and *holier than thou*. We will need to look at the differences of usage in some detail. Some are quite subtle, but there is one obvious, highly unsubtle, one that must be stated at the start. There is a difference of number. If the referent is plural, it has to be *you*; *thou* cannot be used when you are talking to more than one person. Questions of usage occur because both forms can be used in the singular: if you are talking to one person, you could use either *thou* or *you*. When do you use one and when the other? That is the question.[5]

5.5.2 When does Shakespeare use *thou* and when *you*?

In what is often called The Gravediggers Scene (Ham 5.1), Prince Hamlet comes across two gravediggers (actually called First and Second Clown) at work. During the conversation he discovers that the grave they are digging is for his girl-friend, Ophelia, who has drowned. Here is Hamlet asking about the grave. The banter which follows begins with elaborate punning on the word *lie*. Look at this exchange in terms of the use of *thou* and *you* (and associated forms like *thine* and *yours*). Think particularly about the status of the characters, and try to relate that to the forms they use. Is there perhaps a 'rule of use' that suggests itself?

Hamlet:	*Whose grave's this, sirrah?*
First Clown:	*Mine, sir . . . . .*
Hamlet:	*I think it be thine indeed, for thou liest in't.*
First Clown:	*You lie out on't, sir, and therefore it is not yours. For my part, I do not lie in't and yet it is mine.*
Hamlet:	*Thou dost lie in't sir, and say 'tis thine; 'tis for the dead, not for the quick; therefore thou liest.*
First Clown:	*'Tis a quick lie, sir: 'twill away again, from me to you.*

This scene illustrates one of the main determinants in the *thou/you* choice: status or class. Here are four situations stated in status/class terms:

- a high status/class person speaking to another high status/class person (high → high)
- a low status person speaking to another low status person (low → low)
- a high status person speaking to a low status person (high → low)
- a low status person speaking to a high status person (low → high)

In the Gravediggers Scene we find high → low when Hamlet addresses the gravediggers, and low → high when the gravediggers address him. Activity 5 (*Thou and you, high and low*) offers examples of the other possible permutations. Do this Activity before you look at the table below (**NP**).

The examples from the Gravediggers Scene and from Activity 5, taken together, show that the usage is like this (the table is from Activity 5):

high → low	*thou*
low → high	*you*
high → high	*you*
low → low	*you/thou*

Notice that with low → low, either pronoun seems acceptable. Activity 5's example of the mutual use of *thou* involved the gravediggers talking to each other. Though such examples exist, we will see at the end of this section that the mutual use of *you* is much more common.

Status/class is only one of the determinants. A second important one is intimacy. Some languages like French and German have forms which behave like the *thou* and *you* in Shakespeare. Examples are *tu* and *vous* in French, *du* and *Sie* in German. Changing from *vous/Sie* to *tu/du* indicates growing intimacy. It is rather like changing from surname to first name used to be in Anglo-Saxon societies, though nowadays first names have started being used more commonly, even on first meeting. In French there is a verb *tutoyer* which means 'to give the *tu* form', interpreted as a sign of becoming more friendly. As we shall see, there was an English equivalent in the Renaissance: 'to thou'.

The transition from *you* to the intimate *thou* is found in Shakespeare. Juliet, for example, begins by using *you* to Romeo. When they first kiss she tells him: *you kiss by th' book* (meaning 'expertly'; RJ 1.5.110). But by the time we reach the famous balcony scene, where Romeo is beneath the balcony where Juliet stands, she uses *thou* when talking to herself about Romeo (*wherefore art thou Romeo*), then when he arrives: *How cam'st thou hither, tell me, and wherefore?* she asks (RJ 2.2.62).

It is natural that there will sometimes be a 'conflict' between familiarity and status/class. What happens when two higher-status people marry? Or between upper-class siblings? Look back to Activity 5 (*Thou and you, high and low*) where you have upper-class Desdemona and her upper-class husband, as well as two upper-class daughters of King Lear. Though the rule is not firm, there is a tendency for class to be more important than familiarity. Hence wife Desdemona uses *you* to husband Othello and vice versa. Similarly sister Goneril uses *you* with sister Regan, and vice versa.

Is gender a relevant factor? Certainly sometimes you find men using *thou* to women (reflecting a perception of high to low status current at the time), while women use *you* back, (as perceived low to high). We saw earlier that Juliet uses *you* when she first meets Romeo. Take a look at Act 1 Scene 5 (where the future lovers first meet) and check out what pronoun Romeo uses to Juliet. It is *thou*.

Switching to the wrong form could be an insult. In *Twelfth Night* (3.2.43) Sir Toby Belch is trying to goad Sir Andrew Aguecheek into having an argument with Cesario. Belch's advice: *If thou thou'st him some thrice, it shall not be amiss*; 'call him *thou* a few times', he is saying, 'and that should do the trick'. This is a use of the verb 'to thou' mentioned earlier; the first *OED* mention of it was 1440, so it was not a Shakespearean coinage.

As well as the 'status *thou*' and the 'intimate *thou*' there is the 'non-human *thou*', used when addressing some non-human agent. Here are some examples:

- to ghosts: *Go on, I'll follow thee* Hamlet says to his father's ghost (Ham 1.4.79).

- to spirits: In *Richard III* (1.2.7), Lady Anne addresses the body of her dead father-in-law thus: *thou bloodless remnant of that Royal blood*. And when Lady Macbeth evokes the spirit of the night (Mac 1.5.48) she says: *Come, thick night,/ and pall thee in the dunnest smoke of hell*. Later in the same speech is a reminder that whoever is being addressed, *you* must be used if there is more than one of them. *Come . . . you murd'ring ministers*, she says.

- to inanimate objects: In *The Merchant of Venice* (2.9.34) the Prince of Aragon talks to the silver casket he is about to open: *Why then [I turn] to thee, thou silver treasure-house*.

- to gods: Coriolanus's friend Menenius is delighted when he hears the former is returning home: *Take my cap, Jupiter, and I thank thee* (Cor, 2.1.100).

In what we have considered so far, there is a degree of 'stability' in the use of *thou/you*. Statuses remain the same over time (as do ghosts, spirits, objects and gods), so if *you* is appropriate on one occasion, it is likely to be appropriate on the next. It is true that, as we have seen, *you* can change to *thou* as intimacy develops, though once the change has been made, it may remain. But the picture is complicated considerably by more 'unstable' uses of the pronouns – when a character will call someone *you* on one occasion and *thou* on another. Here is an example. In *The Taming of the Shrew*, Petruchio marries the 'shrew-like' Kate, whom he succeeds in 'taming'. Towards the end of the play there is a competition between the male friends to see who has the most obedient wife. The three husbands involved send for their wives, requiring them to stop what they are doing and come running to their husbands immediately. Kate shows how tame she has become by being the only wife to obey. When she comes, Petruchio asks her where the wives of his friends, who failed to obey, are. Notice Petruchio's *your* here (5.2.99):

Kate: *What is your will, sir, that you send for me?*
Petruchio: *Where is your sister, and Hortensio's wife?*

But then, a few lines later (5.2.129) he asks Kate to tell her women friends to be more obedient to their husbands:

Petruchio: *Katherine, I charge thee tell these headstrong women*
             What duty they do owe their lords and husbands.

Why the *thou* here? Perhaps he is feeling particularly affectionate towards her because she has obeyed him. Because the relationship between Kate and Petruchio is a particularly stormy one, there are plenty of interesting examples of changes from *you* to *thou* and back again. If you want to consider one in detail, take a look at Act 4, Scene 5. In this scene, Petruchio uses the *thou* with Kate when he is pleased with her, but otherwise stays with the *you*.

Then there is the 'angry *thou*'. Lady Macbeth usually addresses Macbeth with *you*. But here she is angry with him because he is having second thoughts about the agreed plan to kill Duncan:

From this time
Such I account thy love. Art thou afeard
To be the same in thine own act and valour
As thou art in desire?
(Mac 1.7.38)

Her anger subsides a little, and in her next speech, just a few lines later, she is back to *you*.

Barber's example[6] of what he calls the 'sardonic and contemptuous *thou*' is from the first scene of *Richard III*, where Richard uses *you* to his brother, the Duke of Clarence. But in his immediately-following soliloquy he switches to *thou*. It is a chilling speech where he expresses his intention of killing the duke:

Go, tread the path that though shalt ne'er return.
Simple, plain Clarence, I do love thee so
That I will shortly send thy soul to heaven,
(1.1.117)

At the other end of the emotional spectrum is the 'grateful *thou*'. Brown and Gilman's example is from Act 4, Scene 3 of *Macbeth*, when Malcolm is talking to Macduff. Usually he uses *you*, but at this point he wants to show gratitude that Macduff is on his side against 'devilish Macbeth':

> but God above
Deal between thee and me! For even now
I put myself to thy direction . . .
(4.3.120)

The word used earlier to describe these uses of *thou* was 'unstable'. Brown and Gilman's (1989) word is 'retractable', and they point out that English is strange in this respect. In French, German, and other languages which have similar distinctions, the move to familiar forms is more stable: once the change to the equivalent of *thou* has been made, it tends to stay.

We have already mentioned examples from *The Taming of the Shrew* of changes from *you* to *thou*. To what extent can the various types of *thou* discussed in this section account for all uses? At the very beginning of this book (1.1) we briefly considered a longer example of how *thou*'s and *you*'s pass back and forth between Petruchio and Kate: here is the passage again. Petruchio is announcing to the astonished Kate that he intends to marry her (and to keep himself warm in her bed) whether she likes it or not (2.1.260):

Marry, so I mean, sweet Katherine, in thy bed.
And therefore, setting all this chat aside,
Thus in plain terms: your father hath consented
That you shall be my wife; your dowry 'greed on,
And, will you, nill you, I will marry you.
Now, Kate, I am a husband for your turn,
For by this light, whereby I see thy beauty,
Thy beauty that doth make me like thee well,
Thou must be married to no man but me,
Enter Baptista, Gremio, Tranio [disguised as Lucentio]
For I am he am born to tame you, Kate,
And bring you from a wild Kate to a Kate
Conformable as other household Kates.
Here comes your father. Never make denial,
I must and will have Katherine to my wife.

An explanation for the *you/thou* shifts in terms of intimacy is just about possible. When talking about her bed and her beauty, one might argue, *thou* forms are appropriate, though not perhaps when discussing dowries and marriage arrangements – as well as when others are present (after Baptista and the others enter). But overall – taking all the plays into account – such explanations are not always convincing. This is a topic which Wales (1983) considers, and her conclusion is that from the thirteenth century onward *you/thou* shifts may 'occur within the same sentence, so that contextual changes are often hard to justify' (p. 114). Such shifts may do no more than indicate a change in register (*you* being more formal, *thou* more informal). Wales's argument is a warning: though on some occasions there may be credible explanations for the 'unstable', retractable use of *thou* in terms of affection, anger or the like, we will come to grief if we try to account for all uses in such terms.

Another conclusion Wales reaches is that overall *you* is the <u>unmarked</u> form, and *thou* the <u>marked</u> one, which is the linguist's way of saying that *you* is normally used, unless there is a particular reason for using *thou*. This is suggested by some interesting statistics Wales gives, related to the drama of the time, that:

- *thou* forms are far outnumbered by *you* forms;
- momentary shifts from *you* to *thou* are more frequent than shifts from *thou* to *you*.

Statistics like these show the inexorable movement towards the state of the language today – *you* universally used and *thou* hardly at all.

To conclude this section, look at Activity 6 (*Thou in love and hate*). This is a lengthy Activity which looks in detail at one scene from *Richard III* and brings together a number of the points made here.

5.6 Implicature

When people communicate, they often 'mean something different than the words they use'. We have already seen an example of this in the sentence *It's cold in here* which might be interpreted as meaning 'Close the window'. Another example, from Yule (1996) is *The President is a mouse*. The sentence is clearly literally untrue, yet most listeners would have no problem interpreting it, to mean that the President is a timid person. The term <u>conversational implicature</u> is used to define the 'additional unstated meaning that has to be assumed' if a conversation is to progress.[7] One of the main areas of pragmatics is to study how conversational implicatures 'work' – how speakers and hearers attach meanings to sentences which go beyond what the words actually say.

In order to understand the process of conversational implicature, think about Yule's mouse sentence from the point of view of someone who hears it. A first reaction might be to try and interpret it literally – that the President is a small mammal that squeaks. But you would immediately conclude that this cannot be what the speaker intended. It is precisely because this literal interpretation cannot be true that the hearer's mind goes looking for other interpretations. In Yule's words: 'if someone says . . . something that is literally false, the hearer must assume the speaker means to convey more than is being said' (1996: 128).

The British philosopher Paul Grice looked at conversational implicature in terms of what he called the <u>Cooperative Principle</u> (the CP). This is a statement of assumptions which participants in a conversation will follow if their communication is to proceed smoothly. The principle can be stated in terms of a number of 'maxims':

- Maxim of quantity: be as informative as required – no more, no less;
- Maxim of quality: do not lie;
- Maxim of relation: be relevant;
- Maxim of manner: be perspicuous (brief, orderly, unambiguous, clear).

To discuss the details of the CP and its maxims would take us beyond where we can go in this chapter; from our point of view the relevant point is that 'flouting maxims' is the mechanism by which we alert hearers to the presence of possible implicatures. Here is an example from *The Taming of the Shrew*.[8] Petruchio has come to ask Baptista for his daughter's hand in marriage. The daughter is the shrewish Kate (Katherina). Petruchio asks (2.1.42):

Petruchio: *And you, good sir. Pray have you not a daughter*
                 Called Katherina, fair and virtuous?
Baptista: *I have a daughter, sir, called Katherina.*

Petruchio is asking whether Baptista has a daughter called Katherina, but also whether she is fair and virtuous. Baptista's reply confirms the daughter's name, but makes no mention of fairness and virtue. It therefore flouts the Maxim of Quantity, since it provides less information than requested. Petruchio will notice this of course, and it will lead him to seek implicatures. The one he will doubtless pick up is that Kate is neither fair nor virtuous.

Shakespeare is indeed a master of the conversational implicature, and nowhere is this clearer than in the utterances of his 'Machiavellian' characters – evil schemers like Richard III and Iago, both of whom have great expertise in malicious implication (Activity 7 gives information about who Machiavelli was). The following discussion builds on Coulthard's (1985) consideration of a truly remarkable scene in *Othello*: Act 3, Scene 3. Here Iago manages over the space of a few lines to persuade Othello that his wife Desdemona is being unfaithful to him with his trusted lieutenant Cassio. At the beginning of the scene, 'Othello is perfectly happy in his marriage; at the end he has decided to murder Desdemona and Cassio'.[9]

The pragmatic issue facing Iago can be put like this. Imagine you (Iago) want to do as much harm as possible to someone (Othello), and decide to do it by suggesting that his wife (Desdemona) is being unfaithful with one of his friends (Cassio). You have two problems. One is that the man you want to harm is your boss, so you have to tread very carefully, and work in very indirect ways. Secondly, the boss loves his wife dearly, and also very much trusts the man you are accusing of seduction. It will take all your ingenuity to overcome these problems, and you will have to rely heavily on implicature – 'secondary meanings' – to achieve your wicked aim.

Here is part of how Iago does it. He sees Desdemona and Cassio finishing a conversation together. Perfectly innocent, perhaps, but Iago wants to plant a seed of suspicion in Othello's mind, that the conversation is between lovers. So he says:

Iago: *Ha! I like not that.*
Othello: *What dost thou say?*
Iago: *Nothing, my lord; or if – I know not what.*
Othello: *Was not that Cassio parted from my wife?*
Iago: *Cassio, my lord? No, sure, I cannot think it*
            That he would sneak away so guilty-like,
            Seeing you coming.
Othello: *I do believe 'twas he*
(Oth 3.3.35)

Desdemona and Othello then have a conversation in which it becomes clear that it was indeed Cassio she was talking to. Then Desdemona exits, and Iago continues to poison Othello's mind (3.3.92). It helps to know, incidentally, that Iago knew very well that Cassio helped Othello woo Desdemona and also that Othello would know that Iago knew this. Iago is dissembling when he pretends not to know:

Iago: *My noble lord –*
Othello: *What dost thou say, Iago?*
Iago: *Did Michael Cassio,*
            When you wooed my lady, know of your love?
Othello: *He did, from first to last. Why dost thou ask?*

Iago:	*But for a satisfaction of my thought –*
	No further harm.
Othello:	*Why of thy thought, Iago?*
Iago:	*I did not think he had been acquainted with her.*
Othello:	*O yes, and went between us very oft.*
Iago:	*Indeed!*
Othello:	*Indeed? Ay, indeed. Discern'st thou aught in that?*
	Is he not honest?
Iago:	*Honest, my lord?*
Othello:	*Honest? Ay, honest.*
Iago:	*My lord, for aught I know.*
Othello:	*What dost thou think?*
Iago:	*Think, my lord?*
Othello:	*Think, my lord! By heaven, he echoes me,*
	As if there were some monster in his thought
	Too hideous to be shown. Thou dost mean something.

When you read these passages, you cannot fail to see the 'game' Iago is playing, as well as being impressed at how well he plays it. But analysing exactly what he is doing is not so easy. Part of his strategy is to answer (or, more to the point, fail to answer) questions in such a way as to suggest he is being evasive, 'as if there were some monster in his thought, too hideous to be shown'. He must suggest some hideous meaning, without actually stating anything hideous. Activity 7 (*How to be a Machiavel*) plots the pragmatic mechanisms whereby he achieves this aim.[10]

5.7 The need for pragmatic awareness

The Englishman in China, mentioned at the beginning of this chapter, illustrated two points. One is that in many situations utterances like *How are you?* or *Have you eaten?* do not perform the speech act they may literally appear to perform. In the case of these two utterances, they would often not be intended as *requests for information* but as *greetings*. The other is that ways of performing speech acts like *greeting* are not universal, but vary from culture to culture. These points may be transported into the world of Shakespeare. There, as in the modern world, the speech acts which utterances perform are not necessarily obvious. And just as there are differences between cultures, so too are there differences between ages; many speech acts are expressed differently now from then. It is for these two reasons that pragmatic issues in Shakespeare require attention, why this chapter is here, and why its key phrases are 'different from today', and 'requiring attention'. The chapter's message is that an awareness of the pragmatic dimension to language is useful when you read or listen to Shakespeare today, and that you must be prepared to ask not just what difficult Shakespearean words 'mean', but also what speech acts the utterances of his characters are performing. Perhaps like the Englishman in China, this may not be something that you would naturally expect to have to think about.

Activity section

1 Asking someone to get up, politely   (AS)

(i)   Here are some Modern English ways of asking someone to get up out of bed – a parent, perhaps, talking to a child who has decided to have a lie-in. Some of these ways are taken from Givón (1993). They differ considerably in terms of politeness. How would you grade these in order of politeness? Write [1] beside the least polite, [8] before the most polite:

_____   *Please would you get up*
_____   *Get up*
_____   *It'll be lunch time in twenty minutes*
_____   *Get up, will you!*
_____   *Would you mind getting up*
_____   *Up*
_____   *Won't you get up, please?*
_____   *Do you think you could get up?*

(ii) Here are some possible Shakespearean ways of fulfilling the same function as in (i) above. In *A Midsummer Night's Dream* (5.1.318) **Flute**, the bellows-mender, is acting Thisbe. She (or in fact a he dressed as a she) finds Pyramus motionless. Perhaps he is asleep. *O Pyramus, arise*, (s)he says. This is an authentic example, but the following are mostly made up:

_____   *Arise*
_____   *Arise, prithee*
_____   *From bed, sirrah*
_____   *If it please you, arise now.*
_____   *With every thing that pretty is, my lady sweet, arise*
_____   *Arise now, I beseech you*
_____   *Come, sir, the guests are within and 'tis almost time to dine.*
_____   *Will you not arise now, sir?*

Put these in order of politeness, as for the PDE examples earlier. Then consider the differences between the Early Modern and PDE ways. There are some similarities, but also some differences.

(iii) Finally, looking at both PDE and EModE examples, consider what features contribute to making a directive more or less polite.

2 Exclamations and the pragmatic mind-set (AS)

Here are examples, questions and explanations related to eight Shakespearean exclamations:

(a) *Fico* (and *foh*)

> Pistol: *'Steal'? Foh,*
>   *A fico for the phrase!*
>   (MWW 1.3.26)

A word the swashbuckling character Pistol likes to uses is *fico*, the Italian for a specific fruit. He also on one occasion (in *Henry V*) uses the Spanish version of this word: *figo*. The word expresses contempt, and may often be accompanied by an obscene gesture. The English word for the same fruit is also used in PDE as an expression of contempt. What is the English name, and what is the expression? When is it used in PDE? Incidentally, the example above also contains another exclamation: *Foh*. It is a variant of *faugh* which is used even today to express disgust, especially of a smell (a 1700 example from the *OED* is: *Faugh, the nauseous fellow! he stinks of poverty . . .*)

(b) *Fie*

You are probably familiar with a common Shakespearean interjection – *fie*. Use the following three examples to help describe the emotion it expresses:

(i) In *Much Ado About Nothing* (3.4.25), **Margaret** makes a rather risqué comment. **Hero** replies: *Fie upon thee, art not ashamed?*

(ii) The comedy in *The Comedy of Errors* comes about because it involves two sets of twins who are constantly being confused. So when the **Merchant** says the following to Antipholus of Syracuse, it is really meant for his twin brother: *Fie on thee, wretch. 'Tis pity that thou livest/To walk where any honest men resort.* (CE 5.1.27)

(iii) And here is **Hamlet**, at the beginning of one of his big soliloquies, using the word twice:

How weary, stale, flat, and unprofitable
Seem to me all the uses of this world!
Fie on't, ah, fie, 'tis an unweeded garden
That grows to seed.
(Ham 1.2.133)

(c) *Go to*

Polonius: *Ay, 'fashion' you may call it. Go to, go to.*
(Ham 1.3.112)

This is another common Shakespearean exclamatory phrase. It is often used to express either impatience or disbelief, and (like a number of exclamations) is often said twice. **Polonius** is expressing disbelief when his daughter Ophelia tells him that Hamlet has wooed her 'in honourable fashion'. How might we express this in modern English? There are various ways, some of which also involve a verb of movement, and might be said twice.

(d) *Oh me*

Henry IV is lying ill:
And now my sight fails, and my brain is giddy.
O me! Come near me. Now I am much ill.
(2H4 4.4.110)

Italian has a word *oime* or *ohime* which expresses lamentation (found quite often in Italian opera). The Shakespearean example above sounds similar to the Italian word, and means roughly the same. How might it be translated? The **Queen** in *King Edward III* (5.1.157) uses a variant when she arrives in France and hears the news that her son may be dead: *Ah me, is this my welcome into France?*

(e) *Pish*

An expressive word, this, used in just two plays, *Othello* and *Henry V*. But what does it mean? The following two examples may help.

(i) **Othello** (4.1.41) is in a bewildered state, thinking about how his wife Desdemona lost the precious handkerchief he gave her, and how she committed adultery with Cassio. He is about to have a fit: *It is not words that shakes me thus! Pish! Noses, ears, and lips. Is't possible? Confess? Handkerchief?*

(ii) **Nym** and **Pistol** are always exchanging insults. Here they are in *Henry V* (2.1.38) with swords drawn. An Iceland dog is a kind of sheepdog with pointed ears, and a reputation for snapping:

Nym: *Pish!*
Pistol: *Pish for thee, Iceland dog! thou prick-eared cur of Iceland!*

According to the *OED*, *pish* may be derived from *push*. The semantic idea
is that when you disdain something, you push it off or away.

(f) **Tush**

At the beginning of *Hamlet*, the two watchmen, Marcellus and
Barnardo, tell Horatio about the ghost they have seen. Will it come
again tonight? **Horatio** is sceptical. He says (1.1.30): *Tush, tush, 'twill not
appear*
This is another exclamation which is often said twice, as in the example
above. What kind of emotion is being expressed here? How might one
express it in Modern English?

(g) **Heigh-ho (hey-ho)**

The words *heigh-ho* (or *hey-ho*) are readily associated with Shakespearean
songs, which seem full of them. For example, in **Amiens'** song 'Blow,
blow thou winter wind' in *As You Like It*, which has in the chorus:
*Hey-ho, sing hey-ho, unto the green holly,/ Most friendship is feigning,
most loving mere folly*. But the words are also sometimes used in PDE,
sometimes spelt *hey ho*. In what sense? In the example below, the
modern sense might also be said to apply:
In *Much Ado About Nothing* (2.1.293), **Beatrice** is lamenting that she
does not have good looks (dark-skinned or *sunburnt* was not regarded as
attractive) and would never marry:

Beatrice: *Good Lord, for alliance! Thus goes every one to the world but I,
              and I am sunburnt; I may sit in a corner and cry 'Heigh-ho for a
              husband'!*
Don Pedro: *Lady Beatrice, I will get you one.*

(h) **Buzz, buzz**

The example below contains a strange exclamation, not used today at
all, and with a very explicit meaning. Does the context provide any clue
as to what it might mean?
Polonius (whom Hamlet regards as rather a tedious old fool) informs
Hamlet that the actors have arrived. *The actors are come hither, my lord*
he says (Ham 2.2.391). Hamlet's reply is: *Buzz, buzz.*
The expression is used to express impatience at being told something
already known. It is interesting to consider how one might express the
same idea today. What might a twenty-first century Hamlet have said
here?

3 Who would say it, to whom? When?

Table 5.1 shows some common (and not so common) forms of address you will find in Shakespeare's plays. The middle column gives a short example, and the right-hand column makes comments or suggests other points to consider.

Even if you are just guessing, think about what these forms might mean, and when they might be used. The words are discussed in the text.

4 *You* and *ye*

Look at these examples of Shakespeare's use of *you* and *ye*. Whenever one of these words is used, say whether the case is 'nominative' or 'other'. On the basis of these examples, what generalisation can you make about Shakespeare's use of the pronouns in relation to case?

(a) In *The Tempest* (1.2.323), **Caliban** is cursing Prospero:
A southwest [wind] blow on ye/And blister you all o'er

(b) Here, Speed and Valentine are being accosted by **outlaws** (TGV 4.1.3):
Stand, sirs, and throw us that [what] *you have about ye./If not, we'll. . . . rifle you.*

(c) Fearing he is going to be tortured, **Parolles** (AW 4.3.122) tells his captors he has no more information for them:
If ye pinch me like a pasty I can say no more.

(d) In *Henry VI, Part I* (5.3.126) **Suffolk** is asking **Margaret** whether she would be prepared to marry Henry:
How say you, madam? Are ye so content?

5 *Thou* and *you*, high and low

The graveyard scene extract looks at low → high and high → low interactions. But what about high → high and low → low? Mark the following five situations as high → high or low → low, and note whether *thee* or *you* is used.

(a) **Othello** (a high-ranking military man) is happy to see his wife Desdemona (2.1.177). He says: *It gives me wonder great as my content/ To see you here before me. O my soul's joy!* Then, later in the play, here is **Desdemona** trying to persuade Othello to reinstate his lieutenant Cassio, whom she describes thus: *A man that all his time/Hath founded his good fortunes on your love,/ Shared dangers with you* (Oth 3.4.91)

TABLE 5.1 Forms of address in Shakespeare plays

Form of address	Example	Comment
sirrah	**Cloten**: *Who is here? What, are you packing, sirrah? Come hither: ah, you precious pandar! Villain* (Cym 3.5.81)	In passing: if you do not know what the word *pandar* means, you may wish to look it up. What is its origin?
cousin/coz	**Glendower**: *Why, I can teach you, cousin, to command the devil.* **Hotspur**: *And I can teach thee, coz, to shame the devil* (1H4 3.1.53)	Exactly what family relationship does the word *cousin* describe today?
mistress	**Slender**: *Mistress Anne Page? She has brown hair, and speaks small like a woman?* (MWW 1.1.44) AND **Falstaff**: *Mistress Ford, by my troth, you are very well met. By your leave, good mistress.* (MWW 1.1.178)	Used to all women, or just particular types of women? What is the modern meaning? What might *speaks small* mean?
bully	**Flute** (to **Bottom**): *O sweet bully Bottom* (MND 4.2.18) AND **Host** (to **Falstaff**): *Bully knight! Bully Sir John!* (MWW 4.5.14)	Can you think of a modern use of the word *bully* that has nothing to do with the common modern meaning of someone who intimidates people (and nothing to do with 'bully-beef' either)?
chuck	**Macbeth**: *Be innocent of the knowledge, dearest chuck, Till thou applaud the deed.* (Mac 3.2.45)	Any ideas/guesses about the word's derivation? (Clue: it is to do with birds, and involves a change of vowel)
master	**Hostess**: *Master Fang, have you entered the action?* (2H4 2.1.1)	A word with very many modern meanings (the main *OED* heading has over 20 sub-heads). What might some of the main ones be?
wench	**Prospero** (to his daughter): *Well demanded, wench* (Tem 1.2.139)	What does the word mean today? In EModE to what sort of person do you imagine you might use this address?
your worship	**Dogberry** (the Constable, to Leonato, the Governor): *your worship speaks like a most thankful and reverend youth, and I praise God for you.* (MA 5.1.301)	To whom would you use this form today?
nuncle	**Fool**: *Prithee, nuncle, be contented; 'tis a naughty night/to swim in* (KL 3.4.106)	Take the 'n' away and you have the derivation. But how might the 'n' have got there? Clue: it is to do with the word *mine*.

(b) Hamlet's gravediggers again. Here they discuss whether someone who has taken their own life (Ophelia in this case) is to receive a Christian burial. The First Clown asks this question, and the **Second Clown** replies: *I tell thee she is*. A few lines later, the Second Clown suggests Ophelia is only to get the Christian burial because she is upper class. The **First Clown** agrees: *Why, there thou says't* he says. (Ham 5.1.26)

(c) King Lear's daughters **Regan** and **Goneril** have agreed to take turns having their father to stay. They discuss the arrangement, and comment on how impetuous the old man has become. (KL 1.1.284)

Goneril: *I think our father will hence tonight.*
Regan: *That's most certain, and with you: next month with us.*
Goneril: *You see how full of changes his age is. . . .*

(d) In *A Midsummer Night's Dream*, **Quince** the carpenter, **Bottom** the weaver, and other craftsmen, decide to put on a play (1.2.11). Here is the idea being mooted.

Quince: *Marry, our play is 'The most lamentable comedy and most cruel death of Pyramus and Thisbe'.*
Bottom: *A very good piece of work, I assure you, and a merry. Now, good Peter Quince, call forth your actors by the scroll. Masters, spread yourselves.*
Quince: *Answer as I call you. Nick Bottom, the weaver?*
Bottom: *Ready.*

(e) **Brutus** tells **Cassius** that he (Brutus) loves honour more than he fears death. Cassius replies (JC 1.2.90): *I know that virtue to be in you, Brutus.* Later in the same scene, Brutus states that he is in no doubt ('nothing jealous') of Cassius's feelings about him: *That you do love me, I am nothing jealous.* (JC 1.2.161)

Use the information in this Activity, plus the graveyard extract you saw in the text, to fill in the right-hand column showing which form, *thou* or *you*, would be used in these situations:

high → low	
low → high	
high → high	
low → low	

6 *Thou* in love and hate   (AS)

Barber (1981) looks at the use of *thou* and *you* in *Richard III*. One of the scenes he considers in detail is Act 1, Scene 2. One of the two main characters is Richard, who is brother to the king (Edward IV), and hence high-born. The other main character is also high-born – Anne is daughter-in-law to the previous king (Henry VI). Anne has every reason to hate Richard since he had a hand in the death of her father, her husband and her father-in-law . . . no less! Early in the scene she vents her disgust by spitting at him. Yet such is Richard's guile that by the end of that same scene there is the suggestion they may marry.

The scene is rich in its use of *thou* and *you*, and Barber (1981) talks through the uses. The main ones are described below. Take careful note of what forms are used (not just the words *thou* and *you* of course, but all associated forms like *thee* and *your*, etc.). Try to account for each choice of pronoun. It is not always easy. Before getting involved in highly complex explanations of emotional states, remember that whenever the addressee is plural, the form must be *you*; *thou* cannot be used in the plural.

At the start of the scene, **Anne** is accompanying the funeral cortege of her murdered father-in-law. She addresses his ghost (5-8):

(a) *Poor key-cold figure of a holy king,*
Pale ashes of the house of Lancaster,
Thou bloodless remnant of that royal blood,
Be it lawful that I invoke thy Ghost.

She instructs the bearers to proceed with the coffin (29, 32):

(b) *Come, now towards Chertsey with your holy load/ . . . Rest you, whiles I*
lament King Henry's corpse

But **Richard** enters and orders the bearers to stop (33):

(c) *Stay, you that bear the corpse, and set it down.*

One of the bearers seems ready to disobey, and Richard is firm (39):

(d) *Unmannered dog, stand'st thou when I command*

Anne knows that Richard had a hand in her father-in-law's death. She launches into a denunciation of him (46-8):

(e) *Avaunt, thou dreadful minister of hell!*
Thou hadst but power over his mortal body,
His soul thou canst not have: therefore be gone

Richard's replies are conciliatory (68-70):

(f) Richard: *Lady, you know no rules of charity,*
                    Which renders good for bad, blessings for curses.
    Anne: *Villain, thou know'st nor law of God nor man:*

They continue addressing each other in this way for a long time. But at one point during this interchange Richard attempts intimacy (81-2):

(g) *Fairer than tongue can name thee, let me have*
    Some patient leisure to excuse myself.

But this is fleeting. A change of address which lasts longer occurs at line 131. Barber calls it an 'important switch', as Richard's charm offensive begins in earnest:

(h) Anne: *Black night o'ershade thy day, and death thy life*
    Richard: *Curse not thyself, fair creature; thou art both.*

After a considerable time, Richard bares his breast and offers Anne his sword to put him to death. She wavers (192-8):

(i) Anne: *I would I knew thy heart*
    Richard: *'Tis figured in my tongue.*
    Anne: *I fear me both are false.*
    Richard: *Then never man was true.*
    Anne: *Well, well, put up your sword.*
    Richard: *Then say my peace is made.*
    Anne: *That shalt thou know hereafter.*
    (202-8)

It seems that Anne is won over. He puts a ring on her finger, and as their conversation ends, he asks her to grant him the favour ('boon') of forgiving him (217-20):

(j) Richard: *For diverse unknown reasons, I beseech you,*
    Grant me this boon.
    Anne: *With all my heart, and much it joys me too,*
    To see you are become so penitent.

7 How to be a Machiavel   (AS)

Niccolò Machiavelli (1469–1527) was an Italian political thinker whose most famous book was called *The Prince*. It describes the means a prince has to employ to stay in power, and it led to Machiavelli's name being associated with the use of expediency over morality. Some of Shakespeare's ruthlessly evil characters (the best examples being Richard III and Iago) are called 'machiavels': very clever, hugely resourceful, utterly evil.

Here are the six question episodes from *Othello* Act 3, Scene 3 discussed in the text:

(a) Iago: *Ha! I like not that.* [Probably spoken softly]
     Othello: *What dost thou say?*
     Iago: *Nothing, my lord; or if – I know not what.*

(b) Othello: *Was not that Cassio parted from my wife?*
     Iago: *Cassio, my lord? No, sure, I cannot think it*
               That he would sneak away so guilty-like,
               Seeing you coming.

(c) (Iago has just asked whether, in the days that Othello was wooing Desdemona, Cassio knew about it)
     Othello: *He did, from first to last. Why dost thou ask?*
     Iago: *But for a satisfaction of my thought –*
               No further harm.

(d) Othello: *Why of thy thought, Iago?*
     Iago: *I did not think he had been acquainted with her.*

(e) Othello: *Indeed? Ay, indeed. Discern'st thou aught in that?*
               Is he not honest?
     Iago: *Honest, my lord?*

(f) Othello: *What dost thou think?*
     Iago: *Think, my lord?*

(i) Here are five possible ways of answering (or failing to answer) questions so as to arouse suspicions in the mind of your hearer. Associate each of these with one of the questions above (there are five ways and six questions because one way is use twice). Specify as precisely as possible what the effect on your hearer will be when each of these techniques is used. What will they lead the hearer to think?

    1 Ask a question to which you already know the answer, and the hearer knows you already know the answer. Then refuse to say why you asked it.

    2 Respond to a question by questioning part of it, in a strange or silly way.

    3 Say something a little risqué/suggestive/malicious in a low voice, so the hearer does not entirely hear it. Then when asked what you said, refuse to divulge it.

    4 Answer a question with a lie which you know the hearer will recognise as a lie.

    5 Answer a question with a lie, suggesting that the true answer would suggest something suspicious.

(ii) Now focus on Questions (a), (c) and (d) above. Look back to the text (in 5.6) to remind yourself of Grice's Maxims, and the idea that getting hearers to seek for implicatures can be done by flouting maxims. Which maxims do Iago's answers flout? It will perhaps help to ask questions associated with each of the Maxims: is he being as informative as required? Is he lying? And so on.

Extended activities

1   In 5.1 the sentence *It's cold in here* was mentioned. It seems on the surface to be a statement about temperature, but in some circumstances it could be said – and understood – as a directive (to close the window or door, to put the heating on). Think of some other examples of 'indirect speech acts' in PDE, where what is 'said' and what is 'intended' are rather indirectly linked.

2   5.1 also talks about 'rules of use'. Again focusing on PDE, think about the structure of one or more of the following acts, considering such issues as who speaks first, what kinds of things are said, in what order:
   - the first few utterances of a phone conversation. Think perhaps of a call to a friend, and another to an official (e.g. in a bank)
   - meeting a friend in the street whom you have not seen for a very long time
   - asking a not-very-close friend a big favour, for example to lend you £100 to make a purchase because you have left your credit card at home.

3   Concentrate on a Shakespeare play that particularly interests you. Select one or more of the following speech acts:
   - expressing gratitude
   - greeting
   - saying goodbye (leave taking)
   - inviting
   - asking for permission.

   Skim through parts of the play collecting together examples of the speech act. Then look up your examples on an internet site that has a collocation facility (e.g. 'Shakespeare's Words' or 'Open Source Shakespeare'). Can you make any general statements about the contexts in which the examples may be used (without doubt, degree of formality will be one of the variables you will want to consider).

Answer section

Use of *la* (section 5.2)

The word is used as an <u>intensifier</u>, and means something like 'indeed'. Onions' explanation is closely based on the *OED*: 'exclamation formerly used to introduce or accompany a conventional phrase or an address, or to call attention to an emphatic statement'. An earlier glossary, Phin (1902) gives 'look' or 'there now'. The first uses given in the *OED* are from Shakespeare.

You and *ye* in the Tyndale passage (section 5.5.1)

Blessed are <u>ye</u> when men revile <u>you</u> and persecute <u>you</u>, and shall falsely say all manner of evil sayings against <u>you</u> for my sake . . . <u>ye</u> are the salt of the earth . . . <u>ye</u> are the light of the world.

Activity 1 Asking someone to get up, politely

(i)   Here is one possible order (though others are certainly possible). Following the order on the page: 6, 3, 7, 1, 8, 2, 4, 5.

(ii) Again, more than one order is possible: 2, 3, 1, 5, 8, 4, 7, 6.

Activity 2 Exclamations and the pragmatic mind-set

(a) The fruit is of course the fig. In PDE it is still sometimes used in expressions like *He doesn't give a fig* meaning 'He couldn't care less'.

(b) *Fie* (often followed by *on*) expresses disgust or indignation. There is no word in PDE that directly translates it.

(c) 'Come come', 'come now', 'come off it' are ways of expressing it in PDE.

(d) It can express lamentation or surprise. In the first sense, it is like 'alas' (though this is not used today), or 'oh dear' (though the sense is often rather stronger. In the second sense, it can mean 'goodness me'.

(e) *Pish*: the *OED* states that it expresses contempt, impatience or disgust. No PDE equivalent springs to mind.

(f) *Tush* is used to express impatient disbelief or disparagement. In PDE one might on occasions say 'come off it', or even 'don't be silly'.

(g) In PDE *hey ho* is used to express weariness, resignation, disappointment.

(h) One (but not the only) use of the PDE phrase *So what's new?* is to express this idea.

Activity 6 *Thou* in love and hate

In (a) Anne uses *thou* because she is addressing a spirit (that of the dead king). In (b) *you* is used because she is addressing the group of men (i.e. it is plural). The same is true of Richard's use in (c). In (d) Richard is addressing just one of the bearers. It is an example of high → low. Anne expresses her contempt for Richard in (e) and (f) by using *thou*, while (in (f)) Richard stays with the polite *you*. Then, when he feels it the time to try intimacy, he switches to *thou* (g). (h) shows *thou* being used to express contempt (by Anne) and intimacy (by Richard) together, but by the time (i) is reached, Anne's feelings are moving from contempt to intimacy. In (j) they are back on a more formal footing, using the polite *you* to each other.

Activity 7 How to be a Machiavel

(i)   1 = (c); 2 = (e) and (f); 3 = (a); 4 = (d); 5 = (b).

In 1. the fact that the hearer knows you already know the answer will make them look for a reason why you asked the question. Your refusal to say why you asked it will lead them to think the reason suggests something suspicious.

In 2. responding in a strange and silly way will make the hearer think that you are avoiding answering the question, which will lead them to wonder why. Their conclusion may be that the answer involves something suspicious.

In 3. the hearer will wonder first why you spoke in a soft voice, and second why you refuse to divulge the question. This leads them to wonder what the question is and, again, to think that it suggests suspicious behaviour.

In 4. since the hearer knows you are lying, they will be led to wonder why it is necessary to avoid the truth. The suggestion is that the truth is unpleasant.

In 5. since the answer given is clearly untrue, the hearer will wonder why you are avoiding the truth. They are led towards the conclusion that it is because the truth involves something unpleasant.

(ii) In (a) and (c) the maxim of quantity is being flouted, and in (d) it is the maxim of quality.

Notes

1 The example is from Quirk and Greenbaum (1973).

2 A number of examples and points in the following paragraphs are taken from Replogle (1973).

3 The quotation is from Busse (2008: 88), who is citing Givón (1993). What follows is based on the analyses of Busse (2008) and Brown and Gilman (1989), who look at directives in Shakespeare.

4 The quotation is from Baugh and Cable (2002: 243).

5 To simplify discussion, from this point on *you* will be used to encompass *you, ye, your* and *yours*. Similarly, *thou* stands for all the forms: *thou, thee, thy* and *thine*.

6 From Barber (1981: 170).

7 The definition is from Yule (1996: 128).

8 The example is taken from Thomas (1995) which contains other vivid illustrations.

9 The quotation is from Muir (1968), and is cited by Coulthard (1985: 185).

10 Gilbert (1997) contains further examples of cooperative maxims being flouted in Shakespeare.

Further reading

As introductions to Pragmatics, there are Yule, G. (1996) *Pragmatics*, Oxford: Oxford University Press, and Leech, G. (1983) *Principles of Pragmatics*, London: Longman. The first has a section, and the second a chapter, on politeness. Jucker's edited collection (Jucker, A. H., ed. (1995) *Historical Pragmatics*, Amsterdam: John Benjamins) does not restrict itself to EModE, but provides a comprehensive picture of how the field is developing. Culpeper, J. and Kytö, M. (2010) *Early Modern English Dialogues: Spoken Interaction as Writing*, Cambridge: Cambridge University Press, contains much discussion of pragmatic matters.

CHAPTER 6

Rhetoric: 'Sweet and honeyed sentences'

Key phrases:
stylistic intermingling; stylistic richness

6.1 Complicated sentences

On the internet there are numerous so-called answer-sites, which aim to provide answers to questions on any number of subjects, including Shakespeare. 'Why is Shakespeare hard to read?', one site asks; and another: 'Why is William Shakespeare so hard to understand?'. The answers to such questions often refer to two elements which are the concern of this chapter: figures of speech and complicated sentences. Here is one: 'Shakespeare's dialogue is . . . full of . . . metaphors, similes and other figures of speech, and long and complicated sentences'. A second reads: 'Shakespeare uses metaphors, similes and personification . . . Sometimes he uses long and complicated sentences'.[1]

This chapter is about rhetoric. For many, this primarily means using figures of speech, like the metaphors and similes mentioned above; techniques to make sentences persuasive, as well as 'sweet and honeyed' (the description of Henry V's speech given by the Archbishop of Canterbury – H5 1.1.50). But in fact rhetoric means a lot more than this. It includes the shapes of sentences, how they are structured, how long they are, and detailed issues like whether it is better to put the main point at the sentence's beginning or its end.

Sentence complexity makes a good starting-point. Many of Shakespeare's characters have a taste for long and complicated sentences. Here, to illustrate the point, is part of a famous speech from *Hamlet*. Because of what is said in its second line, we shall it call the 'vicious mole' speech. It occurs at a point when Hamlet hears sounds of revelry in the court. This 'fault' (too much revelry, over-carousing) can detract, he is saying, from other virtues that people may have. The extract is just one sentence – all fourteen lines of it (and in fact in some editions the sentence continues further). Later you will be invited to produce a 'translation' of the speech in PDE. For the moment, it is enough to grasp the general sense of the passage, and Activity 1 (*Particular men*) encourages you to do this (**NP**).

So oft it chances in particular men
That – for some vicious mole of nature in them,
As in their birth, wherein they are not guilty,
Since nature cannot choose his origin –
By the o'ergrowth of some complexion,
Oft breaking down the pales and forts of reason,
Or by some habit that too much o'er-leavens
The form of plausive manners – that these men,
Carrying, I say, the stamp of one defect,
Being nature's livery or fortune's star,
His virtues else, be they as pure as grace,
As infinite as man may undergo,
Shall in the general censure take corruption
From that particular fault.
(Ham 1.4.23)

In order to understand something about the structure of Shakespeare's sentences (including the 'vicious mole' example), it will be useful to look at the linguistics of 'complicated' sentences. The next section deals with the following concepts: what a clause is, co-ordinate and subordinate clauses, compound and complex sentences, some main clause types, identifying ante-cedents of subordinate clauses. If you are familiar with these areas already, skip the section.

6.2 Compound and complex sentences

In 4.4 we touched on the notion of a <u>phrase</u>, as a group of words which 'go together' to form a recognisable part of a sentence (what are called <u>constituents</u>). In the sentence *John and Mary ran down the hill at great speed*, *John and Mary* is a phrase, as is *down the hill* and *at great speed*. But the group of words *hill at great* is not a phrase, because the words do not go together to form a recognisable unit. Phrases (as we also saw in 4.4) can contain verbs, and the words *ran down the hill at great speed* make up a phrase.

There is a special kind of phrase known as the clause. Defining the clause rigorously is difficult, and there are many different types. As a rule of thumb, one may say a clause has a verb in it, in some form or another (which is not at all true of all phrases). It often has a subject and perhaps an object as well. Many sentences consist of just one clause, so it is possible to say that a clause can be a sentence. *Jane is tall*, for example, is a one-clause sentence. But several clauses can be linked together to make a sentence. The words used to link clauses together are called conjunctions or connectors. The sentence *Sally is tall and she lives in London* has two clauses linked together by the conjunction/ connector *and*. In examples like this the clauses might stand as separate sentences (*Sally is tall. Sally lives in London)*, where the sentences have equal importance. This form of joining together is called co-ordination, and sentences which have it (like the one about Sally living in London) are known as compound sentences.

Look now at this example: *I'll speak to you when I get home.* The sentence has two clauses: *I'll speak to you* and *when I get home.* But, one might say, the clauses are not of equal importance. *I'll speak to you* is the main clause and could stand independently – it is a sentence in its own right. *When I get home* is regarded as a subordinate clause, 'depending on' the main clause – indeed the phrase dependent clause is also sometimes used. Sentences containing a subordinate clause are called complex sentences. Notice incidentally that sentences can be both compound and complex. For example: *John liked the cinema and went to a film once a week, where he often met Peter.*

Common subordinating conjunctions are *in order to, before, where, which, because, that, if, when, like, although, so.* Activity 2 (*Common clause types*) identifies the main clause types associated with these conjunctions, and provides practice in recognising them.

So far all the clauses we have considered contain 'normal' finite verbs, which means that they have tenses, and change their form according to the subject of the sentence. So in *Jane is tall* the tense is present, and the subject (*Jane*) is singular so the verb form is present singular (*is* and not *was* or *are*). But there is another class of verb forms which are called non-finite, and these carry neither tense nor person. There are four forms commonly used in non-finite clauses:

1   The infinitive (the very word carries the notion of 'non-finite') preceded by *to* (to go)

2   The infinitive by itself, without *to* (go)

3   The *-ing* form (going)

4   The past participle form, sometimes called the *-en* form (gone), though in most English verbs the ending is *-ed*.

As you go through the examples below, decide whether the non-finite verb form in each is (1), (2), (3) or (4) above (**AS**):

(a) *She helped him answer the question*

(b) *Considered too inexperienced to play, he was dropped from the team*

(c) *To reach the theatre, turn left at the traffic lights*

(d) *Entertaining relatives can be a boring activity*

(e) *It would be a disaster for him to miss the plane*

(f) *Holding his bag tightly he made for the exit*

(g) *Beaten by his opponent he left the ring in disgrace*

(h) *He saw the thief run away*

In order to understand how complicated sentences are constructed, it is often useful to identify the <u>antecedents</u> of subordinate clauses – what they 'refer to'. Often the antecedent is both obvious and stated. In the sentence *John, who liked chocolates, ate some every day*, the *who* clearly refers to *John*, so the antecedent of the relative clause is *John* (relative clauses are discussed in 4.5.4). But sometimes the antecedent is an idea not specifically expressed in so many words. Consider for example this sentence: *She married Michael, which was unexpected*. The subordinate clause is *which was unexpected*. Clearly the *which* does not refer to *Michael*, but to the idea *her marrying Michael*. This type of antecedent can be difficult to pin down. Activity 3 (*The vicious mole*) invites you to do some operations on the Hamlet speech, including pinning down antecedents.

So far in this chapter the focus has been on linguistic matters, and Shakespeare has hardly been mentioned. But the information discussed will very much come into play when we look at his work. First, though, some history . . .

6.3 The history of rhetoric in a nutshell

There have always been those ready to give rhetoric a bad press, suggesting excessive floweriness, artificiality, and lack of sincerity. Quite recently, the American political thinker, Thomas Sowell, talked about the 'cheap price of rhetoric' in relation to the cost of freedom and blood: 'Freedom has cost too much blood and agony to be relinquished at the cheap price of rhetoric'.[2] Rather a nice piece of rhetoric in itself! Go back some 130 years and here is how the British politician Disraeli described his rival Gladstone: 'a sophistical rhetorician: inebriated with the exuberance of his own verbosity'. We will find similar views below in our consideration of Renaissance rhetoric. But there is another standpoint according to which rhetoric was a very serious business indeed. Aristotle wrote his treatise called *Rhetoric* in the fourth century BC. In Greek and then Roman times, rhetoric was the study of techniques of 'persuasion', initially in law courts but soon passing into politics. The Romans were responsible for disseminating the ideas of rhetoric through their Empire. In mediaeval universities, rhetoric was one element of the intro-ductory (or 'lower') liberal arts programme called the 'Trivium'; the word signals a division into three parts, the other two elements being grammar and logic. Incidentally, the association of the word trivium with the 'lower' programme gives us the adjective 'trivial'.

The whole notion of 'renaissance' (the word means 'rebirth') involves looking back to classical times, and bringing the virtues of that time into the present. One influential Renaissance figure – John Colet, who founded St Paul's School in London (which still exists today) – captures the Renaissance view of European history very well. He saw it as falling into three stages: the 'Golden Age' of classical civilisation, the present day which was striving to recreate the 'Golden Age', and between the two, the 'Middle Ages' which he saw as barbaric (he calls it a 'blind world'; more common is the term 'dark ages'). The way that Colet, together with the Dutch humanist philosopher Erasmus, 'strove to recreate the Golden Age' was by means of a huge educa-tional effort to increase knowledge of Latin, and at the same time to 'improve' English in the direction of classical models.[3]

In terms of language (which were very much the terms in which those like Colet thought), the 'Golden Age' was much associated with the period of Latin history from about 190 to 19 BC, which became a kind of linguistic model for the Renaissance to aim towards. A major figure of that period (his dates were in fact 106–43 BC) was the Roman philosopher Marcus Tullius Cicero, commonly known as Cicero, or Tully. He wrote several books about rhetoric. One of most influential for Renaissance times was *De Inventione*, a kind of handbook for orators (for a translation see http://classicpersuasion.org/pw/cicero/dnv1-1.htm). Also popular in the Renaissance was an anonymous book about rhetoric addressed to one C. Herennius, a person whose identity was uncertain. Hence the title *Ad Herennium* (*To Herennius*). There is a version online at http://penelope.uchicago.edu/Thayer/E/Roman/Texts/Rhetorica_ad_Herennium/1*.html. The online versions of these are worth a glance, to see what manner of animal they are.

'The great justification for the study of rhetoric in the Renaissance', Vickers writes, 'was that it was not "theoretical" (a term of abuse to most Humanists), but useful, of practical value: it taught you how to win over friends, and either persuade enemies or make them look ridiculous'.[4] Indeed, so important was rhetoric to Renaissance England that several English writers produced their own handbooks of rhetoric, including Thomas Wilson (*The Arte of Rhetorique* – 1553), George Puttenham (*The Arte of English Poesie* – 1589) and John Hoskins (*Directions for Speech and Style* – 1599). Notice that two of these three books appeared in Shakespeare's lifetime, and one not long before. Rhetoric was clearly a subject of much interest, and as a result Renaissance England was a hotbed of styles. In a moment we will look at some of these in detail, but here is a sketch of the overall scene.

Cicero had a huge influence. The hallmarks of his style were complexity, elegance and balance. But as the 1500s came to an end, there was a reaction against the style, towards something more spontaneous, less contrived and florid – an attempt to get away from what some saw as the 'insidious preference for words over "matter"'.[5] What was wanted, in the words of Gertrude to the verbose Polonius in *Hamlet*, was 'more matter, with less art'. The search for an alternative style again looked partly back towards classical times, and here the Roman rhetorician, Seneca, provided a model for some (though not all) seventeenth-century styles. Some call these emerging styles 'baroque', and they reached their zenith around the 1620s. It is the same reaction against floridness, in favour of 'true plain words', that was mentioned earlier in relation to Sowell and Disraeli. Here is a Shakespearean expression of it, in his Sonnet 82. 'They' in the first line refers to the poet's words, and 'sympathized' means 'depicted'. The poet is saying that his love's true beauty does not need colouring by rhetoric, which is more suitable for a pallid and sallow lover, 'where cheeks need blood':

> *yet when they have devised*
> *What strained touches rhetoric can lend,*
> *Thou truly fair wert truly sympathized,*
> *In true plain words, by thy true-telling friend.*
> *And their gross painting might be better used*
> *Where cheeks need blood; in thee it is abused.*

The trend against floridness and for plain speaking continued after Shakespeare. In the box (*Puns in and out of fashion*) in 3.1.2, Cowley's 1656 attack on puns was mentioned. This was part of the spirit of the age. In the 1640s the British Royal Society was formed and they made great efforts to banish all forms of florid English from scientific writing. One of the Society's founders, Thomas Sprat, asks: 'Who can behold, without indignation, how many mists and uncertainties, these specious Tropes and Figures [rhetorical devices] have brought to our knowledge'. And in 1651, the English philosopher Thomas

Hobbes wrote a book about the structure of society, called *Leviathan*. In it, he attacks the use of any form of metaphor as being 'deceptive' and 'confusing', and thus he argues that metaphors should be banished from the discourse of science. Incidentally, seventeenth-century writers like John Dryden found Shakespeare's writing over-rhetorical: 'his whole style is so pestered with figurative expressions, that it is as affected as it is obscure' is what Dryden said. The latter sought to 'improve' Shakespeare by cutting down on the floridness. Activity 4 (*Shakespeare: the bare bones*) looks at how Dryden did this.

6.4 Some Renaissance styles

6.4.1 The Ciceronian style

Because part of this chapter deals with the structure of passages, the examples we use to illustrate some of the points made are long. There is therefore a Text Page at the end of the chapter, which contains example passages. The first four, together with Hamlet's 'vicious mole' speech that we have already considered, will help focus on the main characteristics of the Ciceronian style. It is worth looking through the four Text Page passages before reading on.

One of the writers who made the style popular in England was Sir Philip Sidney, particularly in his romantic and pastoral prose work *Arcadia*, published in 1590 – a year when Shakespeare was working on his earliest plays. *Arcadia* is a collection of stories, from which Shakespeare on occasions borrowed plot lines. Its opening pages exemplify one striking characteristic of the Ciceronian style: a love of long sentences. *Arcadia's* first two sentences are no less than twenty-nine lines in length. Hamlet's 'vicious mole' speech provides a good Shakespearean example of the same characteristic: as we have already noted, it is a fourteen-liner. You can find a number of other very long sentences in Texts 1–4.

Ciceronian sentences are complex as well as long, containing many phrases, much subordination, and liberal amounts of coordination. Hamlet's 'vicious mole' speech again illustrates this well. It contains several clauses using the *-ing* form of the verb (*breaking*, *carrying*, *being*); there are relatives introduced by *wherein* and *that* (as well as several other *that* clauses); there is a *since* clause, and one beginning with *be they* – and this list is not complete. Text 1 – a sonnet – is also worth looking at from this point of view; try making a list of its clauses (**AS**).

Sometimes the impression is given that the authors themselves get lost in the complexities of their own sentences. Here is example from Spenser:[6]

> *As when the fiery-mouthed steeds, which drew*
> *The sun's bright wane to Phaeton's decay,*
> *Soon as they did the monstrous Scorpion view*
> *With ugly craples crawling in their way,*
> *The dreadful sight did them so sore affray,*
> *That their well-known courses they forwent*
> (Faerie Queene 5.8.40)

If you attempt to <u>parse</u> this sentence (analyse it into its constituent parts), you may decide that the main sentence is 'The dreadful sight did them so sore affray . . .'. You would also conclude that *them* in the fifth line refers to *steeds*. But what is the verb of which *steeds* is the subject? There does not seem to be one. The sentence seems syntactically confused.

Because of this passion for subordination, conjunctions were naturally used a lot, and a look through Texts 1–4 will reveal a long list of them. In this convoluted style, parentheses were also favoured, though these were not always marked with brackets. The 'vicious mole' speech includes some clauses that one could imagine being in brackets. Lines 3–4 are one possible example (*As in their birth, wherein they are not guilty/Since nature cannot choose his origin*). You may be able to find another example later in the same speech (**AS**).

Ciceronian sentences had their own characteristic 'shape'. They tended to be what are referred to as <u>periods</u>, a 'particular type of complex sentence, in which the main clause is completed at, or towards the end of, the construction, having been preceded or interrupted by one or more subordinate clauses'.[7] The effect is a 'piling-up' of clauses. Texts 1–4 are (or contain) examples of this. In Text 2, the 'pile-up' is of phrases rather than clauses. The main verb is *encountered*, occurring in the form *had been encountered*. Between the *had* in the first line, and the *been encountered* in the last, come the subject (*these gentlemen, Marcellus and Bernardo*) plus two or three adverbial phrases (depending on how you count) – *on their watch* and *in the dead waste/in the middle of the night*. The main verb is the very last word. Hamlet's 'vicious mole' speech is a more complex example, and Activity 5 (*Clause and phrase clusters*) asks you to consider it from that point of view.

Text 2 and the 'vicious mole' speech show that it is not just a question of 'piling up', but also of 'holding back'. The endings of sentences were important in Ciceronian rhetoric. The aim was to finish in a climactic way, and often this involved keeping the main verb to the end. This is what occurs in the two texts we have just been considering, and you will able to find other examples in Texts 1–4. Yet another good example, which you may wish to look up, occurs in a well-known speech delivered by the dying John of Gaunt in *Richard II* (2.1.40). He is bemoaning the fact that England is going to ruin. The sentence in which he expresses this view is no less than twenty-one lines long. A short paraphrase of its contents might read: 'England has been leased out like a tenement building'. The first nineteen lines are taken up with elaborate descriptions of England, among them: *this royal throne of kings, this other Eden, this precious stone set in the silver sea, this dear dear land*. So nineteen lines of the sentence are its subject. The verb *leased out* – and the rest of the sentence – is held back until line 20.

Also characteristic of Ciceronian style were sentences which have 'some well-defined turning point, with phrases and clauses tending to mass themselves in parallel formation on both sides of the turning point'.[8] Once again there is an example in the 'vicious mole' speech. The first eight lines include a series of clauses on the topic of 'men with vicious moles'. The return to the subject at the end of line 8 (*that these men . . .*) is the turning point, leading into another series of clauses. You may be able to find a turning point in Text 3, a piece of prose taken from *Henry IV, Part 1*. This same passage exemplifies another aspect of the Ciceronian 'shape' – the tendency to finish with a 'summary' statement: *I see no reason why thou shouldst be so superfluous to demand the time of the day* just about sums up Prince Hal's point in Text 3. Another example of the summary sentence is in Sonnet 29 (Text 1) where the final couplet (as two consecutive lines which rhyme are called) is a kind of summary. Indeed, you could argue that the sonnet form in general was a vehicle particularly suited to the Ciceronian style. Text 1 displays not just a summary sentence, but a long preceding one (the first twelve lines), with both 'piling up' and 'holding back'. This sonnet also has a clear turning point, which coincides with the appearance of the main verb, in line 10.

Prince Hal's answer to Falstaff (Text 3) also shows how full of rhetorical devices Ciceronian sentences could be. The first sentence here uses the *-ing* form to list three actions of Falstaff, in the order they would usually happen – drinking, unbuttoning, sleeping. Then in the last sentence, no less than five associations are set up: between hours and cups of wine, minutes and capons, clocks and bawds, dials and brothels, the sun and wenches. Why should cups of wine be related to hours, and capons with just minutes, one wonders? Perhaps it reflects the relative amount of time Falstaff spends on these activities. The order in which the items are listed is also of interest; certainly, finishing with the sun, you might regard the rhetorical devices as moving up to a climax. In its use of rhetorical devices, Prince Hal's speech has elements of yet another style which was particularly popular in Shakespeare's day, and which is described in the box below. All in all, Text 3 is a very well-constructed piece of discourse, entirely worthy of a future king.

The style of 'another Tully'

One of the most fashionable Elizabethan styles was developed by the writer John Lyly, born around 1553. His best-known book was *Euphues, or the Anatomy of Wit* (1578), which has been described as the first English novel. The plot is very flimsy and is accompanied by large quantities of philosophy and moralising. It is about the adventures of an Athenian man (Euphues, meaning *elegant* in Greek) who goes to Naples and falls in love.

Euphues gave his name to the prose style – euphuism. It was one of the very florid styles which was extremely popular in Shakespeare's early years, but which began to grow out of fashion as more down-to-earth styles came to be preferred. Euphuism is elaborate and complex like Cicero's style, and indeed Lyly was described as 'another Tully' (Tully being one of Cicero's names). A characteristic of the style is the use of phrases of equal length appearing in succession. The elements in the phrases are balanced and matching, often having the same structure. But structural similarities are offset by the use of <u>antithesis</u> – ideas standing in strong contrast to each other. Alliteration (words beginning with the same sound – a kind of 'front rhyme') is sometimes also used, and there is a predilection for exotic imagery (particularly zoological allusions). The following example from *Euphues* well illustrates balanced, matching phrases and strongly contrasting ideas. There is even a little alliteration (*most miserable most happy*):

It is virtue, yea virtue, gentlemen, that maketh gentlemen; that maketh the poor rich, the base-born noble, the subject a sovereign, the deformed beautiful, the sick whole, the weak strong, the most miserable most happy. There are two principal and peculiar gifts in the nature of man, knowledge and reason; the one commandeth, and the other obeyeth . . .

One of the Shakespearean characters who uses a euphuistic style is Polonius in *Hamlet*. He is a pompous, tedious man much taken to speechifying. Here is part of his advice to his son, who is about to go abroad. These four lines clearly illustrate balance and antithesis at work:

Give every man thine ear, but few thy voice:
Take each man's censure, but reserve thy judgement:
Costly thy habit as thy purse can buy,
But not expressed in fancy; rich, not gaudy
(Ham 1.3.68)

The character of Moth, a Page in *Love's Labour's Lost*, also uses euphuism. As you will recall from 2.2.3, *Love's Labour's Lost* is a play about excesses of language, and it is not surprising that the fashionable euphuism should come in for some parody.

Now for our own summary sentence, listing the characteristics of Ciceronian style that have been discussed. They are:

- long sentences
- complex sentences with many subordinate clauses
- many parentheses
- 'piling-up'
- 'holding back'
- a 'turning point'
- rhetorical devices
- summary sentences.

Take a look at Text 4, which offers a good short example of the style. Most (though not quite all) of the points above are present in this extract from *Hamlet*. And there are many other examples of Ciceronian passages in Shakespeare. To establish this, a look through the sonnets will reveal a number which have long complex sentences concluding with the main clause in line 11 or 12. It will also pay to skim through a few pages of a play like *Hamlet*. The result may be astonishment at how much of Shakespeare is Cicero. But not only Shakespeare. To illustrate how popular the style was at this time, here is a final example from Bacon's *Advancement of Learning* (which appeared in 1605, probably the year in which *King Lear* was written).[9] First consider the passage as an example of Ciceronian style, with its elegantly balanced clauses; it even has a Ciceronian 'turning point' – where? (**AS**).

> . . . *men began to hunt more after words than matter; more after the choiceness of the phrase, and the round and clean composition of the sentence, and the sweet falling of the clauses, and the varying and illustration of their works with tropes and figures, than after the weight of matter, worth of subject, soundness of argument, life of invention, or depth of judgement.*

Now look at the passage in terms of what is being said. Bacon is talking about the excesses of Ciceronian rhetoric in his age, and justifying the introduction of other styles. So he is parodying the very style he is attacking.

What Bacon is saying in this passage illustrates how the end of the sixteenth century saw something of a reaction against Ciceronianism. We will now look at the styles which began to replace it.

6.4.2 'Baroque' styles[(10)]

You may have come across the word *baroque* to describe a particular type of florid architecture, painting or musical style, full of flourishes and whimsical ornamentation. The word comes from the Portuguese *barroco* which means 'a rough, irregularly shaped pearl'. Take a look at Texts 5, 6 and 7 on the Text Page. Two of these passages are from Shakespeare and one from his contemporary, the playwright Ben Jonson. Read through these to get some feel for baroque styles. Record any first impressions about how they differ from Texts 1–4. Is it clear why the word 'baroque' should be applied to these styles?

The classical figure whose name is most associated with baroque styles is the Roman rhetorician Seneca, born about eleven years before Cicero died. In France there were a number of writers also using the styles, particularly the Renaissance essayist, Michel de Montaigne, whose works Shakespeare certainly knew. Bacon and Jonson in England also favoured the styles, and a near-contemporary of Shakespeare, John Donne (1572–1631) was a master of them. They were reactions against the proportioned, elegant style of Cicero. Symmetrical, well-balanced sentences were replaced by asymmetrical, uneven ones, and the aim was not to express finished, rounded thoughts, but to give the impression of 'the mind at work' – the fits and starts of thought processes: not thoughts themselves, 'but a mind thinking'.[(11)] One consequence of this desire to capture thoughts in action was for the writing to appear to be spontaneous, and this led to a disdain for the practice of revising and polishing sentences before they appeared. Other consequences were a jerky, uneven style, characteristic of un-worked-out thought, and an absence of anything that was not essential to getting the message across. Here are two vivid descriptions which capture these characteristics. One comes from the seventeenth-century British writer John Aubrey, who cites Dr Kettle (a president of Trinity College, Oxford) as saying that Seneca 'writes as a Boare does pisse, by jirkes'. The second is that the style 'is as hard-bitten, as free of soft and superfluous flesh, as "one of Caesar's soldiers"'.[(12)]

Notice that we have so far referred to baroque styles, in the plural. There were in fact two main ones which could be distinguished, even though they had much in common, and often indeed 'run into each other'.[(13)] To understand the differences, the styles can be seen as different ways of reacting to a central characteristic of the Ciceronian style – the elaborate use of subordinate clauses, together with the connectors that introduce them. If one wishes to escape from these, there are two possibilities. One is to eliminate connectors as much as possible, producing a series of short simple sentences, or longer sentences where the links between the clauses are left unspecified, often relying on punctuation to join the parts together. The result will be a feeling of 'curtness', which is what leads this to be called the <u>curt style</u>. Notice the short sentences in Text 5. The passage is indeed quite difficult to understand, because the connections between the sentences are not immediately clear. Text 6 is also made up of simple sentences, joined together by punctuation (commas and semi-colons).

Text 5 is from *Measure for Measure*, a play dated 1603–4. Some of Shakespeare's later plays, particularly *The Winter's Tale* (1609–10) and *Cymbeline* (1610-11) display an even 'curter' style, and this is certainly one reason why many readers find particular difficulty with the language of these plays: too much curtness leads to bare, almost telegraphic speeches which are sometimes difficult to interpret.

But short sentences were not a necessary hallmark of baroque styles, and indeed the sentences could be as long as in Ciceronian style. This is because the second way of reacting against Ciceronian subordination is to continue using connectors but to link clauses together in a loose and casual manner. This style came to be called the <u>loose style</u>. It tends to use a small number of common link words like *and, or, which, whereto, wherein* and these are repeated many times. You also find many clauses using what are called <u>absolute-participle constructions</u>. These constructions use an *-ing* or an *-ed* form in a clause which stands independently from the rest of the sentence (the Latin word *absolutus* meaning 'complete' conveys this sense of independence). One characteristic of these phrases (which are not very common in PDE) is that their relationship with the rest of the sentence is often rather loose or unclear. For example, a sentence like *The clock striking six, we went home* can suggest a reason ('because the clock struck six we went home' – i.e. it was late) or maybe just an 'attendant circumstance' ('the clock struck six and we went home'). Text 7, from Jonson, illustrates this style. There are quite a few connectors, but they produce coordination rather than subordination.

The linking of sentences and parts of sentences together in the loose style is described above as 'loose and casual'. A technique which helps to create this impression is the use of 'immediately preceding reference'. This is where a clause (introduced for example by a relative like *which* or *that*) follows on from the last idea mentioned in the previous clause. There is a good example of this in Hamlet's 'vicious mole' speech. Notice there how in the third line (*As in their birth, wherein they are not guilty*) the clause beginning *wherein* relates to the immediately preceding word *birth*. Doing this a lot leads to the impression that the sentences are made up of a sequence of loosely linked parts, one following on from the other. As Coleridge puts it, talking of Seneca, the phrases are 'strung like beads, without any causation or progression'.[14]

Notice that the above example is taken from a speech used earlier in this chapter to characterise not baroque but Ciceronian style. How can one passage illustrate two so diametrically-opposed styles? The answer is that such was the richness of rhetorical styles at the time, that authors had a tendency to mix them, and it is rare to find passages which are pure examples of one style or another. One of the key phrases of this chapter is therefore 'stylistic intermingling'.

We noted earlier that Ciceronian style placed emphasis on sentence ends, with the reader being kept in 'suspense' until the end of the sentence. Partly as a reaction against this, baroque style writers often began with the main point, what Montaigne called *le dernier poinct*, the point aimed at. Subsequent sentences develop, and re-express this main point, often viewing it from different perspectives. Texts 5 and 6 on the Text Page illustrate this well. The first sentence of Text 5 is the summary sentence and expresses the main point Lucio is making. In the same way, the second sentence of Text 6 is simply an expansion of what is said in sentence 1. In the next paragraph, two further characteristics of baroque styles are discussed. These are also considered in parts (i) and (ii) of Activity 6 (*Some 'boar-like' qualities*). If you wish to do this Activity, do so before reading the paragraph, but leave part (iii) until later (**NP**).

Another baroque characteristic that contributes significantly to the jerky, inelegant feeling to sentences, is that clauses and sentences often have different subjects. But if inelegant sentences are the result, they are also ones which more closely capture the (jerky, inelegant) way people actually talk. Text 6 is a good example. If we consider the semicolons as functioning like full stops (as discussed later in 8.3.5), then each sentence has a different grammatical subject (*I, he, the earth, the basest horn*). The same characteristic is found in Text 5 to an extent, though here not every new sentence has a new subject. This text also illustrates another characteristic that interrupts the smooth flow which was so important to the Ciceronian style – that there are sharp changes from literal to metaphorical and back again. The 'metaphorical' sentence in Text 5 is the second, about sparrows. Before and after it are 'literal' sentences about the desirability of the Duke's return. Text 7 on the Text Page shows particularly well the jerky rhythm of baroque prose ('as a Boare does pisse', allegedly). Part (iii) of Activity 6 invites you to paraphrase Text 7.

Here, finally, is a description of baroque sentences taken from an influential essay written in 1929 by the American scholar, Morris Croll. In it, he mentions anacoluthon. This is a rhetorical device (the topic of the next section) where a sentence is not grammatically well-constructed, and passes 'from one construction to another before the former is completed' (*OED*). 'The syntactic connections of a sentence become loose and casual', Croll says, 'great strains are imposed upon tenuous, frail links; parentheses are abused; . . . anacoluthon is frequent and passes unnoticed; even the limits of sentences are not clearly marked, and it is sometimes difficult to say where one begins and another ends' (1929: 108).

6.5 Rhetorical devices

The origins of rhetoric, as we have seen, were associated with the law, centring round verbal oratory and the art of persuasion: 'it taught you how to win over friends, and either persuade enemies or make them look ridiculous'.[15] Mediaeval rhetorical handbooks instructed people how to deliver an argument (recall that in mediaeval European universities, rhetoric was one of the 'trivium' of basic subjects). So the handbooks included areas – all with Latin names – like 'structuring your argument' (*Dispositio* in Latin) and 'delivering an argument using appropriate voice techniques and gestures' (*Pronunciatio*). By far the most popular area was *Elocutio* which entailed looking at 'stylistic ornaments' or 'rhetorical devices'. Most Renaissance rhetorical handbooks focused on this area.

The devices themselves usually had Greek or Latin names, and some were very obscure indeed. When for example did you last use the rhetorical device of *bdelygmia*?[16] Obscure it may be, but a search on an internet search engine gives no fewer than 3720 hits. For the record, *bdelygmia* is delivering a 'litany of abuse', usually through a series of pejorative adjectives. Here is an extreme example in an 1859 letter from Edward Lear to Lady Strachey where he describes a lady to whom he did not take: 'A vile beastly rottenheaded foolbegotten brazenthroated pernicious piggish screaming, tearing, roaring, perplexing, splitmecrackle crashmecriggle insane ass of a woman is practising howling below-stairs with a brute of a singingmaster so horribly, that my head is nearly off'. Shakespeare contains a number of such litanies (though not necessarily based around adjectives. At a certain point in *A Midsummer Night's Dream*, for example, the fact that Hermia is a small lady is the subject of discussion. Here is how Lysander addresses her (3.2.328): *Get you gone, you dwarf;/ You minimus, of hindering knot-grass made;/ You bead, you acorn* ('knot-grass' was a weed which if digested was supposed to stunt growth). As mentioned in 2.1, where elaborate, colourful, lengthy insults are concerned, Thersites in *Troilus and Cressida* has no rivals.

Puttenham tried to provide English names for the rhetorical devices. Thus there is one device called *syllepsis*, which is where two expressions using the same verb (but with a slightly different meaning) are joined together. For example, the British comedy singers Flanders and Swann (popular in the 1950s) have a song about a lady being seduced by a man. She is nervous and takes a drink. She raises (Flanders and Swann say) 'her glass, her courage, her eyes and his hopes'.[17] Here the verb *raise* has four objects (glass, courage, eyes and hopes). But it means something different in *raise her glass* and *raise his hopes*. Benedick in *Much Ado About Nothing* uses syllepsis when he says *Let's have a dance ere we are married, that we may lighten our own hearts and our wives' heels* (5.4.115). Puttenham calls *syllepsis* 'the double supply', because the single verb 'supplies' two or more objects.

When you come across lists of rhetorical devices, you may well wonder whether it is worth learning about them. Will we really understand Shakespeare better if we know what a *zeugma* or a *polyptoton* is? Certainly this is of restricted value. Shakespeare's work is so much more than a museum of dead rhetorical figures. But it is worth knowing something about the devices because they were part of the scenery of Renaissance intellectual life. Vickers (1970: 133) talks of the number of rhetorical texts in the Renaissance, and says that 'if each text was issued in an average of 1000 copies, and if each copy was read by anything from one reader to the dozens using a school text, then we have a total of several million Europeans who had a working knowledge of rhetoric'. European interest in the area went far beyond the Renaissance indeed; as Vickers also says: 'every person who had a grammar-school education in Europe between Ovid and Pope knew by heart, familiarly, up to a hundred figures, by their right names'.[18] Ovid was born in 43 BC, and Pope died in 1744, so we are talking about a massive span of history. Puttenham's *Arte of English Poesie* (a book mentioned earlier, in 3.1.1, 6.3 and elsewhere) appeared in 1589, and it is a book that Shakespeare doubtless knew.

Rhetorical devices are sometimes divided into <u>tropes</u> (also called turns), and <u>figures</u> (or schemes). The former involve some 'change of meaning'. An example might be the trope of *litotes* which is a kind of understatement. If you say *Shakespeare is no ordinary writer* you are using the phrase *no ordinary* to mean *extraordinary*. Figures may also involve changes of meaning, but their basis is to do with patterning – for example using repetitions or parallel phrases for rhetorical effect. As an illustration: in *isocolon*, phrases of the same length are used in parallel, as in this passage from *Richard III*:

She for an Edward weeps, and so do I:
I for a Clarence weep, so doth not she.
These babes for Clarence weep, and so do I:
I for an Edward weep, so do not they.
(2.2.82)

There is a good website http://www.virtualsalt.com/rhetoric.htm which contains examples of the main rhetorical devices, and is worth a look. Many books on Renaissance/Shakespeare's language contain lists of devices, as do books dealing with rhetoric (like Leith, 2011). Activity 7 (*Tropes and figures*) provides definitions and examples of six common ones.

It is not necessary to know the names of the rhetorical devices to appreciate Shakespeare's huge command of them. To end this section, we can illustrate his command by looking in detail at part of a famous speech from *Julius Caesar* (the one beginning *Friends, Romans, countrymen, lend me your ears*). Julius Caesar has been murdered by Brutus and his fellow conspirators. Antony, Caesar's friend, gives the speech at the dead ruler's funeral. He wants to condemn the murder, but has to be careful how he does so, because Brutus is now the man in charge. How does he manage these two tasks simultaneously – praising Caesar (as is appropriate at his funeral) while at the same time aiming to avoid upsetting his killers? Activity 8 (*All honourable men*) invites you to consider the rhetorical shape of the speech in detail. If you want to do this Activity, do so now, before reading the paragraph after the speech. It is useful background information to know that earlier (on the Lupercal feast day – 15th February) Antony offered to make Caesar king, and he refused three times (**NP**).

The noble Brutus

Hath told you Caesar was ambitious.
If it were so, it was a grievous fault,
And grievously hath Caesar answered it.
Here, under leave of Brutus and the rest –
For Brutus is an honourable man;
So are they all, all honourable men –
Come I to speak in Caesar's funeral.
He was my friend, faithful and just to me;
But Brutus says he was ambitious,
And Brutus is an honourable man.
He hath brought many captives home to Rome,
Whose ransoms did the general coffers fill:
Did this in Caesar seem ambitious?
When that the poor have cried, Caesar hath wept;
Ambition should be made of sterner stuff:
Yet Brutus says he was ambitious,
And Brutus is an honourable man.
You all did see that on the Lupercal
I thrice presented him a kingly crown,
Which he did thrice refuse. Was this ambition?

Yet Brutus says he was ambitious,
And sure he is an honourable man.
(JC 3.2.78)

Antony is of course here indulging in irony, though the extent to which this is made plain in the speech's delivery on stage will differ from production to production. He is probably being ironical when he calls Brutus *noble*, but the most ironical of phrases is *And Brutus is an honourable man/So are they all, all honourable men*. Notice the way this phrase keeps being repeated, the repetitions adding to the heaviness of the irony.

A major feature of the structure of Antony's speech is that he mentions some example of Caesar's unambitious behaviour, asks whether the behaviour shows ambition (which it clearly does not), then says that Brutus considered it so, which is followed by a piece of irony. This pattern occurs a number of times. A clear example starts in line 12, where Antony points out that Caesar caught many prisoners and collected ransoms for them. Was this ambitious, Antony asks? Brutus says so, he claims two lines later (17). Then comes the irony (*And Brutus is an honourable man*).

A number of words which are syntactically or semantically similar occur in close succession in the speech, serving to emphasise points being made and to create a balanced structure to the discourse. Examples are *grievous* and *grievously* in lines 3 and 4; the word *all* repeated in 7 and elsewhere; *cried* and *wept* in 15, and *thrice* in 20 and 21.

6.6 Energy and growth

When we consider, as we have done in this chapter, characteristic Shakespearean sentences and uses of rhetorical devices, we are not saying nearly all that could be said about his 'style'. He is, of course, a dramatist, and the styles of his speeches are the styles of the characters who make them: it is not (on one level at least) Shakespeare talking, but Macbeth, Hamlet, Falstaff and the rest. But it is certainly useful to know something of the styles of the age, if only to get some sense of how listeners and readers in his time would have reacted to what his characters say.

The chapter has two key phrases. One is 'stylistic richness'. As we have seen, there was much interest in rhetoric and the 'art of writing' in Renaissance England, and the result is a variety of styles, many of which – at some point or another – make their way into Shakespeare's works. The other key phrase is 'stylistic intermingling'. Though different styles dominate at various times, you certainly do not find one play written in Style X and another in Style Y, and often elements of various styles are found in the same speech, let alone the same play. It is just as we found in Chapter 2 in relation to lexis. 'Creative chaos' was the phrase used there. What we encounter in relation to rhetoric too is not purism, but energy and growth.

Text page

Text 1

Sonnet 29

> *When, in disgrace with Fortune and men's eyes,*
> *I all alone beweep my outcast state,*
> *And trouble deaf heaven with my bootless cries,*
> *And look upon myself and curse my fate,*
> *Wishing me like to one more rich in hope,*
> *Featured like him, like him with friends possessed,*
> *Desiring this man's art and that man's scope,*
> *With what I most enjoy contented least;*
> *Yet in these thoughts myself almost despising,*
> *Haply I think on thee, and then my state*
> *(Like to the lark at break of day arising)*
> *From sullen earth sings hymns at heaven's gate;*
> > *For thy sweet love remembered such wealth brings*
> > *That then I scorn to change my state with kings.*

Text 2

Horatio is describing to Hamlet how the watchmen saw a ghost (which turns out to be the ghost of Hamlet's father; Ham 1.2.196):

Two nights together had these gentlemen,
Marcellus and Barnardo, on their watch
In the dead waste and middle of the night
Been thus encountered:

Text 3

Falstaff's very first words in Shakespeare (in the second scene of *Henry IV, Part I*: 1.2.2) are met by a barrage of (highly elegant!) abuse from **Prince Hal**, later to become Henry V. Falstaff is doubtless suffering from a hangover:

Falstaff: *Now Hal, what time of day is it lad?*
Prince Hal: *Thou art so fat-witted with drinking of old sack, and unbuttoning*
                thee after supper, and sleeping upon benches after noon, that thou
                hast forgotten to demand that truly which thou wouldst truly
                know. What a devil hast thou to do with the time of the day?
                Unless hours were cups of sack, and minutes capons, and clocks
                the tongues of bawds, and dials the signs of leaping-houses, and
                the blessed sun himself a fair hot wench in flame-coloured taffeta,
                I see no reason why thou shouldst be so superfluous to demand the
                time of the day.

Text 4

Here are **King Claudius'** first words in *Hamlet*, at the beginning of Act 1,
Scene 2. He is talking about the death of his brother, King Hamlet (the hero's
father). Claudius says that while it is necessary to be sorrowful, we also need
to think about ourselves and the future:

Though yet of Hamlet our dear brother's death
The memory be green, and that it us befitted
To bear our hearts in grief, and our whole kingdom
To be contracted in one brow of woe,
Yet so far hath discretion fought with nature
That we with wisest sorrow think on him
Together with remembrance of ourselves.
(Ham 1.2.1)

Text 5

In *Measure for Measure*, the Duke goes away leaving his deputy Angelo in
charge, who passes a decree against sexual misadventure in the province.
No-one is happy with this decree, as **Lucio** here complains (3.2.163):

I would the Duke we talk of were returned again. This ungenitured agent will
unpeople the province with continency. Sparrows must not build in his house-eaves
because they are lecherous. The Duke yet would have dark deeds darkly answered.
He would never bring them to light. Would he were returned.

Text 6

In *Henry V* (3.7.15), the French **Dauphin** is praising his horse:

When I bestride him, I soar, I am a hawk. He trots the air; the earth sings when he touches it; the basest horn of his hoof is more musical than the pipe of Hermes.

Text 7

In Jonson's play *Every Man out of His Humour* (1600), Delirio is besotted by his own wife, and wishes to please her. In this extract, Macilente suggests a way in which Delirio might ingratiate himself with his wife (5.5.14):

Your wife's brother, signior Fungoso, being at supper to-night at a tavern, with a sort of gallants, there happened some division amongst them, and he is left in pawn for the reckoning. Now, if ever you look that time shall present you with an happy occasion to do your wife some gracious and acceptable service, take hold of this opportunity, and presently go and redeem him; for, being her brother, and his credit so amply engaged as now it is, when she shall hear, (as he cannot himself, but he must out of extremity report it,) that you came, and offered yourself so kindly, and with that respect of his reputation; why, the benefit cannot but make her dote, and grow mad of your affections.

Activity section

1 Particular men   (AS)

(i)   Use the glossary to ensure you understand the meaning of all the individual words in the 'vicious mole' passage.

(ii) In order to help clarify the structure and meaning of the passage as a whole, write one sentence that captures its main point. Using Hamlet's words (rather than writing paraphrases), make your sentence as short as possible, capturing only the main idea. The sentence might begin 'It chances that particular men . . .'

2 Common clause types

The common subordination conjunctions mentioned in the text are;

in order to	*before*	*where*	*which*
because	*that*	*if*	*when*
like	*although*	*so*	

(i)   Here are just some of the common clause types: we can speak of relative clauses, conditional clauses, purpose clauses and so on. Associate the conjunctions above with these types:

(a) relatives

(b) conditionals (talking about something which may happen)

(c) purpose

(d) reason

(e) result

(f) time

(g) place

(h) manner

(i) concession (expressing some kind of qualification)

(ii) Now look at these examples from PDE and associate each with one of these clause types:

(a) He arrived early so that he wouldn't miss the train.

(b) Before he went online, he did his homework

(c) She ran fast, as though her life depended on it

(d) Although it rained hard, he managed to stay dry

(e) The pen that I used was John's

(f) If Mark swims well, he'll win the competition

(g) She worked hard before the exams because she wanted to go to university

(h) Where she lived, the weather was always good

(i) She finished her work, so she left early

3 The vicious mole   (AS)

Look back at the 'vicious mole' speech from *Hamlet*. Here are some operations to perform on the text which may help to reveal (and hopefully unravel) the complexities of the speech:

(i) Identify three connectors used in the passage.

(ii) Here are some specific questions, mostly concerned with identifying antecedents:

(a) One possible meaning of *wherein* is 'of which'. Of what?

(b) *Since* can be used to offer an explanation. What is being explained here?

(c) *By the o'ergrowth of some complexion* describes the manner in which something happens. What?

(d) What breaks down the *pales and forts of reasons*?

(e) Who carry the *stamp of one defect*?

(f) What is described as *nature's livery*?

(g) What does *they* in line 11 refer to? (More than one answer possible here).

(iii) Now that you have looked in detail at the structure of the 'vicious mole' speech, write a 'translation' of it in PDE.

4 Shakespeare: the bare bones

In this speech of Prospero's from *The Tempest*, he admits that it is time he told his daughter, Miranda, more about recent and past events. Below the speech is Dryden's version of it, intended to clear away unnecessary rhetoric. Compare the two versions, identify the changes Dryden has made, and consider his reasons for making them.

Shakespeare's version

'Tis time

I should inform thee farther. Lend thy hand,
And pluck my magic garment from me. – So,
Lie there, my art. – Wipe thou thine eyes. Have comfort.
The direful spectacle of the wrack, which touched
The very virtue of compassion in thee,
I have with such provision in mine art
So safely ordered, that there is no soul –
No, not so much perdition as an hair
Betid to any creature in the vessel
Which thou heard'st cry, which thou sawst sink. Sit down.
For thou must now know farther.
(Tem 1.2.22)

Dryden's version

I should inform thee further: Wipe thine eyes, have comfort; the direful spectacle of the Wreck, which touched the very spirit of compassion in thee, I have with such a pity order'd that not one creature on the ship is lost.
Summers (1966)

5 Clause and phrase clusters   (AS)

The 'vicious mole' speech is a good example of the way clusters of clauses and phrases occur in Ciceronian sentences. Look first at the last seven lines, and assume that the subject is *these men*. Identify the main verb, and note where in the sentence it comes. Notice the clauses and phrases 'piling up' before it.

Then, to see the full extent of the 'piling-up', look at the clauses and phrases in the first half of the passage.

6 Some 'boar-like' qualities   (AS)

(i)   A characteristic of baroque styles about to be discussed in the text is that the grammatical subjects often change from one sentence to the next, creating the sense of shifting focuses. Consider this in relation to Text 6. Count the semicolons as full stops, and note what the subjects are for each sentence.

(ii)   Another characteristic about to be discussed in the text is the way the style can quickly shift from the literal to the metaphorical and back again. Find an example of this in Text 5, where there is one clearly metaphorical sentence.

(iii) Try and produce a PDE paraphrase of Text 7. Doing this will enable you to focus on the sentence structures in a detailed way, and gain an appreciation of how 'jerky' the style is (**AS**).

7 Tropes and figures   (AS)

Here are six rhetorical devices taken from a list provided by Brook (1976). Below the definitions are examples of each. Match the definitions and examples:

Definitions

1   *Alliteration*: We have already come across this (in 6.4.1), in relation to euphuism. It is 'front rhyme', where the beginnings of words (rather than their ends) have the same sound.

2   *Parison*: Repeating a word or structure 'in which within adjacent clauses or sentences word corresponds to word (either repeating the same word, or else grouping noun with noun, adjective with adjective etc.)' (Vickers 1970). Puttenham, by the way, who gave English names to rhetorical devices, called *Parison* the 'figure of even'.

3   *Diaeresis*: 'the logical division of a genus into its species. Each species is briefly described and this description provides a definition' (Brook, 1976). In short, a list of subcategories.

4   *Hendiadys*: Words (often nouns or adjectives) are linked together by *and*. An interesting one, this, discussed in a paper by Wright (1981), who says Shakespeare uses it no less than 300 times, most of all in *Hamlet*. Take a random look through *Hamlet* and you will soon come across examples.

5   *Hypallage*: Taking words which normally go together and mismatching them with others in a list.

6   *Hyperbole*: The *OED*'s definition: 'A figure of speech consisting in exaggerated or extravagant statement, used to express strong feeling or produce a strong impression, and not intended to be understood literally'.

Examples

(a) These two phrases from *Hamlet* illustrate the same rhetorical device:
     The abstract and brief chronicles of the time (2.2.522)
     The book and volume of my brain (1.5.103)

(b) **Rivers** remembers Queen Margaret's curses when her son was killed (R3, 3.3.17):
     Then curs'd she Richard, then curs'd she Buckingham,
     Then curs'd she Hastings.

(c) Here is **Portia** expressing her love for Bassanio (MV 3.2.150):
     though for myself alone
     I would not be ambitious in my wish
     To wish myself much better, yet for you
     I would be trebled twenty times myself,
     A thousand times more fair, ten thousand times
     More rich,

(d) **Bottom** (in MND 4.1.209) often has trouble with words. Here he is describing (or failing to describe!) his dream:
     The eye of man hath not heard, the ear of man hath not seen, man's hand is not able to taste, his tongue to conceive, nor his heart to report what my dream was!

(e) In *As You Like It* (4.1.10) **Rosalind** describes Jaques as a 'melancholy fellow'. He is anxious to explain just what kind of 'melancholy' he has:

I have neither the scholar's melancholy, which is emulation; nor the
musician's, which is fantastical; nor the courtier's, which is proud; nor
the soldier's, which is ambitious; nor the lawyer's, which is politic; nor the
lady's, which is nice; nor the lover's, which is all these: but it is a melancholy
of mine own . . .

(f) **Pyramus** prepares to kill himself in the play put on by Bottom and
friends near the end of *A Midsummer Night's Dream* (5.1.145):
Whereat, with blade, with bloody blameful blade,
He bravely broached his boiling bloody breast

Many of these devices are figures rather than tropes. Identify some figures.

8 All honourable men

The aim of this Activity is to develop some understanding of how Antony's
speech is structured, as he tries to praise dead Caesar without antagonising his
killers. To do this, it is not necessary to have very much specialised knowledge
of the names of parts of speech (though you do need to know what irony is).

One of his main tools is of course irony. Specify the points where you suspect Antony of being ironical.

At a number of points in the speech, examples of Caesar's behaviour are
given, and Antony asks whether these show ambition; this is followed by a
statement that Brutus considered it so, and a piece of irony. Identify the
sequences where this happens.

There is a sentence which is repeated several times. Identify it. What
rhetorical purpose is served by its repetition?

There are a few examples where words which are structurally or semantically
similar are repeated. Find these.

Extended activities

1   Not for the first time in this book, 6.1 asks the question: why is
    Shakespeare so hard to read and understand? Think now about how
    you would answer this question (perhaps to someone who has just
    encountered Shakespeare for the first time).

2   6.3 talks about the notion of 'renaissance', and looking back to an
    earlier time in history as a 'Golden Age'. To appreciate how steeped in
    classical times Shakespeare was, find a list of his plays online; there
    are several sites which also give details of the plots (for example:

http://www.shakespeare-online.com/plots/). Come up with a percentage of how many of the plays are set in classical times, or are situated geographically in Greece, Italy or other areas associated with the classical world.

The very notion of 'looking back to a "better", earlier time' (especially with the degree of obsession displayed in the Renaissance) may be a little curious to us today. Or is it? Is there a Golden Age today that people look back to?

3   6.4.1 provides a list of characteristics associated with the Ciceronian style. Focusing on a play of your choice, find passages which exhibit some of these characteristics. Or, if the play is one of the later ones, you may wish to search instead for 'baroque' characteristics, as discussed in 6.4.2.

4   6.5 deals with rhetorical devices. But no definition of rhetorical device is given. Find definitions (on the internet or elsewhere). Then skim through a play of your choice looking for examples of rhetorical devices in action. Identify the tropes and figures that are exhibited in the examples you find.

Answer section

Non-finite verbs (section 6.2)

Example (a) is type 2; (b) is 4; (c) 1; (d) 3; (e) 1; (f) 3; (g) 4; (h) 2.

Clauses in Sonnet 29 (section 6.4.1)

These are: When . . . I all alone beweep; and trouble deaf heaven . . . ; and look upon myself . . . ; wishing me like . . . ; Featured like him . . . ; like him with friends possessed; desiring this man's art . . . ; and (desiring) that man's scope; With what . . . contented least; Yet . . . myself almost despising; Haply I think on thee; and then my state . . . sings; at break of day . . . arising; thy sweet love remembered . . . ; then I scorn.

Brackets in 'vicious mole' speech (section 6.4.1)

Being nature's livery or fortune's star might be in brackets. Another possibility might be *be they as pure as grace.*

'Turning point' in Bacon passage (section 6.4.1)

This occurs at the words 'than after the weight'. The passage is based on a 'more . . . than' structure. Before the 'turning point' it is the 'more' that is being developed; thereafter the sentence focuses on the 'than' part.

Activity 1 Particular men

(ii) One possibility: 'It chances that particular men shall take corruption from a particular fault'. It is also possible that the subject of *shall* in line 13 is 'virtues', in which case the sentence might read: 'It chances that the virtues of particular men shall take corruption from a particular fault'.

Activity 3 The vicious mole

(i)   Connectors are 'that', 'wherein', 'since'.

(ii) (a) of their birth; (b) why the men are not guilty; (c) such men's virtues are swamped and they take corruption; (d) the excessive growth of some natural trait; (e) the men being referred to ('these men'); (f) any defect they possess; (g) either 'these men', or their virtues.

(iii) One possible version:
'So it often happens in particular people that because of some vicious defect in their nature, like their birth (which they are not guilty of, because we can't choose where we come from), through the excessive growth of some natural trait, which often destroys the boundaries and defences of reason, or through some habit which encroaches too much on the form of pleasing behaviour – that these men, having, as I have said, the mark of one defect, being nature's uniform or predestined by fortune, whatever other virtues he has, even if they are as pure as virtue and as infinite as is possible for a human, shall in the general opinion become corrupted by that single fault.'

Activity 5 Clause and phrase clusters

The main verb is 'take (corruption)', and it occurs almost at the end of the passage. The pile-up of clauses and phrases between the subject 'these men' and the verb 'take (corruption)' include: 'carrying . . . the stamp of one defect', 'being nature's livery or fortune's star', 'his virtues else', 'be they as pure as grace', 'as infinite as man may undergo', 'in the general censure'.

The clauses and phrases in the first half of the passage are 'oft it chances . . . that', 'for some vicious mole . . .', 'as in their birth', 'wherein they are not guilty', 'since nature cannot choose his origin', 'by the o'ergrowth of some complexion', 'oft breaking down . . . of reason', 'or by some habit', 'that too much o'er-leavens . . . plausive manners'.

Activity 6 Some 'boar-like' qualities

(iii) A loose, colloquial paraphrase might be:

> 'Your wife's brother, Signor Fungoso, was having supper tonight in a tavern with a group of fops. They had a disagreement, and he was in danger of having to pay the bill. If ever you had a good chance to do your wife some gracious and welcome service, this is it. Seize the opportunity and go and help him out. Because it's her brother, and his finances are tied up at present. She'll hear – and when push comes to shove he will have to tell her – that you have turned up and kindly offered your services, because you are so concerned about his reputation. When she does so, you will benefit because it will make her dote on you, and she'll grow mad with affection.'

Activity 7 Tropes and figures

(a) is an example of 4; (b) of 2; (c) 6; (d) 5; (e) 3; (f) 1.
Alliteration, parison, diaeresis, hendiadys are figures rather than tropes.

Notes

1 The two sites are http://www.brandshome.com and http://wiki.answers.com

2 Sowell (1979: 118).

3 This account is based on Adamson (1999).

4 Vickers (1970: 134).

5 Colney (1900: 167).

6 The example is taken from Ronberg (1992).

7 Adamson (1999: 584).

8 Barish (1960: 117).

9 The passage is cited by Hussey (1982).

10 This section owes much to the account of Croll (1929).

11   The phrase is Croll's (1929: 87), who also uses the word 'asymmetrical'.

12   The first quote is taken from Ronberg (1992). The second is from Croll (1929). The comparison with Caesar's soldiers come from Daniello Bartolli's 'Dello stile, dell' uomo di lettere'. In *Opere*. Venice (3, 101).

13   Croll (1929: 88).

14   From Raysor (1936: 217).

15   The quote is from Vickers (1970:134), who is here talking about the Renaissance interest in rhetoric.

16   This is one of the rhetorical devices which Vickers (1970) discusses.

17   The song's title is *Madeira M'Dear*.

18   Vickers (1970: 394).

Further reading

Histories of rhetoric (providing background which goes well beyond the Elizabethan period) are found in Vickers, B. (1970) *Classical Rhetoric in English Poetry*, Basingstoke: Macmillan, and (more recently) Leith, S. (2011) *You Talkin' To Me?: Rhetoric from Aristotle to Obama*, London: Profile Books, which manages to be both light-hearted and serious at the same time.

Comprehensive coverage, focusing on the period 1476–1776, is provided by Adamson, S. (1999) 'Literary Language', in Lass, R. (ed.) (1999) *Cambridge History of the English Language, Volume 3*, Cambridge: Cambridge University Press, 539–653. For a central focus on Shakespeare, there is Hussey, S. S. (1982) *The Literary Language of Shakespeare*, London: Longman.

Vickers, B. (ed.) (1999) *English Renaissance Literary Criticism*, Oxford: Oxford University Press, is a useful book to dip into. It contains excerpts from important literary texts of the period.

CHAPTER 7

Verse and Prose: Iambic pentameters all the time?

Key phrases:
dissimilitude in similitude; ducking in and out

7.1 Blank verse

7.1.1 What makes poetry special?

M. Jourdain is the main character in Molière's play, *The Bourgeois Gentleman*. He is a man of limited breeding who aspires to be a 'gentleman'. He wants to write a letter to a lady he has fallen for, and seeks advice about whether to write in verse or prose. The distinction is new to him, and he is surprised to learn that 'what isn't verse is prose, and what's not prose is verse'. When told that prose is used for everyday communication, his reaction is: 'Oh, really? So when I say: "Nicole bring me my slippers and fetch my nightcap," is that prose? . . . Well, what do you know about that! These forty years now, I've been speaking in prose without knowing it!'[1]

Except for the likes of M. Jourdain, everyone knows that poetry and prose are different. But it is not that easy to articulate what the differences are. Activity 1 (*What makes poetry special?*) invites you to think about these differences, and to identify characteristics of some poetry forms (**NP**).

Your answer to the question 'What makes poetry special?' may well involve issues of content and vocabulary – poetry is often associated with a particular type of subject matter (love, death, etc.), and diction (a word which came in for discussion in 3.2). But the examples in Activity 1 indicate that poetry is different in form from prose, as well as showing that many more than one type of form are associated with poetry. These different forms or genres are fashionable at different times. Passage (a) in Activity 1 is an example of alliteration, a technique mentioned earlier in 3.5. It was popular in the Old English period, though it has had a revival in more recent times, for example in the poetry of Gerard Manley Hopkins (1844–1889). Passage (b) is 'rap' – a type of music developed in the 1970s, which has strong rhythm and beat. Example (c) is written in pairs of rhyming lines (heroic couplets), a form very popular in the eighteenth century. Example (d) is a limerick.

Passage (e) is an example of blank verse, a verse form popular in Shakespeare's time. It uses a rhythmic scheme known as the iambic pentameter (or IP as we shall call it). In a documentary about Shakespeare in modern times, one of Al Pacino's informants expresses himself thus: 'everybody says, all the time, iambic pentameter, Shakespeare, iambic pentameter – what is that supposed to mean?'.[2] The purpose of this section is to explain what it is 'supposed to mean'. This will take us into the fundamentals of metre, starting with the notion of a syllable. If you already know these fundamentals, then simply skip the section (or portions of it). Also, the chapter has rather more activities than others, and you may decide to miss out some of these where they deal with areas you are familiar with.

7.1.2 Syllables

It is quite easy to recognise syllables. Most people can do it most of the time without difficulty. But as with many linguistic concepts, it is not all as simple as it looks. It is, for example, often difficult to say where one syllable begins and ends. Also, to define the syllable rigorously is anything but easy. The box below discusses:

Syllables explained . . . in words of one syllable

The phonetician David Abercrombie (1967) makes the point that 'most people seem able to say, without much difficulty, how many syllables are contained in a given word or utterance'. But, he goes on to say, 'writers on linguistics have nevertheless not found it at all easy to say *what* a syllable is' (1967: 34).

One major theory associates it with a pulse of air pushed out from the lungs with muscular pressure. To understand this theory you need to realise how vowels and consonants (the units that make up syllables) differ in the way they are produced. With a vowel, none of the vocal organs (tongue, teeth, palate, lips, etc.) are touching each other or are close to each other. Air escapes with relative freedom from the mouth. But with a consonant, the air stream is blocked or partially blocked by organs which touch or nearly touch. To appreciate the difference, say a vowel like [e], as in the word *bet*. Then say a consonant like [p] as in *pit*. Notice that with the consonant two vocal organs (in this case the lips) are touching as you pronounce the sound.

A syllable can potentially have three parts. The 'centre' comes when air escapes relatively freely out from the mouth, without being restricted by any vocal organs blocking that exit by touching each other. Thus, as Abercrombie puts it, 'a vowel is the nucleus or central part of the syllable' (1967: 39).

The vowel is central to most syllables, and some syllables are made up of just a vowel. The word *I*, for example, consists of just the vowel/diphthong – [ai]. But sometimes consonants come before and/or after the central vowel. You can think of the consonant coming before the vowel as the release of air which leads into the vowel (and indeed this consonant is sometimes called the <u>releasing consonant</u>). In the word *see*, for example, the [s] leads into the vowel [i:]. There may also be an <u>arresting consonant</u> after the vowel. In the word *cease*, both the releasing consonant and the arresting consonant are [s]. This one-syllable word has three elements – CVC (for Consonant – Vowel – Consonant).

As is clear from this explanation, syllables may be broken down into constituent parts – vowels and consonants. Many writing systems use these component parts as their bases. But for some, the unit is the syllable. Symbols in Japanese stand for syllables. Societies like the ancient Greeks develop symbols for vowels and consonants, the component parts. These are <u>alphabets</u>. An advantage over syllable-based systems is that they require fewer symbols.

Here is some advice to help with syllable recognition. The central thing to listen for is a vowel. There is such a thing as the 'vowel-less syllable' – the word *Sh!*, for example.[3] But usually counting syllables is largely a question of counting vowels. So *hat* is a one-syllable word (a monosyllable), *hated* a two-syllable word (a disyllable), and *ignoring* a trisyllable. As the box shows, syllables can start with a vowel instead of a consonant (*at* instead of *hat*). Be warned, though, that we are here talking about spoken, not written vowels. So though the word *hate* has two vowels in the written language (*a* and *e*), the second one is unpronounced, and the word thus has one, not two syllables. The word *hate* also shows that diphthongs count as single units. *Hate*, in phonetic script, is [heɪt]. This shows the vowel sound has two elements: [e] and [ɪ]. It is a diphthong. But it is pronounced as one sound, so the word is a monosyllable (diphthongs are discussed in more detail in 9.4.1). If you need practice at counting syllables, look at Activity 2 (*Counting syllables*). Do just part (i) at the moment.

Syllables in Shakespeare are more or less as in PDE. There are some small differences. It is likely, for example, that *Henry* could be pronounced as *Henery* – as a trisyllable, that is. But there is an inflexion that needs special attention. It is the *-ed* ending, used in the simple past tense and in past participles, including when they function as adjectives (as in *tired* for example). In PDE the *-ed* ending sometimes adds a syllable to a a word it is attached to, sometimes not. In the case of *help → helped* for example, the ending is pronounced as [t], without a vowel, so the number of syllables stays the same. But with *want – wanted* the *-ed* is pronounced [ɪd] Since the ending contains a vowel, the word changes from monosyllable to disyllable. There are also some special cases in PDE where we pronounce the ending [ed], and put an accent over the 'e' in spelling, to indicate this. An example is *blessed*, as in the biblical *Blesséd are those who mourn*). If you want practice at working out whether the *-ed* ending adds a syllable to a word or not in PDE, do Activity 3 (*Modern -ed*).

In Shakespeare it was possible to put in a vowel or not, so the word *helped* could be pronounced [helpt] or [helped], the second being like in *blessed* as discussed above. Sometimes scriveners would put in an apostrophe to indicate it is not pronounced – *help'd*; (look back to 1.5 for discussion about the role of scriveners and others in the transmission process). Later in this chapter we shall see that metrical considerations can determine how *-ed* is pronounced.

Being able to recognise syllables is the first step towards understanding how IPs work. Next comes the notion of stress.

7.1.3 Stress

In words, some syllables are given more prominence, or <u>stress</u>, than others, which means that they are pronounced with more force. If you are a native speaker of English, it is usually easy to identify where the stress in a word comes just by saying it aloud, perhaps in an exaggerated way. The first word in Activity 2 is *introducing*. The stress here comes on the *duc* syllable. One way of marking this would be to underline the vowel in the stressed syllable: *intro<u>du</u>cing*. More commonly, an accent [´] is put over the vowel in the stressed syllable – introdúcing. When the word is monosyllabic, the stress falls of course on the one vowel; as in *hít* – the third word on the Activity 2 list. Part (ii) of Activity 2 practises identifying and marking the stressed syllable in PDE words.

Stress plays a more important role in English than in some other languages. To gain a sense of this, listen to a piece of English being spoken on the radio. It is easy to pick up the way that some syllables are stressed and others not – resulting in a kind of 'unevenness' of delivery. You may wish to do the same with French (there are plenty of websites, including www.listenlive.eu/

france.html which will give you access to French radio stations). The delivery is much more even; it is much more difficult to identify stressed syllables.

Sequences of stressed and unstressed syllables are important for understanding metre in poetry. Using the sign / to indicate a stressed syllable, and x to show an unstressed one, the stress sequence in the word *introducing* is: x x / x. This shows that the third syllable is stressed, and the others are unstressed. If you wish to familiarise yourself with this way of marking stress sequences in individual words, do part (iii) of Activity 2.

So far we have been concentrating on individual words. But the idea of stressed and unstressed elements applies to larger units as well. Consider the phrase *the man*. In normal circumstances (with language use it is always of course easy to find exceptions) the word *man* is stressed, but not the word *the*; in other words the sequence is x /. Now consider a whole sentence: *The man went to the office*. There are three main stresses here, on the words *man, went* and *office*. So a representation of the sentence in terms of stress would be: x / / x x / x. For practice at representing stress sequences in phrases and sentences, look at Activity 4 (*Marking stress sequences*).

The example we have just considered (and others in Activity 4) show that it is what are called <u>content words</u> which are normally stressed – the nouns and verbs, adjectives and adverbs which carry the main sense of the sentence – while the arguably less important <u>grammatical words</u> ('joining' the content words together) tend to be unstressed. The Activity's last sentence is *Mary and her brother saw the film in the evening*. The content words *Mary, brother, saw, film* and *evening* are stressed, while the grammatical words *and, her, the* and *in* are unstressed.

As usual when discussing language, words of warning are necessary, because the above description has been simplified. First of all, which words get stressed will depend a lot on context and what the speaker wants to say. For example, normally the word *and* in the sentence about Mary above would be unstressed; it is a grammatical word. But it would not be difficult to imagine a context in which it might receive high stress. For example, if someone asked *Did Mary see the film, or was it her brother?*, the answer might come back *Mary <u>and</u> her brother saw the film*, where it would be quite legitimate to stress the normally unstressed word *and*. Secondly, it is an oversimplification to say that syllables either carry stress or not. In many words it is possible to identify a <u>secondary stress</u>, coming between main stress and unstressed. Take the word *anatomic* for example. The main stress is on the syllable containing *o*. The second syllable (containing the second *a*) and the last (with *i*) are unstressed, but the initial syllable (like many words with more than three syllables) has a secondary stress. If you say the word aloud, this will become clear.

Earlier in this chapter we considered ways in which poetry made itself special; ways, in other words, that distinguish poetry from normal speech – prose. One difference is that in prose you do not usually find stress sequences which are regular, sentence after sentence. Speakers are just not concerned to speak in such a way that their stress patterns are regular; they are much more focused on getting their message across. Activity 4's last sentence (*Mary and her brother saw the film in the evening*) reveals this. The stress sequence here is /xxx/x/x/xx/x; the distribution of stressed and unstressed syllables is not at all regular. The first stressed syllable is followed by three unstressed ones, the second and third stressed syllables by one unstressed one each, and the fourth by two. Compare this quickly with the stress sequence in a line from Activity 1's Passage (e) – Shakespeare's *In peace there's nothing so becomes a man* which gives x/x/x/x/x/ and the difference will be clear. For further evidence of the lack of regularity of stress in prose, take a look at part (i) of Activity 5 (*Stress sequences in prose and poetry*).

Focusing now on poetry: very often (though not always, as a look back to the examples in Activity 1 will confirm) poetry imposes a pattern on the stress sequences, and this pattern is known as a metre. If you now look at part (ii) of Activity 5, you will detect a regularity in the stressed, unstressed sequences. It is true that the regularity is not total, and you will certainly be able to find sequences that do not follow a strict pattern; part (iii) asks you to do this. We shall deal with the exceptions in a moment. But despite occasional irregularities, the examples show an overwhelming pattern of regularity.

A common way of analysing lines of poetry involves a unit of analysis which takes into account stressed/unstressed sequences. The unit is hence larger than the syllable and smaller than the line; it is called the foot. A full list of the possible feet in English would be long. A common one is the trochee, which is a stressed syllable followed by an unstressed one: /x. The witches in *Macbeth* use a series of four trochees in succession in their line (4.1.10):

/ x / x / x / x
Double, | double, | toil and | trouble

Notice in this example the use of a vertical line | to mark off feet, rather as bars are marked off in music. Other common feet are the phyrric (two unstressed syllables: xx) and the spondee (two stressed syllables //). The first two feet from this line of Hamlet's (3.1.59) show a phyrric followed by a spondee:

x x / /
Or to | take arms | against | a sea | of troubles

But look at the next two feet in this line (*against* and *a sea*). These illustrate the foot which is without doubt the most common one in Shakespeare's verse, and indeed in much of English poetry. It is called the <u>iamb</u> and has an unstressed syllable followed by a stressed one: x/. Henry V's *In peace there's nothing so becomes a man* (3.1.3) is another illustration of a series of iambs. Activity 6 (*Iambic or trochaic?*) provides practice at identifying iambs and trochees in single disyllabic words.

7.1.4 IPs

So, at long last, we have arrived at Shakespeare, and the 'iambic' part of the IP formula. Look now in detail at the *Henry V* passage (e) in Activity 1. The lines were chosen because they well illustrate sequences of iambs, as you will discover if you mark the stress sequence in the same way as you did for the limerick in part (ii) of Activity 5. The lines also well illustrate that to make the lines entirely regular you have to be prepared to exaggerate a little – to read them with a certain lilt, sometimes stressing syllables that would otherwise take secondary stress or even no stress at all, at other times not giving due stress on a content word where you otherwise might expect it. In the first line, for example, your 'lilting' read might put more stress on the *to* in *unto* than in usual speech. But with these little adjustments, the underlying regularity of the metre is apparent:

Once more unto the breach, dear friends, once more   x/x/x/x/x/

So here we have a sequence of iambs. But there is another sort of regularity which is apparent in these lines. It is that the number of stresses per line is five. Hence the word <u>pentameter</u>, from the Ancient Greek *pente* meaning five. The lines are iambic pentameters. We have arrived! In order to develop a stronger feel for the IP, try DeDUMming the lines – saying De for an unstressed syllable, DUM for a stressed. So *Once more unto the breach, dear friends, once more* becomes DeDUM deDUM deDUM, deDUM, deDUM.

In a moment we shall be looking at ways in which Shakespeare often deviates from strict IPs. Before we do this, it is important to gain a feeling for the regular IPs that pervade his work. Take a look at Texts 1–3 on the Text Page. They are passages predominantly written in IPs, taken from different periods of Shakespeare's writing life. Read through these passages now to develop a sense of what IPs are like.

Also before looking at deviations, it is worthwhile thinking of one of a number of measures Shakespeare takes to create regular IPs. In 7.1.2 we looked at the pronunciation of *-ed* in PDE, and noted that in Shakespeare's time it could count as an extra syllable or not. Whether or not it counted as a syllable would depend on whether the line required an extra syllable or not. Activity 7 (-*ed in Shakespeare*) explores this.

7.1.5 Common variations

The IP is the basis of much of Shakespeare's verse. In his early plays, as well as those written at about the same time by contemporaries like Christopher Marlowe, the IPs tended to be regular almost to the point, on occasions, of monotony. But as time passed, more and more variation was introduced – to an extent indeed that often upset later writers (especially in the eighteenth century) who liked their poetry to follow more hard-and-fast rules. Not so Shakespeare. Part of his strength is that he is prepared to break the rules, to produce a flexibility capable of conveying different moods, different characters, different events. What the IP provides is a broad framework, and no more than that. In terms of quantity, the variations are very many, and according to one scholar, 'the lines in Shakespeare's later plays diverge from what we think of as regular meter about twenty percent of the time'.[4] That is one in five lines, and it is certainly true that you can look at almost any speech in any play and find parts of lines which bend the IP rules in various ways. But how can variation be achieved? One way is by changing the stress sequence, so that not all feet are iambs. Another method is to add or miss out syllables, so that not all lines are pentameters. These (and others besides) are used by Shakespeare, and we shall deal with them in turn below. In preparation for this, look again through Texts 1–3 on the Text Page. They were presented earlier as examples of regular IPs. But there are irregular lines even in these passages. Identify the lines which, in one way or another, deviate from the strict IP pattern (**NP**).

Text 1 on the Text Page contains the following line from *The Taming of the Shrew*: *Beggars that come unto my father's door*. The line is a pentameter, and each foot is an iamb except for the first. But this first foot is a trochee which, as we saw earlier in this chapter, follows the sequence *stressed + unstressed*. One way of considering the trochee is as an 'inverted iamb', because it inverts the iamb's order x/ to give /x. Inverting iambic x/ by using trochaic /x is called trochaic inversion, and it is very common in Shakespeare. One way of recognising it easily is to look at the trochee and the iamb that usually follows it. Two iambs together give x/x/. With the inversion you find /xx/, recognisable by the two unstressed syllables coming together in the middle. In DUMdeDUM terms, you have DUMdedeDUM instead of deDUMdeDUM. Take another look through Texts 1–3, and find an example of a line which begins with trochaic inversion (**AS**). This line-initial position is common; here is what Wright (1988: 9) says about trochees: 'Renaissance poets use them especially often at the beginning of the line or at midline following a pause, where they were welcome as a metrical flourish that could enliven the usual pattern'. Activity 8 (*Recognising inversion*) gives practice at finding inversion not just in line-initial positions, but in the middle of lines also.

The second method of creating variation mentioned above, is by adding or taking away syllables, so that lines are no longer strictly pentameters. One of the lines in Text 2 is: *And husht with buzzing night-flies to thy slumber.* If when reading you are prepared to put a main stress on *to* but not on *flies*, then this is a regular IP – until you get to the final foot, which has an extra (unstressed) syllable. DeDUMming the line gives DeDUM deDUM deDUM deDUM, deDUMde. This extra final unstressed syllable is known as a feminine ending. Perhaps the most famous example is Hamlet's: *To be, or not to be, that is the question* (3.1.56) where the line also finishes with /x.). Here is how Puttenham describes this phenomenon in *The Arte of English Poesie*: 'the sharpe accent falles upon the *penultima* or last save one sillable of the verse, which doth so drowne the last, as he seemeth to passe away in manner unpronounced, and so make the verse seem even'.[5] George Puttenham's treatise appeared in 1589, and it was indeed the 1590s when the feminine ending reached popularity. His book was a highly influential treatment of poetic forms. Shakespeare himself certainly knew it, and his use of the feminine ending increased over time. In one study, Shakespeare's working life is divided into four chronological periods, and the number of feminine endings used in each are counted. The percentage figures show a steep increase over the years. They are: 10.8, 18.4, 26.9, 32.9.[6]

Shakespeare sometimes also omits syllables. This may occur at the beginning of lines when an initial unstressed syllable is missed out. In *Romeo and Juliet*, when Mercutio is looking for his friend Romeo, he says (2.4.1): *Where the devil should this Romeo be?* The line has five stressed syllables, and is an IP in every respect except that there is an unstressed syllable missing at the beginning of the line. Where this happens, the line is called headless. When the missing syllable is from within the line, it is called broken-backed. Here is an example:

Now o'er the one half-world
Nature seems dead, and wicked dreams abuse
The curtained sleep. Witchcraft celebrates
Pale Hecat's offerings;
(Mac 2.1.49)

The relevant line is the third. In the middle of the line, two stressed syllables come face to face: in *sleep* and *witch*. One way to <u>scan</u> the line (to analyse its metre, that is) would be to say that there is an unstressed syllable missing between the two. If that syllable were there, the line would be a regular IP. One might even want to say that the pause between the two words is acting as a syllable. The <u>scansion</u> (metrical analysis) is:

```
  x   /   x     /   (x)   /   x   /   x   /
The curt|ained sleep|.   Witch|craft cel|ebrates
```

Activity 9 (*Identifying variations*) will give you practice at recognising feminine endings, headless and broken-backed lines.

A look through Text 3 reveals that Shakespeare's deviations from the IP norm can be quite substantial. There is one line – the fifth – which is very much shorter than the others. Indeed, it is just one iamb long. The line is *'Tis gone*.[7] Wright (1988: 119) shows how short lines increase over Shakespeare's writing career. He cites figures derived from Chambers (1933). In the early plays *The Comedy of Errors* and *A Midsummer Night's Dream* there are only 17 and 5 respectively. In the much later *Timon of Athens* there are 171, and in *King Lear* as many as 191. A middle-period play which has quite a few is *Julius Caesar*, where overall, Shakespeare seems to be experimenting with metre and the IP.

In this section we have covered a number of irregularities – inversions, feminine endings, headless and broken-backed lines. What purpose do these irregularities serve? Where metre is concerned, variety is often indeed the spice of life, and variations from the regularity of straight IPs save the verse from monotony. The variations add vigour, keep the verse humming along, give it movement. But there are also many times when Shakespeare is clearly aiming at some special dramatic effect related to the emotional state of his characters and what they are saying. This is clear in the *Othello* example just considered. Leech (1969: 120) talks about 'the temporary sense of disorienta-tion, almost of shock' which is caused by the inclusion of this very short line among the more or less regular IPs. An even more dramatic example occurs in *King Lear*, when Lear, crazed with madness, fantasises about the revenge he will take on his sons-in-law who have treated him badly. He will, he says, creep up on them silently with cavalry, and murder them. The chilling final line is about as far from a regular IP as you can imagine:

It were a delicate strategem, to shoe
A troop of horse with felt. I'll put 't in proof,
And when I have stol'n upon these son-in-laws,
Then kill, kill, kill, kill, kill, kill.
(KL 4.6.185)

In this section we have considered a number of variations to standard IP lines. Various activities have provided practice at identifying some of these. If you wish to take a closer look at IP variations, try scanning some of the passages on the Text Page. This will provide further examples of some of the irregularities we have covered; it will also reveal other variation types not mentioned here. In addition, it will show that scanning is no simple activity. Looking in detail at any passage will almost certainly throw up lines which are difficult to scan, or which can be scanned in more than one way. Incidentally, alternative possibilities will often mean that there is more than one way for an actor to deliver a line. How you scan often dictates how you say.

7.1.6 End-stopping and enjambment

This section will consider another way of adding variety to blank verse. To explore this through an activity look at Activity 10 (*Changing prose into end-stopped lines*) (**NP**).

This method of adding variety is to do with the relationship between grammatical units and lines of poetry. Look again at Text 1, taken from the early play, *The Taming of the Shrew*. The first lines are: *The more my wrong, the more his spite appears. / What did he marry me to famish me?* In these lines, and in the passage as a whole, there is a strong connection between grammatical units (phrases, clauses, sentences) and the lines of poetry. The end of a line corresponds with a phrase, clause or sentence end. When the ends of lines and grammatical units coincide, this is called <u>end-stopping</u>.

One of the 'advantages' of end-stopping is that if you are listening to (as opposed to reading) a passage you will have a clear idea of where lines start and finish (and if the passage is IP then of course number of stresses helps a lot too!) A 'disadvantage' is that continual end-stopping becomes predictable and tedious, with each line end corresponding with a grammatical break. A further disadvantage, from the writer's point of view, is that the lines have to be constantly manipulated to ensure that end-stopping happens, making all the words and thoughts fit – snugly but unnaturally – into pentameters. Shakespeare's early plays in particular are full of end-stopping. In fact, looking at the amount of end-stopping in a play often gives a rough (but by no means fool-proof) indication of how early or late it was written.

Look now at a passage from *As You Like It*, written about nine years later. It is part of the famous *All the world's a stage* speech, where the melancholic Jaques (whom we first met in 1.1) is describing the seven 'ages of man'. Here are the second, third and fourth ages:

And then the whining school-boy with his satchel
And shining morning face, creeps like snail
Unwillingly to school. And then the lover,
Sighing like furnace, with a woeful ballad
Made to his mistress' eyebrow. Then, a soldier,
Full of strange oaths, and bearded like the pard,
Jealous in honour, sudden, and quick in quarrel,
Seeking the bubble reputation
Even in the cannon's mouth. And then the justice
. . . .
(AYLI 2.7.146)

There is much less end-stopping here. Throughout, the full stops come in the middle of lines rather than at their ends. Looking specifically at the description of the school-boy, notice that it is one sentence, where both the subject and the object 'run across' line boundaries. In Jaques' speech, instead of end-stopping there is what is called <u>enjambment</u> (from the French *enjamber* meaning 'to stride over') – the syntax 'strides over' the line ending.

When lines and grammatical units do not coincide, there are logically three configurations possible. They can run from full line to in-line – starting at the beginning of a line and finishing before the end of a line. Or they can run in-line to in-line, or in-line to full line.[8] Consider for example this passage from *The Winter's Tale*, a late play (c. 1609):

I am not prone to weeping, as our sex
Commonly are; the want of which vain dew
Perchance shall dry your pities; but I have
That honourable grief lodged here which burns
Worse than tears drown. Beseech you all . . .
(WT 2.1.108)

Here, the sentence as a whole (from *I am not prone* to *than tears drown*) is full line to in-line, and within this sentence there are clauses that run in-line to in-line – *as our sex/Commonly are*, for example.

When the syntactic break is in-line, whereabouts in the line does it occur? Earlier in this chapter we mentioned broken-backed lines, defining them as where there is the lack of an unstressed syllable after the midline pause. The word <u>caesura</u> is often used to describe the midline pause: Crystal and Crystal's (2005: 51) definition of *caesura* as 'a rhythmical break in a line of verse, often in the middle'. It can be quite easy to identify the caesura in a line by looking at the punctuation, as you will see if you look back at the Jaques passage we have just considered.[9] You will be able to find several lines where the caesura point is very obvious: after *school* in line 3, *eyebrow* in line 5, *mouth* in line 9, for example. As Crystal and Crystal's definition says, they are indeed usually roughly in the middle of the line. To find out exactly how central to the lines they are, count the syllables before and after the caesura in the lines you have identified. In nearly all cases the caesura comes within a syllable or two of the mid point. But this is not always true in Shakespeare. As his career progressed, he tended more and more to put the caesuras in a variety of places, not always near the mid point at all. This means that the points at which the grammatical units finish vary also. The passage from *The Winter's Tale* above illustrates this. Concentrate on the second, third and fifth lines. As with the *As You Like It* lines earlier, work out after what syllables the in-line break comes. In fact, these are but a few of the number of possibilities Shakespeare uses. Activity 11 (*Identifying the caesura point*) shows the full gamut. Changing the point where grammatical units finish is another way of adding variety to the verse.

To develop more of a feel for how Shakespeare's lines run in the later plays (and for some more practice at identifying different lines types), look at Text 4. Notice how common enjambment is here. There are some end-stopped lines, but not so many. Incidentally, while looking at the passage, find an example of line-initial inversion, and of a feminine ending. Look also for examples of the four line types discussed in the text (mid to mid, mid to full, full to mid, full to full). To do this, you will sometimes have to look at sentence endings, sometimes clause and sometimes phrase endings (**AS**).

Text 4 contains examples of another characteristic of Shakespeare's in-line to in-line sequences. Count the stressed syllables in these sequences (in both cases the first word is stressed):

Come, you spirits
That tend on mortal thoughts!

nor keep peace between
The effect and it!

There are five, and the sequences therefore might be regarded as IPs. In other words as well as having full lines which are IPs, we also have in-line to in-line IP sequences cutting across those full lines. Leech calls these latter ghost lines, noting that others use the phrase straddled lines for the same phenomenon.[10] You may wish to attempt a definition of what a ghost line is. Also, look back to the Jaques' speech we considered earlier and find a ghost line in that (**AS**).

The large amount of enjambment that Shakespeare uses, as well as the existence of ghost lines, means that when you listen to a speech containing these, it is particularly difficult to work out (if you cannot see the text) where the lines on the page begin and end. As Leech (1969: 127) puts it, 'often . . . enjambment is so frequent that the line-divisions can scarcely be followed by the ear unaided by the eye'. This is quite a different state of affairs from the early Shakespeare and from the verse of the playwright Christopher Marlowe, who was writing at the same time Shakespeare was producing those early plays. There you have predominantly end-stopped lines, where you can hear exactly where lines begin and end. To remind yourself of such end-stopping, look back to Text 1 (from Shakespeare's early play, *The Taming of the Shrew*), and the Marlowe passage in Activity 10.

As we have seen, the essence of enjambment is that syntactic and metrical units do not begin and end together. One might say that a 'tension' is set up between the structure of the verse (which deals in the unit of the line) and the syntactic structure, which cuts across that metrical unit. Leech (1969: 126) talks about syntactic and verse finality (where syntactic and metrical units end), and says that 'if either occurs without the other, some structural expectation is still unfulfilled; the reader has, as it were, arrived at a halting-place, not a destination.' There is, in Wright's phrase this time, a 'counterpoint of line and sentence' (p. 213), where the two elements (verse and syntax) weave across and around each other, but do not coincide. Leech considers this issue particularly in relation to the poet John Milton, whose life just overlapped Shakespeare's (Milton was eight years old when Shakespeare died). Leech describes the aesthetic satisfaction which occurs when, in Milton's poetry, this counterpoint is resolved by metre and syntax finally coming together. He compares the effect to 'the perfect cadence at the end of a Bach fugue'. Occasionally this is also found in Shakespeare. The example Wright gives is of the Jaques speech considered earlier. We focused on the second, third and fourth 'ages of man'. The evocation of all the seven ages except for the second, Wright notes, begins in-line. But here is how the speech ends:

> *Last scene of all,*
> *That ends this strange eventful history,*
> *Is second childishness and mere oblivion,*
> *Sans teeth, sans eyes, sans taste, sans everything.*
> (AYLI 2.7.164)

Syntax and lines come together at the end, creating Leech's Bach-like perfect cadence. But this type of ending is, in later Shakespeare, the exception rather than the rule. He more often prefers the effect of finishing on the half line. Look back, for example, to the end of Lady Macbeth's speech in Text 4. It ends in-line. In fact that is not strictly true, because Lady Macbeth continues speaking: Macbeth enters and she ends the line by addressing him: *Great Glamis! worthy*

Cawdor. But this is a change of subject, and the big speech itself finishes on the half line. Wright (1988: 127) notes that in *Julius Caesar* (a play where – as noted earlier in 7.1.5 – Shakespeare appears to be doing a lot of experimentation in terms of verse lines) no fewer than twenty-three speeches end with short lines, 'and a great many more . . . in half lines completed by the next speaker'.

7.1.7 Metre and speech patterns

As Al Pacino's informant put it: 'Everybody says, all the time, iambic penta-meter, Shakespeare, iambic pentameter – what is that supposed to mean?' We have been considering what it is supposed to mean. A big part of the message is that IP is the norm, but that there is plenty of variation. What we have is 'IP plus, plus' – plus all those lines where the syntactic units run across line units; plus all those lines that are, technically speaking, too long or too short, or where the feet are not quite as iambic as they should be. Irregularities, as we have seen, prevent the verse from being monotonous, and there are also spe-cial effects which are often heightened by metrical variation. But there is another reason for the irregularities, not so far mentioned. It is related to the differences between prose and poetry considered at the beginning of this chapter. Prose, we noted, was not marked by regular rhythms. Poets desire, of course, to be 'poetical', and this leads them to impose stress patterns (metre) onto what their characters say. But at the same time, they often require a degree of realism, wishing to capture something of the irregular rhythms of everyday speech. Look again at Marlowe's Dr Faustus speech in Activity 10, and at Shakespeare's *Henry IV* speech in Text 2. Beautiful poetry they both may be, but it might be said that real people do not speak like that. Compare this with the edgy prose you find in the following passage from one of Shakespeare's last plays, *Cymbeline*. Cloten, the queen's son, has been found dead. He should, Belarius argues, be properly treated in death:

Great griefs, I see, medicine the less, for Cloten
Is quite forgot. He was a queen's son, boys,
And though he came our enemy, remember
He was paid for that; though mean and mighty rotting
Together, have one dust, yet reverence –
That angel of the world – doth make distinction
Of place 'tween high and low.
(Cym 4.2.243)

It is not just the metre which is distorted here, but the syntax as well – just as syntax is often distorted in real-life communication. The passage is a good example of the 'curt' style considered in 6.4.2, and this is no accident. Recall from the chapter that the aim of the 'curt' style was to move away from rounded Ciceronian balance towards showing 'the mind at work'. The result was a style nearer to the rhythms of real speech than achieved by the symmetry of Ciceronian rhetoric.

Shakespeare is, we have said, 'IP plus, plus'. But though a great deal of his work does use IPs, there is more besides. Non-IP verse as well as prose add to the overall variety. The rest of this chapter will concentrate on the parts of Shakespeare that are not written in IP.

7.2 Verse and prose

7.2.1 Rhymed verse

At the end of *Love's Labour's Lost* (5.2.883) is a song in two parts – one presented by the allegorical figure for 'Spring', the other by 'Winter'. Take a look at Text 5 on the Text Page, which is a verse (or stanza as they are called) from Winter's contribution. A more vivid, descriptive gem of a verse you could not ask for. If you want to look up a few more impressive examples of verse, there are several in *Twelfth Night*; try 2.4.50 for *Come away, come away, death, / And in sad cypress let me be laid*, or *When that I was and a little tiny boy, / With hey-ho, the wind and the rain* (5.1.386). Then there are the more sinister witches' verses from *Macbeth*, one of which is given on the Text Page as Text 6. Or there is the 'willow song' Desdemona sings shortly before she is murdered by her husband Othello (Oth 4.3.38): *The poor soul sat sighing, by a sycamore tree, / Sing all a green willow* – a song which Verdi made much of in his opera *Otello*, based on the Shakespeare play. There are many more besides, with *A Midsummer Night's Dream* and *The Tempest* also being particularly rich in examples.

The types of rhymed verse in Shakespeare are many. If you scan Text 5's lines, you will find that they are predominantly iambs, with the usual irregularities and variations. But they are tetrameters rather than pentameters, meaning there are four, not five, stresses per line (*tetra* is from the Greek word for 'four'). Since the lines are rhymed, we need a way of indicating what the rhyme scheme is, and the conventional way of doing this is by using letters of the alphabet, with rhyming lines using the same letter. In the case of Text 5 this gives *ababccdd* (accepting *note* and *pot* as a rhyme). A particularly common verse form in the Renaissance is the sonnet. Take a look back to Chapter 6's Text Page, where Text 1 is a sonnet (number 29). This sonnet follows the conventional sonnet rhyme scheme. Before reading the next paragraph, scan the sonnet and work out the rhyme scheme (**NP**).

Sonnets are traditionally fourteen lines long. They are usually divided into three four-line stanzas, called <u>quatrains</u> (also derived from a word meaning 'four', from French this time), followed by a final two lines. The rhyme scheme of each quatrain is *abab*, and the final two lines rhyme with each other (as was seen in 6.4.1, the final couplet of a sonnet often acts as a summary statement). So the rhyme scheme for an entire sonnet is *ababcdcdefefgg*. The lines are usually IPs.

Three of the parameters we have so dealt with in this chapter are types of feet (iambs, trochees etc.), number of feet per line (pentameter, tetrameter), and rhyme schemes (couplets, *abab* etc.). Take a look now at Texts 6–9 on the Text Page. In each case scan the lines and work out the rhyme schemes. These will be considered in the following paragraphs (**NP**).

Earlier in this chapter (7.1.3), the first line of Text 6 (the *Macbeth* witches' incantation) was used as an example of trochees rather than iambs in a verse. The lines which follow this carry on in the same vein. They are <u>trochaic tetrameters,</u> and you may have found another text on the Text Page which uses the same form. It is often used in chant- or incantation-like verses.

Text 7, from *The Rape of Lucrece*, is in iambic pentameters. The poem's stanzas have seven lines, rhyming *ababbcc*. The form was used much by Chaucer in narrative poems, including in four of his *Canterbury Tales*. It came to be known as <u>rhyme royal</u>, probably because King James I of Scotland, who was something of a poet, also used the form. One reason for the form's popularity was because there were several ways of grouping the lines by rhyme: thus you could regard it as *aba* followed by two couplets, *bbcc*; or as an *abab* pattern with a final *bcc*.

Couplets are also found in Text 8's trochaic tetrameters. Shakespeare uses couplets a lot, particularly in the early plays. There are more than 500 rhyming couplets in the early *Love's Labour's Lost* (written around 1594), and none at all in the late *The Winter's Tale* (dated 1609–10).[11] In plays written late in his career, Shakespeare often marked the end of a scene with a couplet. At the end of 2.2 in *Hamlet*, for example, Hamlet has formed the idea of having a play performed which will expose the crime of his uncle, now king. The final words of the scene are (2.2.602):

> *The play's the thing*
> *Wherein I'll catch the conscience of the King.*
> Exit

One of the most interesting characteristics of Shakespeare's use of verse (both rhymed and blank) is the way he 'ducks in and out' of it as he sees fit. An excellent example occurs in *Romeo and Juliet*, a play written predominantly in blank verse and prose. But for the moment when the two lovers, Romeo and

Juliet, first meet – and leading up to The First Kiss – something special is reserved. Text 9 is the passage in question. It is a sonnet – that verse form much associated (particularly then but also now) with love poetry – embedded in a scene which is mostly in blank verse. Notice particularly how the lines are shared between the characters: each has a quatrain to themselves at the beginning; they share the third quatrain, and a line each of the final couplet. There are more examples of Shakespeare ducking in and out of verse in Activity 12 (*Ducking in and out of verse*). Look at this now (**NP**).

Later in the play, Romeo has only to think about Juliet to break into verse. Passage (a) in Activity 12 shows this well, and also how sudden the change from prose to verse can be. Then there is the character of Beatrice in *Much Ado About Nothing*. She is a down-to-earth lady and an inveterate prose speaker. But when love is in the air, as Passage (b) shows, she breaks into verse. Incidentally, this is the only time Beatrice uses the *thou* form in the whole play (see 5.5 on the *thou/you* distinction).[12]

Though lyrical expressions of love are most likely to bring on sudden bursts of rhyme, particularly couplets, there may be other reasons for this. One is when snippets of wisdom are being put forward, pieces of advice are being given, or in 'philosophical debate'. It can also be used in rapid dialogue to give energy.[13] Both of these reasons may be what causes the burst of couplets in Passage (c). After this piece of quick-fire dialogue, the 'debate' continues with longer passages in couplets. Then, when other characters come on the scene, it is back to blank verse.

Jack Cade's speech in Passage (d) is in verse because of its 'noble' subject matter. It is a call to arms, much like Henry V's famous *Once more unto the breach, dear friends* (a speech also intended to stir the troops into battle). Though Cade is a person of low social rank, who normally communicates in prose, the topic is sufficiently elevated here to drive him into verse. Incidentally, notice in passing the word *shooen* in the passage. It was mentioned in 4.5.2 as the irregular plural of *shoe*. There is only one other instance of it in Shakespeare (by Ophelia in *Hamlet*).

7.2.2 Prose

Prose: the language that M. Jourdain spoke all his life without knowing it. Though the vast majority of Shakespeare's plays have more verse than prose, the latter is by no means lacking. And Shakespeare is also very good at it. Take a look back to Text 3 on the Text Page of Chapter 6 (Prince Hal talking to Falstaff) to find an impressive piece of prose, indicating that Shakespeare could excel at this as well as poetry. Comparing this text with others on that page raises another issue that it is worth facing early on: how you tell prose from verse. If you are listening rather than reading, and the verse is rhymed, the rhymes will give it away. In the case of blank verse, the rhythm of iambs is of course a guideline. If you are reading, there are some typographical conventions which distinguish verse from prose. The most obvious difference between Text 3 and, say, Text 4 (still on Chapter 6's Text Page) is that each line of the latter begins on a new line of text, while in the case of Text 3 in prose, the text just continues without break. Notice also that each line of verse in Text 4 begins with a capital letter.

That there is more verse in Shakespeare's plays than there is prose reflects the Greek and Roman view that prose was not a suitable medium for literature. The same view held sway in England until into Renaissance times. As Puttenham, writing in 1589, puts it: verse is 'a manner of utterance more eloquent and rethorical then the ordinarie prose'.[14] But by then we are beginning to find prose making an appearance in literary works. When does Shakespeare use prose? Thinking first about his career as a whole, take a look at the chart below which plots the use of prose in the plays, listed in chronological order. Some questions to ask: which of the plays have no prose at all? Which play has the most? What are the top four plays for prose use? What can be said about the use of prose in the early plays? In addition, choose two comedies that you know, and two tragedies; is there more prose in your chosen comedies or the tragedies? This section will deal with the reasons why Shakespeare chose to use prose on occasions. Based on your answers to the questions above, do you have any initial thoughts about possible reasons (**NP**)?

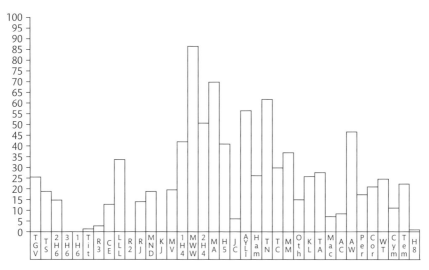

FIGURE 7.1 Percentage distribution of prose in Shakespeare's plays. Adapted from Vickers (1968: 453)[15]

Figure 7.1 reveals large differences in the use of prose over Shakespeare's writing career. Some plays like *Henry VI, Part 1*, *King John* and *Richard II* are without prose, while *The Merry Wives of Windsor* is written almost entirely in prose, with just an occasional piece of verse. The early plays tend to have less prose, and it is only with *Henry IV, Part 1* (written around 1596) that the use of prose really takes off. An exception is the early *Love's Labour's Lost*, which sticks out rather obviously on the chart. The middle period seems to be the heyday of prose, with some tapering off towards the later period.

There are a number of factors which control how much prose is used. Many of them revolve around the notion that verse is high, sublime, poetic, while prose is low, mundane and, well, . . . prosaic. Before you read what follows, look at Activity 13 (*Ducking in and out of prose*) which invites you to speculate on the use of prose and verse in some specific passages (**NP**).

One relevant factor is genre. Verse was considered the correct medium for tragedy, while prose was permissible in the less elevated genre of comedy. The chart above suggests this. It is why, in the chart, the comedy of *Love's Labour's Lost* sticks out like a sore thumb among the early works. The top four plays for prose use are all comedies: *The Merry Wives of Windsor*, *Much Ado About Nothing*, *Twelfth Night* and *As You Like It*. Conversely, the plays with little or no prose are tragedies or histories. But genre is far from being the only factor. Another is the class or status of the speaker. The general rule (followed particularly in the early plays) is that higher status speakers use verse, lower status ones prose. It is for this reason that the Porter in *Macbeth* (Passage (a)) is one of the few characters to use prose in that play. The princes, lords, kings talk to each other (and even to their spouses) in blank verse.

But Activity 13 reveals that there are many exceptions even here. There are some mental states that are particularly associated with prose, the obvious one being madness. So much so that high-status king's son, Hamlet, drops into prose when feigning madness (Passage (b)). This is true also of another kingly figure – King Lear, who talks prose in his madness, verse in his sanity. There is another interesting case in *Macbeth*. Most of the time Macbeth and his wife, the infamous Lady Macbeth, use blank verse with each other. But at a certain point Lady Macbeth, crazed with guilt, goes sleepwalking, hallucinating as she walks. Here she talks in prose – clearly the appropriate medium for mad, bad dreams.

It is not just the status of the speaker that is important. The status of the person spoken to (the interlocutor) is also relevant. A clear example (Passage (c)) involves another king's son – Prince Hal, soon to become Henry V. When addressing his father and other important personages, he uses blank verse. But a number of scenes in *Henry IV, Parts 1 and 2*, show Prince Hal slumming it in taverns with Falstaff and his cronies. In these conversations with such 'low-life' characters, he uses prose. Then there is Hamlet, who uses prose not just when feigning madness but also when talking to the lowly – the gravediggers for example (Chapter 5 has an example of Hamlet and the gravediggers talking prose; in section 5.5.2). One special type of interlocutor is oneself, and when most characters are soliloquising, they do so in blank verse. An interesting contrast occurs in *Hamlet*, 3.2. Hamlet is talking to the courtiers Rosencrantz and Guildenstern. He uses prose because he is feigning madness; perhaps also because he disdains the two courtiers, regarding them as a kind of 'low life'. Whatever the reasons, as soon as Rosencrantz and Guildenstern exit and Hamlet begins to soliloquise (*'Tis now the very witching time of night/ When churchyards yawn and hell itself breathes out/Contagion to this world*; 3.2.395) he uses blank verse. But sometimes a character is so 'low' and comic that he is not even allowed to soliloquise in verse. Falstaff is such a one. In a soliloquy in which he sings the praises of sherry-wine (2H4 4.3.85; one of literature's most famous defences of drinking alcohol), he uses prose.

We have already seen that characters break into verse when the subject matter and mood are right. There are also times when they 'break into prose'. Today we find it strange that married couples talk to each other in blank verse, but this is what they do in Shakespeare, if they are of high birth. This is what Hotspur and his wife are doing just before Passage (d). But, as they banter with each other, they descend for just a moment into prose.

Or is it prose? At the beginning of this section it was said that one of the ways the listener can distinguish between blank verse and prose was by the presence of regular iambs, which indicate verse. But this is not a foolproof criterion, because prose can also sometimes be iambic. Some regard the iambic pattern (unstressed + stressed: x/) to be natural to the rhythm of English speech. As noted at the beginning of this chapter, prose does not usually follow a consistent rhythmical pattern. But prose passages can show a predominance of iambs, just because iambs are so natural to English. Some, for example, have noted that Dickens (possibly under the influence of Shakespeare) has passages of iambic prose, particularly in his early novels – take a look at http://www.librarything.com/topic/11337 for such a claim. The same has been said about the prose of Shakespeare's Pistol – the flamboyant mate of Falstaff whose idiolect we considered in 3.5). The existence of iambic prose, and indeed of any prose that exhibits rhythmical regularities, makes it on occasions difficult to know whether a passage was intended as verse or prose. The lines of Hotspur and his wife in Passage (d) are a case in point. Some modern editors have these lines in prose, but in the First Folio they are in verse. Another example shows the contrary situation. We have already noted that as a comic character, Falstaff was seldom 'allowed the honour' of speaking verse. One of the occasions when modern editors give him a few lines of blank verse is when he is speaking to a high-bred person: one of the king's sons, Prince John of Lancaster. There are the lines as they appear in the Arden edition:[16]

My lord, I beseech you give me leave to go
Through Gloucestershire, and when you come to court
Stand my good lord, pray, in your good report
(2H4 4.3.80)

Not quite iambs, but the editor says 'the feeling is of verse', and there is a rhyme. But the First Folio has the passage in prose, without capitals for *Through* and *Stand*. Verse or prose? The choice is yours.

7.3 Blank, rhyme and prose: the mix

In this chapter we have seen that though IPs are the predominant verse form in Shakespeare, he often deviates from the strict IP. This is partly to create variety, but is often for particular artistic effects. A statistic mentioned in 7.1.5 is that one in five lines is divergent. 'Dissimilitude in similitude' is a key phrase which captures the two facts – firstly that IPs are the norm (the similitude), but secondly that there is much variation (the dissimilitude).[17] In the later sections of the chapter we have seen that Shakespeare also uses rhymed verse and prose. A characteristic noted is that he often 'ducks in and out' (another key phrase for the chapter) of both verse and prose. It is emphatically not the case that one play is written in blank verse, another in rhyme, and a third in prose. The vast majority of plays contain elements of all these three.

In 7.2.2 we noted that there are differences in appearance on the page between prose and verse. The next chapter will concentrate on 'appearance on the page'. It will focus on the written word, with particular attention given to spelling and punctuation.

Text page

Text 1

The Taming of the Shrew is an early play, written before 1592. In this passage, the 'shrew', **Katherina**, is complaining about her husband Petruchio, who is treating her badly – not letting her eat and sleep:

The more my wrong, the more his spite appears.
What did he marry me to famish me?
Beggars that come unto my father's door
Upon entreaty have a present alms,
If not, elsewhere they meet with charity.
But I, who never knew how to entreat,
Nor never needed that I should entreat,
Am starv'd for meat, giddy for lack of sleep,
With oaths kept waking, and with brawling fed.
(TS 4.3.2)

Text 2

Henry IV, Part 2 was written around 1598. Here **the King** is lamenting the fact that he cannot sleep:

How many thousands of my poorest subjects
Are at this hour asleep! O sleep, O gentle sleep,
Nature's soft nurse, how have I frighted thee,
That thou no more wilt weigh my eyelids down,
And steep my senses in forgetfulness?
Why rather, sleep, liest thou in smoky cribs,
Upon uneasy pallets stretching thee,
And husht with buzzing night-flies to thy slumber,
Than in the perfum'd chambers of the great,
Under the canopies of costly state,
And lull'd with sound of sweetest melody?
(2H4 3.1.4)

Text 3

Othello is dated 1603–4. **Othello** has been persuaded that his wife Desdemona has been unfaithful. In this passage he is lamenting the loss of love, and swearing vengeance:

O, that the slave had forty thousand lives!
One is too poor, too weak for my revenge.
Now do I see 'tis true. Look here, Iago;
All my fond love thus do I blow to heaven:
'Tis gone.
Arise, black vengeance, from thy hollow cell!
(Oth 3.3.439)

Text 4

Just before this well-known speech from *Macbeth*, **Lady Macbeth** has learned that the King, Duncan, is to visit her castle. She and her husband intend to murder the King. Here she is steeling herself for the deed (1.5.39):

> *The raven himself is hoarse*
> *That croaks the fatal entrance of Duncan*
> *Under my battlements. Come, you spirits*
> *That tend on mortal thoughts! unsex me here,*
> *And fill me from the crown to the toe top full*
> *Of direst cruelty; make thick my blood,*
> *Stop up the access and passage to remorse,*
> *That no compunctious visitings of nature*
> *Shake my fell purpose, nor keep peace between*
> *The effect and it! Come to my woman's breasts,*
> *And take my milk for gall, you murdering ministers,*
> *Wherever in your sightless substances*
> *You wait on nature's mischief! Come, thick night,*
> *And pall thee in the dunnest smoke of hell,*
> *That my keen knife see not the wound it makes,*
> *Nor heaven peep through the blanket of the dark,*
> *To cry 'Hold, hold!'*
> (Mac 1.5.36)

Text 5

Part of 'Winter's Song' from the end of *Love's Labour's Lost*:

> *When icicles hang by the wall,*
> *And Dick the shepherd blows his nail,*
> *And Tom bears logs into the hall,*
> *And milk comes frozen home in pail,*
> *When blood is nipped, and ways be foul,*
> *Then nightly sings the staring owl:*
> *'Tu-whit Tu-who!' – a merry note,*
> *While greasy Joan doth keel the pot.*
> (LLL 5.2.901)

Text 6

The **witches** in *Macbeth* are dancing round their cauldron, muttering spells:

All: *Double, double, toil and trouble;*
                  Fire burn, and cauldron bubble.
Second witch: *Fillet of a fenny snake*
                  In the cauldron boil and bake;
                  Eye of newt, and toe of frog,
                  Wool of bat, and tongue of dog,
                  Adder's fork, and blind-worm's sting,
                  Lizard's leg and howlet's wing,
                  For a charm of powerful trouble,
                  Like a hell-broth, boil and bubble.
                  (Mac 4.1.10)

Text 7

This passage is from *The Rape of Lucrece*, a narrative poem written in 1593 or 1594. This stanza describes Lucrece, the beautiful and chaste wife of Collatinus:

> *Beauty itself doth of itself persuade*
> *The eyes of men without an orator;*
> *What needeth then apology be made*
> *To set forth that which is so singular?*
> *Or why is Collatine the publisher*
> *Of that rich jewel he should keep unknown*
> *From thievish ears, because it is his own?*
> (Luc.29)

Text 8

In *A Midsummer Night's Dream* the spirit **Puck** has been ordered by his master Oberon to find a man dressed as an Athenian and to put a magic potion into his eyes:

Through the forest have I gone,
But Athenian found I none
On whose eyes I might approve
This flower's force in stirring love.
Night and silence. – Who is here?
Weeds of Athens he doth wear.
This is he my master said
Despised the Athenian maid;
And here the maiden, sleeping sound
On the dank and dirty ground.
(MND 2.2.72)

Text 9

Romeo and Juliet are exchanging their first words, soon to be followed by their first kiss:

Romeo: *If I profane with my unworthiest hand*
           This holy shrine, the gentle sin is this.
           My lips, two blushing pilgrims, ready stand
           To smooth that rough touch with a tender kiss.
Juliet: *Good pilgrim, you do wrong your hand too much,*
           Which mannerly devotion shows in this.
           For saints have hands that pilgrims' hands do touch,
           And palm to palm is holy palmers' kiss.
Romeo: *Have not saints lips, and holy palmers too?*
Juliet: *Ay, pilgrim, lips that they must use in prayer.*
Romeo: *O, then, dear saint, let lips do what hands do!*
           They pray: grant thou, lest faith turn to despair.
Juliet: *Saints do not move, though grant for prayers' sake.*
Romeo: *Then move not while my prayer's effect I take.*
He kisses her
(RJ 1.5.93)

Activity section

1 What makes poetry special?

Before looking at the six pieces of poetry below, consider these general questions: how is poetry different from prose? What makes poetry special? Then read through the examples, identify the particular characteristics of each, and consider what it is that makes them poetry. Pay particular attention to what they look like on the page, and how they sound when read aloud.

(a) These lines come from the poem *Beowulf*, written anonymously between the eighth and eleventh century. The passage (translated into Modern English by Michael Alexander) describes how the monster Grendel sought his prey:

> *Girt with God's anger, Grendel came gliding*
> *over the moors beneath misty mounds.*
> *The man-scather sought someone to snatch*

from the high hall. He crept under cloud
until he caught sight of the king's court
whose gilded gables he knew at a glance.

(b) Attridge (1995: 91) cites and discusses these lyrics, from the group EPDM's song *It's My Thing*, as an example of rap:

They mean business, no time for play
If you bite a line, they blow you away
The more you bite, your body gets hot
Don't get too cold because you might get shot
Knowin' that my rhyme's like a poisonous rat
Don't play dumb boy, you're smarter than that
It's my thing

(c) This passage is taken from a poem written by Alexander Pope. The poem is a philosophical consideration of the nature of man, and is called *An Essay on Man*. It was published in 1734.

All nature is but art unknown to thee,
All chance, direction which thou canst not see;
All discord, harmony not understood;
All partial evil, universal good;
And, spite of pride, in erring reason's spite,
One truth is clear, 'Whatever IS, is RIGHT.'

(d) This poem by Jacqueline L. Fuller is called *The Boy from Lake Trout*:

There once was a boy from Lake Trout
Who thought he could eat a Girl Scout
He took a big bite,
Chewed with much might
But ended up spitting her out

(e) And now for some Shakespeare. These famous lines are taken from *Henry V*, dated 1598–9. The king is encouraging his soldiers before they go into battle:
Once more unto the breach, dear friends, once more;
Or close the wall up with our English dead!
In peace there's nothing so becomes a man
As modest stillness and humility:
But when the blast of war blows in our ears,
Then imitate the action of the tiger;
(H5 3.1.1)

2 Counting syllables   (AS)

(i)   How many syllables does each of these words have? Write 1, 2, 3 or 4 in the first space on the right.

       introducing   <u>4</u>   x x / x

(a) *apron*   ——   ——

(b) *hit*   ——   ——

(c) *matter*   ——   ——

(d) *announcer*   ——   ——

(e) *rope*   ——   ——

(f) *anchorage*   ——   ——

(g) *unconsoling*   ——   ——

(h) *abbreviate*   ——   ——

(ii) Go through the words putting an accent over the vowel in the stressed syllable.

(iii) Show the stress sequence in each word by writing the symbols x and / in the rightmost column.

3 Modern -*ed*   (AS)

As discussed in the text, sometimes in PDE -*ed* is pronounced as a separate syllable, sometimes not. The examples given were *helped* (where the -*ed* is not pronounced with a vowel) and *wanted* (where there is a vowel sound). Say the words below aloud to ascertain whether the -*ed* vowel is pronounced or not:

(a) *loved*   (b) *added*   (c) *liked*   (d) *raided*

(e) *initiated*   (f) *caged*   (g) *adulterated*   (h) *scattered*

Any speculation as to what controls whether the vowel is pronounced or not?

4 Marking stress sequences   (AS)

Read the phrases and sentences on the left in a 'normal' way. Use the symbols 'x' and '/' to show the sequence of syllables in each case. Of course, the examples include words of more than one syllable (like *Peter*, which is /x). Be sure to show <u>all</u> the syllables.

the man	x /
(a) *John and his dog*	_____
(b) *John and Peter*	_____
(c) *John, Peter and Mike*	_____
(d) *Mary and her brother*	_____
(e) *John and the man went to the bar*	_____
(f) *Mary and her brother saw the film*	_____
(g) *Mary and her brother saw the film in the evening*	_____

5 Stress sequences in prose and poetry   (AS)

(i) Here is part of a (prose!) conversation. Using the symbols 'x' and '/', write down the sequences of stressed and unstressed syllables for some or all of it. Then look at the relationship between stressed and unstressed syllables. Is there always the same number of unstressed syllables between each stressed one? Is there any regularity at all?

When I bumped into Annie yesterday I immediately saw that she was upset. Really upset, I'd say. You could tell it by the way she was speaking. So I thought I'd ask her outright why. So I said: Is anything the matter, Annie. Then she blurted it all out – how she and George had had an argument and how he had walked out, just like that.

(ii) Look back to the limerick in Activity 1. Read it aloud, emphasising the rhythm as much as possible. Then mark the stress sequences beside each line. The first line will be: x/xx/xx/ (notice here that the word *Lake* is marked as unstressed, which is how it will sound if you read the line with a 'lilt').

Is there any regularity here in the relationship between stressed and unstressed syllables? There certainly is. Express what it is.

(iii) Though there is a pattern (in the limerick's stress sequences), there are some syllable sequences which do not quite conform to it. Identify these and try to express these irregularities in words.

6 Iambic or trochaic?   (AS)

(i) Are these words iambic or trochaic – x / or / x?

discuss	x /	*water*	/ x
(a) *amble*	_____	(b) *arrange*	_____
(c) *alike*	_____	(d) *lighting*	_____
(e) *capture*	_____	(f) *cancer*	_____
(g) *announce*	_____		

(ii) Now do the same for these sequences of words, thinking in terms of
    normal usage (in 7.1.3 the point is made that exceptions can be found
    in particular contexts). Sometimes extra words are given below in
    brackets to indicate the intended sense.

(a) *a man*   _____
(b) *waste not (want not)*   _____
(c) *help us*   _____
(d) *he came*   _____
(e) *look it (up in a dictionary)*   _____
(f) *it's dark*   _____
(g) *write to (your mother)*   _____
(h) *John and (Helen)*   _____

7 -*ed* in Shakespeare   (AS)

Shakespeare, like other Elizabethan poets, would count the -*ed* form as an
extra syllable where the verse required it. When it was not pronounced as an
extra syllable, this was often signalled by the use of an apostrophe – *chang'd*
not *changed*. Below are some lines from the opening speech of *Richard III* – the
one which begins with the famous lines *Now is the winter of our discontent /
Made glorious summer by this son of York*. In it, the future Richard III is apparently heralding the time of peace which has now come to England. For the
purposes of this Activity, there are no apostrophes, and the full -*ed* forms are
given (as indeed is done in some modern editions). Decide which of the -*ed*
forms would have been pronounced [ed] (as if they were written *changéd* in
PDE), in order to provide a required extra unstressed syllable. The -*ed* forms to
concentrate on are shaded:

(a) *Our bruised arms hung up for monuments,*

(b) *Our stern alarums changed to merry meetings*

(c), (d) *Grim-visaged War hath smoothed his wrinkled front:*

(e) *And now, instead of mounting barbed steeds*

(f) *But I, that am not shaped for sportive tricks*

(g) *I, that am rudely stamped, and want love's majesty*

(h) *Deformed, unfinished, sent before my time*

(i) *I am determined to prove a villain*

(j) *Brother, good day; what means this armed guard*

8 Recognising inversion   (AS)

Often inversion occurs at the beginning of a line, but it is also common to find it in the middle. Here are some examples. Identify the inversion in each and note whether it is line-initial or line-medial.

(a)   *Methinks I hear*
     Antony call; I see him rouse himself
     (AC 5.2.282)

(b) *Nothing will come of nothing: speak again*
     (KL 1.1.90)

(c) *To give them seals, never my soul consent*
     (Ham 3.2.406)

(d) *And lose the name of action. – Soft you now!*
     The fair Ophelia! Nymph, in thy orisons
     Be all my sins remember'd.
     (Ham 3.1.88)

(e)   *and then his state*
     Empties itself, as doth an inland brook
     (MV 5.1.95)

(f) *To follow still the changes of the moon*
     With fresh suspicions? No; to be once in doubt
     Is once to be resolved.
     (Oth 3.3.176)

9 Identifying variations   (AS)

Three sorts of variations discussed in the text are represented here: feminine endings, headless lines, and broken-backed lines. Decide which of these variations each of the following passages exemplifies (in some cases it is more than one). The lines to concentrate on are in italics (other lines are given to provide context):

(a) Spur post, and get before him to the king,
     And beg thy pardon ere he do accuse thee,
     I'll not be long behind.
     (R2 5.2.113)

(b)   the hour prefix'd
     Of her delivery to this valiant Greek
     Comes fast upon. Good my brother Troilus
     (TC 4.3.1)

(c) And too soon marr'd are those so earthly made,
     Earth hath swallowed all my hopes but she,
     She is the hopeful lady of my earth
     (RJ 1.2.13)

(d)   he has been bred in the wars
     Since he could draw a sword, and is ill school'd
     In bolted language; meal and bran together
     He throws without distinction.
     (Cor 3.1.318)

(e)   [these blazes . . .]
     You must not take for fire. From this time
     Be somewhat scanter in your maiden presence;
     (Ham 1.3.120)

(f) *They were all in lamentable cases*
     The king was weeping-ripe for a good word.
     (LLL 5.2.273)[18]

10 Changing prose into end-stopped lines

This Activity involves a speech from a play written in the early 1590s by Shakespeare's contemporary, the playwright Christopher Marlowe. The play is called *The Tragical History of Dr Faustus*. In this speech, Dr Faustus is attempting to invoke devils. Like Shakespeare, Marlowe wrote in IPs, but look first at part of the speech 'translated' into prose:

Now that the gloomy shadow of the earth, longing to view Orion's drizzling look, leaps from th'Antarctic world unto the sky, and dims the welkin with her pitchy breath: Faustus, begin thine incantations, and try if devils will obey thy hest, seeing thou hast prayed and sacrificed to them.

This passage is made up of two sentences (assuming that the colon (:) after *breath* is acting as a full stop – the use of colons as full stops is discussed in the next chapter, 8.2.2). But each sentence is quite long and complex, being divided into a number of clauses. Divide the passage into clauses by putting a line (|) at the end of each clause.

Now look at the speech divided up into lines (IPs) as it appears in the play:[19]

Now that the gloomy shadow of the earth,
Longing to view Orion's drizzling look,
Leaps from th'Antarctic world unto the sky,
And dims the welkin with her pitchy breath:
Faustus, begin thine incantations,
And try if devils will obey thy hest,
Seeing thou hast prayed and sacrificed to them.
(1.3)

What is there to notice about the relationship between the lines of poetry and the grammatical clauses you have identified?

11 Identifying the caesura point   (AS)

(i) Wright (1988: 209) illustrates how Shakespeare varies the position of the caesura, by providing nine examples with the caesura occurring after the first syllable, the second – and so on. Here are Wright's examples. Write down after how many syllables the caesura occurs. In (a), for example, it occurs after the first syllable, and in (b) after the sixth. Notice how much variation these examples reveal.

   Of course, punctuation often gives the game away by making the caesura point obvious. So after the first three examples below the punctuation has been removed, to make the task more challenging.

   (a) *Love! His affections do not that way tend*   _____
        (Ham 3.1.163)

   (b) *Love looks not with the eyes, but with the mind*   _____
        (MND 1.1.234)

   (c) *Why speaks my father so ungently? This*   _____
        (Tem 1.2.445)

   (d) *My thought whose murder yet is but fantastical*   _____
        (Mac 1.3.138)

(e) *If music be the food of love play on*   _____
     (TN 1.1.1)

(f) *Her father lov'd me oft invited me*   _____
     (Oth 1.3.127)

(g) *Then trip him that his heels may kick at heaven*   _____
     (Ham 3.3.93)

(h) *If you have tears prepare to shed them now*   _____
     (JC 3.2.170)

(i) *I come to bury Caesar not to praise him*   _____
     (JC 3.2.75)

(ii) Pick a speech from a Shakespeare play at random and notice (by looking
     at the punctuation) where the caesurae fall. You will see that it is most
     common towards the middle of the line. But not nearly always so.

12 Ducking in and out of verse

In the following passages, you might expect prose, but instead you find verse
– blank or rhymed. Why? Develop some thoughts on why verse is used. All
the examples are discussed in the text.

(a) *Romeo and Juliet* 2.4 is a scene almost entirely in prose. Towards the end,
     the **Nurse** enters seeking **Romeo**, who has a message for her to convey
     to her mistress Juliet. It is that he wishes to marry Juliet that very
     afternoon. The passage starts in prose but ends up in blank verse. Why?

     Romeo: *Nurse, commend me to thy lady and mistress. I protest unto*
               thee –
     Nurse: *Good heart, and I'faith I will tell her as much. Lord, Lord, she*
               will be a joyful woman.
     Romeo: *What wilt thou tell her, nurse? Thou dost not mark me.*
     Nurse: *I will tell her, sir, that you do protest, which, as I take it, is a*
               gentlemanlike offer.
     Romeo: *Bid her devise*
               Some means to come to shrift this afternoon;
               And there she shall at Friar Lawrence's cell,
               Be shrived and married.

     (RJ 2.4.168)

(b) Beatrice and Benedick are two witty young things who spend much of
     Much Ado About Nothing intellectually sparring with each other in prose.

But suddenly, **Beatrice** has reason to believe that Benedick actually loves her. She is here talking to herself. Why in verse?

And, Benedick, love on. I will requite thee,
Taming my wild heart to thy loving hand.
If thou dost love, my kindness shall incite thee
To bind our loves up in a holy band.
(MA 3.1.111)

(c) In *The Comedy of Errors*, the ladyfolk, **Adriana** and **Luciana**, are discussing their menfolk. Just before, the passage is blank verse, but suddenly they break into rhyme:

Adriana: *Why should their liberty than ours be more?*
Luciana: *Because their business still lies out o' door.*
Adriana: *Look when I serve him so he takes it ill.*
Luciana: *O, know he is the bridle of your will.*
(CE 2.1.10)

(d) In *Henry VI, Part 2*, a major character is the populist people's leader **Jack Cade** – a kind of fifteenth-century militant trade unionist. He uses prose nearly all the time. In the lines below he is inciting the crowd to battle – in verse. Why verse?

And you that love the commons, follow me:
Now show yourselves men, 'tis for liberty.
We will not leave one lord, one gentleman:
Spare none but such as go in clouten shooen.
(2H6 4.2.172).

13 Ducking in and out of prose

In these passages, you might expect verse, but instead you find prose. Why? Develop some thoughts on why prose is used. All the examples are discussed in the text.

(a) The **Porter** in *Macbeth* is one of the few characters in the play to use prose. Macbeth and his wife have killed the king in their castle. There is a loud, persistent knocking at the door. The Porter grumbles (*old* here has the sense of 'frequent'):

Here's a knocking, indeed! If a man were Porter of Hell Gate, he should have old turning the key. [Knocking] *Knock, knock, knock. Who's there, i'th' name of Belzebub?*
(Mac 2.3.1)

(b) **Hamlet** (who is a prince) uses verse much of the time, but here he is feigning madness. He is being questioned by old **Polonius** (a character plentifully lacking in wit, one might say) about what he is reading:

Polonius: *What is the matter, my lord?*
Hamlet: *Between who?*
Polonius: *I mean the matter that you read, my lord.*
Hamlet: *Slanders, sir, for the satirical slave says here that old men have grey beards, that their faces are wrinkled, their eyes purging thick amber or plum-tree gum and that they have a plentiful lack of wit, together with weak hams:*

(Ham 2.2.194)

(c) **Prince Hal**, the future king, is slumming it – as is his wont – in *The Boar's Head Tavern*. Here he is talking to Francis, a drawer (barman) about the possibility of Francis cheating on his master:

Wilt thou rob this leathern-jerkin, crystal-button, not pated, agate-ring, puke-stocking, caddis-garter, smooth-tongue Spanish pouch?
(1H4 2.4.67)

(d) For most of *Henry IV, Part 1*, **Hotspur**, who is an earl's son, talks in blank verse, including to his wife, **Lady Percy** (who replies in the same way). Here he teasingly asks her to sing, and she continues the banter by saying no:

Hotspur: *Come Kate, I'll have your song too.*
Lady P: *Not mine, in good sooth.*
Hotspur: *Not yours, in good sooth! Heart, you swear like a comfit-maker's wife – 'not you, in good sooth!', and 'As true as I live!', and 'As God shall mend me!', and 'As sure as day!'.*

(3.1.239)

Extended activities

1   As we have seen in this chapter, the major part of Shakespeare's dramatic writing is in verse; prose, though not absent, is not used nearly so much. Yet it is hard to imagine a twenty-first-century playwright using anything other than prose. This is quite a major change. Why do you think it came about? What led playwrights to all but abandon the use of verse in drama? What is gained? What is lost?

2 (i) Focus on a play that particularly interests you. Do your own rough statistical analysis of how much of the play is in blank verse, how much in rhymed verse and how much in prose. Are there clear reasons why each of these forms is used when they are?

   (ii) If the play uses blank verse, what proportion of this is end-stopped? Does the figure fit roughly into the statement made in 7.1.6, that earlier plays have a lot of end-stopping, later plays less?

   (iii) Assuming the play uses verse (blank or rhymed), select a substantial speech from it (say over ten lines). What proportion of the lines follow an absolutely regular metrical pattern? What proportion show some irregularity? Are any of the irregularities of the sorts discussed in 7.1.5?

Answer section

Example of initial inversion (section 7.1.5)

In Text 2: *Nature's soft nurse, how have I frighted thee.*

Inversion and other characteristics in Text 4 (section 7.1.6)

Under my battlements is an example of initial inversion; there are feminine endings on the words *nature* and *ministers*; as well as the example of mid-to-mid given in the next paragraph, there is also *nor keep peace between/The effect and it!* Mid-to-full: *Come, thick night, / And pall thee in the dunnest smoke of hell.* Full-to-mid: *Nor heaven peep through the blanket of the dark, / To cry 'Hold, hold!'* Full-to-full: *That my keen knife see not the wound it makes.*

Ghost line in the Jaques speech (section 7.1.6)

This is *creeps like snail/Unwillingly to school.*

Activity 2 Counting syllables

(i) and (iii)   (a) 2, /x; (b) 1, /; (c) 2, /x; (d) 3, x/x; (e) 1, /; (f) 3, /xx; (g) 4, xx/x; (h) 4, x/xx.

Activity 3 Modern -ed

yes = pronounced; no = not pronounced:
(a) no; (b) yes; (c) no; (d) yes; (e) yes; (f) no; (g) yes; (h) no.
The vowel is pronounced when the last sound of the verb is [t] or [d].

Activity 4 Marking stress sequences

(a) /xx/; (b) /x/x; (c) //xx/; (d) /xxx/x; (e) /xx/xxx/; (f) /xxx/x/x/; (g) /xxx/x/x/ xx/x.

Activity 5 Stress sequences in prose and poetry

(ii) x/xx/xx/
     x/xx/xx/
     x/xx/
     /xx/
     x/xx/xx/

(iii) An irregularity is that while all other lines begin with x/, the fourth loses the first x. The result is that it has only four syllables, while the other short line – the third – has five.

Activity 6 Iambic or trochaic?

(i)   (a) /x; (b) x/; (c) x/; (d) /x; (e) /x; (f) /x; (g) x/.

(ii) (a) x/; (b) /x; (c) /x; (d) x/; (e) /x; (f) x/; (g) /x; (h) /x.

Activity 7 -ed in Shakespeare

yes = pronounced, no = not pronounced:
(a) yes, (b) no, (c) no, (d) no, (e) yes, (f) no, (g) no, (h) no, (i) yes, (j) yes.

Activity 8 Recognising inversion

(a) *Anthony call* (initial); (b) *Nothing will come* (initial); (c) *never my soul* (medial); (d) *Nymph, in thy orisons* (medial); (e) *Empties itself* (initial); (f) *No, to be once* (medial).

Activity 9 Identifying variations

(a) feminine; (b) broken-backed + feminine; (c) headless; (d) feminine; (e) broken-backed; (f) headless + feminine.

Activity 11 Identifying the caesura point

(i) (a) 1; (b) 6; (c) 9; (d) 2; (e) 8; (f) 5; (g) 3; (h) 4; (i) 7.

Notes

1 The translation is taken from a verse adaptation by Timothy Mooney, available on http://moliere-in-english.com/bourgeois.html

2 Al Pacino's documentary is called *Looking for Richard* (Fox Searchlight Pictures, 1996).

3 The example is taken from Abercrombie (1967: 41).

4 Wright (1988: 105).

5 p. 59 in the 1971 edition of Puttenham's work.

6 Much of the information in this paragraph, including the Puttenham quote, is taken from Wright (1988: 160). The study mentioned is Tarlinskaja (1987).

7 This is the example Leech (1969: 120) uses.

8 These possibilities are discussed by Wright (1988) particularly in relation to Shakespeare's later plays. These paragraphs owe much to his discussion.

9 Recall, though, the point made in 1.5, that punctuation was often subject to a scrivener's or compositor's intervention.

10 Leech (1969: 125).

11 This information was taken from http://www.shakespeare-online.com/plays/hamlet/hamletversehudson.html

12 The point is made by Crystal (2008: 212).

13 The example is taken from McEvoy (2006: 43).

14 Puttenham, *The Art of English Poesie* (1589) Chapter 3.

15 Vickers' chart has been adapted to fit the chronological order (and play title abbreviations) used in this book.

16 Humphreys (2007).

17 The phrase is Wordsworth's. He uses it in his Preface to the *Lyrical Ballads* (along with the phrase 'similitude in dissimilitude') to describe characteristics found in artistic creations.

18 This is as the lines appear in the First Folio. Some editions put *O!* at the beginning of the line, which makes it no longer headless.

19 The word *incantations* in line 5 would have had five syllables in EModE, so the line would be an iambic pentameter. There are a number of EModE words which would have been pronounced with more syllables than the PDE equivalent. Another example is *Henry*, which in EModE would have been pronounced with three syllables (as if it were written 'Henery').

Further reading

Attridge, D. (1995) *Poetic Rhythm: An introduction*, Cambridge: Cambridge University Press, provides a guide to verse and metre in general, while the following two books have useful chapters on the topic: Leech, G. (1969) *A Linguistic Guide to English Poetry*, London: Longman, and Short, M. (1996) *Exploring the Language of Poems, Plays and Prose*, London: Longman.

Specifically on verse and Shakespeare, there is a succinct account in McDonald, R. (2003) 'Shakespeare's verse' in Wells, S., and Orlin, L. C. (eds) (2003) *An Oxford Guide to Shakespeare*, Oxford: Oxford University Press, 79–92, while Wright, G. T. (1988) *Shakespeare's Metrical Art*, Berkeley: University of California Press, provides more detailed coverage. Vickers, B. (1968) *The Artistry of Shakespeare's Prose*, London: Methuen, is the standard work on Shakespeare's prose.

CHAPTER 8

Shakespeare on the Page: 'Wryting englysh treu'

Key phrases:
the taste and fancy of the speller; standardisation attempts

8.1 Taste and fancy

In Charles Dickens' novel *The Pickwick Papers*, one of the characters – Sam Weller – appears before a judge, who asks him his name:

> *'Sam Weller, my Lord,' replied that gentleman.*
> *'Do you spell it with a "V" or a "W"?' inquired the Judge.*
> *'That depends on the taste and fancy of the speller, my Lord', replied Sam . . .*
> *'I spells it with a "V".'*

This chapter is about what Shakespeare looks like when he is written down. Spelling is a main topic, but we shall also be looking at punctuation and the use of some letters of the alphabet (an area called graphology). One conclusion will be that what appeared on the page was often subject to 'the taste and fancy' of the user. Attitudes were quite relaxed, and a great deal of variation in spelling and punctuation was tolerated without apparently raising eyebrows. Where Shakespeare's texts are concerned, we need to remember that the 'user' may very well not be the writer himself, but some of the many hands involved in the transmission process. To remind yourself of this process, and the roles played by scriveners, compositors and editors, look back to 1.5.

8.2 Spelling

8.2.1 Some background

The short passage shown in Figure 8.1, taken from *The Merry Wives of Windsor* (2.1.71), gives an initial example of variation.[1] It contains three common words each spelt in two different ways in the space of these few lines. One of them is *he* which is also spelt *hee*; find the other two, which show the same *e/ee* difference. The passage is taken from the First Folio. Ignore for the moment the 'ſ' form used here; it is a type of 's' and will be discussed later in this chapter, as will the use of 'v' when today we would have 'u'. The context is that Falstaff has written the same love letter to Mistress Ford and to Mistress Page (both married women), and they have found out. Mistress Page is speaking. *Turtles* were turtle doves, symbols of faithfulness. *I will find you twenty lascivious turtles ere one chaste man* – what a great line!

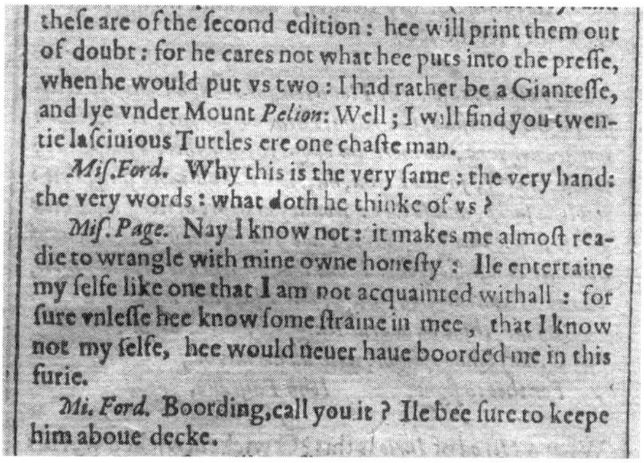

theſe are of the ſecond edition : hee will print them out of doubt : for he cares not what hee puts into the preſſe, when he would put vs two : I had rather be a Gianteſſe, and lye vnder Mount *Pelion*: Well ; I will find you twen- tie laſciuious Turtles ere one chaſte man.

   Miſ.Ford. Why this is the very ſame : the very hand: the very words : what doth he thinke of vs ?

   Miſ.Page. Nay I know not : it makes me almoſt rea- die to wrangle with mine owne honeſty : Ile entertaine my ſelfe like one that I am not acquainted withall : for ſure vnleſſe hee know ſome ſtraine in mee , that I know not my ſelfe, hee would neuer haue boorded me in this furie.

   Mi. Ford. Boording, call you it ? Ile bee ſure to keepe him aboue decke.

FIGURE 8.1 Spelling variations within early Shakespeare manuscripts

In 2.2.1 we discussed the precarious state of English, and how it was struggling for recognition against the forces of French and Latin. The struggle had its effect on spelling and punctuation. When a language is just beginning to come into accepted use, very few 'rules' for matters like spelling and punctuation will have been established by the community. There is likely to be a very long period when people 'do as they please', spelling and punctuating as they wish without fear of anyone telling them they are wrong. One huge force for standardisation did occur in the mid fourteen hundreds – the invention by the German Johannes Gutenberg of the first movable type printing press.

William Caxton brought the machine to England in 1476. It is easy to imagine how the establishment of printing helped to standardise spelling. But language use is an area in which standardisation is notoriously slow to happen, and written English had been in accepted use for only a century and a half by the time Shakespeare was born. Not so long in linguistic terms. Hence the spelling and punctuation 'free-for-all' which was normal in the late fifteen-hundreds.

In the *Merry Wives of Windsor* passage, the spellings *he, me* and *be* stand alongside *hee, mee* and *bee*. There are very many more examples of spelling variation in the period. In Baugh and Cable (2002: 209 – an excellent history of the English language) an example is the word *coney*. Literally it means 'a rabbit'; *coney-catching* means 'trickery', and 'coney-catching pamphlets' were a type of Elizabethan crime story describing the activities of vagrants. In Robert Greene's 1591 *A Notable Discovery of Coosenage* ('deception'), *coney* is spelt *cony, conny, conye, conie, coni, cuny, cunny, cunnie*; just in that one book. Even Shakespeare's own name makes the point. A look at two websites[2] comes up with the following spellings (among others – according to Bryson, 2007, there are more than 80 spellings in all) of William and his father's surname during their lifetimes:

Shackspeare	*Shakspeare*	*Shaxpeare*
Shakspeyr	*Shackesper*	*Shagspere*
Shaxspere	*Shakysper*	*Shackspere*
Shackespeare	*Shakespear*	*Shakespere*
Shaxper	*Shakspere*	*Shackespere*
Shexpere	*Shakespeare*	*Shacksper*
Shaksper	*Shaxpere*	*Shakyspere*

The list above is not in any kind of order. Look through it and establish at what points in the word the variations can lie, tabulating the various possibilities at each point. For example, all spellings have the initial 'sh' – there is no variation. But one point where there *is* variation is in the following vowel, sometimes written 'a', sometimes 'e', and sometimes in other ways.

All in all, it is no wonder that the English educator John Hart, in his 1569 book called *An Orthographie* (which puts forward ideas for spelling reform), talks about 'confusion and disorder' in English spelling. The newness of the accepted use of English for writing is enough to explain the degree of variation, but there are other reasons. As we saw in 2.2.1, another characteristic of the time was the large number of Romance words coming into the language, and this added to the confusion – no-one really knew how to spell many of the foreign-sounding words. Another important factor was that in the middle of the fifteenth century (again, not so far back in linguistic terms), English had gone through major pronunciation changes, called the <u>Great Vowel Shift</u>. This, as the name suggests, changed how English vowel sounds were pronounced. But although the sounds themselves had changed, in Shakespeare's time not all of these changes had made their way into writing. So sometimes spelling reflected the pre-Vowel Shift pronunciation, sometimes the newer pronunciation. Then there was the fact that when Caxton set up his printing press in London, he had to use foreign compositors, and they brought with them their own spelling conventions, plus a great preparedness to waive rules when convenient. They were, for example, quite capable of shortening words if there was not enough room for the full word on the page. Crystal's (2008) example is the word *sonne*. In one line in *The Taming of the Shrew* it is spelt just like that, which was the norm. But a few lines later we find *son* coming at the end of a line, probably simply because there was not enough space for the full form (TS 5.1.80).

At the beginning of this chapter it was said that 'apparently' no eyebrows were raised at variation in spelling. 'Apparently' only, however, because John Hart's comment that there was 'confusion and disorder' in spelling clearly constitutes a raised eyebrow. It shows that not everyone was happy with the situation, and another characteristic of the age was in fact the efforts that were made to move towards standard ways of spelling. Early attempts at standardisation included a 1530 spelling manual, which now exists only in fragments. It gave directions on how 'one may lerne to spel & to rede & how one shud wryte englysh treu'.[3]

What ways are available to go about standardising spelling? One is to base the system on how words are pronounced, trying to use a different writing symbol for each distinct sound. 'One sound, one symbol' is not of course what happens in PDE. Think, for example, about the use in writing of 'ou'. It represents many more than one sound. In fact, it is used for all the vowel/diphthong sounds in the words *tough, bough, cough,* and *dough,* all of which are quite different. The fact that different sounds can be represented by the same symbol like this is a major reason why many – both native and non-native speakers of the language – find English spelling difficult to master. In *An Orthographie,* John Hart tried to introduce a new 'phonetic' alphabet for writing. In his system, each distinct sound would be represented by a different written symbol. Figure 8.2 is a short example of the phonetic path Hart wanted spelling to follow. Try to work out what some of the individual words are (**AS**):

*/bikauz de voëls and konsonants ar devci-
ded intu suG parts az befor, dis tabd dufi
kip dem in de leik order : tu-uit first a,e,i,
o, u, and den de four perz huiG ar mad uid*

FIGURE 8.2 Example of Hart's phonetic alphabet

Hart was by no means the last in history to try introducing 'one sound, one symbol'. Most failed because they usually ended up having to use many symbols unfamiliar to readers, making the spelling system difficult to learn. Difficulty for the learner is a sure recipe for failure, and this was the fate met by Hart's system.

A similar fate awaited William Bullokar's 1580 *Booke at Large for the Amendment of English Orthographie*. He tried to keep to existing letters but used diacritics – 'accents' like [´] which could be put above a symbol (as in á) to indicate a specific sound – and this did not go down well with readers either. More successful were the efforts of two schoolmasters. Richard Mulcaster's *The Elementarie* (1582) contained a list of no fewer than 8500 spellings. But the length of the list helped to make it a long book, and hence expensive to buy. Incidentally, some people have suggested that Mulcaster may have been the model for the pedant Holofernes in *Love's Labour's Lost* – a character we met in 3.1.3. Most popular of all was Edmund Coote's *The English School-Maister* (1596), which was much shorter than Mulcaster's work. It contains a brief dictionary at the end. Just how rare dictionary use was in those days is suggested by this extract (Figure 8.3) from Coote's 'directions for the unskilfull' on how to look up words in a dictionary:

*Directions for the
unskilfull.*

IF thou haft not been acquainted with fuch a table as this following, and defireft to make vfe of it, thou muft get the Alphabet,
that is, the order of the letters as they ftand, without Booke perfectly : to know where euery letter ftandeth, as (*b*) neere the beginning, (*m*) about the middeft, and (*v*) toward the end. Therefore if the word thou wouldeft finde, begin with (*a*) looke in the
beginning of the Table, if with (*t*) looke toward the end : Againe,
if thy worde beginne with (*ba*) looke in the beginning of the
letter (*b*) but if with (*bu*) looke toward the end of that letter, and
if thou obferueft the fame for the third and fourth letters, thou fhalt
finde thy word prefently. Secondly, thou muft know the caufe of

FIGURE 8.3 Example of Coote's directions for using a dictionary

8.2.2 Some graphology and spelling differences between then and now

Now to detail. The famous 'Seven Ages' speech of Jaques from *As You Like It* (2.7.140) will be used as the basis for our discussion of graphology and spelling – a speech already considered in 7.1.6. Here it is, in a version adapted from Wells and Taylor's (1986) 'original spelling' edition (also mentioned before, in 4.5.1).[4] As you read, note the spellings and uses of letters which are different from today's.

Iaques   All the world's a ſtage,
And all the men and women, meerely Players;
They haue their Exits and their Entrances,
And one man in his time playes many parts,
His Acts being ſeuen ages. At firſt the Infant,
Mewling, and puking in the Nurſes armes:
Then, the whining Schooleboy with his Satchell
And ſhining morning face, creeping like ſnaile
Vnwillingly to ſchoole. And then the Louer,
Sighing like Furnace, with a wofull Ballad
Made to his Miſtreſſe eyebrow. Then, a Soldier,
Full of ſtrange oaths, and bearded like the Pard,
Ielous in honour, ſudden, and quicke in quarrell,
Seeking the bubble Reputation
Euen in the Canons mouth: And then, the Iuſtice
In faire round belly, with good Capon lin'd,
With eyes ſeuere, and beard of formall cut,
Full of wiſe ſawes, and moderne inſtances,
And ſo he playes his part. The ſixth age ſhifts
Into the leane and ſlipper'd Pantaloone,
With ſpectacles on noſe, and pouch on ſide,
His youthfull hoſe well ſau'd, a world too wide,
For his ſhrunke ſhanke, and his bigge manly voice,
Turning againe toward childiſh trebble pipes,
And whiſtles in his ſound. Laſt Scene of all,
That ends this ſtrange euentfull hiſtorie,
Is ſecond childiſhneſſe, and meere obliuion,
Sans teeth, ſans eyes, ſans taſte, ſans euerything.

Some (though not all) of the differences are discussed below. Before reading on, you may wish to look at Activity 1 (*Graphology and spelling differences*), which asks questions about these differences (**NP**).

As regards uses of letters, possibly one of the first things you noticed is the presence of a letter we no longer have: ſ. It is a form of 's' and is derived from the Roman form used in everyday writing. It is often called <u>long s</u>, to distinguish it from the <u>short s</u> which we use today, and which is also found in the passage. The two letters do not represent different sounds. What distinguishes them is that short *s* is used in word-final positions (at the ends of words), and word-initially when the word has a capital letter. ſ is used word-initially and medially, never finally or as a capital letter.

The difference between 'u' and 'v' also relates to where in the word the letter comes. In PDE these two letters represent different sounds: the former is a vowel, the latter a consonant. But Jaques does not differentiate the letters in this way. Both can stand for either vowel or consonant. 'v' is used at the beginning of words, for both lower and upper case. 'u' occurs within or at the end of words. The first example of the modern-day vowel/consonant distinction was noted in a book published in 1634, eighteen years after Shakespeare died, and eleven years after the First Folio appeared.

There is one letter which we now have but which was not much found in Shakespeare's day: *j*. In the passage, there are three examples of words which today we would write with a 'j': *Iaques, Ielous* and *Iuſtice*, for *Jaques, Jelous* and *Justice*. As it happens all these letters are capitals in the passage; it would be the same if they were in lower case – 'i' would be used rather than 'j'. The latter started to be used around 1630, and in fact the Third Folio (1664) has *Justice* instead of *Iustice* in this passage.

Most of the other differences we shall discuss relate to how vowels are represented, but one consonant-related difference is that some words in the passage have a consonant repeated where we would have just one letter. This is called <u>consonant doubling</u>. Most of the examples of this in the passage involve a doubling of 'l' at the end of a word – *Satchell, woefull*, and so on. Such unnecessary repetition was lamented by reformers like Mulcaster (1582) who complains about 'the dubling of consonants at the end of a word . . . and a thousand such ignorant superfluities'. This was common practice, and Mulcaster has a rather quaint theory that it was 'the swiftness of the pen sure, which can hardly stay upon the single ending *l*, that causeth this doubling'. The pen just cannot stop. Lass (1999a: 11) says the doublings were often just 'typographical decorations'.

Another of Mulcaster's 'superfluities' is the final 'e'. You will have found plenty of examples in the passage of words ending in *e* which would have no final *e* in modern English – words like *snaile, schoole, mistresse, quicke, faire*. In fact a final *e* can be anything but superfluous, and the letter can indeed play an important role in spelling. It is worth taking a moment to consider such cases, even though they do not include the words above. Look at the PDE word pairs below, distinguished only by a final *e*. Say the words to yourself and note what difference the final *e* signals regarding the pronunciation of the preceding vowel:

hat	*hate*	*not*	*note*
mad	*made*	*strip*	*stripe*

In the words taking the final *e* the preceding vowel is pronounced as a diphthong. It is often, in fact, pronounced in the way that we say the names of the vowels today (a,e,i,o,u). Because of this effect on the nature of the preceding vowel, modern-day spelling teachers sometimes talk about the 'magic *e*'. The *e* in EModE could be equally magical, and in fact two of the word pair examples above (*mad/made* and *strip/stripe*) are also used by Mulcaster, whose description of the *e* comes close to calling it magic. It is, he says, a 'letter of maruellous vse in the writing of our tung' because it 'sometime altereth the vowell'.[5] (Mulcaster himself seems here to be indulging in 'ignorant superfluity' with that doubled 'l' in *vowell*!)

But in her discussion of the final *e*, Salmon (1986) notes that often the final *e* is functionless, and this is the case in the examples given earlier (*snaile, schoole*, etc.). Why is it there? Sometimes, Salmon says, it is a remnant from an earlier form of the language. The old verb *walken* ('to walk'), for example, over time became *walke*. The final *e* was pronounced until about 1400, then it disappeared from speech but stayed on in the spelling. This is indeed a very common reason why English spelling can be so bothersome. Earlier in this chapter we noted that a result of the Great Vowel Shift was that discrepancies arose between how words were said and how they were written, so that pronunciation becomes an unreliable guide to spelling (and vice versa). The final *e* on words like *walke* is another example.

Salmon has another interesting observation to make about the final *e*. Recall the passage from *The Merry Wives of Windsor* cited at the beginning of this chapter. Three words appeared there with a final *e* added: *be, he* and *me* became *bee, hee* and *mee*. According to Salmon, EModE preferred words to have a minimum of three letters, though exceptions were made for prepositions and pronouns. She goes on to say that this preference even exists in English today. You can roughly test the truth of this by taking a random paragraph from this book. You will find the paragraph contains an overwhelming majority of words with three or more letters. Also that the one- and two-letter words are very often (though not always) prepositions or pronouns. Note that two out of the three words in the *Merry Wives of Windsor* passage (*hee* and *mee*) are in fact pronouns, which suggests that the 'preference for a minimum of three' might operate on these too.

There are two words in the passage – *meerely* and *meere* – where you find 'ee'. Here are some more examples from the First Folio of *All's Well That Ends Well*:

neere	*deere* (the animal)	*Trophee*
atcheeve	*heere* (the adverb of place)	*breefe*

The spelling 'ee' was used to represent a variety of 'i' related sounds ([iː] being the vowel in PDE *see*). These examples show that 'ee' was indeed used to cover what has become a variety of modern spellings. To appreciate this, go through the list above noting how the vowel in each word would be written today; for example, in *neere* it would be 'ea'.

The PDE versions of two of the words on the list above – *atcheeve* and *breefe* – are spelt with an 'ie'. There are two 'ie' spellings in the passage which you would not find in PDE. One is in *ielous* for *jealous*, which we have already discussed. The other one is *hiſtorie* where today we would have a final *y*. Using 'ie' for our final 'y' was very common in EModE, and once again Mulcaster has something to say about it: 'When . . . *i* is it self the last letter . . . it is qualified by the *e*, as *manie, merie* . . . where the verie pen, will rather end in the *e*, then in the naked *i*.'[(6)] But, Mulcaster goes on to note, *y* is used when the stress falls on the final syllable – so we have *deny, cry*, not *denie, crie*. Incidentally, there are occasions in modern English when we add a suffix to a word ending in *y*, which then becomes *ie*. So we 'change' *y* to *ie* when we add an *s* to it. This happens when we form a plural noun. For example, *history* becomes *histories*. We do the same when a verb takes a final *s*: we write *to deny*, but *he denies*.

There are three examples in the passage of words where a letter is missing, replaced by an apostrophe. They are *lin'd, ſlipper'd* and *ſau'd*. In all three cases, the missing letter is 'e', and these are indeed examples of the unstressed *-ed* ending that we discussed in 7.1.2. In modern English we replace a letter with an apostrophe in the same way in words like *can't, didn't,* and also less commonly in abbreviations like *gov't* for *government,* and *'till* for *until* (though this is now very rare). The use of the apostrophe as a 'letter replacer' was more widespread in EModE. Here are some more examples, mostly taken from *The Merry Wives of Windsor*:

o'my life	*do's*	*'tis*	*desp'rate*
wil't	*sland'rous*	*sh'adulterates*	*th'ther day*
o'er	*for't*	*auis'd*	*reueng'd*
y'haue	*thou'rt*	*w'are*	

As a general rule, letters which are pronounced very lightly are the ones that tend to get missed out. Here are some of the common contexts for this. You may like to fit the examples above into these categories (**AS**):

- The vowel sound of an *-ed* verb ending;

- some lightly pronounced medial vowel;

- letters in a preposition, a pronoun or the definite article;

- parts of common verb sequences, particularly using the verbs *do*, *be* or *have* – here either part of the pronoun or part of the verb goes.

Finally in this section, you probably noticed that the passage uses capital letters in a way that is different from today. Think first about modern use of the capital. When do we use it? Perhaps you have come across another modern language where the usage is different from PDE. One is mentioned at the end of the next paragraph, which also provides information about capitals in Jaques' speech. Before reading on, look at Activity 2 (*Upper and lower case*) which asks questions about this (**NP**).

In EModE, capital letters are used at the beginning of each line in blank verse. In fact (as we saw in 7.2.2), when you are looking at a piece of text, sometimes the easiest way of recognising whether it is in prose or blank verse is by this feature. As in PDE, the letter following a full stop is always a capital, but sometimes (as we will see in the next section) in EModE colons or semi-colons are used where today we might have a full stop, and there you will also find a following capital. The example in the passage is *And* in line 15, after a colon.

But in the passage there are words which start with a capital even though not at the beginning of a sentence or a blank verse line. Sometimes in Shakespeare they are adjectives. For example, in *Henry V* the King says the traitors *receyu'd the Golden Earnest of Our death*. Blake (2002) hypothesises that *Golden* is capitalised to suggest the noun *gold*, while the capital on *Our* suggests royalty. But mostly, as in the Jaques speech, the capitalised words are nouns. Yet not all nouns have capital letters – in the passage *man, oaths*, *eyebrow* do not. Why some and not others? It has been suggested that capitals are used to mark out certain types of words. 'Important' nouns, for example; but why should *oaths* be less important than *Players*? Because *players* are people? Some say that only nouns describing animate objects have capitals. But *Exits and Entrances* provide counter-evidence, and certainly there are animate nouns (like *man*) which do not have capitals. The truth of the matter is that it is indeed nouns that tend to take capitals; but not by any means all nouns, and it is difficult to find any rhyme or reason in their use. Salmon (1986) argues that there was movement at this period towards the eighteenth-century situation when capitals were used for nearly all nouns. A language you may have come across where all nouns begin with a capital letter is German.

Activity 3 (*The Fourth Folio*) involves comparing the version of Jaques' speech given earlier with a later one, as it appeared in the Fourth Folio, dated 1685. This illustrates how spelling was moving rapidly towards PDE forms.

8.3 Punctuation

8.3.1 Punctuation on the move

Perhaps you come to this section with the idea that punctuation is something trivial and easy to understand. The latter is certainly not always true at all: some of the rules of punctuation are very difficult indeed to apply as a writer, let alone to explain. Before considering EModE punctuation, you may like to think a little about the modern system. Activity 4 (*Punctuation today*) allows you to do this.

Sam Weller's point about spelling depending on the 'taste and fancy' of the user applies equally to Elizabethan punctuation. Here again 'variation' is an important feature of Elizabethan punctuation, and for much the same reason – that writing in English was comparatively new, and rules had yet to be established. 'Flux' is another important feature. Punctuation was on the move. In Caxton's time (c. 1415–c. 1492), for example, there was a punctuation mark known as the 'virgule', written as a slash (/) and roughly equivalent to the modern comma (French speakers will recognise the word as meaning 'comma' in modern French). Here are the opening lines of Caxton's book *The Game of the Chess* (1483) showing use of this punctuation mark:[7]

> *Amonge all the euyll condicions and signes that may be in a man the first and y'e grettest is when he feereth not/ ne dredeth to displese and make wroth god by synne/ and the peple by lyuyng disordynatly/ whan he reccheth not/ ner taketh hede unto them that repreue hym and his vices/ but fleeth them/ In suche wyse as dide the emperour Nero/ whiche dide do slee his maister seneque*

By Shakespeare's day the virgule was out, but on the way in were the apostrophe and the full stop.

A matter of 'taste and fancy'. Here is how one writer puts it: 'In those days', Flatter (1948) says, 'people strutted about displaying bright colours in their doublet and hose, wearing feathers in their hats and rings in their ears: everyone who wanted to show his importance sported his own fashion and style not only in his clothes but in everything else – and something of that multifarious liberty and gay individualism is mirrored in the Elizabethan punctuation'. But again as with spelling, standardisation was on the way, and writers like Mulcaster also turned their attention to punctuation: his *Elementarie* had a section on the topic.

8.3.2 Punctuation for actors

In Activity 4 you were asked to think about the uses of punctuation marks in PDE. Doubtless many of the uses you considered were of the sort that might be called <u>grammatical</u>. That is, they indicate something about sentence structure. The comma, for example, is often used to separate phrases, the semicolon can divide clauses; and, of course, the full stop marks the end of a sentence. You can certainly find this grammatical use of punctuation in Shakespeare's day, but another function was predominant then. Here is a quotation from Mulcaster which suggests this function. He is talking about the comma, which he quaintly describes as: 'a small crooked point, which in writing followeth some small branch of the sentence, & in reading warneth vs to rest there, & to help our breth a little.' The first use he mentions – 'in writing' – is a grammatical function. But the second use ('in reading') is what has been called <u>rhetorical</u> or <u>elocutional</u>; it says something about how the sentence is to be uttered, when reading aloud for example. In fact Mulcaster makes this writing/reading distinction in discussing a number of punctuation marks. The 'writing point' is often to do with grammar, and the reading point with 'elocution'. Here for example is part of what he says about brackets: 'parenthesis is expressed by two half circles, which . . . in reading warneth us, that the words inclosed by them, ar to be pronounced with a lower & quikker voice . . .'. A main elocutional use of some punctuation marks – especially the semicolon, full stop and comma – is to mark pause length. Before reading the next paragraph, consider the relative pause length suggested by these three punctuation marks. It is not difficult to work out which one suggests the longest pause, which the shortest (**NP**).

The order in which George Puttenham (whose 1589 *Art of English Poesie*, as noted several times earlier, Shakespeare certainly knew) puts the 'three manner of pauses' is, in increasing order of length: comma, colon and full stop. Another author, the John Hart we met in 8.2.1, uses a musical analogy to make the same point. The comma, he says, is like a crotchet, and the colon like a minim (by which declension the full stop would perhaps be a semibreve).[8]

Hart's musical analogy suggests a role for punctuation in 'performance', and leads to the claim that in various ways, Renaissance punctuation marks help actors deliver their lines. The suggestion has been around for a long time. Here is Dover Wilson in 1921: 'the stops, brackets, capital letters in the [Shakespeare] Folio and Quartos are in fact stage-directions, in shorthand. They tell the actor when to pause and for how long, they guide his intonation, they indicate the emphatic word.' Sixty years later, Graham-White (1982) explores the punctuation of an anonymous comedy drama written in the 1550s, *Gammer Gurton's Needle*. He concludes that the marks help actors pace their speeches by giving information about how long pauses should be. Much more recently, Crystal (2008) suggests that some present-day directors see punctuation in the same way. He tells how in 2005 he attended rehearsals of The Globe Theatre's production of *Troilus and Cressida*. 'I can affirm,' he says, 'that there were many discussions between director and actors over precisely how much value to attach to a comma' (p. 69).

Here is a clear example of Shakespeare using punctuation in a rhetorical way. It comes from *Julius Caesar* (2.1.18). Brutus is trying to justify his part in the conspiracy to kill Caesar. He is being very hesitant, and the high number of commas in the First Folio increases this sense of hesitancy:

Th' abuse of Greatnesse, is, when it dis-ioins
Remorse from Power: And to speake truth of Caesar,
I haue not knowne, when his Affections sway'd
More then his Reason.

Some modern editors think there is too much punctuation here, and get rid of some of the commas to permit more fluency. But in doing so perhaps they destroy the sense of hesitancy.[9]

8.3.3 From light to heavy, rhetorical to grammatical

In the above example from *Julius Caesar*, the First Folio text has more punctuation marks than modern editors use. But usually it is the other way round – the original punctuation is 'lighter' than in later editions. In fact you can often date an edition by looking at how 'heavy' its punctuation is. It is perhaps surprising to the modern reader to learn how much compositors, as well as later editors, allowed themselves to make massive changes to an author's work. McKenzie (1959) focused on *The Merchant of Venice* and looked in detail at differences between one Quarto version and the First Folio. The statistics are staggering: compositors made 3200 changes in all from one version to the other, and no fewer than 715 of these involved punctuation. Commas were added, semicolons changed into full stops, question marks into commas. Is nothing sacred?

Why the increase? It seems partly to do with a shift in the predominant role of punctuation from primarily rhetorical in the Renaissance, to primarily grammatical today. Earlier, when we were talking about spelling, we noted that standardisation came about very slowly, as much linguistic change does. It is surprising then that the move from rhetorical to grammatical punctuation was so rapid. The punctuation in Shakespeare First Folios is noticeably more grammatical than in the earlier Quartos.[10] Part of the effect of this change was to increase the amount of punctuation, marking off phrases and clauses, indicating grammatical relationships – functions it had not previously been called on to fulfil.

Graham-White's *Gammer Gurton's Needle* study, mentioned a moment ago, involved comparing different versions of the play. A number of other studies have plotted punctuation changes by the same method. One, for example, does it for versions of *The Merchant of Venice* in different Quartos, while another focuses on three Shakespeare soliloquies, comparing Folio and five modern editions.[11] To try it yourself, take a look at Activity 5 (*From light to heavy*) which asks you to compare a First Folio passage with a Victorian version. The Victorians were particularly known for adding in lots of punctuation.

The list of PDE punctuation marks in Activity 4 had twelve items – too many to look at in detail. So three have been chosen for a closer look – the apostrophe, the exclamation mark, and italics. This is followed by a few briefer observations on seven more.

8.3.4 Some punctuation marks in detail

We have already seen, in 8.2.2, how an apostrophe is used to replace a missing letter. Indeed the word itself comes originally from the Greek *apostrophos* meaning 'the turning away or rejection of a letter'.[12] Another common PDE use is to mark possession. So *The boy's desk* means 'the desk of the boy'. As discussed in 4.2, the general 'rule' (which has a number of exceptions) is that *'s* is put on the end of a singular noun. If the noun is plural and already has a final *s*, you add an apostrophe to that; so *The boys' desk* means 'the desk of the boys'. There are no uses of the possessive *'s* in the Jaques passage, though you may have noted some points where we would use it in PDE: *Nurſes* and *Miſtreſſe* for example. The use was not unknown in Shakespeare's time, but it was infrequent, and found irregularly. Look for example at this passage from *Antony and Cleopatra* (2.2.5),[13] where you find the possessive apostrophe in one line, but not two lines before. The lines also contain an example of an apostrophe used to replace a missing letter:

Let Anthony looke ouer Caesars head,
And speake as lowd as Mars. By Iupiter,
Were I the wearer of Anthonio's Beard,
I would not shaue't to day.

There is an article by Cavella and Kernodle available online at http://www1. american.edu/tesol/wpkernodlecavella.pdf which gives information about the history of the apostrophe. You may perhaps have noticed that many people today tend not to use it when they 'should', or to put it in where it is not needed, as on the fruit market sign which reads: *Apple's £1.65*. Perhaps this punctuation mark is on the way out. But not if the Apostrophe Protection Society (website: http://www.apostrophe.org.uk/) has its own way!

Now to exclamation marks. In Activity 5 (*From light to heavy*) you will have noticed the Victorian predilection for the exclamation mark. In fact in Shakespeare's time, it was not used that much, and some plays have none at all. Look at a copy of the First Folio on the internet (one source is mentioned in 1.4). It will not be difficult to find a play that has no exclamation marks at all. When exclamation marks do appear, their use is very much according to the preferences of individual compositors. Crystal (2008) notes that one of the plays which shows a more sophisticated use is *A Midsummer Night's Dream*. Before reading on, take a look at Activity 6 (*Exclaiming in A Midsummer Night's Dream* – **NP**).

The Activity 6 examples from *A Midsummer Night's Dream* show that the exclamation mark is indeed used for exclamations, and the word *O* seems almost automatically to trigger its use. Sometimes, though, you find questions ending with *!* rather than *?* Perhaps the compositors themselves found it difficult to distinguish questions from exclamations. Understandably so, because it is not always easy, as a couple of the *A Midsummer Night's Dream* examples show. Are the following (all found in Activity 6) questions or exclamations?

> *oh how fit a word / Is that vile name, to perish on my sword!* (2.2.112)
> *My Oberon, what visions haue I seene!* (4.1.75)

More clearly questions are:

> *To what, my loue, shall I compare thine eyne!* (3.2.138)
> *Eyes, do you see! How can it be!* (5.1.272)

The confusion worked the other way as well. In 8.3.5 below you will find a question mark used where we would today expect an exclamation mark.

When are italics used in PDE? Consider when you would put something into italics in your own word-processed writing. Then look at Activity 7 (*Italics in Troilus and Cressida*) which provides examples of italics in Shakespeare and invites you to consider why they are used (**NP**).

One use of italics, today as in Elizabethan times, is wherever there is a desire to make a piece of text stand out in some way. In this book, for example, actual words being discussed are put in italics, to distinguish them from the rest of the text. Italics can also be used for emphasis; again, it is a way of making a word or phrase stand out. A list of some specific occasions when

Shakespeare uses italics is given below, though because of inconsistencies in spelling and punctuation at the time, it is not difficult to find many exceptions in Shakespeare texts.[14] The uses (exemplified in Activity 7) are:

(a) for stage directions;

(b) for foreign words;

(c) for names of people;

(d) for the words of songs;

(e) for proverbs or maxims;

(f) for names of places – but you find an example in the *Troilus and Cressida* passages where the name of a place is neither in italics nor even has a capital letter!

(g) in prologues or epilogues;

(h) to emphasise a particular word;

(i) in parentheses.

8.3.5 Other punctuation: A 'Rough Guide'

By far the most useful and detailed recent consideration of Shakespearean punctuation is Chapter 4 of Crystal (2008). Salmon (1986) also has a short but authoritative discussion on the topic, as does Blake (2002). Here are some of the points these authors make about aspects of punctuation not so far covered.

Colon. Called a *pause* in Ben Jonson's *English Grammar*. Often used to mark a break or a grammatical juncture longer or more important than a comma, but less than a full stop (though it was often used instead of a full stop; look back to the 'Seven Ages' speech in 2.1.2 to find an example of this).

Here is Shylock in *The Merchant of Venice* 2.5.35): *By Iacobs staffe I sweare/ I haue no minde of feasting forth to night:/ But I will goe:* (to the Clowne) *goe you before me sirra,/ Say I will come.*

Semicolons were used in roughly the same way as the colon, though suggesting a shorter pause.

Comma. New in the sixteenth century. It has a variety of uses marking off parts of a sentence. It suggests less of a break (or a less important break) than a colon, semicolon or full stop. Many uses are as in PDE – but would we use a comma here today: *Thou know'st, that we two went to Schoole together* (*Julius Caesar* 5.5.26 – the example is Blake's)? Here the comma is marking off a *that* clause acting as the object of a sentence.

The comma is sometimes used for a hyphen in compounds: *active, valiant* (for what some editors interpret as *active-valiant); well, aimed* (for *well-aimed*). See 2.3.5.

Hyphen. Becoming common in the 1570s. One use was at ends of lines, when the second half of a word appears on the next line. (*yon-der* is one of Crystal's examples). Also used in compounds ending in *-ing* or *-ed*, like *life-preserving, ill-faced*. Also after affixes like *a-: a-board*. There is huge variation per compositor.

Inverted commas (quote marks). These started to appear in the 1590s, but were not common till the late 18C. You often find the 'opening' commas, but not the 'closing' ones. Belarius in *Cymbeline* (4.2.26) says: *"Cowards father Cowards, & Base things Syre Bace/ "Nature hath Meale, and Bran; Contempt, and Grace.* Here each line of the 'saying' has opening but not closing marks. Used commonly for proverbs or maxims (look back to Activity 7 for an example). Incidentally, one method of indicating direct speech was to put the reporting verb in brackets. Here is Cornelius reporting the words of Cymbeline's wife: *If Pasanio/ Haue (said she) giuen his Mistris that Confection/ Which I gaue him for Cordiall, she is seru'd,/ As I would serue a Rat.* (Cym 5.5.245).

Question mark. Questions intended to be exclamatory had a question mark, as could any sentence beginning with a question word. A couple of examples from *Hamlet*: the first is Hamlet himself in one of those famous soliloquies: *How weary, stale, flat, and vnprofitable/ Seemes to me all the vses of this world?* (1.2.133). This begins with a question word (*How*) but is not really a question. Similarly when Polonius says *How pregnant (sometimes) his Replies are?* (2.2.209).

Logograms. (Symbols standing for words) were often used to save space. Most common is the ampersand [&] standing for *and*. [&c] is also common, for example in stage instructions: *Exit Duke &c.*

Tilde. This symbol (~) is sometimes put over a letter to indicate that a following letter (often an *m* or *n*) is omitted. There is an example in Prospero's passage in Chapter 10.1, where *stāding* is used for *standing*.

8.4 A look at the First Folio

Most of our consideration of spelling and punctuation has been based on the Jaques speech, in the original-spelling version of Wells and Taylor. This version uses various early manuscripts. To end the chapter, Figure 8.4 is a chance to look at an extract from the First Folio itself. Read through it looking for examples of some of the points made in this chapter. The passage is taken from *Romeo and Juliet* (3.5.1). Day is dawning and the lovers must part, which they do, oh so reluctantly. . . . (**NP**)

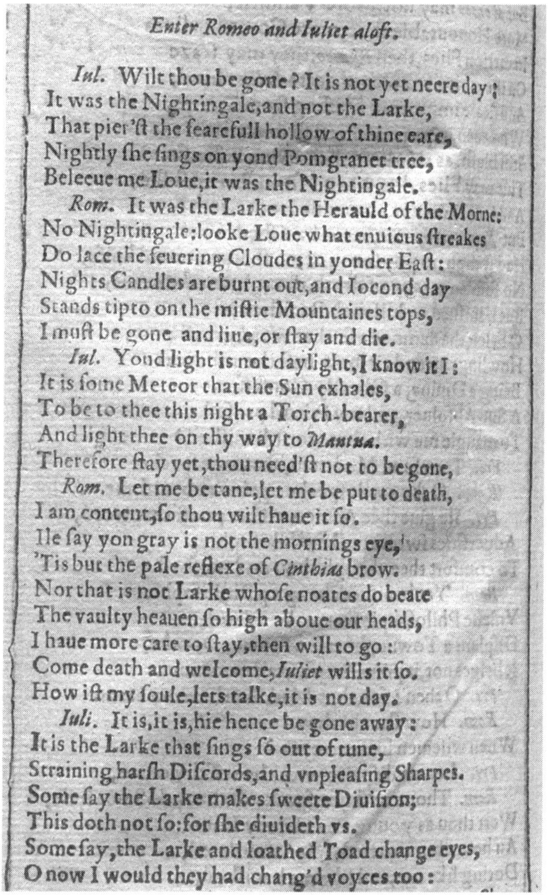

FIGURE 8.4 First Folio, *Romeo and Juliet*

Here are some points you may notice:

- *ee* spelling for an 'i' type of sound
- word-final consonant doubling;
- *v* at the beginning of a word (where PDE would have *u*); *u* in a word where we would today have *v*;
- italics for a place name, for a person's name, for stage directions;
- an apostrophe for some missing letters (which letters?);
- absence of the possessive *'s*.

The passage also has an example of an adjective with a capital letter (*Iocond* – the first letter looks like a *J*, but is probably an *I* with a damaged base).[15]

8.5 Variation and standardisation

This chapter started with Sam Weller, from Dickens' novel *The Pickwick Papers*. He talked about 'the taste and fancy of the speller', and this is one of the chapter's key phrases. It captures the variation in matters graphological that we find in Shakespeare's time. But there were, as we have seen, many attempts to put some order into the chaos of Renaissance spelling and punctuation, with educationalists and spelling reformers producing a variety of schemes intended to simplify these areas, often by regularising the relationships between how words were pronounced and how they were written. For this reason 'standardisation attempts' deserves to be a second key phrase.

But how were words pronounced in Shakespeare's time? Did the Renaissance Englishman sound like the Englishman today? Thereby hangs a tale, and enough of one to make a new chapter.[16]

Activity section

1 Graphology and spelling differences

Here are some questions intended to focus attention on some of the differences between PDE and EModE that are found in the Jaques passage. Almost all these issues are discussed in the text.

(a) 'ſ' is a form of 's'. The difference between the two is not to do with pronunciation, but with where in the word the letter comes. What might the rule be?

(b) What is the difference between 'u' and 'v' in PDE? How are these letters used in the speech? (Note: word position is also relevant here).

(c) In Shakespeare's time, the letter 'j' was rare. What is used instead?

(d) In the text, we discuss <u>consonant doubling</u>. What characteristic found in the speech might this refer to?

(e) Find the three words in the speech where *-ed* is replaced by *'d*. In 7.1.2 we saw that the vowel in *-ed* is sometimes pronounced, sometimes not. What about in these three cases?

(f) In PDE an apostrophe is sometimes used to indicate that a letter is omitted. Think of some examples. What letters are omitted in your examples? Then identify the apostrophes in the Jaques speech and say what letters they are replacing.

2 Upper and lower case

Look at the Jaques speech, concentrating solely on capitals and lower case letters at the beginning of words. Here are some statements about the use of capitals in this 'original' version. Which of the statements are true, which false? In all statements except for the first two, do not consider capitals at the beginning of lines or sentences.

(a) In blank verse, each line begins with a capital letter.

(b) The letter following a full stop is always a capital.

(c) The full stop is the only punctuation mark followed by a capital letter.

(d) All nouns have capital letters.

(e) Only nouns have capital letters.

(f) Only important nouns have capital letters.

(g) Only nouns describing animated objects have capital letters.

The 'answers' are contained in the text.

3 The Fourth Folio

The version of Jaques' speech given in 8.2.2 is based on Wells and Taylor (1986), with some changes made. This edition is based on early versions of the text. Below are the first fifteen lines of the same speech as they appear in the Fourth Folio, taken from the Internet Shakespeare Editions site (http://internetshakespeare.uvic.ca/), with the same changes made. The Fourth Folio is dated 1685, 62 years after the First Folio appeared. Compare the spelling of the two versions of the speech, and notice how much movement towards PDE has taken place during those 62 years.

Iaques   *All the world's a ſtage,*
And all the men and women, meerly Players;
They haue their Exits and their Entrances,
And one man in his time playes many parts,
His Acts being ſeuen ages. At firſt the Infant,
Mewling, and puking in the Nurſes arms:
Then, the whining School boy with his Satchel
And ſhining morning face, creeping like ſnail
Unwillingly to ſchoole. And then the Lover,
Sighing like Furnace, with a woful Ballad

Made to his Miſtreſs eye-brow. Then, a Soldier,
Full of ſtrange oaths, and bearded like the Pard,
Jealous in honour, ſudden, and quick in quarrel,
Seeking the bubble Reputation
Even in the Canons mouth.

4 Punctuation today

A list of some of the main uses of punctuation marks in PDE is given in Table 8.1. Cover the column on the right and decide which punctuation mark is being described in each row. Be warned, though: the explanations are always only partial, and sometimes also rather vague.

TABLE 8.1 PDE punctuation: some principal uses

separates phrases or clauses, or items on a list	,
indicates the end of a sentence	.
comes at the end of a direct question	?
indicates an alternative between two or more elements	/
separates independent clauses or sentences which are closely related	;
comes before a list, or some development/explanation of something just mentioned	:
indicates that a letter is missing; also used together with a final *s* on the end of a noun to indicate possession	'
introduces a secondary element which you do not want to emphasise	( )
comes at the end of a declaration, interjection or command	!
separates off a part of a sentence, often to develop/explain something	–
indicates something directly said by someone	" "
indicates that words have been missed out, e.g. from a quotation	. . .

5 From light to heavy (AS)

Here are two versions of a famous speech from *Romeo and Juliet* (2.2.1). The first (Figure 8.5) is taken from the First Folio, the second from a Victorian edition – Singer (1875).

(i) Count the number of punctuation marks in each (a sequence like *!* – would count as two). Which has more (if you are mathematically inclined you can state this in percentage terms)?

(ii) Say what the differences are. Why do you think the Victorian editor made these changes? What effect do they have?

The First Folio

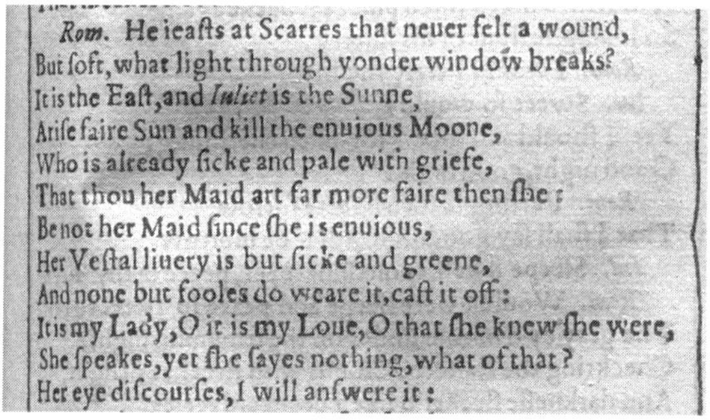

> *Rom.* He ieafts at Scarres that neuer felt a wound,
> But foft, what light through yonder window breaks?
> It is the Eaft, and *Iuliet* is the Sunne,
> Arife faire Sun and kill the enuious Moone,
> Who is already ficke and pale with griefe,
> That thou her Maid art far more faire then fhe :
> Be not her Maid fince fhe is enuious,
> Her Veftal liuery is but ficke and greene,
> And none but fooles do weare it, caft it off :
> It is my Lady, O it is my Loue, O that fhe knew fhe were,
> She fpeakes, yet fhe fayes nothing, what of that ?
> Her eye difcourfes, I will anfwere it :

FIGURE 8.5 First Folio, *Romeo and Juliet*

Singer's version

Rom. *He jests at scars, that never felt a wound.—*

But, soft! what light through yonder window breaks?

It is the east, and Juliet is the sun!—

Arise, fair sun, and kill the envious moon,

Who is already sick and pale with grief,

That thou her maid art far more fair than she:

Be not her maid, since she is envious;

Her vestal livery is but pale and green,

And none but fools do wear it; cast it off.—

It is my lady; O ! it is my love :

O, that she knew she were!—

She speaks, yet she says nothing. What of that?

Her eye discourses, I will answer it.

6 Exclaiming in *A Midsummer Night's Dream*

The examples below are all from the First Folio of *A Midsummer Night's Dream* (1.1.136). There is one word which overwhelmingly (here and in Shakespeare as a whole) appears in the context preceding an exclamation mark. What is it? Notice also that compositors sometimes used an exclamation mark instead of a question mark (probably through their own confusion). Find examples of this by looking for questions. You will find a few cases where it is not clear whether something is an exclamation or a question. But the examples include at least two unambiguous questions:

(a) *O crosse! too high to be enthral'd to loue.*

(b) *O spight! too old to be ingag'd to yong.*

(c) *O hell! to choose loue by anothers eie. /Demetrius loues you faire: O happie faire!*

(d) *oh how fit a word/ Is that vile name, to perish on my sword!*

(e) *Lord, what fooles these mortals be!*

(f) *You doe aduance your cunning more & more, /When truth kils truth, O diuelish holy fray!*

(g) *To what, my loue, shall I compare thine eyne!*

(h) *O how ripe in show, /Thy lips, those kissing cherries, tempting grow!*

(i) *O spight! O hell!*

(j) *My loue, my life, my soule, faire Helena. / Hel. O excellent!*

(k) *O how I loue thee! how I dote on thee!*

(l) *My Oberon, what visions haue I seene!*

(m) *Oh, how mine eyes doth loath this visage now!*

(n) *Gods my life!*

(o) *O most couragiovs day! O most happie houre!*

(p) *But stay: O spight!*

(q) *Eyes do you see! How can it be!*

(r) *O dainty Ducke: O Deere!*

(s) *Thy mantle good; what staind with blood!*

(t) *O Fates! come, come:*

7 Italics in *Troilus and Cressida*

Here are nine short passages from *Troilus and Cressida*, taken from Wells and Taylor (1986). Consider why italics are being used in each; you will probably be able to explain some but not all uses. Then look at the list of uses given in the text, and match uses and examples:

(a) Cressida: Therefore this *maxim* out of loue I teach,
                     "*Atchiuement is command: vngained beseech*"
                     (1.2.292)

(b) Thersites: I will see you hang'd like *Clatpoles*, ere I come any more to your tents
                     (2.1.116)

(c) Thersites: You scuruy Lord.
    Aiax: You curre.
                   [Strikes him]
                   (2.1.50)

(d) Thersites: As will stop the eye of *Hellens* needle, for whom he comes to
fight.
(2.1.79)

(e) Pandarus: In good troth it begins so.

Song

Loue, loue, nothing but loue, still loue still more:
For o loues bow,
Shoots Bucke and Doe . . .
(3.1.111)

(f) Prologue: *In Troy there lyes the Scene; From Iles of Greece*
. . . .
(1.1.1; Opening lines of the play)

(g) Nestor: But that *Achilles* weare his braine as barren,
As banks of libia *(though* Apollo *knows*
'Tis dry enough) will . . .
(1.3.327)

(h) Troylus: her bed in *India* there she lies, a pearle
(1.1.102)

(i) Thersites: Lo, lo, lo, lo, what *modicums* of wit he vtters . . . and his *pia
mater* is not worth the ninth part of a sparrow.
(2.1.67)

Extended activities

1   In 8.2.1 it is suggested that many people continue today to find English
spelling difficult. There have certainly have been a number of times in
the history of English since the Renaissance when spelling reform has
been considered. Think what the arguments for and against spelling
reform might be. You may also wish to find out about some of the
spelling reform attempts that have been made in the past.
    There is one recent innovation which is actually creating its own
kind of spelling reform. This is text messaging. Why should this be so?
List some specific examples of words that might be spelt differently in
text messages than in other situations.

2   8.2.1 mentions a number of Renaissance figures concerned with
spelling reform (and the development of writing skills). Use the
internet or some other source to find out more about the work of
one of these figures.

Again using whatever sources you have available, find out something more about the Great Vowel Shift mentioned in 8.2.1.

3   8.3.1 makes the point that punctuation rules can be very difficult to explain. Focus on the use of the semicolon in PDE. Try to set out rules for its use, in a way that distinguishes it from the comma and the full stop.

4   Find a folio text of a play of your choice. Select a passage and find examples of differences in spelling and punctuation from today. You are likely to find some that have not been discussed in this chapter. If you have the resources to do so, find out something about these differences and what rules govern the EModE usage.

The Internet Shakespeare Editions (http://internetshakespeare. uvic.ca/), contains more than one version of plays – different folios and sometimes quartos. Look at various versions of the passage you have chosen, and note what differences in spelling and punctuation there are between them.

Answer section

Hart's phonetic writing (section 8.2.1)

'because the vowels and consonants are divided into such parts as before, this table does keep them in like order: to wit first 'a', 'e', 'i', 'o', 'u', and then the four pairs which are made with . . .'

The apostrophe as 'letter replacer' (section 8.2.2)

- *-ed* verb ending: *auis'd*; *reueng'd*

- lightly pronounced medial vowel: *desp'rate*; *sland'rous*

- in a preposition, a pronoun or the definite article: *o'my life*; *sh'adulterates*; *th'ther day*; *o're*; *for't*

- common verb sequences, with *do, be* or *have*: *wil't*; *y'haue*; *thou'rt*; *w'are*; *do's*; *'tis*.

Activity 5 From light to heavy

There are 20 punctuation marks in the First Folio, 30 in the Singer version – i.e. 50 % more.

The changes from early to late are: comma and colon (on one occasion) become full stop or exclamation mark plus dash; exclamation marks are added; commas are added; commas become semicolons; colons become full stops.

Notes

1 Because of this chapter's subject matter, all of the Shakespeare quotations are given in original spelling (which has largely been avoided in earlier chapters).

2 The sites are http://shakespeareauthorship.com/name1.html and http://languagelog.ldc.upenn.edu/nll/?p=1314

3 These attempts at standardisation are described in Salmon (1986).

4 A few changes have been made to the Wells and Taylor text: italics have been eliminated; words have been separated or joined where they would be separated or joined in modern English (this includes eliminating some hyphens); some EModE spellings that are not discussed in the text here have been written as in PDE. For example: *sixt* for *sixth*, *honor* for *honour*, and *sodaine* for *sudden*; apostrophes have been added where they would occur in PDE; 's' has been replaced by 'ſ' where the First Folio has the latter.

5 This quotation is cited in Salmon (1986) whose discussion is used as the basis for this section on final *e*.

6 Cited in Salmon (1986).

7 Taken from http://www.gutenberg.org/files/10672/10672-h/10672-h. htm#bk1ch1

8 Puttenham and Hart are cited on this point by Crystal (2008).

9 Warren (1977), from whom the example comes, argues this.

10 The point is made by Graham-White (1982).

11 The studies are by McKenzie (1959) and Warren (1977) respectively.

12 According to Partridge (1964).

13 From the Wells and Taylor (1986).

14 The list is based on discussions in Crystal (2008) and Salmon (1986).

15 Thanks to Geoffrey Leech for pointing this out.

16 The phrase 'thereby hangs a tale' is from a speech by Jaques (AYLI 2.7.20). It was quoted in 1.1.

Further reading

On the topic of transmission – discussed in 1.5 but very relevant to this chapter – the following two articles provide accessible, brief accounts: Murphy, A. (2010) 'The transmission of Shakespeare's texts'. In De Grazia, M. and Wells, S. (eds) (2010) *The New Cambridge Companion to Shakespeare*, Cambridge: Cambridge University Press, 61–76, and Maguire, L. (2003) 'Shakespeare published', in Wells, S. and Orlin, L. C. (eds) *An Oxford Guide to Shakespeare*, Oxford: Oxford University Press, 582–594.

A good short introduction to the field is given by Salmon, V. (1986) 'The spelling and punctuation of Shakespeare's time'. In Wells, S. and Taylor, G. (eds) (1986) *Shakespeare: The complete works (original spelling edition)*. A whole book on the topic is Partridge, A. C. (1964) *Orthography in Shakespeare and Elizabethan Drama*, London: Edward Arnold. There is a section of Salmon, V. and Burness, E. (eds) (1987) *Reader in the Language of Shakespearean Drama*, Amsterdam: Benjamins, devoted to punctuation.

CHAPTER 9

Sounds: The 'tongue's sweet melody'[1]

Key phrases:
not so different; 'researchable'

9.1 How different . . . and why bother?

If by some magic you were transported to Shakespeare's time, into the presence of the Bard himself, and his company of actors, and could hear them speak, what would they sound like? How easy would his version of English pronunciation be to understand? It seems likely that the man himself spoke with a slight West Country accent, not unlike the Warwickshire accent of today.[2] But just how different from today Elizabethan pronunciation was is a subject of scholarly disagreement. If you look at the 'Shakespeare's pronunciation' page on the 'Internet Shakespeare Editions' site (http://internet shakespeare.uvic.ca/Library/SLT/literature/language/pronunciation.html), the first sentence you will read is 'Elizabethan pronunciation differed significantly from our own'. But Baugh and Cable's opening sentence on the same topic could not be more different (2002: 234): 'Shakespeare's pronunciation, though not ours, was much more like ours than has always been realised'. Helge Kökeritz, one of the major authors in the Shakespearean pronunciation field, comes down on the 'not so different' side. Those who expect what is called 'original pronunciation' (OP) to be alien will, he says, 'have to reconcile themselves to the fact that they would be able to understand Shakespeare. . . . with little effort'.[3] Crystal expresses a similar view when he says 'people generally expect OP to be much more different from Modern English than in fact it is, and it comes as a bit of a surprise to realise that it is in many respects identical' (2005: 36). It is indeed a question of just what your expectations are, of course. As this chapter will show, there are a good number of differences between PDE and EModE. But not so many as to impede comprehension severely, and we can at least conclude that there is a body of opinion in support of one of this chapter's key phrases: 'not so different'.

What scholastic differences do suggest is that we need to approach the question of how words were pronounced more than 400 years ago with caution. In the latter half of this chapter we shall look at ways in which evidence about pronunciation has been collected. Though some methods are quite reliable, it is important to realise that pronunciation is, of its very nature, a variable thing. Attend two performances of the same modern play and you are likely to find differences (perhaps even considerable ones) in the pronunciation of the actors. People pronounce words differently, not just according to where they come from, but also following their own personal styles and idiosyncrasies. So it was in Shakespeare's day too, and it would be foolish to lay down strict 'laws' about how words were pronounced. Add to this fact that in Shakespeare's time there did not exist any strong sense of a 'Received Pronunciation' – a socially accepted norm that we have had in more recent times. Thus in the huge social mix of sixteenth-century London, you are likely to have met a huge variety of pronunciations – more variety even than we saw in the last chapter in relation to spelling and punctuation. Incidentally, in this chapter we will regularly refer to RP (for Received Pronunciation), often called 'BBC English' or 'the Queen's English'. It identifies a particular variety of present-day British English pronunciation, originating in the southern counties and accepted by some as a 'standard'. You will find in the chapter that we often talk about RP pronunciations, sometimes comparing them EModE. If the version of English you use is not RP, you need to be aware that statements made will sometimes (frustratingly perhaps) not apply to your version of English at all. You will certainly soon realise that RP can be substantially different from other spoken varieties of English – British dialects, Australian and American English, for example.

So we will never be sure exactly how the actors in Shakespeare's first performances said their lines. But does this matter? For some reason, studying historical pronunciation causes more people to ask 'why bother?' than the historical study of other aspects of language. Why should we want to know how Shakespeare was pronounced? Brook (1976) gives three reasons. One is that if we are to appreciate 'the melody of Shakespeare's verse', knowing about pronunciation will be useful. Secondly, there may be times when editorial decisions about how a word should be spelt, or which of two possible words is right in a given context, will be helped by information about pronunciation.

The third reason is in order to appreciate examples of word play. Many puns depend on words being pronounced in the same (or very similar) ways. These are what are called <u>homophones</u>. Examples of homophonic pairs in RP are *bold* and *bowled*, *morning* and *mourning*, *soul* and *sole*. Shakespeare is full of homophonic pairs like these being used for puns. At the beginning of *Julius Caesar*, for example, a citizen is stopped in the street and asked what his job is. *A trade, sir, that I hope I may use with a safe conscience*, he replies, *which is, indeed, sir, a mender of bad soles* (1.1.14). His answer hints that he may be a churchman ('mending' souls), while in fact he is a cobbler (mending soles). But because pronunciation changes over time, it is not surprising that some words which were homophones in Shakespeare's day, are today pronounced differently. In other words, they could be puns then, but are not now. We came across an example in 1.1. involving a pun which made melancholic Jaques in *As You Like It* laugh for an hour. It hinges round the words *hour* and *whore* which were homophones in EModE but which are not today. *And so from hour to hour we ripe, and ripe*, the jester Touchstone says, *And then from hour to hour we rot, and rot* (2.7.26). The joke will be lost to us today, unless we know something about EModE pronunciation.

Pronunciation changes will also, of course, lead to words which today are homophones, but which may not have been so in EModE. *Board* and *bawd* are a case in point.[4] In the former word, the 'r' would have been pronounced, so the words were not quite homophones, as they are in RP (though not in many other versions of PDE).

Unless you are an actor, you will not be interested in learning about how Shakespeare was pronounced in order to pronounce it like that yourself. But perhaps you will find that actually pronouncing words is a good way of learning something about EModE pronunciation. That is why, below, it will be sometimes suggested that you try pronouncing individual words, or reading a passage, aloud. There have been productions of Shakespeare plays where OP has been attempted. A major one was undertaken by London's Globe Theatre in 2004 when for three days *Romeo and Juliet* was performed using OP. The guiding linguistic spirit behind this project was David Crystal, and his book (Crystal, 2005) describes in detail how the project was conceived and realised. A site which contains audio samples of Crystal reading Shakespearean passages in OP, together with transcriptions and notes, is mentioned in the next section.[5]

9.2 A first look (or listen)

By far the best way of approaching Shakespearean pronunciation is to start by listening to an example. If you have access to the internet, you can find examples at the following two sites:

- http://www.npr.org/templates/story/story.php?storyId=4761275
  As well as performing *Romeo and Juliet* in OP, London's Globe Theatre has also done *Troilus and Cressida*. Here the actor Peter Forbes is reading that play's Prologue.

- http://www.pronouncingshakespeare.com/op-recordings/ This is David Crystal reading several passages: the Prologue to *Romeo and Juliet*, Sonnets 1 and 116, *Troilus and Cressida* 1.1.[6]

Choose a passage and listen to it several times, noting any major differences between what you hear and RP (or whatever PDE pronunciation you use as a model). Later sections focus on distinct areas of difference between EModE and RP. At this stage it is enough to form an impressionistic view of the differences between then and now.

If you do not have internet access, very much a second best is to look at a phonetic transcription of a text and try to read it for yourself.[7] Table 9.1 shows the Prologue to *Romeo and Juliet* (1.1.1), spoken by the Chorus figure (one of the passages that Crystal reads on the second website mentioned above). You will notice that the Prologue has the form of a sonnet (like the passage discussed in 7.2.1 where Romeo and Juliet first meet). On the left is the written text, and on the right a phonetic transcription.[8] If you have no access to the internet, and do not want to work with phonetic transcription, the alternative is to omit this section and go straight to the detailed

TABLE 9.1 Prologue to *Romeo and Juliet* with phonetic transcription

Two households, both alike in dignity,	tuː əʊsoːldz, boːθ əlaɪk ɪn dɪgnɪtəɪ,
In fair Verona, where we lay our scene,	ɪn fɛːr vəroːnə, hwɛːr wɪ leː əʊr seːn,
From ancient grudge break to new mutiny,	frəm eːnʃənt grɤdʒ breːk tə njuː mjuːtnəɪ,
Where civil blood makes civil hands unclean.	hwɛːr sɪvɪl blɤd meːks sɪvɪl andz ənkleːn.
From forth the fatal loins of these two foes	frəm foːrθ ðə feːtl ləɪnz əv ðeːz tuː foːz
A pair of star-crossed lovers take their life;	ə pɛːr əv staːr krɒst lɤvrz teːk ðɛːr ləɪf;
Whose misadventured piteous overthrows	huːz mɪsədventərd pɪtjəs oːvərθroːz
Doth with their death bury their parents' strife.	dɤθ wɪð ðɛːr deθ berəɪ ðɛːr pɛːrənts strəɪf.
The fearful passage of their death-marked love	ðə fiərfəl pæsɪdʒ əv ðɛːr deθ maːrkt lɤv
And the continuance of their parents' rage,	ənd ðə kəntɪnjʊəns əv ðɛːr pɛːrənts reːdʒ,
Which, but their children's end, naught could remove,	hwɪtʃ, bɤt ðɛːr tʃɪldrənz end, naːt kʊd rəmɤv,
Is now the two hours' traffic of our stage;	ɪz nəʊ ðə tuː əʊrz træfɪk əv əʊr steːdʒ;
The which if you with patient ears attend,	ðə hwɪtʃ ɪf juː wɪð peːʃənt iːrz ətend,
What here shall miss, our toil shall strive to mend.	hwɔt iːr ʃəl mɪs, əʊr təɪl ʃəl strəɪv tə mend.

description of sounds beginning in 9.3. Phonetic symbols are used there (so cannot be avoided entirely), but to a restricted extent. The phonetic symbols used in this book are given before the main text of this book. There is also a box at the beginning of 9.4.1 (*Classifying vowels*) which provides some guidance regarding the pronunciation of a few selected sounds.

9.3 Looking at some consonants

9.3.1 [r]

If you have been listening to an audio recording, one of the first things you may have noticed is the pronunciation of the sound [r]. This is always a problematic but an interesting sound in English. It is one that can be pronounced in a variety of ways. Indeed, there is even a word (though admittedly not in common use) – 'rhotacism', which the *OED* defines as the 'unusual pronunciation or pronounced production' of [r]. MacCarthy (1950: 134) warns foreign learners of English that native speakers find mispronunciation of the RP 'r' 'to be the most noticeable and most objectionable of all the mistakes of pronunciation'. Consider first the situation in the RP and Australian versions of PDE. Activity 1 (*Pronouncing and not pronouncing an 'r'*) looks at this (**NP**).

What Activity 1 shows is that in RP today the letter is sometimes pronounced and sometimes not. Where it occurs at the beginning of a word (word-initially) or before a vowel, it is pronounced, as in *run, recent, enrol, acronym, arrive*. But it is not pronounced at the end of a word (word-finally), or in the middle of a word (word-medially) before a consonant. The words in Activity 1 like this are *teacher, arm, cart, fair* and *fewer*. Languages or dialects which do not pronounce the 'r' before a consonant or in word-final position are called <u>non-rhotic</u>. But not all 'Englishes' are non-rhotic. Examples of rhotic versions of English are American and Scots, and here the 'r' is pronounced almost wherever it is written. Another such language is EModE, which is why you find so many 'r' sounds in whatever example of OP you have been considering. Consequently it is easy to know when to pronounce the 'r' in EModE. The rule of thumb is 'if there is an "r" in the spelling, pronounce it'.

But how is it pronounced? A phonetician would describe the sound as a <u>post-alveolar fricative</u>. The tip of the tongue comes quite close to the back (the 'post' part of the description) of the teeth ridge (sometimes called the alveolum) and the sound is caused by the friction of breath between the two (a fricative). But there are very many variations. Some [r] sounds are 'trilled', an effect achieved by vibrating the tip of the tongue (as for example in the Italian word *terra*). Others are called 'retroflex', meaning that the tip of the tongue is slightly bent backwards. If you pronounce the word *bird* as an American might, or as someone from the British West Country in England (the accent of Devon or Somerset for example), you may be able to experience what a retroflex [r] feels like to make.[9] Indeed, your initial reaction to hearing OP might be how much it sounds like West Country British. If so, your impression will doubtless have a lot to do with when and how the 'r's are pronounced, with a hint of retroflexion given to them.

We do not know, though, exactly how 'r' was pronounced in Shakespeare's time. One of his contemporaries, Ben Jonson, was best known as a play-wright, but he also wrote a book entitled *English Grammar* in which he describes 'r' as the 'dog's letter' (*littera canina* in Latin), because it sounds like a growl. Indeed, in *Romeo and Juliet* (2.4.204) the Nurse (talking about the first letter of Romeo's name) calls it *the dog's name*. Jonson provides a detailed description of how to make the sound, with 'the tongue striking the inner palate, with a trembling about the teeth. It is sounded firme in the beginning of words, and more liquid in the middle, and ends; as in *rare* and *riper*'. From this description, it sounds as if initial [r] may have been a little trilled. Notice also that Jonson's description distinguishes initial [r] from the medial and word-final versions (and according to Kökeritz, 1953: 314, he was the first to do so). There is, as we have seen, a distinction between two types of 'r' which is relevant to PDE pronunciation: the word-initial and word-medial pre-vocalic 'r' which we pronounce today in RP, and the word-medial preconson-antal and word-final 'r' which we do not pronounce. Kökeritz describes this second as a 'weakly sounded' version. Though Jonson talks only about word-initial, medial and final positions, and does not mention preconson-antal or prevocalic positions, perhaps he has the same distinction in mind. If so, his 'more liquid' may mean the same as Kökeritz's 'weakly sounded'.

Sometimes phonetic transcriptions distinguish the two sorts of 'r'. The symbol [r] is used to represent the one we pronounce in RP today, while the 'weakly sounded' medial preconsonantal as well as word-final versions (not pronounced in RP today, though it is in many other versions of modern English) are represented by [ɹ]. Look through the transcription of the *Romeo and Juliet* Prologue given earlier and consider where the symbol [ɹ] could be used. In the second line, for example, [fɛːɹ] could replace [fɛːr]. You may also wish to read the passage again to yourself, concentrating on the 'r' sounds and being sure to pronounce them all.

9.3.2 [h]

Look again at the *Romeo and Juliet* passage (or listen to an OP passage from the internet) and concentrate on consonants only this time. Identify any major differences between EModE and PDE pronunciation (there are not many), and articulate as far as possible what those differences are (**NP**).

As we have seen, people can be very particular about the way [r] is pronounced (positively 'neurhotic' one might say). The same is true about [h]. In RP it is frequently dropped when in an unstressed position, so a sentence like *Hand him his hat* is likely to be pronounced as if it were *Hand im iz hat* where the initial 'h' of the unstressed words *him* and *his* is dropped.[10] But in EModE it was common for it to be omitted at the beginning of a stressed syllable, which is not normal today. For some people today, 'dropping your aitches' (saying '*ouse* instead of *house*, for example) is considered a mark of lack of education. But this view only began in the nineteenth century, and in Shakespeare's day there was no such derogatory association. As Kökeritz puts it, 'the correct use of *h* had not yet become a shibboleth of gentility'.[11] Examples of missing 'h's in the *Romeo and Juliet* transcription are in the words *households* (two 'h's gone there) and *hands*. But it is pronounced (though rather lightly) in the word *whose*. Notice that sometimes in both EModE and PDE an initial 'h' that is written is never pronounced – the example in the passage is the word *hours*. There is no 'h' sound in PDE here.

According to Crystal (2004) dropping the 'h' can be done for emotional reasons. The example he gives is from *Romeo and Juliet*, when Capulet is angry with his daughter Juliet for disobeying him (3.5.164). According to this view, not many 'h's would be pronounced in the last two lines:

My fingers itch. Wife, we scarce thought us blest
That God had lent us but this only child.
But now I see this one is one too much,
And that we have a curse in having her.
Out on her, hilding!

9.3.3 [hw]

The pronunciation of 'wh', when it comes at the beginning of a word, is interesting. In RP, initial 'wh' in words like *what* and *which* (but not *who* and *whose*) is pronounced [w]. In EModE it was pronounced [hw]. So *witch* and *which* were not homophones, because the second would start with [hw]. You can find five examples of [hw] pronunciations in the *Romeo and Juliet* passage. This sound comes from OE, where it was reflected in the spelling. The OE 'hw' became reversed in the twelfth century, to give 'wh'. Perhaps the reason for the reversal was an analogy with other consonantal combinations like *th* and *ch* where the 'h' comes second. Some modern versions of English (like

Scottish) still maintain the [hw] pronunciation for words like *what* and *where*. By way of a digression (not related to pronunciation at all!), the box below discusses an OE word where the [hw] is written 'hw' rather than 'wh'. It is *hwæt*, predecessor to today's *what*:

Listen up

The first word of the best-known OE poem, *Beowulf* (turned into a 'motion capture' film in 2007) was *hwæt*. It is used there as a means of attracting the audience's attention, meaning something like 'listen up'. It is interesting to note that *what* is occasionally used in this attention-attracting sense in Shakespeare. For example, when Prospero in *The Tempest* (4.1.33) calls his servant he says *What, Ariel*), and the Nurse calls Juliet in *Romeo and Juliet* (1.3.4) by saying *What, Juliet*.

Another variation you may have come across is the greeting/attention-attracting *what ho*, used a lot in the early twentieth century, though not today. In fact, the BBC used the title *What ho! Jeeves* for a series of radio adaptations of stories by the author P. G. Wodehouse. Actually the phrase goes back to Chaucer, where the form was *what how*.

What is not the only 'wh' word used to attract attention or summon someone. In *The Merchant of Venice* Shylock impatiently calls his daughter Jessica by saying *Why Jessica I say* (2.5.6). *When* is also used as an exclamation of impatience. Here Brutus is using it (as well as *what*) to call his servant: *When, Lucius, when? Awake, I say! What, Lucius!* (JC 2.1.5).

9.4 Some vowels and diphthongs

9.4.1 'Monophthongs then, diphthongs, now'

'Trying to tell people about sounds on paper', Culpeper (2005: 28) observes, 'is tricky at the best of times'. He is right, and this section may show just that, as we look in detail at some of the sound changes that have occurred between Shakespeare and now. Seat belts need to be fastened!

So far in this book, we have talked about vowels and consonants, and the box in 7.1.2 (*Syllables explained . . . in words of one syllable*), briefly described what a vowel is and the central part it plays in the syllable. Here is another box which discusses how vowels can be classified.

Classifying vowels

One important dimension for the classification of vowels relates to tongue position. When a vowel is pronounced, the tongue makes a 'hump' in the mouth. The highest point of that hump will change according to the vowel pronounced. Two axes are relevant here. One is high → low, and vowels are classified as <u>close</u>, <u>half-close</u>, <u>half-open</u> and <u>open</u>, according to the position of the highest part of the tongue in relation to the top or bottom of the mouth. The other axis describing the hump's position is front → back, and along this dimension vowels are described as <u>front</u>, <u>central</u> or <u>back</u>. In the word *seat*, where the vowel is [iː], the highest point of the tongue is in the top front section of the mouth. So the vowel is described as 'close front'. The [ɑː] vowel in the word *car*, on the other hand, is pronounced with the highest point of the tongue in the bottom back section, and the vowel is therefore 'open back'.

Phoneticians use a diagrammatic chart to represent the mouth, so that the individual vowels can be marked on it according to tongue position. Figure 9.1 is a common version of it, with a few vowels (to be discussed below) shown.[12]

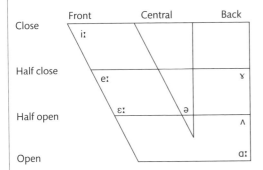

FIGURE 9.1 Vowel classification: tongue positions

The diagram shows the position of the vowels [iː] and [ɑː] discussed above. It also shows why diphthongs discussed in 9.4.2 are called 'centralised', their first element being the central vowel [ə].

There is one sound shown here which does not occur in the *Romeo and Juliet* transcription. It is the RP vowel [ʌ], found in words like *shut, cut* and *grudge*. This last word occurs in line 3 of the *Romeo and Juliet* Prologue, and you will see that it is transcribed using the symbol [ɣ]. The diagram shows that this sound is slightly more closed that the RP [ʌ]. If possible, listen again to Crystal's reading of the Prologue. You may be able to discern that his pronunciation of the vowel in *grudge* is very slightly more close that it would be in RP.

Another two sounds that are not so easily distinguishable are the [ɛ:] in [fɛːr], and the [eː] in [seːn], both in line 2 of the transcription. Again, a careful listening to Crystal's transcription will suggest what the chart shows, that [ɛ:] is the slightly more open of the two.

Tongue position is not the only dimension important in classifying vowels. Another is 'perceived length'. English vowels are often described as 'short' or 'long'. The short [æ] in *cat* and the long [ɑː] in *cart* are examples, and the symbol [ː] is often used to indicate a long vowel. The word 'perceived' is important because in purely acoustic terms the principles governing actual sound length are in fact extremely complex – in some circumstances a long vowel may not in fact be that long, nor a short vowel that short.

Another classificatory dimension is lip position, with 'rounded' and 'unrounded' being the two commonly identified positions. Compare the rounded lip position in the sound [uː] in 'two' (the first word in the transcription), and the unrounded position of [ɪ] in the fifth word.

It will now be useful to distinguish between 'pure' vowels (also called <u>monophthongs</u>), and <u>diphthongs</u>. The sound [e] in RP *get*, the [æ] in *cat*, and the [ɑː] in *cart* are monophthongs. As you produce these vowels, the sound remains relatively constant throughout, however long the sound is continued. For example, if you artificially extend, for as long as you have breath, the vowel [ɑː] in the word *bah* ('bɑːɑːɑːɑːɑːɑːɑːɑː'), the vowel sound will remain more or less the same. But in a diphthong, the sound 'deliberately' changes direction – you 'glide' from one sound to another. Examples are the [eɪ], [əʊ] and [ɪə] in RP *pay, low* and *peer*. A diphthong may be regarded as 'one sound' which changes in the middle; or it may be seen as two vowels combined, as long as it is understood that they occur together in the same syllable. In RP the second element of a diphthong will be an [ɪ], [ʊ], or [ə], as in the examples above.

You will have noticed in the *Romeo and Juliet* Prologue (or whatever passage of Shakespeare you have been considering) that some sounds which are today diphthongs were then monophthongs. One example is the word 'fair'. In RP this is pronounced with the sound [eə], while in EModE it was [ɛ:] – the introduction to this book, giving a list of phonetic symbols, contains an indication of how that sound is pronounced. In the *Romeo and Juliet* transcription, you will find another eleven examples of RP [eə] pronounced as [ɛ:] (some of these eleven being in the same word repeated more than once) (**AS**). 'Monophthongs then, diphthongs, now' is indeed a common phenomenon; as Kökeritz (1953: 161) says: 'one of the major differences between [RP] and late 16th-century pronunciation is the absence in the latter of certain diph-thongs and diphthonging tendencies which characterize our speech today'.

Another example of 'monophthong then, diphthong now' is modern [eɪ] being pronounced [eː]. This happens in the word 'fatal' (line 5 of the tran-scription). Today we would pronounce the word with a diphthong: [feɪtl]. But in EModE it was a monophthong ([feːtl]). Again you are invited to find the other eight examples in the passage (but note that there are in addition a fur-ther three words having the [eː] sound which would not be pronounced [eɪ] today) (**AS**). A third case is the RP word 'foes', which today we pronounce with the diphthong [əʊ] – [fəʊz]. You will see from the transcription that it was pronounced with [oː]. Find the other four examples of this in the passage (again bearing in mind that there are other instances where the RP sound would not be [əʊ]) (**AS**). Incidentally, there are a number of present-day British English accents which have monophthongs where RP has a diph-thong, and [eɪ] is a case in point. Thus many speakers of Yorkshire dialects pronounce words like *mate* with the monophthong [eː].

9.4.2 Centralised diphthongs

Despite the 'monophthongs then, diphthongs, now' tendency, EModE was far from being diphthong-free. Activity 2 (*Dip and mono, then and now*) explores some EModE diphthongs. Indeed, it looks at one case of 'diphthong then, monophthong now'. This is the RP sound [ɪ] which in EModE was sometimes pronounced as the diphthong [əɪ]. There are plenty of occurrences of this diphthong in the *Romeo and Juliet* transcription, though only three where in RP we would find the monophthong [ɪ] – at the end of the words *dignity, mutiny* and *bury* (**NP**).

One way in which we can gain evidence about EModE pronunciation is by looking at rhymes. Here are three lines from Sonnet 62. They include a rhyme which is relevant because it involves the word *remedy* which in RP at least is pronounced with the same (word-final) vowel as in *dignity, mutiny* and *bury*:

> *Sin of self-love possesseth all mine eye,*
> *And all my soul, and all my every part;*
> *And for this sin there is no remedy*

If we first assume that the word *eye* was pronounced as it is today (with the diphthong [aɪ]), the suggestion is that the final sound in *remedy* was also a diphthong in EModE. And if *remedy* finishes with a diphthong, then so too perhaps do *dignity, mutiny* and *bury*, which is just what the *Romeo and Juliet* transcription shows. But which diphthong? The RP diphthong which makes up the word *eye* is [aɪ]. So if *eye* and *remedy* are to rhyme, we would expect the final diphthong of *remedy* to be [aɪ] also, giving the pronunciation [remədaɪ]. So too, one might expect, in *dignity*, *mutiny* and *bury*. But the transcription does not show [aɪ] in these words. It has [əɪ] instead: *dɪgnɪtəɪ, mjuːtnəɪ* and *berəɪ*. This suggests that today's RP diphthong [aɪ] was pronounced as [əɪ] in EModE.

The evidence of rhyme plays a part in this argument, relating to words (*eye* and *remedy*) which do not rhyme today. In 9.1, we considered words which were homophones in EModE, but are no longer so. Homophones, like rhymes, can also provide valuable information about pronunciation, including in the case of the diphthongs we are considering here. In 1687 (admittedly a little after Shakespeare's time),[13] the educationalist Christopher Cooper wrote a book entitled *The English Teacher* which contains a useful list of homophones. Two from his list are *line* and *loin*. Homophones mean possible puns, and so it is in the *Romeo and Juliet* Prologue line: *From forth the fatal loins of these two foes*. Since *lines* and *loins* were pronounced in the same way, this could be referring to *loins* in the meaning which the word carries today, or it might refer to *lines*, meaning 'ancestry'. But notice how the diphthong in *loins* is transcribed in the *Romeo and Juliet* extract. It is not [ɔɪ] as it is today, nor is it [aɪ] as in *lines*. It is the same diphthong found in *dignity*, *mutiny* and *bury*: [əɪ].

The EModE diphthongs we have been considering (and others which Activity 2 draws attention to) have [ə] as their first element. This sound is called a <u>central vowel</u>, and the box (*Classifying vowels*) at the beginning of this section explains why. Central vowels are relevant here because it is a phonetic feature of EModE that some diphthongs started with more centralised vowels than today. The examples given in Activity 2 show this. Along with *dignity*, *mutiny, bury*, and *loins* discussed above (as well as *boy*, containing the same diphthong as *loins*), there are four words in the transcription – *alike, life, strife* and *strive* – where we find EModE [əɪ] for RP [aɪ]. We also find *our, now, hours* and <u>household</u> with [əʊ] for RP [aʊ].

Incidentally, Activity 2 also includes one example of 'monophthong then, monophthong now', but where the monophthong has changed. This is the RP [iː] found in *scene, unclean* and *these*. The transcription shows [eː] for these sounds.

9.5 Some EModE pronunciation 'practice drills'

A lot of detail has been covered in this chapter, so (before seat belts are finally unfastened) here is a summary, together with some pronunciation 'practice drills' to provide the opportunity to say the sounds we have been discussing. The practice words have mostly been taken from the beginning of Act 4 of *Henry V* (starting with the Chorus' speech talking about *A little touch of Harry in the night*. A great speech, and well worth a look – 4.1.1).

(a) [r] Unlike in RP, 'r' is pronounced wherever it is written. The areas to look out for are medially before a consonant and word finally, because this is where it is not pronounced in RP but would be in EModE. Words to practise:

conjecture   *third*   *morning*   *danger*   *umbered*

(b) [h] There was no shame in 'dropping your aitches' even in a stressed position. Words to practise:

hum   *hammers*   *horrid*   *host*   *head*

(c) [hw] Words which have an initial 'wh', now pronounced [w] in RP (though not in some versions of PDE).

when   *where*   *which*   *why*   *what*

(d) [ɛː] For the RP [eə]. Do not forget to pronounce the 'r's in the examples below.

where   *care*   *despair*   *chair*   *rare*

(e) [eː] For the RP [eɪ]. A long monophthong where RP has a diphthong.

lake   *cage*   *pay*   *obey*   *age*

(f) [oː] Where RP has [əʊ]. Monophthong for diphthong again.

go   *slow*   *odour*   *though*   *show*

(g) [əɪ] For RP word final [ɪ]. Diphthong for monophthong this time.

army   *paly*   *drowsy*   *tediously*   *patiently*

(h) Centralised diphthongs. The first element of some PDE diphthongs is the central vowel [ə]. So the [aɪ] in RP *die* is [əɪ]; the [aʊ] in RP *how* is [əʊ], and the [ɔɪ] in RP *joy* is [əɪ].

wide	*fire*	*foul*	*hour*	*toy*
destroy	*sounds*	*night*	*foils*	*time*
drowsy	*royal*			

Finally in this section, here is the opportunity to read a passage of Shakespeare aloud, following OP as much as possible. It is Sonnet 116. This is one of the passages Crystal reads on http://www.pronouncingshakespeare.com/op-recordings/ and if you have access to the internet you can listen to his version (perhaps <u>after</u> you have formulated your own).

> *Let me not to the marriage of true minds*
> *Admit impediments. Love is not love*
> *Which alters when it alteration finds,*
> *Or bends with the remover to remove.*
> *O no, it is an ever-fixed mark*
> *That looks on tempest and is never shaken;*
> *It is the star to every wand'ring bark,*
> *Whose worth's unknown, although his height be taken.*
> *Love's not Time's fool, though rosy lips and cheeks*
> *Within his bending sickle's compass come;*
> *Love alters not with his brief hours and weeks,*
> *But bears it out even to the edge of doom.*
> *If this be error and upon me proved,*
> *I never writ, nor no man ever loved*

9.6 Shakespearean pronunciation: how do we know?[(14)]

One question which often arises when issues of historical pronunciation are discussed is: how on earth do we know? When dealing with areas like grammar and lexis, we have the words on the page to provide evidence. But sounds are acoustic waves which once said disappear, literally, into thin air. Yet scholars speak about how given words were pronounced four hundred years ago. How can they know? In fact, a number of the types of evidence used have already been mentioned in this chapter. Before reading what follows, look back at the evidence that has been referred to so far (**NP**).

9.6.1 Passing comments

One source of information comes from contemporary accounts – what people of the time say about pronunciation matters. Sometimes the information comes almost in passing, through incidental mentions of pronunciation. An oft-quoted example is from *Love's Labour's Lost*, the Shakespeare play which (as we noted in Chapter 2) particularly focuses on curious language uses. In

2.2.3 we considered a speech of the schoolmaster Holofernes. He is known for his linguistic pedantry, and thereby provides useful evidence of what was pedantic at the time. Here again is part of his outburst against Don Adriano de Armado, described in various *Dramatis Personae* lists as 'an affected Spanish Braggart', or 'a fantastical Spaniard'. Holofernes is scathing about him (LLL 5.1.16):

He [Don Adriano] draweth out the thread of his verbosity finer than the staple of his argument. I abhor such fanatical phantasimes, such insociable and point-device companions, such rackers of orthography, as to speak 'dout' sine 'b' when he should say 'doubt', 'det' when he should pronounce 'debt' – d, e, b, t, not d, e, t. He clepeth a calf 'cauf', half 'hauf'; neighbour vocatur 'nebor', neigh abbreviated 'ne'. This is abhominable, which he would call 'abominable'. It insinuateth me of insanie.

If you look up *debt* in the *OED*, you will find that in the thirteenth century it was written *dete*, without the 'b'. The first *OED* example of a spelling with 'b' is dated 1548, and this seems to have been the work of spelling reformers who noted that the word comes from the Latin *debitum*. The way of acknowledging this Latin source was, they appear to have believed, to put a 'b' into the spelling. There are always those who believe you should pronounce as you spell, including Holofernes. So he, like others of his pedantic ilk, then translated the spelt 'b' into a pronounced one. Another word he mentions is *calf*. This is different since the 'l' was always there in the spelling. But it had stopped being pronounced in colloquial English, and we find rhymes in Shakespeare that suggest the silent 'l' in similar words – *hawk* and *baulk* are for example rhymed.[15] But one authority of the time, the schoolmaster and spelling reformer Alexander Gill, says that 'many learned men pronounced this "l" in reading and sometimes in speaking'. It is such learned men that Shakespeare is satirising through Holofernes.

9.6.2 Orthoepists and other writers on language

Spelling reformers like Gill fall into a group of people who provide much more than passing comments on Elizabethan pronunciation. They are known as orthoepists. The *OED* defines an orthoepist as 'a person who studies the pronunciation of words; [specifically] any of a group of 16th- and 17th-century writers who sought to establish a standard pronunciation of English and usually to reform the spelling system in accordance with it'. The concern of such people was to capture the purest forms of language. John Wallis, in his 1653 *Grammatica linguae anglicanae*, says they were looking at 'pure and genuine pronunciation'. It is amusing to us today to read that this led Wallis to be careful not to pay attention to 'individual local dialects, or the absurdities affected by flighty women, or other such barbarisms'.[16] One of the earliest orthoepists was one John Cheke; he was cited in Activity 1 of Chapter 2, where he showed himself to be on the 'purist' side of the Inkhorn Controversy. Here is a box with more information about him.

Caned for Greek pronunciation?

Dobson (1957) describes at length the work of John Cheke (1514–1557), one of the first people to show an interest in spelling reform at the time. He was a scholar working in Cambridge, where in 1540 he was made Professor of Greek. At that time, the pronunciation of Greek was based on the models provided by contemporary Greeks; it was in fact really 'modern Greek'. Using the modern form of the language as a model was challenged by such eminent scholars as Erasmus, who argued that classical Greek should be the version taught. Cheke agreed, and from around 1534 he (together with Sir Thomas Smith, whose work was mentioned in 2.2.1) used the classical forms in his classes with, he claims, a great increase in student interest and motivation. But the change incurred the wrath of the authorities, particularly the Chancellor of Cambridge, one Bishop Gardiner. In an acrimonious exchange of letters, Gardiner stands firmly on his dignity as Chancellor, and tries to ridicule Cheke. Gardiner argues that languages get better with time, so that by teaching the most modern version of Greek one is using the best version. He also looks with alarm (and some prescience) to the future, arguing that if Cheke reforms Greek, English will be next in line. Which indeed it was.

In 1542 Gardiner issued a decree forbidding use of the classical pronunciation, on pain of 'expulsion from the Senate, loss of honours or scholarships, or caning' (Dobson, p. 39). Cheke was forced to obey, the result being, he claimed, a fall in his class attendance from 200 to 40.

In his arguments with Gardiner, Cheke took some of his linguistic examples from English words, and certainly the argument about Greek led to the articulation of views about the relationship between spelling and pronunciation which applied as much to English as to Greek. Cheke did not write a book about spelling reform in English, but his translations, of St Matthew's Gospel and the first chapter of St Mark's among others, show elements of reform.

Orthoepists were systematic in their approach to spelling, and often tried to use phonetic description. They also sometimes used their own 'phonetic' way of writing to capture sounds more accurately than normal spelling did. In 8.2.1 we saw an example of the phonetic script John Hart used in his 1569

Orthographie. Here he is describing the pronunciation of [t] and [d].[17] You make the sounds, he says, 'bei leing ov iur tung full in ðe palet ov iur mouθ, and tučing hardest of iur for- tiθ' (by laying of your tongue full in the palate of your mouth, and touching hardest of your fore-teeth'). It has been said that the best of Hart's phonetic descriptions are as 'good as anything modern' – that is, in modern phonetics. Another example from Hart is how he describes a way of working out the tongue position of vowels (a topic covered above in 9.3.3). By 'holding the top of your finger betwixt your teeth, you shall the more sensiblye feele that they are so made'. Try it yourself for the vowels [iː], [e] and [ɑː], as in the words *see, get, father*. We have already seen another example of phonetic description from Jonson. You will find it in 9.3.1.

Dobson (1957) mentions twelve sixteenth- and seventeenth-century spelling reformers, including Cheke, Hart, Bullokar, Mulcaster, and Gill. There were also sources like rhyming dictionaries, books on shorthand systems, and books for foreigners learning English. Dobson also mentions seventeenth-century phoneticians, one of which was none other than Sir Isaac Newton who, when not grappling with problems in physics, was also dabbling in phonetics.

Another figure Dobson mentions in this context was Christopher Cooper. His book (already mentioned in 9.4.2) was *The English Teacher*, subtitled *The Discovery of the Art of Teaching and Learning the English Tongue. Fitted for the Use of Schools, and necessary for all those that desire to Read, Write, or Speak our Tongue with Ease and Understanding*. As noted earlier, it contains another type of source of possible use to those interested in historical pronunciation: a list of homophones. Cooper's includes: *jester/gesture; order/ordure; pickt her/picture; Ile (I'll)/isle; mile/moil; line/loin; coffing/coffin; jerking/jerkin*. The motive for such homophone lists was to help pupils learn to spell, so they concentrated on difficult words. Such lists should be very useful as guides to pronunciation of the period, but their use is in fact restricted because (being intended as no more than rough guides to pupils) they often contain words that are not exact homophones.[18]

9.6.3 Rhymes and spellings

Crystal's Globe Theatre OP project and the book describing it (Crystal, 2005) have already been mentioned. In the latter he considers another source of information in detail. These are rhymes. There are various lists of Renaissance rhymes available. One of them is an Appendix to Kökeritz's (1953), and Wyld (1923) is another useful source. Like homophone lists they are potentially very valuable, but not always entirely trustworthy. One has to be careful what conclusions are reached. If a writer uses two words to rhyme with each other, this suggests something about their pronunciation. But what exactly is suggested? The problem can be illustrated by means of an example used earlier. The relevant lines (from Sonnet 62) are: *Sin of self-love possesseth all mine eye,/ And all my soul, and all my every part;/And for this sin there is no remedy.* 'If we assume', we said, 'that the word *eye* was pronounced as it is today', then this tells us something about the pronunciation of *remedy*. But can we make this assumption? What if *remedy* were pronounced as today? This would suggest that *eye* were pronounced [ɪ]. As Crystal succinctly puts it: 'if we know that A rhymes with B, all we know is that the two words sounded the same: we do not know whether A sounded like B or B sounded like A'.[19] It is also possible, of course, that neither A nor B were pronounced as today.

Then there are what are called <u>eye rhymes</u>. These are words which are spelt in a similar way and hence look as if they should rhyme, but do not. PDE examples might be *bough* and *though*, *heard* and *beard*, *love* and *prove*. Writers can be forgiven for using the visual similarity between such pairs to employ them as rhymes, even though strictly speaking they are pronounced differently. Because writers, including Shakespeare, indulge in eye rhymes on occasions – and are in other ways sometimes a little 'loose' in their criteria for making rhymes – we have to be careful about using apparent rhymes as conclusive evidence for pronunciation.

For these reasons, evidence from rhymes often suggests possible pronunciations, but scholars look for other sorts of evidence to provide confirmation. Sometimes this other source of evidence is spelling. How a word is spelt can suggest something about how it is pronounced. What is called <u>occasional spelling</u> is particularly useful here. This is when someone – a scribe perhaps, who may be working very quickly – misspells a word in a way that suggests how it might be pronounced. An example is the word *shrew*. Throughout all of *The Taming of the Shrew*, the word is spelt with a 'e' in the First Folio, but in the final lines of the play we read (5.2.187):

Hortensio: *Now goe thy wayes, thou haſt tam'd a curſt Shrow*
Lucentio: *Tis a wonder, by your leaue, ſhe wil be tam'd ſo.*

Is *shrew* pronounced like RP *so*, or *so* like RP *shrew?* Perhaps the scribe's misspelling above suggests the former.[20]

9.7 More on puns and homophones

At the beginning of this chapter (9.1) we saw an example of a pun which only emerges when you learn something about Renaissance pronunciation. It involved the homophones *hour* and *whore*. Kökeritz's book is a treasure trove for the homonymic pun seeker, and contains a long list of them. Activity 3 (*Puns and pronunciation*) gives some examples which reflect differences of pronunciation between then and now. One particularly interesting pun involves the sixteenth-century word *jakes*, still used today in slang to refer to a lavatory. The *OED* is unsure of the origin of the word, but it seems connected with the name Jack as a common name, a kind of 'everyman'. This usage is found several times in Shakespeare, for example in *A Midsummer Night's Dream* (3.2.461) where Puck says *Jack shall have Jill*, meaning 'the man will get the woman', or in *Love's Labour's Lost* (5.2.864) where the opposite sentiment is expressed: *Jack hath not Jill*. Thus 'Jack's place' is perhaps the meaning of *jakes*. Bearing this in mind, consider these lines from Thersites in *Troilus and Cressida*. As mentioned a number of times before, this character is one of the greatest Shakespearean masters of insult: Agamemnon describes him as 'rank Thersites'. Here is what he has to say about the warrior Ajax:

But yet you look not well upon him: for whomsoever you take him to be, he is Ajax. (TC 2.1.62)

There is a pun here. Knowing that, it is possible to guess how the name *Ajax* is pronounced. Elsewhere Shakespeare plays with the name *Jaques*, the character in *As You Like It* whom we have met several times, in relation to *jakes*. And Kökeritz (1953: 91) includes another example of an *Ajax* pun which, he says, 'no Elizabethan would have missed', given the close proximity of the words *close stool*. The words are spoken by Costard in *Love's Labour's Lost* (5.2.573):

. . . your Lion that holds his poleaxe sitting on a close stool, will be given to Ajax'.

Poleaxe, stool, Ajax. Shakespeare can be very rude. Indeed, Kiernan (2006) is a whole book devoted to showing just how rude Shakespeare's puns can be, while Williams (2006) provides an extensive glossary of Shakespeare's sexual language.[21]

9.8 Stress

This chapter has at several points mentioned pronunciation changes. Stress as well as pronunciation changes with time. You can see stress changes happening as you watch, today. For example, dictionaries of British English a few decades back distinguish the noun and verb forms of the word *contrast* in terms of stress. In the noun, the stress used to be (and still is for some) on the first syllable: *cóntrast*, while the verb form took the stress on the second syllable: *contrást*. More recent dictionaries reflect the fact that many people today put the stress on the first syllable for both forms. How can we find out where the stress lay in EModE words? In the case of verse, but not prose, the metre can of course provide information. But care is needed because, as mentioned at various points in Chapter 7, verse is rarely entirely regular in its metre. Activity 4 (*CONtrite or conTRITE?*) looks at some examples where useful information about stress can be gleaned from stress sequences.

9.9 Pronunciation and comprehension

This chapter started by claiming that Shakespeare's pronunciation is more similar to today's than one might fear, and 'not so different' is one of the chapter's key phrases. There are of course a few puns which can only be understood if you know something about Elizabethan pronunciation, and this is one reason for looking at the area. But in general the differences between then and now are sufficiently minor to make it possible to watch an OP production of a Shakespeare play without suffering major comprehension problems.

In the latter part of the chapter, we considered how scholars can know about the pronunciation of people four hundred years ago. Books on the subject (like Kökeritz, 1953) are always careful to admit that there is much uncertainty surrounding Elizabethan speech. But, as we have seen, there are various methods available to the researcher for finding out quite a lot about how sounds were said. For this reason 'researchable' is the other key phrase for the chapter.

Activity section

1 Pronouncing and not pronouncing an 'r'

In RP and Australian PDE an 'r' is sometimes pronounced, sometimes not. Here are some words containing the letter 'r'. If you speak one of these versions of PDE, establish when the 'r' is pronounced, and try to work out the 'rule' which controls whether it is pronounced or not (hint: the relevant factors are the position of the letter in the word, and the surrounding sounds):

run	*teacher*	*arm*	*recent*	*enrol*
cart	*acronym*	*fair*	*arrive*	*fewer*

2 Dip and mono, then and now   (AS)

(i) EModE diphthongs were often different from RP ones, and occasionally what is now a monophthong was a diphthong then. Column 1 in Table 9.2 shows five RP sounds, with an example PDE word using the sound given each time. Read through the *Romeo and Juliet* passage in 9.2 and write down, in Column 2, all words where we would today use each of these sounds. For example, the sound [aɪ] is found in the RP pronunciation of *alike*, so that word would be written in the second row. Then use the transcription to find out how the EModE version of each sound in Column 1 is pronounced, and write this in Column 3.

TABLE 9.2 Diphthongs in PDE and EModE

RP sounds	RJ instances	EModE pronunciation
[ɪ] sit	(a) (b) (c)	
[aɪ] right	(a) (b) (c) (d)	
[ɔɪ] boy£	(a) (b)	
[aʊ] how	(a) (b) (c) (d)	
[iː] see	(a) (b) (c)	

(ii) Concentrate now on Column 3, showing EModE sounds. Most, but not all, of the sounds there will be diphthongs. Look first at the monophthongs. Based on the few examples given, you can make a statement about how one sound in RP could be pronounced in EModE. What is the statement? Now focus on the diphthongs. What do you notice about these?

3 Puns and pronunciation   (AS)

Here are some examples of puns which involve pronunciation points. Questions are asked about each.

(a) *Ache* as a noun could apparently be pronounced with the 'ch' sound as in the RP *Rachel*; the phonetic symbol for this sound is [tʃ]. In battle, Antony notices that his follower Scarus is bleeding. The latter says he had a T-shaped wound. Explain the pun in the second line:

I had a wound here that was like a T,
But now 'tis made an H
(AC 4.7.7)

(b) *Harden* was a coarse fabric, used to make cheap clothing. Arriving in the Forest of Arden, Touchstone, dressed (in disguise) as a peasant, says

I, now am I in Arden, the more fool I
(AYL 2.4.13)

What pronunciation point covered in this chapter makes this pun possible?

(c) In *Twelfth Night* (2.5.2), a practical joke is being played and Fabian, a member of Olivia's household, does not want to lose a moment (a 'scruple') of the fun ('sport'). To appreciate the pun you need to know that bile was said to cause melancholy.

. . . if I lose a scruple of this sport,
Let me be boil'd to death with melancholy.

Explain the pronunciation basis of the pun (this will involve looking back in the text to where the pronunciation of RP [ɔi] and [aɪ] were discussed).

(d) In *The Taming of the Shrew* (1.2.8), Petruchio asks his servant Grumio to knock on the door to announce his arrival. Grumio deliberately misunderstands. The joke works because then, as in RP, *me* can (very colloquially) be used instead of *my*. What is the pronunciation point behind the pun involving the word *here*?

Petruchio: *Villain I say, knock me here soundly*
Grumio: *Knock you here sir? Why sir, what am I sir, that I should knock you here sir?*
Petruchio: *Villain I say, knock me at this gate.*

(e) There are two puns in this passage. One is based on the two meanings of the word *medlar*, which was a fruit, but also a prostitute. The other revolves round the word *eat*, where the vowel was pronounced [eː]. The second word involved in the pun would be pronounced without its initial 'h'. What is it?

Apemantus: *There's a medlar for thee, eat it.*
Timon: *On what I hate, I feed not.*
Apemantus: *Do'st hate a Medlar?*
Timon: *Ay, though it look like thee.*
(TA 4.3.307)

(f) The two RP sounds involved in the following pun are [eɪ] and [iː]. In EModE both could be pronounced [eː]. Find the points in the text where both these EModE → RP changes are discussed. In *The Comedy of Errors* (3.2.98), Dromio of Syracuse describes the kitchen maid Nell like this:

Marry, sir, she's the kitchen wench, and all grease

Consider how *grease* might have been pronounced, and identify the homophone involving another RP vowel.

4 CONtrite or conTRITE? (AS)

In these examples, some taken from Crystal (2008: 134), you are asked to decide which of two possible stresses is the likely one, based on metrical evidence:

(a) *And on it have bestowed more contrite tears* (H5 4.1.289)
<u>Con</u>trite or con<u>trite</u>?

(b) *That old and antique song we heard last night* (TN 2.4.3)
<u>An</u>tique or an<u>tique</u>?

(c)   *But his body*
And fiery mind illustrate a brave father (TNK 2.4.21)
<u>Il</u>lustrate or il<u>lus</u>trate?

(d) *And proofs as clear as Founts in July, when* (H8 1.1.154)
<u>Ju</u>ly or Ju<u>ly</u>?

(e) *'Tis no sinister nor no awkward claim* (H5 2.4.85)
<u>Sin</u>ister or sin<u>is</u>ter?

Extended activities

1 (i) In 9.1 some arguments in favour of knowing something about Shakespearean pronunciation are put forward. But what about entire performances in OP? Of what benefit might these be? Is there any point?

   (ii) As well as 'original' pronunciation, there are other ways in which performances might be made 'original'. One is to use 'original' theatres, reconstructed as far as possible on the lines of Elizabethan theatres. The Globe Theatre in London is an example. What do performances in such theatres add? What do they lose (in comparison with performances in modern theatres)?

(iii) Another possible area of 'originality' would be to return to the acting styles used by Elizabethan actors. Use an internet search engine to find out something about these styles (there is also a book dedicated to the subject, Joseph (1964), for those particularly interested). Give a thought to what would be added, what lost, in a Shakespearean performance using OA ('Original Acting').

2   Use the internet or some other source to find out about one or more of the following people mentioned in this chapter: John Cheke, Christopher Cooper, John Hart, Alexander Gill.

3   (i)   Focus on a play of your choice. It is likely, though not certain, that the play will contain some rhymed verse. Find examples of words which are made to rhyme, but which do not rhyme today. Consider what possibilities these rhymes might suggest regarding Elizabethan pronunciation of the words.

(ii) Look at the summary in 9.5 of detailed pronunciation points made in this chapter. Look for examples of each in the play of your choice.

Answer section

EModE [ɛː] for RP [eə] (section 9.4.1)

Apart from *fair*, the other words are: *where* (× 2), *pair*, *their* (× 6), *parents* (× 2).

EModE [eː] for RP [eɪ] (section 9.4.1)

Apart from *fatal*, the other words are: *take, rage, stage, patient, lay, break, make, ancient*. The three words with EModE [eː], but RP pronunciation other than [eɪ] are *scene, unclean* and *these*.

EModE [oː] for RP [əʊ] (section 9.4.1)

Apart from *foes*, the other examples are *both, Verona, overthrows*, and *overthrows*.

Activity 2 Dip and mono, then and now

(i)   Table 9.3 shows the answers to Table 9.2.

(ii) The generalisation is that RP [iː] could be pronounced [eː] (it is not
      <u>always</u> pronounced in this way, though!). The first element of all
      diphthongs in the EModE examples is the central vowel [ə].

TABLE 9.3 Answers to Table 9.2

RP sounds	RJ instances	EModE pronunciation
[ɪ] *sit*	(a) dignity (b) mutiny (c) bury	[əɪ]
[aɪ] *right*	(a) alike (b) life (c) strife (d) strive	[əɪ]
[ɔɪ] *boy*	(a) loins (b) toil	[əɪ]
[aʊ] *how*	(a) our (b) now (c) hours (d) household	[əʊ]
[iː] *see*	(a) scene (b) unclean (c) these	[eː]

Activity 3 Puns and pronunciation

(a) The wound has changed shape from T-shaped to H-shaped. It also now
     aches.

(b) The relevant point is that an initial 'h' need not be pronounced, so
     harden could be pronounced as *Arden*.

(c) *Boil* and *bile* would be homophones because the first element of the
     diphthong in both would be centralised to [ə]. The pun depends on
     assuming that the noun *bile* can be a verb, meaning something like 'fill
     with bile'.

(d) The pronunciation point behind the pun is based on the fact that
     an initial 'h' need not be pronounced, so that the two words *ear*
     and *here* could be homophones. Thus *knock me here* could mean
     knock my ear.

(e) The second pun is *eat* and *hate*. This and the *medlar* pun continue through the lines.

(f) The homophone is *grace*. Both *grease* and *grace* would have been pronounced with the vowel [eː].

Activity 4 CONtrite or conTRITE?

(a) *con<u>trite</u>*; (b) *an<u>tique</u>*; (c) *il<u>lus</u>trate*; (d) *<u>Ju</u>ly*; (e) *si<u>nis</u>ter*.

Notes

1 In *A Midsummer Night's Dream* (1.1.189), Helena expresses envy for Hermia's attractive qualities, which include her 'tongue's sweet melody'.

2 The British Library has an archive of sound recordings, including examples of Warwickshire dialect. Details online at http://sounds.bl.uk/BrowseCategory.aspx?category=Accents-and-dialects

3 Kökeritz (1953: 6).

4 The example is from Barber (1997).

5 Crystal's notes have been used on a number of occasions in the following discussion. His 2005 book also contains interesting reactions from the actors regarding OP use, adding a different and valuable perspective to the 'why bother?' question.

6 A further example of OP can be found online at http://www.youtube.com/watch?v=dWe1b9mjjkM, a recording based on an OP performance of *A Midsummer Night's Dream*, also involving David Crystal, given at the University of Kansas in 2010.

7 Kökeritz (1953) contains proper phonetic transcription of no fewer than twenty passages.

8 The transcription is based very much on Crystal's reading as available online. He himself provides a transcription of the first four lines (in Crystal, 2005: 37), and this has been used, though some modifications have been made. Stress, for example, is not marked, and the symbol [ɹ] is not used at all (the symbol is discussed in the text). Some other changes reflect perceptions of his pronunciation in the online reading.

9 The word 'rolled' is also used, to describe another 'r' sound, usually when the back of the tongue vibrates against the uvula at the back of the throat, as in the French word *arrivé*.

10 The example is from MacCarthy (1950).

11 Kökeritz (1953: 308).

12 The position of these vowels is only approximate (and in fact various positions are associated with the sounds, depending on a number of phonetic factors).

13 There is indeed some disagreement in the literature as to when diphthong centralisation took place. Some argue for a later, post-Shakespeare, date.

14 Chapter 6 of Crystal (2008), as well as Part 1 of Kökeritz (1953), provide discussions on this issue, and together these form the basis of this section.

15 The example comes from Kökeritz (310), who also cites Alexander Gill.

16 Wallis is cited by Lass (1999b: 59), from whom the quotation is also taken. The translation is also by Lass.

17 In these paragraphs, the examples and the quotations (plus the rendition of Hart into RP) are taken from Lass (1999b).

18 The point is made by Dobson (1957).

19 Crystal (2005: 52).

20 The example is Crystal's (2008: 129). The two lines cited are given as in the First Folio. The Folio also has two examples of the adjective *shrew'd* (meaning 'shrew-like') spelt *shrow'd*.

21 Crystal (2008) as well as Kökeritz discusses the *jakes* pun.

Further reading

Kökeritz, H. (1953) *Shakespeare's Pronunciation*, New Haven: Yale University Press provides comprehensive coverage, as does Cercignani, F. (1981) *Shakespeare's Works and Elizabethan Pronunciation*, Oxford: Clarendon Press. As regards size, however, both pale in comparison with Dobson's massive study: Dobson, E. J. (1957) *English Pronunciation: 1500–1700*, Oxford: Oxford University Press. Barber, C. (1997) *Early Modern English*, Edinburgh: Edinburgh University Press has a chapter on sounds.

As well as Crystal, D. (2008) *Think on my Words*, Cambridge: Cambridge University Press (a book recommended in relation to all chapters), there is also Crystal, D. (2005) *Pronouncing Shakespeare*, Cambridge: Cambridge University Press, which gives a detailed account of the use of OP in a Globe Theatre production of *Romeo and Juliet* in 2004.

CHAPTER 10

Our revels now are ended

10.1 Language points in one passage

The main aim of this brief chapter is to draw attention to how the contents of this book have attempted to add a linguistic dimension to your study of Shakespeare. The very best way of achieving this aim would be for you to look at a piece of Shakespeare that particularly concerns you – a play that you are studying perhaps. Select a lengthy passage, or even a whole scene. Go through it identifying points that have been raised in this book. In relation to some areas you will find nothing or very little: if the text you are using has modern spelling, then there will be no spelling points cropping up, and pronunciation issues may not easily present themselves. But areas like lexis, grammar, pragmatics, rhetoric, verse/prose are likely to throw up many points. It is also, incidentally, more than likely that language points that have not been covered will come to light, and you are encouraged to explore these for yourself.

Looking at an extended piece of text has the advantage that more of the points covered in this book will be represented. But if you do not have a play that particularly concerns you, here is just one short passage to look at. It does not contain anything like all the points made in the book, though you may be surprised at how many interesting language issues occur in even a short extract.

The passage is taken from near the end of the last play that Shakespeare wrote alone: *The Tempest*. In the play, Prospero uses his magic charms to control the island on which he lives, together with its few inhabitants. But in the end he decides to give up these charms, giving the inhabitants the freedom to lead their own lives without any magic interference. In this understandably famous speech, Prospero is stating his intention to abjure magic. His 'revels', he states, 'now are ended'. Some have suggested that Prospero's abjuration of magic is like Shakespeare giving up his 'magical' skills of writing as he moved towards retirement. The speech is given twice. You will probably want to use the modern day version for everything except the identification of spelling, punctuation and graphological points, where the First Folio version (Figure 10.1) will help. Go through the speech (from Tem 5.1.33) identifying as many examples as possible of points raised in the book. The paragraphs which follow review these points (**NP**).

Modern version

Ye elves of hills, brooks, standing lakes, and groves,
And ye that on the sands with printless foot
Do chase the ebbing Neptune, and do fly him
When he comes back; you demi-puppets that
By moonshine do the green, sour ringlets make,
Whereof the ewe not bites; and you whose pastime
Is to make midnight mushrooms, that rejoice
To hear the solemn curfew, by whose aid –
Weak masters though ye be – I have bedimmed
The noontide sun, called forth the mutinous winds,
And 'twixt the green sea and the azured vault
Set roaring war; to the dread rattling thunder
Have I given fire, and rifted Jove's stout oak
With his own bolt; the strong-based promontory
Have I made shake, and by the spurs plucked up
The pine and cedar; graves at my command
Have waked their sleepers, oped, and let 'em forth
By my so potent art. But this rough magic
I here abjure, and when I have required
Some heavenly music – which even now I do –
To work mine end upon their senses that
This airy charm is for, I'll break my staff,
Bury it certain fathoms in the earth,
And deeper than did ever plummet sound
I'll drown my book.

First Folio version

> *Pro.* Ye Elues of hils, brooks, ſtãding lakes & groues,
> And ye, that on the ſands with printleſſe foote
> Doe chaſe the ebbing-*Neptune*, and doe flie him
> When he comes backe: you demy-Puppets, that
> By Moone-ſhine doe the greene ſowre Ringlets make,
> Whereof the Ewe not bites: and you, whoſe paſtime
> Is to make midnight-Muſhrumps, that reioyce
> To heare the ſolemne Curfewe, by whoſe ayde
> (Weake Maſters though ye be) I haue bedymn'd
> The Noone-tide Sun, call'd forth the mutenous windes,
> And twixt the greene Sea, and the azur'd vault
> Set roaring warre: To the dread ratling Thunder
> Haue I giuen fire, and rifted *Ioues* ſtowt Oke
> With his owne Bolt: The ſtrong baſs'd promontorie
> Haue I made ſhake, and by the ſpurs pluckt vp
> The Pyne, and Cedar. Graues at my command
> Haue wak'd their ſleepers, op'd, and let 'em forth
> By my ſo potent Art. But this rough Magicke
> I heere abiure: and when I haue requir'd
> Some heauenly Muſicke (which euen now I do)
> To worke mine end vpon their Sences, that
> This Ayrie-charme is for, I'le breake my ſtaffe,
> Bury it certaine fadomes in the earth,
> And deeper then did euer Plummet ſound
> Ile drowne my booke.   *Solemne muſicke.*

FIGURE 10.1 *The Tempest* 5.1.33

Words were the focus of attention in Chapters 2 and 3, with the former centred around neologisms and how Shakespeare (together with other Renaissance writers) went about word creation. You may have attempted to find neologisms in the Prospero passage. It is of course almost impossible for the modern reader to recognise, just by looking at them, which words were new to Renaissance readers. But it *is* possible to develop hunches about this just by reading a passage. Signs to look for include affixes being attached to words, possibly creating new formations, or words being joined together to form compounds. Words which sound Latin or French in base can also offer a clue. It is in the nature of hunches that they will not always be right, but it can be an interesting linguistic exercise to develop them, checking them if possible by looking in the *OED*. Of course, even this will not give you a definitive answer, for the reason discussed in 2.3.1: sometimes Shakespeare is the first example of a word given in that dictionary, and this suggests – but certainly does not prove – that he may have been its creator.

There are in fact three neologisms, or new word uses, in the Prospero passage. *Printless* (meaning 'leaving no trace') is one; a derivation formed by adding the Germanic suffix -less to a noun. The compound demi-puppet is another. It refers to a small puppet-like figure, and is the only example of the word in the OED. The word spur existed before Shakespeare, but he was the first, in this passage, to use it in the sense of 'principal root of a tree'. There are other words which one might be forgiven for having had hunches about. Azured is a French-based word, formed by derivation from the noun azure. In fact its use as an adjective was relatively new (the OED first mention is 1562), but it was not a Shakespeare neologism. The same seems to be the case with the verb bedim (prefix be plus verb/adjective dim). The first OED mention is 1582, and this passage is the second.

You may also have noted several words which exist today but have changed their meaning or usage slightly, and hence sound strange to modern ears. Airy, for example, is today often associated with buildings and means 'spacious'. In Shakespeare it could mean 'carried by the wind', or 'lofty'. Fly cannot today easily mean 'flee from', which is the sense in the passage. Another interesting case is the verb drown. In EModE it could simply mean 'submerge', and it could be used in relation to objects and not just people. The use of fathom is also odd to us today. It was a measurement of around six feet – the span of outstretched arms, and this was indeed the origin of the word: one of the meanings of the verb to fathom was to 'encircle with outstretched arms'. Today it is used as a measurement, but only of depth in water. In Shakespeare's time it is usually used in that sense, and indeed there is a song earlier in The Tempest (1.2.397) which begins Full fathom five thy father lies, referring to a drowned man. But it can, as in the passage, be used to refer to depth in earth. There are nine instances of fathom and four of fathoms in Shakespeare, according to the 'Shakespeare's Words' website; you may wish to look up these instances and see how many of them do not obviously refer to depth in water.

One of the grammatical areas covered in Chapter 4 related to ways of expressing possession (the genitive). Two of these are found in the passage: elves of hills, and Jove's. The much rarer forms discussed in 4.5.1 do not occur – the split genitive and the form using his. That chapter also discusses relative clauses (4.5.4), and touches on the use of that versus who or which form. It notes that Shakespeare does not always use the distinction as we do today. There are three uses of that in the passage (ye that on the sands, demi-puppets that, and their senses that). These may sound strange to many today, when who and which might be preferred. But the issue is not clear-cut, and an argument for the use of that could be made in each case.

There are several examples in the passage of do used in positive affirmative sentences: there are two in the third line alone – Do chase the ebbing Neptune, and do fly him. In the case of these particular examples they certainly help to maintain the metre of IPs, and this might be why they have been introduced. There is also an example of a negative formed without *do* in the phrase *Whereof the ewe not bites*. This phrase also involves a deviation from more normal word order of *bites not*. Inversion like this occurs in other parts of the passage, for example *the strong-based promontory/Have I made shake*.

There is little of pragmatic interest in the passage. The now obsolete word *ye* is used three times, in each case as part of a summons to spirits of one kind or another. As discussed in 5.5.1, by Shakespeare's time very little distinction was made between *ye* and *you*, and this tallies with the use of *you* in the passage, fulfilling the same grammatical function as *ye*, in the phrase *and you whose pastime*.

The passage provides some good examples of rhetorical points. If one counts full stops as markers of sentence ends (as opposed to colons and semi-colons which could be used in the same way), then the twenty-five-line passage in its modern version has just two sentences, the first being eighteen lines long. There are plenty of co-ordinate and subordinate clauses, so there really is what in 6.4.1 was called a 'piling-up'. Some of the clauses are in parentheses in the First Folio version, and separated off by dashes in the modern version (a feature associated with the Ciceronian style in 6.4.1). The first long sentence is so complex that it is very difficult to work out its syntax. Where does the summons to the spirits end? What is the main clause? At first sight the main clause may seem to be the one starting *I have bedimmed*, but this is in fact the verb embedded in the relative clause beginning *by whose aid*. Perhaps the sentence is a case where the author himself gets lost in the complexities of his own syntax (the example in 6.4.1 was from Spenser). 'Holding back' the main verb to the end is particularly apparent in the second part of the second sentence, beginning *when I have required*. The main verbs *break, bury* and *drown* come a few lines later (the third being the third-to-last word of the passage).

There is similarly much to say about the passage's verse. The lines are IPs, but with many of the deviations discussed in Chapter 7. There are feminine endings (*Do chase the ebbing Neptune, and do fly him*), and trochaic inversions (*Bury it certain fathoms in the earth*). There are no examples of headless or broken-backed lines. As you would expect of a late Shakespeare play, there are many examples of enjambment, with some variation as to where the caesura falls, though with a strong tendency for it to fall in the centre of the line (see 7.1.6). There are also ghost lines, one example being, *and let 'em forth/By my so potent art*. Note also that the speech concludes with a half line. In fact, as in the example of Lady Macbeth's speech given in 7.1.6, it is the same speaker (Prospero in this case) who continues after the half line, but this follows the entry of several characters, and the topic is changed.

You will of course need to read the First Folio version of the speech to look for orthography, spelling, and punctuation points, as covered in Chapter 8. The passage contains examples of the 'ſ' vs. 's' and the 'u' vs. 'v' distinctions discussed there. There are also examples of 'i' used where today we would have a 'j' (*reioyce* for example). Superfluous final 'e's are there too, like *foote* and *warre*, in the latter case combined with consonant doubling. In the word *here* you find the symbols 'ee' used to represent an i-related sound, and indeed this very word was used in 8.2.2 as an example of this phenomenon. There are apostrophes for missing letters ('*em* for *them*), and there is also a tilde indicating a missing letter (*n*) in the word *stāding*. The same line also contains an ampersand (&). There is no apostrophe in the genitive *Ioves* – as discussed in 8.3.4, this was often omitted. The passage also shows the irregular use of capitals considered in 8.2.2.

As regards punctuation, it is interesting to compare modern and First Folio versions. The comparison does not bear out the point that punctuation increased over chronological time, and in fact there are 25 punctuation marks in each excluding dashes or brackets; (however, a version of the same speech in a Victorian edition – Singer, 1875 – has no fewer than thirty-six punctuation marks). Colons in the Folio are replaced by semi-colons in the modern version. Interestingly, there is an extra full stop in the Folio version (after *Cedar*), possibly an example of rhetorical punctuation (8.3.2) suggesting a longer pause than does the modern version's semi-colon. Note also the extra comma in the Folio's version of line 6, again perhaps an example of rhetorical punctuation to suggest a pause. Notice the use of italics in the Folio for the names of people (*Neptune* and *Iove*: see 8.3.4).

In 9.5 you were given the opportunity to read a Shakespeare passage in OP. To draw attention to pronunciation points, you might do the same for the Prospero passage. As an alternative (or an addition), Activity 1 (*Some pronunciation points*) provides a means of looking back over issues raised in Chapter 9.

10.2 After the revels

As mentioned above, not nearly all the language points made in the book are represented in the Prospero passage. If you would like a chance to review the book's contents more systematically, look at Activity 2 (*Looking back through the book*).

Here, very finally, are some issues you might like to consider now that you have finished this book, and the revels really are ended:

(i)   How much has the book convinced you of the value of looking in detail at Shakespeare's language? Have your views on this changed since you started the book?

(ii) As the result of your reading, have you come to regard Shakespeare's language as more or less difficult than you originally thought?

(iii) Look again at the contents page. Which areas have you found the most interesting to study? The least? What areas would you like to know more about? A visit to the library may uncover books that will inform you about these areas.

Activity section

1 Some pronunciation points   (AS)

Here is a list of most of the pronunciation points made in Chapter 9. Find one or more words exemplifying each of these points in the Prospero passage. Pronounce the words to yourself as they would have been pronounced in EModE:

(a) an 'r' which is not pronounced in non-rhotic versions of PDE, but which would be in EModE.

(b) an 'h' which would be pronounced today, but could be dropped in EModE.

(c) a word which includes the EModE sound [hw].

(d) An RP [eə] which would have been [ɛː] in EModE.

(e) a word containing [eɪ] in RP which would have been pronounced [eː].

(f) a word containing RP [əʊ], pronounced [oː] in EModE.

(g) an example of PDE word-final [ɪ] which would have been pronounced [əɪ].

(h) The PDE diphthong [aɪ] which would be centralised in EModE as [əɪ].

(i) PDE [aʊ] centralised as EModE [əʊ].

2 Looking back through the book

Each of the book's chapters (except for the first and last) has two or more key phrases associated with it. These are given below, together with the chapter titles. Look through the key phrases to remind yourself of central points made in each chapter. Where memory fails, look back to the chapters themselves.

2   *Inventing words.*
    Unruly growth; adaptation and innovation

3   *Using words.*
    Artifice; self-consciousness; wordplay

4   *Grammar.*
    Half-way house; settling down; variation

5   *Pragmatics.*
    Different from today; requiring attention

6   *Rhetoric.*
    Stylistic intermingling; stylistic richness

7   *Verse and prose.*
    Dissimilitude in similitude; ducking in and out

8   *Shakespeare on the page.*
    The taste and fancy of the speller; standardisation attempts

9   *Sounds.*
    Not so different; 'researchable'.

Answer section

Activity 1 Some pronunciation points

Just one possibility per category is given; there are others:

(a) *sour* (b) *heavenly*; (c) *when*; (d) *airy*; (e) *lake*;
(f) *though*; (g) *heavenly*; (h) *fly*; (i) *stout*.

Glossary

afflict *v* torment
alarum *n* call to arms
alliance *n* marriage
alms-basket *n* basket containing alms for distribution
annex *v* join
antique *adj* bizarre
apoplexy *n* paralysis
argal *adv* therefore (also *ergo*)
arras *n* tapestry screen
attached *adj* seized
attorneyship *n* proxy
avaunt *interjection* away with you
barbed *adj* armoured
bark *n* ship
barren *adj* unable
bearing *n* behaviour
bear out *v* win
beseech *v* entreat
betide *v* happen
beweep *v* lament
birthdom *n* birthright
blabbing *adj* indiscreet
blastment *n* blight
blind-worm *n* slow worm
blown *adj* blossoming
board *v* make advances to
bolted *adj* refined
boon *n* request
bootless *adj* useless
bounded *adj* confined
bow-case *n* box for keeping the bow of a musical instrument. *Fig* thin person

box *n* vagina (slang)

brave *v* boast

breach *n* gap (in defences)

break forth *v* erupt into conflict

broach *v* pierce

broth *n* frothy liquid

buff *n* a hide leather uniform

bully *n* fine fellow

by gar a favourite expression of the French Dr Caius in *The Merry Wives of Windsor*, meaning 'by God'

by-room *n* side room

caddis *n* woollen tape

capon *n* castrated cock, a delicacy

censure *v* opinion

clatpole *n* clodpole, blockhead

clepe *v* call

clouted, clouten *adj* hobnailed

cog *v* deceive, cheat

come away *v* come here

comfit-maker *n* confectioner

complaint *n* lamentation

complexion *n* natural trait

compunctious *adj* remorseful

concavity *n* hollowness

confection *n* medical preparation; poison

contagion *n* poisonous influence

continency *n* sexual abstinence

counter-seal *v* confirm with a seal of approval

craple *n* grip

crew *n* company, gang

crystal-button *n* buttons worn by barmen

cub-drawn *adj* hungry (sucked dry by cubs)

Dan *n* Sir

deal *v* (in Mac 4.3.121) seal an agreement

degree *n* measured proportion

descant *v* play or sing in harmony with a fixed theme

digt *v* past participle of 'dig' (in speech of Welsh Captain Fluellen)

disbench *v* cause someone to leave their seat

disgracious *adj* disliked

disjoin *v* separate

division *n* modulation (in music)

drawn *adj* drained

dun *adj* dingy brown

dungy *adj* vile

eel-skin (or elf-skin) *n* skinny person

emulation *n* ambitious rivalry

enthral'd *adj* captured

espouse *v* marry

exchange *n* substitution

eyne *n* eyes

fain *adv* willingly

fair befall *interjection* good fortune to

fell *adj* cruel

fenny *n* marshland

figured *adj* represented

flap-dragon *n* raisin

flap-mouthed *adj* with broad hanging lips

flat *n* level ground

forlorn *adj* abandoned

fortune's star *n* destiny as set in the stars

frame *v* create

furnace *v* breathe out as from a furnace

gallant *n* fop, man of fashion

Gallian *adj* French

gauge *v* judge

get goal for goal *v* 'be even with' (Onions, 1986)

giddy *adj* confused

given *adj* inclined

glaze *v* stare

gleek *n* taunt

go *v* 'walk' (one sense)

grace *n* virtue

half-world *n* hemisphere

hilding *n* worthless person

honorificabilitudinitatibus *n* the state of being able to achieve
    honours

horn *n* the substance of which an animal's hoof is made

hose *n* stockings

howlet *n* owl

hunt's up *n* an early morning song (entitled 'the hunt is up')

Iceland dog *n* a type of dog with pointed ears and long hair. Popular as a pet

impiteous *adj* pitiless

in pawn at risk

inkhorn *n* inkwell

insanie *n* madness

insinuate *v* suggest

intrinsicate *adj* intricate

invocate *v* invoke

jack-a-nape *n* boastful person

joy *v* gladden

kate *n* Alternative spelling for 'cate'. A delicacy.

keel *v* prevent from boiling over

key-cold *adj* stone cold

kingdomed *adj* like a kingdom

la *interj* one use is to 'call attention to an emphatic statement' (Onions, 1986); in PDE this would sometimes be equivalent to 'so there you are'

lean *v* depend

leaping house *n* brothel

levy *v* conscript

liable *adj* fit

livery *n* uniform

long of *prep* because of

lottery *n* prize

make love to *v* court

mannerly *adj* decent

mantle *n* cloak

measurable *adj* appropriate

meddle or make *v* interfere

medicine *v* cure

mewl *v* whimper

moil *v* moisten

modicum *n* small amount

mouth-honour *n* insincerely-expressed respect; lip service

naughty *adj* bad, wicked

neat *n* ox-like animal

negligent *adj* due to negligence

nice *adj* delicate; lascivious

nicely *adv* triflingly

nill *v* will not, do not want ('will you, nill you' is associated with the PDE phrase 'willy-nilly')

nod *v* = beckon

not pated *adj* short-haired

o'erleaven *v* excessively pervade

orison *n* prayer

out o' door *adv* out of the house

pale *n* boundary

pall *v* cover

pallet *n* straw bed

palmer *n* pilgrim

paly *adj* pale

pandar *n* go-between (in love matters)

pard *n* leopard

peised *adj* = balanced, poised

perdition *n* loss, destruction

peregrinate *adj* well-travelled

phantaseme *n* fantastic person

pia mater *n* membrane covering the brain (meninges), brain

picked *adj* refined

piping time *n* 'peaceful times in which the music of the pastoral pipe is heard' (Onions, 1986)

pizzle *n* penis

plate *n* money

plausive *adj* praiseworthy

point-device (or **devise**) *adj* precise

poke *n* pocket, bag ('a pig in a poke' is a pig in a bag)

poleaxe *n* battle axe

politic *adj* prudent, cunning

pouch *n* wallet

powdering tub *n* 'sweating tub used for the cure of venereal disease' (Onions, 1986)

prate *v* chatter

presage *v* suggest; predict

prithee *interjection* I pray thee

prompture *n* urging

proof *n* trial

protest *v* declare love

publisher *n* one who makes public

puke *n* dark woollen cloth

purblind *adj* partly blind

purge *v* discharge

quick *adj* alive; sharp

quondam *adj* former

racker *n* torturer

ranged *adj* ordered

rate *v* scold

raught *v* simple past tense and past participle of *reach*

ravening *adj* devouring

reckoning *n* bill

reflex *n* reflection

remover *n* restless person

resort *v* frequent

rifle *v* rob

sack *n* type of wine

safe *v* ensure the safety of

sans *prep* without

saw *n* proverb, saying

sblood *interjection* '(by) God's blood'

scather *n* (in *Beowulf*) harmer

scissor *v* cut with scissors

score *n* tavern bill

scroll *n* list

scruple *n* small part

seeming *n* appearance

seneque *n* Seneca

sheeted *adj* in a shroud

shrift *v* confession

shrive *v* give absolution

signory *n* estate

sine *prep* without (Latin)

smoking *adj* fumigating

snow-broth *n* melted snow

sooth *n* truth

spare *v* avoid

spital *n* hospital

sportive *adj* amorous

stamp *v* beget

staple *n* fibre of wool

starveling *n* emaciated person

stock-fish *n* dried cod

strain *v* produce a melody

strained *adj* excessive

superfluous *n* extravagant

taffeta *n* type of silk

tane *v* (past participle of take), taken

tend on *v* control

thrasonical *adj* boastful

thrift *n* profit; frugality

top full *adj* full to the brim

transmigrate *v* move into another body

trimmed *adj* well-dressed

tuck *n* rapier

turn *n* needs

umbered *adj* darkened

undergo *v* sustain

ungenitured *adj* sterile, impotent

vasty *adj* vast

vengeance of *interjection* a plague on

vestal *adj* virginal

virgin *v* be chaste

wait on *v* accompany

wag *v* proceed

waste *n* desolate time

weeds *n* clothes

weeping-ripe *adj* ready to weep

welkin *n* sky

whoreson *adj* hateful (literally 'son of a whore')

wimpled *adj* blindfolded

window *v* place on display in a window

witching *adj* suitable for witches

withal *adv* with this

withhold *v* restrain

wool *n* fur

wrack *n* wreck

wrangle with *v* deceive

wrong lead *v* mislead

yard *n* measuring rod

References

Abercrombie, D. 1967 *Elements of General Phonetics* Edinburgh: Edinburgh University Press

Adamson, S. 1999 'Literary Language'. In Lass, R. (1999) *The Cambridge History of the English Language, vol. III* Cambridge: Cambridge University Press, 539–653

Alexander, C. M. S. (ed.) 2004 *Shakespeare and Language* Cambridge: Cambridge University Press

Attridge, D. 1988 'Unpacking the portmanteau, or who's afraid of *Finnegan's Wake*'. In Culler, J. (ed.) (1988) *On puns: The foundation of letters* Oxford: Blackwell, 140–155

Attridge, D. 1995 *Poetic Rhythm: An introduction* Cambridge: Cambridge University Press

Barber, C. 1981 '"You" and "thou" in Shakespeare's *Richard III*'. In Meredith, P. (ed.) (1981) *Leeds Studies in English*, 12, 273–289

Barber, C. 1997 *Early Modern English, Revised Edition* Edinburgh: Edinburgh University Press

Barish, J. A. 1960 'Jonson's Dramatic Prose'. In Watson, G. (ed.) (1970) *Literary English since Shakespeare* Oxford: Oxford University Press, 111–155

Bate, J. and **Rasmussen, E.** (eds) 2007 *William Shakespeare: Complete works* London: Macmillan

Baugh, A. C. and **Cable, T.** 2002 *A History of the English Language, Fifth Edition* London: Routledge

Becket, A. 1815 *Shakespeare's Himself Again V1-2: Or the language of the poet asserted* Republished 2008 Whitefish MT: Kessinger Publishing

Beerbohm, M. 1969 *More Theatres: 1898–1903* London: Rupert Hart-Davis

Blake, N. F. 2002 *A Grammar of Shakespeare's Language* Basingstoke: Palgrave

Bland, D. S. 1951 'Shakespeare and the "ordinary" word'. In Salmon, V. and Burness, E. (eds) (1987) *Reader in the Language of Shakespearean Drama* Amsterdam: Benjamins, 237–243

Bolton, W. F. 1992 *Shakespeare's English: Language in the history plays* Oxford: Blackwell

Brewer, C. 2007 *Treasure-House of the Language: The living OED* London: Yale University Press

Brook, G. L. 1976 *The Language of Shakespeare* London: Deutsch

Brown, P. and **Levinson, S. C.** 1987 *Politeness: Some universals in language usage* Cambridge: Cambridge University Press

Brown, R. and **Gilman, A.** 1989 'Politeness theory and Shakespeare's four major tragedies' *Language in Society* 18: 159–212

Bryson, B. 2007 *Shakespeare* London: Harper Press

Burke, P. 1998 *The European Renaissance: Centres and peripheries* Oxford: Blackwell

Busse, U. 2008 'An inventory of directives in Shakespeare's *King Lear*' In Jucker, A. H. (ed.) (1995) *Historical Pragmatics: Pragmatic developments in the history of English* Amsterdam: Benjamins, 85–114

Cercignani, F. 1981 *Shakespeare's Works and Elizabethan Pronunciation* Oxford: Clarendon Press

Chambers, E. K. 1933 *William Shakespeare: A study of facts and problems* Oxford: Clarendon Press

Chantrell, G. 2002 *Oxford Dictionary of Word Histories* Oxford: Oxford University Press

Colney, T. M. 1900 *Rhetoric in the European Tradition* Chicago: University of Chicago Press

Coulthard, M. 1985 *An Introduction to Discourse Analysis, Second Edition* London: Longman

Craig, W. J. (ed.) 1905 *Shakespeare: Complete Works* Oxford: Oxford University Press

Croll, M. W. 1929 'The baroque style in prose'. In Watson, G. (ed.) *Literary English since Shakespeare* Oxford: Oxford University Press, 1970: 84–110

Crystal, D. 2004 'Notes to accompany the transcription of Romeo and Juliet'. On site http://www.pronouncingshakespeare.com/supporting/hello-world/

Crystal, D. 2004a *The Stories of English* London: Penguin Books

Crystal, D. 2005 *Pronouncing Shakespeare* Cambridge: Cambridge University Press

Crystal, D. 2008 *Think on my Words* Cambridge: Cambridge University Press

Crystal, D. and Crystal, B. 2002 *Shakespeare's Words* London: Penguin Books

Crystal, D. and Crystal, B. 2005 *The Shakespeare Miscellany* London: Penguin Books

Culler, J. (ed.) 1988 *On Puns: The foundation of letters* Oxford: Blackwell

Culpeper, J. 2005 *History of English, Second Edition* London: Routledge

Culpeper, J. and Kytö, M. 2010 *Early Modern English Dialogues: Spoken interaction as writing* Cambridge: Cambridge University Press

Davis, P. 2006 'The Shakespeared brain'. In *The Reader*, 23. In collaboration with Roberts, N., Gonzalez-Diaz, V. and Thierry, G.

Davis, R. C. and Lindsmith, B. 2011 *Renaissance People* London: Thames & Hudson

De Grazia, M. and Wells, S. (eds) 2010 *The New Cambridge Companion to Shakespeare* Cambridge: Cambridge University Press

Denison, D. 1993 *English Historical Syntax* London: Longman

Denison, D. and Hogg, R. 2006 'Overview'. In Hogg, R. and Denison, D. (eds) (2006) *A History of the English Language* Cambridge: Cambridge University Press, 1–42

Dillon, J. 1998 *Language and Stage* Cambridge: Cambridge University Press

Dobson, E. J. 1957 *English Pronunciation: 1500–1700* Oxford: Oxford University Press

Dover Wilson, J. 1921 'Textual Introduction' to Quiller-Couch, A. and Dover Wilson, J. (eds) *The Tempest* Cambridge: Cambridge University Press

Ellegård, A. 1953 *The Auxiliary Do. The Establishment and Regulation of its Use in English* Stockholm: Almqvist & Wiksell

Elsness, J. 1994 'On the progression of the progressive in Early Modern English'. *ICAME Journal* 18: 5–25

Empson, W. 1977 *Seven Types of Ambiguity* London: Chatto & Windus

Evans, I. 1964 *The Language of Shakespeare's Plays, Third Edition* London: Methuen

Ferguson, C. A. 1959 'Diglossia'. Reprinted in Giglioli, P. P. (ed.) (1972) *Language and Social Context* London: Penguin Books

Feynman, R. P. 2001 *The Pleasure of Finding Things Out* London: Penguin Books

Fischer, O. and van der Wurff, W. 2006 'Syntax'. In Hogg, R. and Denison, D. (eds) (2006) *A History of the English Language* Cambridge: Cambridge University Press, 109–198

Flatter, R. 1948 *Shakespeare's Producing Hand* London: Heinemann

Freeborn, D. 2006 *From Old English to Standard English: A course in language variation across time, Third Edition* London: Palgrave Macmillan

Garner, B. A. 1982 'Shakespeare's Latinate neologisms'. In Salmon, V. and Burness, E. (1987) *Reader in the Language of Shakespearean Drama* Amsterdam: Benjamins, 207–288

Giglioli, P. P. (ed.) 1972 *Language and Social Context* London: Penguin Books

Gilbert, A. J. 1997 *Shakespeare's Dramatic Speech, Studies in Renaissance Literature* Lewiston, NY: Edwin Mellen Press

Givón, T. 1993 *English Grammar: A function-based introduction* Amsterdam: Benjamins

Görlach, M. 1999 'Regional and social variation'. In Lass, R. (ed.) (1999) *The Cambridge History of the English Language Volume III: 1476–1776* Cambridge: Cambridge University Press, 459–538

Graham-White, A. 1982 'Elizabethan punctuation and the actor: "Gammer Gurton's Needle" as a case study'. In *Theatre Journal* 34/1: 96–106

Greenblatt, S. 2004 *Will in the World: How Shakespeare became Shakespeare* London: Jonathan Cape

Grégoire, S. 2006 'Gender and language change: the case of early modern women'. Paper available online at http://homes.chass.utoronto.ca/~cpercy/courses/6362-gregoire.htm

Hinman, C. 1996 *The Norton Facsimile: The First Folio of Shakespeare* New York: W. W. Norton & Co

Hogg, R. and Denison, D. (eds) 2006 *A History of the English Language* Cambridge: Cambridge University Press

Hope, J. 2002 *Shakespeare's Grammar* London: Methuen Arden Shakespeare

Hopkins, L. 1997 'Household words: Macbeth and the failure of spectacle'. In Alexander, C. M. S. (ed.) (2004) *Shakespeare and Language* Cambridge, Cambridge University Press, 251–265

Hughes, G. 2000 *A History of English Words* Oxford: Blackwell

Humphreys, A. R. (ed.) 2007 *The Second Part of King Henry IV* London: Methuen Arden Shakespeare

Hussey, S. S. 1982 *The Literary Language of Shakespeare* London: Longman

Johnson, K. 2010 'A Globe for the thirties'. *Around the Globe* 44, 36–38. A version is also available online at www.keithjohnsonhome.co.uk

Joseph, B. L. 1964 *Elizabethan Acting* Oxford: Oxford University Press

Jucker, Andreas H. (ed.) 1995, *Historical Pragmatics: Pragmatic developments in the history of English* Amsterdam: Benjamins

Kakietek, P. 1976 'The perfective auxiliaries in the language of Shakespeare'. In Salmon, V. and Burness, E. (eds) (1987) *Reader in the Language of Shakespearean Drama* Amsterdam: Benjamins, 309–317

Kastovsky, D. 2006 'Vocabulary'. In Hogg, R. and Denison, D. (eds) (2006) *A History of the English Language* Cambridge: Cambridge University Press, 199–270

Kermode, F. 2000 *Shakespeare's Language* London: Penguin Books

Kiernan, P. 2006 *Filthy Shakespeare: Shakespeare's most outrageous sexual puns* London: Quercus

Kökeritz, H. 1953 *Shakespeare's Pronunciation* New Haven: Yale University Press

Kraye, J. (ed.) 1996 *The Cambridge Companion to Renaissance Humanism* New York: Cambridge University Press

Lass, R. (ed.) 1999 *The Cambridge History of the English Language Volume III: 1476 to 1776* Cambridge: Cambridge University Press

Lass, R. 1999a 'Introduction'. In Lass, R. (ed.) (1999) *The Cambridge History of the English Language, Vol. III: 1476–1776* Cambridge: Cambridge University Press, 1–12

Lass, R. 1999b 'Phonology and morphology' In Lass, R. (ed.) 1999 *The Cambridge History of the English Language, Vol. III: 1476–1776* Cambridge, Cambridge University Press, 56–186

Leech, G. 1969 *A Linguistic Guide to English Poetry* London: Longman

Leech, G. 1983 *Principles of Pragmatics* London: Longman

Leech, G. and Svartvik, J. 2002 *A Communicative Grammar of English, Third Edition* London: Longman

Lehmann, W. P. and Malkiel, Y. (eds) 1982 *Perspectives on Historical Linguistics* Amsterdam: Benjamins

Leith, S. 2011 *You Talkin' to Me? Rhetoric from Aristotle to Obama* London: Profile Books

Liberman, M. and Pullum, G. K. 2006 *Far from the Madding Gerund* Sherwood, OR: William, James & Company

Lowth, R. 1775/1979 *A Short Introduction to English Grammar, Scholars' facsimiles and reprints* New York: Delmar

Mabillard, A. 2000 *Shakespeare in Print.* Shakespeare Online: http://www.shakespeare-online.com/biography/shakespeareinprint.html

MacCarthy, P. 1950 *English Pronunciation, Fourth Edition* Cambridge: Heffer & Sons

McDonald, R. 2001 *Shakespeare and the Arts of Language* Oxford: Oxford University Press

McDonald, R. 2003 'Shakespeare's verse'. In Wells, S. and Orlin, L. C. (eds) (2003) *An Oxford Guide to Shakespeare* Oxford: Oxford University Press, 79–92

McEvoy, S. 2006 *Shakespeare: The basics, Second Edition* London: Routledge

McKenzie, D. F. 1959 'Shakespearean punctuation: a new beginning'. *Review of English Studies* X: 361–70. In Salmon, V. and Burness, E. (eds) *Reader in the Language of Shakespearean Drama* Amsterdam, Benjamins, 445–454

Maguire, L. 2003 'Shakespeare published'. In Wells, S. and Orlin, L. C. (eds) (2003) *An Oxford Guide to Shakespeare* Oxford: Oxford University Press, 582–594

Mahood, M. M. 1957 *Shakespeare's Wordplay* London: Methuen

Meredith, P. (ed.) 1981 *Leeds Studies in English*, 12

Miola, R. S. 2000 *Shakespeare's Reading* Oxford: Oxford University Press

Muir, K. (ed.) 1968 *Othello* Harmondsworth: Penguin Books

Murphy, A. 2010 'The transmission of Shakespeare's texts'. In De Grazia, M. and Wells, S. (eds) (2010) *The New Cambridge Companion to Shakespeare* Cambridge: Cambridge University Press, 61–76

Nevalainen, T. 1999 'Early Modern English Lexis and Semantics'. In Lass, R. (ed.) (1999) *The Cambridge History of the English Language Vol. III: 1476–1776* Cambridge: Cambridge University Press, 332–458

Nevalainen, T. 2006 *An Introduction to Early Modern English* Edinburgh: Edinburgh University Press

Nevalainen, T. and Raumolin-Brunberg, H. 2003 *Historical Sociolinguistics: Language change in Tudor and Stuart England* London: Pearson Education

Nevalainen, T. and van Ostade, I. T-B. 2006 'Standardisation'. In Hogg, R. and Denison, D. (eds) (2006) *A History of the English Language* Cambridge: Cambridge University Press, 271–311

Onions, C. T. (revised by Eagleson, R. D.) 1986 *A Shakespeare Glossary* Oxford: Clarendon Press

Palliser, D. M. 1992 *The Age of Elizabeth, Second Edition* London: Longman

Partridge, A. C. 1964 *Orthography in Shakespeare and Elizabethan Drama* London: Edward Arnold

Phin, J. 1902 *The Shakespeare Cyclopedia* New York: The Industrial Publication Company

Puttenham, R. 1589 *The Arte of English Poesie* [Reprinted 1971] Amsterdam: Da Capo Press

Quirk, R. and Greenbaum, S. 1973 *A University Grammar of English* London: Longman

Rabb, T. K. 2000 *Renaissance Lives: Portraits of an age* New York: Basic Books

Raysor, T. M. (ed.) 1936 *Coleridge Miscellaneous Criticism* London: Constable

Redfern, W. 2000 *Puns, Second Edition* London: Penguin Books

Replogle, C. 1973 'Shakespeare's salutations: a study in stylistic etiquette'. In Salmon, V. and Burness, E. (1987) *Reader in the Language of Shakespearean Drama* Amsterdam: Benjamins, 101–116

Rissanen, M. 1999 'Syntax'. In Lass, R. (1999) *The Cambridge History of the English Language Vol. III 1476–1776* Cambridge: Cambridge University Press, 187–331

Ronberg, G. 1992 *A Way with Words: The language of English Renaissance literature* London: Arnold

Salmon, V. 1970 'Some functions of Shakespearean word-formation'. In Alexander, C. M. S. (ed.) (2004) *Shakespeare and Language* Cambridge: Cambridge University Press, 79–100

Salmon, V. 1986 'The spelling and punctuation of Shakespeare's time'. In Wells, S. and Taylor, G. (eds) (1986) *William Shakespeare: The complete works, original-spelling edition* Oxford: Clarendon Press, xlii–lvi

Salmon, V. and Burness, E. (eds) 1987 *Reader in the Language of Shakespearean Drama* Amsterdam: Benjamins

Schlauch, M. 1965 'The social background of Shakespeare's malapropisms'. In Salmon, V. and Burness, E. (1987) *Reader in the Language of Shakespearean Drama* Amsterdam: Benjamins, 71–99

Short, M. 1996 *Exploring the Language of Poems, Plays and Prose* London: Longman

Singer, S. W. (ed.) 1875 *The Dramatic Works of William Shakespeare* London: George Bell and Sons

Sokal, B. J. and Sokal, M. (eds) 2000 *Shakespeare's Legal Language: A dictionary* Athlone: Continuum International Publishing Group

Sowell, T. 1979 *Knowledge and Decisions* New York: Basic Books

Spevack, M. 1967 *The Harvard Concordance to Shakespeare* Cambridge, MA: Belknap Press of Harvard University Press

Spolsky, B. 1998 *Sociolinguistics* Oxford: Oxford University Press

Summers, M. (ed.) 1966 *Shakespeare Adaptations* New York: Haskell House

Tanselle, G. T. and Dunbar, F. W. 1962 'Legal language in *Coriolanus*'. In Salmon, V. and Burness, E. (eds) (1987) *Reader in the Language of Shakespearean Drama* Amsterdam: Benjamins, 255–262

Tarlinskaja, M. 1987 *Shakespeare's Verse: Iambic pentameter and the poet's idiosyncrasies* New York: Peter Lang

Taylor, E. W. 1976 'Shakespeare's use of *eth* and *es* endings of verbs in the first folio'. In Salmon, V. and Burness, E. (eds) (1987) *Reader in the Language of Shakespearean Drama* Amsterdam: Benjamins, 349–369

Taylor, G. 1989 *Reinventing Shakespeare: A cultural history from the Restoration to the present* London: The Hogarth Press

Theobald, R. M. 1906 'Word coinage in Shakespeare and others' *Baconiana*, Third series, 239–246

Thomas, J. 1995 *Meaning in Interaction: An Introduction to Pragmatics* London: Longman

Thompson, F. 2003 *Prose: Works of Francis Thompson, Part 3* Whitefish MT: Kessinger Publishing

Traugott, E. C. 1982 'From propositional to textual and expressive meanings: some semantic-pragmatic aspects of grammaticalization'. In Lehmann, W. P. and Malkiel, Y. (eds) (1982) *Perspectives on Historical Linguistics* Amsterdam: Benjamins, 245–271

Ullmann, S. 1964 *Semantics: An introduction to the science of meaning* Oxford: Blackwell

Vickers, B. 1968 *The Artistry of Shakespeare's Prose* London: Methuen

Vickers, B. 1970 *Classical Rhetoric in English Poetry* Basingstoke: Macmillan

Vickers, B. (ed.) 1999 *English Renaissance Literary Criticism* Oxford: Oxford University Press

Wales, K. M. 1983 '*Thou* and *You* in Early Modern English: Brown and Gilman re-appraised'. In *Studia Linguistica* 37: 107–125

Warren, M. J. 1977 'Repunctuation as interpretation in editions of Shakespeare' *English Literary Renaissance* 7: 155–69. In Salmon, V. and Burness, E. (eds) (1987) *Reader in the Language of Shakespearean Drama* Amsterdam: Benjamins, 455–469

Watson, G. (ed.) 1970 *Literary English since Shakespeare* Oxford: Oxford University Press

Wells, S. 2002 *Shakespeare For All Time* London: Macmillan

Wells, S. and Orlin, L. C. (eds) 2003 *An Oxford Guide to Shakespeare* Oxford: Oxford University Press

Wells, S. and Taylor, G. (eds) 1986 *William Shakespeare: The complete works. original-spelling edition* Oxford: Clarendon Press

Wells, S., Taylor, G. and Jowett, J. (eds) 2005 *William Shakespeare: The complete works, Second Edition* Oxford: Oxford University Press

Wermser, R. 1976 *Statistische Studien zur Entwicklung des englischen Wortschatzes (Schweizer Anglistische Arbeiten 91)* Bern: Francke

Williams, G. 2006 *Shakespeare's Sexual Language: A glossary* Athlone: Continuum

Wright, G. T. 1981 'Hendiadys and *Hamlet*' *PMLA* 96:2, 168–93

Wright, G. T. 1988 *Shakespeare's Metrical Art* Berkeley: University of California Press

Wyld, H. C. 1923 *Studies in English Rhymes from Surrey to Pope* London: John Murray

Yule, G. 1996 *Pragmatics* Oxford: Oxford University Press

Index